Migrating to Visual Basic® .NET

Migrating to Visual Basic® .NET

Steve Cisco

M&T Books
An imprint of Hungry Minds, Inc.

Best-Selling Books • Digital Downloads • e-Books • Answer Networks •
e-Newsletters • Branded Web Sites • e-Learning

New York, NY • Cleveland, OH • Indianapolis, IN

Migrating to Visual Basic® .NET

Published by
M&T Books
An imprint of Hungry Minds, Inc.
909 Third Avenue
New York, NY 10022
www.hungryminds.com

Library of Congress Control Number: 2001092921

ISBN: 0-7645-4894-8

Printed in the United States of America

10 9 8 7 6 5 4 3 2 1

1B/QY/QR/QS/IN

Distributed in the United States by Hungry Minds, Inc.

Distributed by CDG Books Canada Inc. for Canada; by Transworld Publishers Limited in the United Kingdom; by IDG Norge Books for Norway; by IDG Sweden Books for Sweden; by IDG Books Australia Publishing Corporation Pty. Ltd. for Australia and New Zealand; by TransQuest Publishers Pte Ltd. for Singapore, Malaysia, Thailand, Indonesia, and Hong Kong; by Gotop Information Inc. for Taiwan; by ICG Muse, Inc. for Japan; by Intersoft for South Africa; by Eyrolles for France; by International Thomson Publishing for Germany, Austria, and Switzerland; by Distribuidora Cuspide for Argentina; by LR International for Brazil; by Galileo Libros for Chile; by Ediciones ZETA S.C.R. Ltda. for Peru; by WS Computer Publishing Corporation, Inc., for the Philippines; by Contemporanea de Ediciones for Venezuela; by Express Computer Distributors for the Caribbean and West Indies; by Micronesia Media Distributor, Inc. for Micronesia; by Chips Computadoras S.A. de C.V. for Mexico; by Editorial Norma de Panama S.A. for Panama; by American Bookshops for Finland.

For general information on Hungry Minds' products and services please contact our Customer Care department within the U.S. at 800-762-2974, outside the U.S. at 317-572-3993 or fax 317-572-4002.

For sales inquiries and reseller information, including discounts, premium and bulk quantity sales, and foreign-language translations, please contact our Customer Care department at 800-434-3422, fax 317-572-4002 or write to Hungry Minds, Inc., Attn: Customer Care Department, 10475 Crosspoint Boulevard, Indianapolis, IN 46256.

For information on licensing foreign or domestic rights, please contact our Sub-Rights Customer Care department at 212-884-5000.

For information on using Hungry Minds' products and services in the classroom or for ordering examination copies, please contact our Educational Sales department at 800-434-2086 or fax 317-572-4005.

For press review copies, author interviews, or other publicity information, please contact our Public Relations department at 317-572-3168 or fax 317-572-4168.

For authorization to photocopy items for corporate, personal, or educational use, please contact Copyright Clearance Center, 222 Rosewood Drive, Danvers, MA 01923, or fax 978-750-4470.

 is a trademark of Hungry Minds, Inc.

 is a trademark of Hungry Minds, Inc.

To my wife, Laura, my two children, and my father, for their support and understanding as I wrote this book. It took a lot of time and effort, and I can never say enough thanks for everything you have done.

Credits

SENIOR ACQUISITIONS EDITOR
Sharon Cox

PROJECT EDITOR
Elizabeth Kuball

TECHNICAL EDITOR
Todd Meister

EDITORIAL MANAGER
Mary Beth Wakefield

SENIOR VICE PRESIDENT, TECHNICAL PUBLISHING
Richard Swadley

VICE PRESIDENT AND PUBLISHER
Joseph B. Wikert

PROJECT COORDINATOR
Maridee Ennis

GRAPHICS AND PRODUCTION SPECIALISTS
Melanie DesJardins
Joyce Haughey
Laurie Petrone
Jill Piscitelli
Betty Schulte
Jeremey Unger
Erin Zeltner

QUALITY CONTROL TECHNICIANS
Laura Albert
Andy Hollandbeck
Carl Pierce
Charles Spencer

PROOFREADING AND INDEXING
TECHBOOKS Production Services

COVER IMAGE
© Noma/Images.com

About the Author

Steve Cisco has a bachelor's degree in Electrical Engineering from Rose-Hulman Institute of Technology in Terre Haute, Indiana. Steve started working with Visual Basic shortly after version 3 was released, creating human-machine interfaces for control systems. At that point, he started the transition from consulting engineering to IT consulting and has worked on a day-in, day-out basis with each subsequent version of Visual Basic as it was released. He has always enjoyed pushing Visual Basic to the edge, surprising many die-hard C programmers with the things that can actually be done in Visual Basic.

Steve currently possesses his MCSD and MCSE certifications from Microsoft and has performed various consulting services for many companies, including Saturn Corporation and HCA — The Healthcare Company. Steve is currently a software engineer for Adaptive Systems, Inc. (www.adaptivesys.com), a software engineering company that is dedicated to designing and creating open, scalable, and supportable software solutions. In addition to designing and developing software, Steve is also responsible for educating and training other developers and clients about Visual Basic .NET. You can reach Steve via e-mail at dearvbguru@hotmail.com or scisco@adaptivesys.com.

About the Contributor

Brian Patterson currently works as a Technical Team Leader for AFFINA, Inc. AFFINA, based in Peoria, Illinois, partners with Fortune 1000 companies and government agencies to provide comprehensive customer relationship management programs integrating inbound telecommunications, Internet, database marketing, market research, closed-loop lead management, and fulfillment services.

Brian has been using Visual Basic since 1988 and can generally be found posting to the Microsoft newsgroups or uploading his latest creation to the Internet. When Brian isn't locked away in his computer room, you can reach him at BrianPatterson@affina.com.

About the Series Editor

Michael Lane Thomas is an active development community and computer industry analyst who presently spends a great deal of time spreading the gospel of Microsoft .NET in his current role as a .NET technology evangelist for Microsoft. In working with over a half-dozen publishing companies, Michael has written numerous technical articles and written or contributed to almost 20 books on numerous technical topics, including Visual Basic, Visual C++, and .NET technologies. He is a prolific supporter of the Microsoft certification programs, having earned his MCSD, MCSE+I, MCT, MCP+SB, and MCDBA.

In addition to technical writing, Michael can also be heard over the airwaves from time to time, including two weekly radio programs on Entercom (www.entercom.com) stations, most often in Kansas City on News Radio 980KMBZ (www.kmbz.com). He can also occasionally be caught on the Internet doing an MSDN Webcast (www.microsoft.com/usa/webcasts) discussing .NET, the next generation of Web application technologies.

Michael started his journey through the technical ranks back in college at the University of Kansas, where he earned his stripes and a couple of degrees. After a brief stint as a technical and business consultant to Tokyo-based Global Online Japan, he returned to the States to climb the corporate ladder. He has held assorted roles, including those of IT manager, field engineer, trainer, independent consultant, and even a brief stint as Interim CTO of a successful dot-com, although he believes his current role as .NET evangelist for Microsoft is the best of the lot. He can be reached via e-mail at mlthomas@microsoft.com.

Preface

Welcome to the world of Visual Basic .NET. If you're reading this book, then you're aware of the latest version of Visual Basic and have either heard about or experienced firsthand the changes and new features that are in Visual Basic .NET. Visual Basic .NET is a full-fledged object-oriented programming language, and using it properly requires some discipline and understanding. Visual Basic .NET is more of a revolutionary release than an evolutionary one. Visual Basic, along with the other languages in Visual Studio .NET, runs on top of the .NET Framework, which is a common set of libraries and routines that abstract the operating system from the code itself. There are no longer separate runtime libraries for applications created in Visual Basic, Visual C++, or Visual C#. There are many changes to the Visual Basic language, and no single book can cover them all. As time passes and developers begin to understand the changes and additions to the language, you'll probably see many books appear that are dedicated entirely to topics covered in individual chapters within this book.

Visual Basic has evolved many times in the past decade, and with each version has come new features and improvements on existing ones. Through its history, the single biggest change was between versions 3 and 4. Visual Basic 4 was rebuilt from the ground up to take advantage of OLE as the underlying architecture. Version 4 introduced classes, which was the first step toward its becoming an object-oriented programming language. The verbal jabs and arguments from developers of other languages started to appear, saying that their language was better than Visual Basic because Visual Basic was not a true object-oriented programming language or that Visual Basic would never be used as much as their language. Never mind the fact that many of those other developers who touted their object-oriented programming languages didn't understand enough about object-oriented programming to use it properly.

During this time, a strange thing happened: Businesses, as well as developers, began to see that even though it lacked certain features and required some workarounds, Visual Basic could be used to get more applications out the door — and in less time than developers using the other languages needed. Although it's true that some types of applications (services, device drivers, console applications, and so on) couldn't be created using Visual Basic, the majority of all business applications are ideally suited for Visual Basic. In most business applications, the majority of time is spent either waiting for the user or a database command to complete. For these types of applications, it really doesn't matter that language A is 15 percent faster than language B, because they both wait for the external responses and inputs at the same speed.

I'm a software engineer, not a full-time author. As I started looking at the .NET Framework and Visual Basic .NET, I was upset at first, because I thought I was going to have to relearn the entire language just to be productive again, as the changes were so far reaching. After I got over the initial shock and the anger, I began to explore the new features and found myself saying, "Cool," "Wow," and, "They finally got it right." I've spent considerable time trying to get up to speed on the changes and thought that if I was having this much trouble, many other developers out there were going to have the same trouble. The .NET Framework's time has come, and I don't see it going away or fading into the sunset. The real question is not whether it will be adopted but how quickly developers and businesses will adopt it.

This book was written by a developer for use by other developers as they try to learn and understand the changes to the Visual Basic .NET platform compared with prior versions. It does not contain a lot of fluff or warm fuzzies to increase the page count so that it meets a target or takes more shelf space. The content in this book sometimes requires a little background information, but the majority of it gets straight to the point. The content is arranged in a logical order that will make sense as you progress through learning the changes in the environment and the language and figure out how to use the new features and capabilities properly.

The book starts off by showing you the basic changes to the Visual Basic .NET language and the common development environment that will make you more productive as a developer. The book then gets progressively more advanced, because after you understand the basics, you'll apply these concepts to the advanced material. Because of the way it's structured, I strongly suggest reading through this book from beginning to end. You can skip Chapters 7 and 8 and come back to them later, because they discuss data access features in Visual Basic .NET. With the exception of these two chapters, the examples included in this book do not assume that you have a database available for use. Visual Basic .NET can co-exist with prior versions of Visual Basic on the same hard drive, in the same partition, and in the same operating system. As a result, it would be wise to install it side by side in the beginning. This way, if you get stuck with a particular concept in Visual Basic .NET, you could create it in a prior version and then run the import wizard on the project and see how the project and code are changed to operate under the .NET Framework.

The content in this book will apply to you the most if you are at least an intermediate-level programmer in one of the existing versions of Visual Basic, preferably versions 5 or 6. I don't waste any time describing the basics like how to place a control on a form, what a text box is used for, what a button is used for, and so on. I assume that you already know that sort of information and want details about what you need to know to become productive in Visual Basic .NET in the shortest amount of time possible. Again, neither this book nor any other single book can be a comprehensive guide to your migration strategies to Visual Basic .NET. Think of this book as your atlas to the Visual Basic .NET language. It gives you an overview of the various changes and new features in Visual Basic .NET, as well as the kinds of details that a normal atlas would have in the form of insets of various cities. If you need more information about a particular feature (like the detailed names of all the city streets that are absent in an atlas), you can get additional help by reviewing the documentation, magazine articles, newsgroups, Web sites, and other books that are published on the specific subjects.

How This Book Is Organized

This book is divided into six parts, outlined in the following sections.

Part 1: Getting Over Shell Shock: Changes from Visual Basic 6

This part of the book quickly covers the most visible changes to Visual Basic .NET from prior versions. Chapter 1 gives you an overview of the sweeping changes in Visual Basic .NET and sets the stage for the rest of the book. Chapter 2 gives you a quick tour of the new development environment, which is finally common with all the other languages in the Visual Studio .NET development platform. Chapter 3 highlights the changes to the syntax of the language itself.

Part II: Understanding New Language Features

Part II covers the features that have been added to the Visual Basic language that will be used by all developers programming in Visual Basic .NET. Chapter 4 discusses how to handle errors in your Visual Basic .NET applications using Structured Exception Handling, which will be a new concept for the majority of Visual Basic developers. Chapter 5 discusses the concept of inheritance and how it's used everywhere within the language. (Understanding inheritance and how it's used in Visual Basic .NET is critical to your understanding of Visual Basic .NET, so it's discussed here, early in the book, even though some of the concepts may be a little more advanced.) Chapter 6 runs you through the toolbox and highlights the new controls as well as how the controls have changed from prior versions.

Part III: Data Access in Visual Basic .NET

This part of the book covers the various data access techniques in Visual Basic .NET. Chapter 7 discusses ADO.NET, shows how to use it to access various data stores, and compares it with "plain" ADO. Visual Basic .NET makes extensive use of XML to store configuration settings for applications as well as for other data stores. ADO.NET uses XML as the internal data storage format, and XML is also used by Web Services to communicate with other Web Services and clients over the Internet. Chapter 8 shows you how XML is used in Visual Basic .NET and how you can use it in your applications to store data and communicate with other applications.

Part IV: Tying It All Together

Chapter 9 walks you through creating a combined application using each of the project types available for use in Visual Basic .NET. Chapter 10 discusses the debugging tools available for use in Visual Basic .NET and how to use them to debug the various types of applications that can be created in Visual Basic .NET. Visual Basic .NET allows applications to be deployed in several different ways. Chapter 11 discusses the new deployment projects and how they're used to create packages for the

Windows Installer. This chapter also shows you how to create a deployment project that will distribute the application suite that is developed in Chapter 9.

Part V: Advanced .NET Topics

This part of the book discusses a few of the more advanced topics in Visual Basic .NET that you may need to know about shortly after you start using it. Chapter 12 covers the topic of free threading in Visual Basic .NET and shows you how to create a thread manager that can be used in your applications to more easily manage the ancillary requirements of using multiple threads in your applications. Chapter 13 discusses the Windows Forms Designer and how the new forms engine creates the forms at runtime as well as at design time by generating Visual Basic code. Graphics programming in Visual Basic .NET has changed drastically from prior versions. Chapter 14 shows you how the various graphics objects and methods can be used to easily create complex graphics operations in Visual Basic .NET.

Part VI: Architecture and Design

With many of the changes like inheritance, free threading, and object-oriented programming techniques, the importance of having a good design and documentation cannot be stressed enough when using Visual Basic .NET. Chapter 16 discusses design and documentation techniques and how they can be applied to Visual Basic .NET to create robust, easy-to-manage applications. Chapter 17 gives an overview of the Project Lifecycle Development portion of the Microsoft Solutions Framework. The Microsoft Solutions Framework can be used in conjunction with the new productivity enhancements in Visual Basic .NET to reduce the development time of applications and help improve their chances of success.

Appendix: Migrating Existing Applications to Visual Basic .NET

This appendix highlights some suggested practices, techniques, and tips for migrating existing applications to Visual Basic .NET and lets you know why you may want to start from scratch instead of upgrading.

Conventions Used in This Book

Each chapter in this book begins with a heads-up of the topics covered in the chapter and ends with a summary of what you should have learned by reading the chapter. Throughout this book, you'll find icons in the margins that highlight special or important information. Keep an eye out for the following icons:

Notes provide additional or critical information and technical data on the current topic.

This icon indicates where in the book you can find more information on the topic at hand.

The Tip icon indicates tidbits that I picked up along the way and want to share with you.

In addition to the preceding icons, the following formatting and typographical conventions appear throughout the book:

◆ Code examples appear in a `fixed width font`.

◆ Other code elements such as data structures and variable names appear in `fixed width`.

◆ File, function, and macro names as well as World Wide Web Addresses (URLs) appear in a `fixed width font`.

◆ The first occurrence of an important term in a chapter is highlighted with *italic* text. Italics are also used for placeholders in file and directory names, which may be different on each computer, depending on where the product was installed.

◆ Menu commands are indicated in hierarchical order, with each menu command separated by an arrow. For example, File → Open means to click the File command on the menu bar and then select Open.

◆ Keyboard shortcuts are indicated with the following syntax: Ctrl+C.

Acknowledgments

First, I would like to thank Microsoft for releasing such a comprehensive development platform and giving the majority of Visual Basic developers everything they have been asking for (and then some) over the last several years. I would like to thank Sharon Cox at Hungry Minds for the opportunity to write this book and for understanding all the changes to the content and scheduling that were required. I would also like to thank everyone else at Hungry Minds who was involved in every aspect of the publication of this book, for keeping the content accurate and concise.

Finally, I want to say thanks to my wife, Laura; my daughter, Jaylynn; and Sullivan, my new son, who was born during the process of writing this book. Writing this book took a lot of effort and time that would have been devoted to other free-time activities on the weekends. I would not have been able to complete this book if it weren't for their understanding and flexibility during the process.

Contents at a Glance

Contents

Part I

Getting Over Shell Shock: Changes from Visual Basic 6

Chapter 1

An Overview of Changes to Visual Basic .NET

IN THIS CHAPTER

- ◆ Overview of IDE changes
- ◆ Overview of language changes
- ◆ Projects and solutions
- ◆ .NET Framework
- ◆ COM interoperability

Since Microsoft first introduced Visual Basic as a programming language, it has continually evolved and been improved upon with each new version. In its history, the jump from version 3 to 4 was probably the most drastic change the language has undergone until now. The underlying architecture of Visual Basic changed, forcing control vendors to basically abandon their VBX controls and introduce a new type of control called OLE custom controls (OCX's, ActiveX, OLE Control, and so on). Although Visual Basic 4 allowed you to create programs to run on either 16-bit platforms or 32-bit platforms, it was clear that at the rate hardware and software were advancing, the days of creating 16-bit programs were numbered. Version 4 introduced the concepts of classes, and forms that could be treated as classes, with a visual interface instead of a separate user interface object. Although there were a lot of aches and groans, the majority of applications that have been developed were eventually transitioned to run as 32-bit programs.

Since version 4 was released, developers have asked Microsoft to incorporate many features into the language, but a large number of the vocal requests kept asking to make Visual Basic a "true" object-oriented language by including inheritance. Other requests were to make it more productive and make the language more powerful without having to resort to using API calls. One of the strengths of Visual Basic is that, although it has grown more complex over the years, it has remained flexible enough that it can be used by developers of all skill levels. In fact, there are more Visual Basic developers in the world than developers of all the other languages from Microsoft combined. The majority of the various versions of Visual Basic have been evolutionary in nature. Each version expanded upon the capabilities of the previous version, providing new features here and there. Developers found certain features very useful, while other features didn't fare so well. Visual

3

Basic .NET incorporates the best ideas and features from previous versions and includes many features that, for one reason or another, weren't incorporated into previous versions.

The Visual Basic .NET version is more revolutionary than evolutionary, as the other releases were. For all those developers who requested it, Visual Basic is now a true object-oriented language. Inheritance is now a fundamental feature of the language, because *everything* in Visual Basic .NET is an object. Microsoft has been working on merging the IDEs of all the languages in the Visual Studio suite for some time now, and the time has finally come. One of the things you may notice is that Visual Interdev is no longer a separate product. Visual Basic .NET now allows you to create Web projects, which allow you to create Web-based applications in a variety of ways. The common IDE is very powerful, and taking the time to understand all it has to offer can make you a more productive developer.

The purpose of this chapter is to give you a brief overview of the many changes in Visual Basic .NET, which later chapters in this book will explain in greater detail. Again, Visual Basic .NET is a revolutionary product release and, as such, there are so many subtle changes everywhere in the product that it would be impossible to cover everything. This book covers the most important concepts that you need to understand in order to migrate your skills to Visual Basic .NET.

An Overview of IDE Changes

The first thing you'll notice about Visual Basic .NET is that the familiar IDE from previous versions has been changed. The changes were required to allow a single IDE to be used with all the languages in the Visual Studio .NET product. When you become familiar with the changes in the IDE, you can take advantage of the customization features in it so that you can get it to do as much work for you as possible, reducing your overall effort when creating applications in Visual Basic .NET.

Getting help when you need it

Almost everywhere you look, there is something about Visual Basic .NET that has changed from prior versions and, as a result, knowing where to go for help when you get stuck or confused is important. One of the changes in Visual Basic .NET is the enhanced help system that is now incorporated into the IDE. The traditional MSDN library help system is still where all the help files reside, but now there is a Dynamic Help feature that automatically displays links for help-file topics that are related to your current activities in the IDE.

The Dynamic Help feature will be very useful as you're learning the language, and it can be customized or even turned off as you learn the changes to the language syntax and the features in the common IDE. The Dynamic Help system can be made available for use by selecting the Dynamic Help option from the Help menu or by pressing Ctrl+F1. As you work with the development environment, look at the Dynamic Help window and see how the contents change in the Dynamic Help window. Click on one of the hyperlinks in the Dynamic Help window and notice how the help system is displayed; the topic that is displayed is the topic you selected in the Dynamic Help window.

As you'll notice, just about every feature of the IDE can be customized to suit your tastes. In order to customize the items in the Dynamic Help window, bring up the Options dialog box by selecting Tools → Options. As shown in Figure 1-1, there are many new options that you may not be used to setting. On the left side of the dialog box is a group of folders. Each folder contains options related to the folder description.

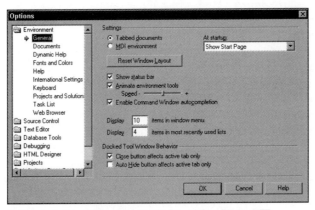

Figure 1–1: The Options dialog box in Visual Basic .NET.

Figure 1-2 shows the options available to you for customizing the Dynamic Help system. You can limit the categories and topic types that are shown, as well as change the order in which they're displayed in the Dynamic Help window. You can also limit the number of general topics shown and limit the number of topics shown for the selected item or the particular piece of the IDE you're working with. By configuring and using the Dynamic Help system to suit your own preferences, you can reduce your time spent searching and waiting for the results of a regular help file search, because the Dynamic Help system will take you right to the topic you're interested in.

The enhancements to the help system go a long way as you're getting acquainted with Visual Basic .NET, but there may be times when you cannot find the information you're looking for in the help files. Should this occur, there are many Web sites on the Internet that may be of assistance. Here is a list of a few sites that contain valuable samples, articles, discussions, and other technical information related to Visual Basic .NET:

◆ msdn.microsoft.com

◆ www.gotdotnet.com

◆ www.devx.com/dotnet

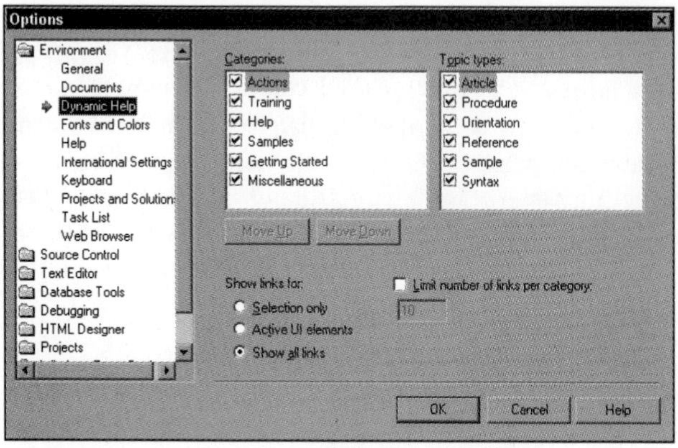

Figure 1-2: Dynamic Help customization options.

Customizing the IDE

One of the great features about the common IDE is that it has many productivity enhancements that can be customized to suit your individual needs. You now have the capability of launching external tools from within the IDE. Go to Tools→ External Tools, and you'll see the External Tools configuration dialog box, shown in Figure 1-3. If you wanted to bring up Internet Explorer and automatically go to a particular Web site, you would browse to the executable for your browser and enter the Web site address as the command line argument. This now adds a menu item to your Tools window that you can click on and that will automatically launch your external tool and supply it any parameters you need.

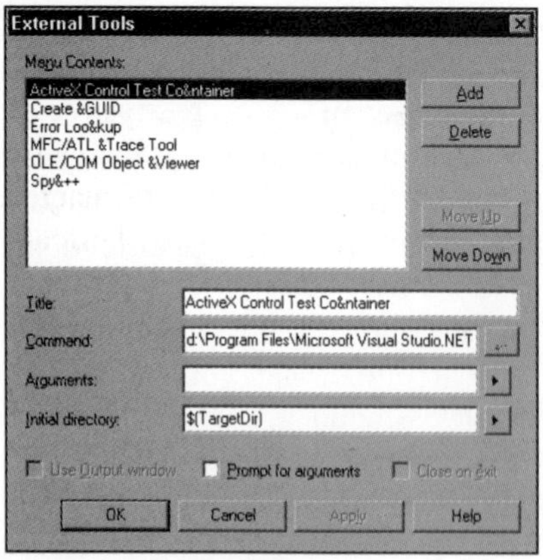

Figure 1-3: The External Tools
configuration dialog box.

As mentioned earlier, the IDE allows you to set developer-specific options through the Options dialog box. Take some time to explore the options available and find out where they're located in this new display structure. You can choose whether you want to view your windows in the new tabbed documents layout or the familiar MDI environment. You can set the desired colors for more windows than just the text editor, and you're no longer limited to the 16 colors that are supplied; you can now select any custom color you desire. Along with the colors, you can set your own fonts for the different windows as well. Through the Options dialog box, you can also set the default grid options that are used by the forms you create, as shown in Figure 1-4.

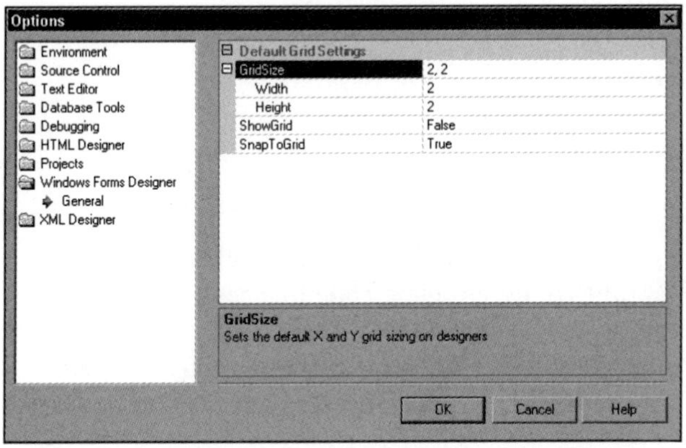

Figure 1-4: Setting the default grid options used by forms.

Default options — such as whether to display the grid, snap controls to the grid, and the grid size — can be set here, but each Windows form has these same options that override the defaults that you set here. Note that the grid size settings are in pixels, not twips. Visual Basic .NET only supports pixels for sizes and positions of controls and forms.

These samples are just the tip of the iceberg when it comes to dealing with customizing the Visual Basic .NET IDE. Later on in this book, you'll see some of the other ways to customize and extend the environment through the use of macros, add-ins, project and file templates, creating and customizing keyboard shortcuts, creating and using aliases for typing commands in the new Command window, and through using other IDE extensibility features.

An Overview of Changes to the Visual Basic Language

As Visual Basic has evolved over the years, it has retained many of its original features, while some features were extended and others were added. Due to the sweeping changes required for the Visual Basic .NET platform and the Common Language Runtime, Microsoft has taken the opportunity to remove some of the redundancy and inconsistencies. According to Microsoft, the changes to Visual Basic .NET are intended to:

◆ Simplify the Visual Basic language and make it more consistent.

◆ Add new features requested by developers.

◆ Make code easier to read and maintain.

◆ Help programmers to avoid introducing coding errors.

◆ Make applications more robust and easier to debug.

◆ Support the common language runtime.

Changes to the language syntax

This section highlights the major changes to the language syntax itself. It's important to understand the changes to the language before programming in Visual Basic .NET so that you won't waste time trying to debug code that may appear to work differently than it did in prior versions of Visual Basic. Understanding the language syntax changes will also allow you to take advantage of the new and changed features in your code, which can reduce the overall amount of effort required when developing an application in Visual Basic .NET.

ARRAYS
In Visual Basic 6, the default lower bound for every dimension of an array was zero. However, this could be changed by using the Option Base statement or by explicitly declaring both the low and high bounds when declaring the array. In .NET, the lower bound of each array dimension is always zero. The `Option Base` statement is no longer supported, and you can't declare both the lower and upper bounds when you declare the array. This doesn't mean that you have to have zero as the lower bound of all arrays in .NET, because you could write a class that simulates the functionality of an alternative-based array by adjusting the index given back to the zero-based array.

Another change to arrays in .NET is that the number of dimensions of the array must be fixed when the array is declared. The `Redim` statement in .NET only allows you to change the size of each dimension in the array; it won't allow you to change the number of dimensions of an array.

REDIM STATEMENT
In prior versions of Visual Basic, the `Redim` statement could be used to serve as the initial declaration of the array, because you didn't have to declare the array in a regular `Dim` statement before it was used with a `Redim` statement. This could lead to some difficult bugs if the spelling of the variable changed in the `Redim` statement from the `Dim` statement, because you would be working with two different arrays at

that point. This is cleaned up in .NET – you have to declare the variable with a regular Dim statement before it can be used with the Redim statement.

FIXED-LENGTH STRINGS

In prior versions of Visual Basic, you could specify the length of a string variable when it was declared, making it a fixed-length string. In .NET, you cannot declare a string variable to have a fixed length. If a project is upgraded from version 6 into .NET, the upgrade wizard will change all declarations of a fixed-length string to use the FixedLengthString compatibility object:

```
Dim strX As String * 100
'Gets converted to
Dim strX As New VB6.FixedLengthString(100)
```

However, you shouldn't start using the object directly, because it's included only for compatibility. In fact, if you just type in the preceding code, it won't compile, because in order to use the object you must add a reference to the compatibility component and then use an imports statement to be able to use the namespace where the object is located. In order to use the compatibility namespace, you first have to add a reference to the Microsoft Visual Basic .NET Compatibility Runtime assembly. The VB6 namespace is then located in the Microsoft. VisualBasic.Compatibility namespace, which would need to be imported into the local namespace. Fixed-lengths strings should be changed to use a regular String object, but this requires you to look at how the string is used everywhere in your code.

INTEGER DATA TYPE

Prior versions of Visual Basic had two signed integer data types called Integer and Long. Integer was a 16-bit signed integer data type, while the Long data type was a 32-bit signed integer value. In Visual Basic .NET, the Long data type is now a 64-bit signed value in preparation for the 64-bit processors that will soon be delivered. The Integer data type is now a 32-bit value instead of a 16-bit value. Because both the Integer and Long types were promoted, Visual Basic .NET needed a new Short data type for the 16-bit signed values. On 32-bit systems, operations with 32-bit integers are faster then 16-bit or 64-bit data types, so they should be used most of the time, as long as the values for the variables are within the proper range for the data type.

UNIVERSAL DATA TYPE

In previous versions of Visual Basic, the ugly Variant served as the universal data type, because it could store values of any data type. Although there were many problems with using variants, it was the best method available at the time for storing data with different types. Visual Basic .NET has eliminated the Variant data type and has replaced it with the new System.Object class. Even though the Object data type was in prior versions, it's not the same data type, as you'll understand later in this book as you read the chapter on inheritance (Chapter 5). In .NET, the `vartype` function is no longer supported either. If you want to know the type of data assigned to a variable, you can check its typecode property, as in the following example:

```
Dim o As Object
Dim TC As TypeCode

o = 5
o = "Hello World"

TC = o.GetType.GetTypeCode(o.GetType)
Select Case tc
    Case TypeCode.Boolean
    Case TypeCode.Int32
    Case TypeCode.String
    Case TypeCode.Double
End Select
```

The sample code illustrates how you can use a variable of the object data type and assign different data types to it. The `Select Case` statement is used to determine what the data type is and allows you to perform different execution paths depending on the data type contained in the variable.

DATA TYPES

The default data type statements (`DefBool`, `DefByte`, `DefCur`, `DefDate`, `DefDbl`, `DefDec`, `DefInt`, `DefLng`, `DefObj`, `DefSng`, `DefStr`, and `DefVar`) in prior versions are not supported in Visual Basic .NET. Furthermore, the `currency` data type is not supported either. The `decimal` data type, which is directly supported by the .NET framework and runtime, should be used to store currency values, because it can handle more digits on both sides of the decimal point. In Visual Basic 6, a date value is stored in a double format using 4 bytes, but Visual Basic .NET uses the `DateTime` data type, which stores the data in an 8-byte integer value. In order to convert from a date value represented in Visual Basic 6, you should use the `FromOADate` method of the `DateTime` class. Similarly, to convert from .NET back to the Visual Basic 6 representation, you should use the `ToDouble` method on the `DateTime` class.

BOOLEAN OPERATORS

Visual Basic .NET improves the way logical expressions are evaluated. Unlike Visual Basic 6, where all operands of all logical expressions are always evaluated, .NET introduces short-circuiting capabilities when performing Boolean operations. If the first operand of an `And` operator evaluates to false, the rest of the expression is not evaluated. Similarly, if the first operand of an `Or` operator evaluates to true, the remainder of the expression is not evaluated. You need to be aware of this difference in behavior from Visual Basic 6, because it can cause some logical errors in your program if you intend for all expressions (particularly function or method calls as an operand) to be evaluated.

DEFAULT PROPERTIES

In Visual Basic .NET, default properties for objects are no longer supported unless they take parameters. These properties are also known as parameterized properties. The major impact of this is if you relied on the default properties for controls and didn't specify default property when reading from or writing to the property:

```
'In VB6 this was valid
lblDescription = "Hello World"

'In VB.NET the above is invalid and requires
lblDescription.Text = "Hello World"
```

The preceding listing also points out another difference you need to be aware of. Visual Basic .NET changed the controls to make them more consistent with each other. As a result, any time you need to set the text of a control, you use the common Text property instead of Text on some and Caption on others. Therefore, in the preceding example, setting the Text property of the label control is valid.

The reason for the default property change was to remove the ambiguity from the code and make the intentions clear to anyone reading the code. Default properties made the Set statement necessary in the Visual Basic language when setting object references, as shown in the following listing:

```
Dim L1 As Label
Dim L2 As Label

L1 = "Some Text"     'Setting the caption property
L2 = L1              'Set the caption of L2 to same as L1
Set L2 = L1          'Store an object reference to L1 in L2
```

Because the default properties have been removed from the language, the Set statements can be eliminated. This not only applies to setting two objects equal to each other but also when creating new objects. In .NET, the L2 = L1 in the preceding listing would set an object reference, and if you wanted the Text properties equal, you would need to include the Text property on each label.

Default properties that take parameters are not ambiguous and therefore are supported in Visual Basic .NET. Think about a Recordset object and how the default properties are used in it. The default property of a Recordset object is a Fields collection, and the default property of the collection is the Field object. The following listing shows both valid and invalid uses of the default properties in Visual Basic .NET:

```
Dim Rs As Recordset

Rs.Fields.Item(1).Value = "Some Text"      'Valid
Rs.Fields(1).Value = "Some Text"           'Valid

Rs(1).Value = "Something"                   'Not Valid
Rs.Fields(1) = "Something"                   'Not valid
```

In the preceding listing, the top two lines of code both represent valid statements, because there is no ambiguity. However, in the second two lines of code, the syntax is invalid, because fields is not parameterized in the first line and the value is not parameterized in the second line. The Item property of the Fields collection is the only parameterized property and, therefore, it's the only one that can be omitted when supplying a parameter value. In prior versions of Visual Basic, you had to go into the Object Browser, select a property, display the properties for the property, and then specify that a particular property was to be the default property. In Visual Basic .NET, you specify a property is the default property by starting its declaration with the Default keyword as long as the property takes a parameter. This approach makes it easier to create and understand how to use default properties, which meets several of the reasons listed earlier in this chapter for why the changes are required in the Visual Basic .NET language.

PROPERTY PROCEDURES
Visual Basic .NET introduces a new unified property declaration syntax that includes the procedures for getting and setting the property's value. This ensures consistency between property attributes such as access level and overloading. The following listing shows how you would create a property procedure that doesn't take parameters in a class:

```
Public Class Thermometer
    Private dblTemperature As Double      'Internal storage

    Public Property Temperature() As Double
        Get
            Return dblTemperature
        End Get

        Set (ByVal Value As Double)
            dblTemperature = value
        End Set
    End Property
End Class
```

Several things need to be pointed out in the preceding listing. First, a Let statement is no longer required because there is no need to determine whether you're setting the object or the default value for the object. Second, notice the use of the `Return` keyword to return the value required. The `Return` statement can be used in Subs and Functions and is a shortcut to setting the return value of the function and then issuing an `Exit Function` statement. If used in a sub, it's equivalent to the `Exit Sub` statement. Here, the `Return` keyword is used to return the value in the `Get` property and exit the property. Notice how we get the value supplied by the property, because we didn't declare a variable to hold the value we're setting it to. The `Value` keyword is an implicit variable that contains the value passed into the property. Notice how the get and set are contained within an overall property procedure. This again makes for cleaner code by keeping the statements together and by allowing the access modifiers to be only required on the property procedure, not the individual `Set` and `Get` statements. You'll see later through overloading a function how you can use one property name that accepts different data types, and you'll understand why it's important and makes it easier to code for when you have situations that require overloading or overriding a function.

STRUCTURE DECLARATIONS

In Visual Basic 6, you could define a structure using the `Type` keyword. Types defaulted to public access for the structure and its members. Visual Basic .NET unifies the declarations for structures and classes, because both can have members and methods unlike a type structure in previous versions. Furthermore, each member can have different access modifiers and, as a result, each member must explicitly declare an access modifier:

```
Structure MyPoint
    Public X As Integer
    Public Y As Integer

    Private intScale As Integer

    Public Sub GenerateScale()
        intScale = x * y
    End Sub
End Structure
```

The preceding listing shows how to create a structure with both public and private members, and it contains a public method as well. Structures are almost identical to classes, however the major difference between a class and a structure is that a structure cannot use inheritance and a structure requires significantly less overhead to store in memory. If you need inheritance, then you must use a class or define interfaces that are implemented by classes.

VARIABLE DECLARATION SYNTAX

In previous versions of Visual Basic, if you declared multiple variables on the same line, unless you specified the data type for each variable, it defaulted to `Variant`.

Visual Basic .NET has simplified the variable declaration syntax to eliminate the requirement that the data type be repeated for each variable:

```
Dim X,Y As Integer
```

In the preceding listing, X would be a variant and Y would be an integer in previous versions, but now in .NET, both X and Y will be integers.

VARIABLE SCOPE

In previous versions of Visual Basic, if you declared a variable in the middle of a procedure, it was available anywhere after the point where you declared it. In Visual Basic .NET, variables now also have block scope. If a variable is declared within a particular block of code, then it's only accessible inside the block:

```
Dim intCounter As Integer
Dim Y As Integer
For intCounter = 1 to 10
    Dim intResult As Integer
    intResult = intResult + intCounter
Next

    Y = intResult
```

In previous versions, the preceding code would work fine and you could get the value of intResult outside of the block. However, the preceding code will fail in Visual Basic .NET because the intResult variable is not accessible outside the block. You'll get an error stating that intResult is not declared on the line where you assign it to the Y variable. It's important to note that even though the variable isn't accessible outside of the block, its lifetime is the same as the lifetime of the procedure.

OBJECT CREATION

In prior versions of Visual Basic, an object variable declared with the As New keywords is initialized to Nothing. Every time the variable is referenced in code, Visual Basic first checked to see if the object was Nothing; if so, then it would automatically create an instance of the object before the line of code executed. If the object was set to Nothing, it would automatically be created again the next time you used it. This behavior wasted processing time, because it had to check each and every time the variable was used. Many programmers were surprised the first time they realized what was actually happening to the object variable. In .NET, there is no implicit object creation when the variable is encountered in code:

```
Dim objEmp As New cEmployee
Dim objEmp As cEmployee = New cEmployee
```

In the preceding code, both lines are equal and the object is created and initialized when the variable is declared. Another feature in .NET is that some classes provide constructors, which can be used to initialize the object:

```
Dim objEmp As cEmployee = New cEmployee(intEmployeeID)
```

The preceding line of code would declare and initialize the Employee object at the same time. As a side note, you'll see later that everything in .NET is an object. For this reason and through providing constructors, the following lines of code create and initialize variables at the same time:

```
Dim intX As Integer = 5
Dim dblPi As Double = 3.14159
```

PROCEDURE DECLARATIONS

In Visual Basic 6, you could declare a procedure parameter as Optional without specifying a default value. If the optional parameter was a Variant data type, you could check to see if the parameter was supplied by using the IsMissing function. However, in Visual Basic .NET, every optional parameter must declare a default value, which will be supplied to the procedure if the calling routine doesn't supply a value for the parameter. As a result, there's no way to tell if a parameter wasn't supplied or if the calling routine passed the default value in for the parameter. The parameter will behave in the exact same way regardless of whether it was supplied or not. Furthermore, the IsMissing function is rendered obsolete and therefore it's not supported in Visual Basic .NET.

If you need to know whether a parameter was supplied, then you need to look at the concept of overloading a function, which will allow you to determine which parameters are supplied to the function.

The concept of overloading functions is introduced later in this chapter but is not discussed in detail until Chapter 3.

Another difference in the declarations of functions is that in prior versions, you could declare a procedure with the Static modifier. This forced every local variable to be static and retain its value between calls. Visual Basic .NET doesn't support the static modifier on a function or a sub statement. Each local variable that you want to be static must be declared with the static attribute.

PROCEDURE CALLING SYNTAX

The inconsistent use of parentheses when calling functions and subs in prior versions led to confusion as to whether they were needed or not. In prior versions, parentheses were required around the parameter list in function calls and sub calls when you used the call statement. If you didn't use the call statement when calling a sub procedure, parentheses weren't allowed. Visual Basic .NET cleans this up by always requiring parentheses around a non-empty parameter list. If you're calling a procedure without supplying any parameters, parentheses are optional and can be left off if so desired.

In prior versions of Visual Basic, you could use the `Return` keyword only to branch back to the code following a `GoSub` statement, and both statements were required to be in the same procedure. The `GoSub` statement isn't supported in Visual Basic .NET so you can't branch to a subroutine within a subroutine. There are many ways that `GoSubs` can be replaced, so I won't go into detail on this. However, by not supporting `GoSubs` anymore, the `Return` statement is freed up for other uses. The use of the `Return` statement was explained earlier in this chapter in the property procedures section.

PASSING PARAMETERS

In Visual Basic 6, if you didn't specify either `ByVal` or `ByRef` for each procedure parameter, the parameters defaulted to passing by reference. This allowed the variable that was passed into the procedure to be modified in the calling procedure. Although passing a parameter by reference has its benefits, it can also lead to unexpected behavior. As a result, Visual Basic .NET defaults to passing parameters by value instead of by reference. If you need to pass a parameter `ByRef`, then you must explicitly state that it's by reference.

If a property was passed as a by-reference parameter to a procedure, the property is copied in to the procedure but it's not copied out. This changes in Visual Basic .NET, as properties that are passed `ByRef` are copied both into and out of the procedure.

In Visual Basic 6, if you used the `ParamArray` keyword to accept an array of variant parameters, they were always passed by reference. In Visual Basic .NET, the parameters in a `ParamArray` are always passed by value and the data type of the parameters in the array must be an Object.

FLOW CONTROL STATEMENTS

As previously mentioned, the `GoSub` statement isn't supported because you can call procedures with the `Call`, `Function`, and `Sub` statements. Furthermore, the computed `GoTo` and `GoSub` statements aren't supported in Visual Basic .NET. The only exception to this is you can still use the `On Error Goto` statement. The `While` loop structure is still valid, but the `Wend` keyword is replaced with the `End While` statement.

CLASSES AND INTERFACES

There are several changes to classes and interfaces in Visual Basic .NET from prior versions. Visual Basic 6 didn't allow you to define and use interfaces directly from within Visual Basic itself. There was a workaround by defining a class with no implementation and then implementing this class module, but it only worked because a default interface was created behind the scenes that included the public members of the class. In Visual Basic .NET you can now explicitly define an interface and use the `Implements` keyword to consume the interface. The `Implements` keyword can only specify an interface, not a class.

In prior versions of Visual Basic, you could set the `Instancing` property to `GlobalSingleUse` or `GlobalMultiUse`, and other components could invoke the properties and methods of the class as if they were global functions instead of requiring an object to be created first. In Visual Basic .NET, you can add shared properties and methods of a class to the system namespace using the `Imports` statement. After doing this, you can call the shared properties and methods without having to create an object before doing so. The `MsgBox` function is a perfect example of a shared member, as it's a shared function located in the Interaction class of the `Microsoft.VisualBasic` namespace, which is imported by default at the project level in the Project Properties dialog box.

In prior versions, you could use the initialize and terminate events of a class module to perform any necessary actions at the time of creation and destruction. The initialize event fired whenever a new object based on the class was created, and the terminate event fired whenever the last reference to the object was destroyed. In Visual Basic .NET, you don't have these events; instead, Visual Basic .NET uses constructors and destructors.

The constructor is used by specifying a sub named `New`, and you can provide parameters in the procedure that are required to be supplied when the object is created. You can use the `New` procedure to initialize your object to a known state at the time of creation. This avoids introducing bugs where the caller forgets to initialize your object properly after creation.

In Visual Basic .NET you cannot rely on the destructor to fire when the last object reference is released. Through the Common Language Runtime, Visual Basic .NET provides support for garbage collection in order to clean up objects and free up memory. Although this behavior may seem strange, it's a more efficient process then the way COM increments and decrements the reference counter and destroys the object when the reference counter goes to zero. Garbage collection walks the reference tree and can effectively clean up objects that have circular references, which were difficult to clean up in prior versions. Furthermore, the garbage collector runs in the background when there isn't as much processing activity going on. This process introduces a new term called Indeterminate Lifetime. Because there is no way of knowing the order in which the objects will be destroyed or the time it takes the garbage collector to traverse the tree and find the objects that aren't referenced by any currently executing code, you have no idea when the object will be destroyed.

PROGRAMMING ELEMENTS REPLACED BY METHODS

Visual Basic .NET no longer supports several programming elements, because the .NET Framework and the Common Language Runtime include functionality that makes them unnecessary. First, the `System.Drawing.Graphics` class and related classes provide extensive graphical support through their methods and other members. Graphics, pictures, images, and icons are probably one of the most difficult things to understand in Visual Basic .NET, and I cover these in detail later on in the book to ensure that you have the basic knowledge to understand how to use the graphics and related classes.

The System.Math class is included to provide extensive mathematical support through its methods and fields. In this class, you may notice that some of the function names have changed to reduce ambiguity in their names. The native functions of Visual Basic 6 are now compatibility functions in the .NET Framework and are located in the Microsoft.VisualBasic namespace. For projects created with Visual Basic, the namespace is imported for you in the project template. Therefore, you do not need to explicitly import this namespace. This is how you can call prior Visual Basic functions without having to qualify them. The methods are shared methods in the VisualBasic namespace and as mentioned previously the Imports statement brings shared members into the system namespace. In fact, since Visual Basic is very customizable, you can set your own namespaces to be imported globally into the project. Bring up the Project Properties dialog box by right-clicking on the project in the Solution Explorer and selecting Properties. Click the Imports item in the folder list, and you see the dialog box shown in Figure 1-5.

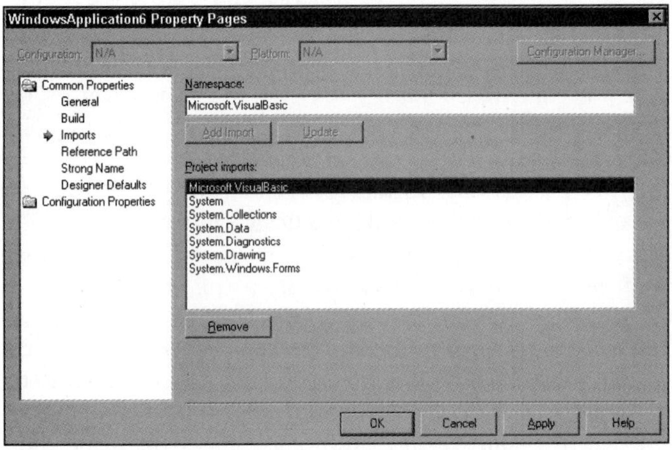

Figure 1-5: The imports section of the Project Properties dialog box.

As you can see, you're free to choose the namespaces that are imported by default into your entire project. After these namespaces have been imported, there is no need to include another imports statement for the listed namespace, because it's there by default even though you don't explicitly see the imports statement in each class or module.

The MsgBox function is replaced by the Show method of the System.Windows.Forms.MessageBox class, which provides extensive capabilities for informing and instructing the user. You should also know that the Microsoft.VisualBasic. Interaction class exposes a MsgBox function that approximates the Visual Basic 6

MsgBox function. The MsgBox function is merely a wrapper around the new MessageBox.Show method.

Because everything is an object in Visual Basic .NET, the string manipulation functions you typically use are now methods of the String class. As a result, any time you declare a variable of the String class (which you're used to thinking of as a data type), you can initialize the string as well as call methods to operate on the string, such as Replace, Join, Split, PadLeft, PadRight, and so on.

PROGRAMMING ELEMENTS SUPPORTED DIFFERENTLY

There are several language elements supported differently in Visual Basic .NET that you need to be aware of. Visual Basic .NET uses the Nothing keyword for a variable that contains no data and to indicate that the variable has not been initialized yet. Prior versions used the Empty keyword for an uninitialized variable and the Null keyword for a variable that contained no data. Therefore, the Empty and Null keywords are no longer supported, and because the Empty keyword is no longer supported, there is no longer any need for the IsEmpty function, which is also no longer supported.

Visual Basic .NET removes the *vb* prefix from all the core language constants and the constants have been moved to keep them with the classes they're used with. For example, in order to set the color of a form to red, you'd have write the following line of code:

```
frmX.BackColor = Color.Red
```

If you use many color constants in your code, you may want to import the System.Drawing.Color namespace into your code either through an explicit imports statement or by setting it in the Project Properties dialog box.

OPTION STATEMENTS

Visual Basic .NET only supports three Option statements. The Option statements you can use are Option Compare, Option Explicit, and Option Strict. By default, if you don't specify otherwise, the Option Explicit command is set to on and the Option Strict command is set to off. The Option Compare default uses the Option Compare Binary option, which forces text comparisons to be completed as a binary operation, and case will matter. If you don't want case to matter when comparing strings, you can set the Option Compare Text statement at the module level and the case of the string won't matter. One of the first things you should do in any project is turn the Option Strict On in the Project Properties dialog box. This helps you to see and understand the type conversions that are required between the variables in your applications.

If you want to turn off the Option Explicit setting (not a good idea), you can include the Option Explicit Off statement in every module. Similarly, if you want to turn off the Option Strict setting, you can include the Option Strict Off statement in every module. With Option Explicit On, all variables must be declared before use. It's generally a good idea to leave this on so that it catches errors that can occur from misspelling a variable. Without enforcing that all variables be declared, you can accidentally create multiple variables with the same intention. This type of programming bug can be very hard to track down; by including the Option Explicit statement, you catch undeclared variables at compile time instead of having to track down the bug at runtime. Visual Basic can perform implicit type conversions automatically of any data type to another. However, data loss can occur when the data is converted to a variable with less precision then the original. Should this occur, a runtime error will occur. The Option Strict statement enforces compile-time checking for these types of conversions so they may be avoided. Conversions of widening type are allowed because the precision of the original variable won't be lost in the conversion. Each data type has a list of data types that it can widen to without any problem. The help file shows a table of the data types and the widening conversions allowed on each type. Search for the Option Strict statement in the help file to view the table.

CONTROL ARRAYS NO LONGER SUPPORTED

In prior versions of Visual Basic, you could create several controls of the same type, give them the same name, and change the Index property of each control, and you'd have a control array. Control arrays were useful for handling the event code for multiple controls in one common location. If you created control arrays, you could write code in the common event routine and you could check the Index property of each control to see which control the event was coming from. This also made it difficult to determine which control in a control array was being manipulated without requiring the developer to look at documentation or the form and figure out which control matched the specified index. The typical workaround was to declare an enumeration that would give meaningful names to the indexes and use the enumeration item when specifying a particular control in the control array.

In keeping with the design goals of Visual Basic .NET, Microsoft removed the direct concept of creating a control array. However, they realized the importance of having common code routines and replaced the concept of a control array with a solution that's easier to understand and maintain by developers. Visual Basic .NET introduces the Handles keyword, which is placed at the end of an event procedure and is used to identify that the procedure will handle the events of other procedures. The best way to understand this is to view a code snippet that shows how to use the Handles keyword. Create a new Windows Application project, add three buttons on the form, and name them btnTrue, btnFalse, and btnGuess. The following code shows the click event of the btnTrue where you will place code:

```
Private Sub btnTrue_Click(ByVal sender As System.Object, _
    ByVal e As System.EventArgs) Handles btnFalse.Click, _
    btnGuess.Click


    Select Case True
        Case Sender.Equals(btnFalse)
```

```
                messagebox.Show("False")
        Case Sender.Equals(btnTrue)
                messagebox.Show("True")
        Case Sender.Equals(btnGuess)
                messagebox.Show("Guess")
    End Select
End Sub
```

You may immediately notice that the button event procedure is different from what you're used to seeing. The sender indicates what object initiated the event, which is obvious for single controls. The e parameter listed will contain any system arguments that you may need. If you were to look at the code for the MouseDown event, you would see a different type for the e parameter. The e object will have several properties such as the coordinates of the mouse position, and whether any other keys were down at the time of the event. All the information you need is packed neatly into an object, which you can query for any property value supported. This common event structure is different from what you've seen in the past, but it doesn't take long to understand how it works.

If you look at the procedure declaration line, you see the keyword handles toward the end of the declaration. After the keyword, you see a list of objects and events on each object that this procedure will also handle. The .NET Framework and runtime place the hooks into the program to automatically handle the click events from the other buttons. Now the sender object makes sense when you're looking at an event procedure that handles many controls. You simply need to check to see what the sender object is, perform any specific logic to that sender, and then include the common logic for all senders.

Additions to the language

Visual Basic .NET introduces a few other key features that enhance the power and capabilities of the language. These include support for inheritance, overloading functions, structured error handling, and free threading.

INHERITANCE

Visual Basic not only supports inheritance, it also takes advantage of it everywhere. In Visual Basic .NET, everything except for an interface definition is an object. There is a base object data type from which everything else in the language is derived. This object data type is not the same object data type as in prior versions. The object data type is an object itself, and it exposes certain functions that can be called on the object itself. The concept of inheritance allows objects to use behavior supplied in the base class without having the code in the derived class. Because every object is derived from the base object, they all contain the same functions exposed in the base object class. One of the principles of inheritance is that the derived objects can provide their own implementation or behavior for a method or property in the base class. This concept is known as being able to override a function that is inherited from a base class. Visual Basic .NET allows you to inherit from other classes, interfaces, forms, and controls. The objects you can inherit from can be from within your local projects or they can be from external assemblies.

 Inheritance is covered in detail in Chapter 5.

OVERLOADING PROCEDURES

Another feature that's very useful is the concept of overloading functions. Overloading a function allows you to define several different procedures or properties — each with the same name, as long as its signature is different. The concept of overloading a function is typically used with constructors but can be used for anything. By overloading a constructor of a class, you can provide different parameters that will allow the object to initialize to different states, depending on the parameters supplied.

In the following listing, we define a class with several different constructors:

```
Public Class MyPoint
    Public X As Integer
    Public Y As Double

    Public Sub New()
        'No parameters, do nothing
    End Sub

    Public Sub New(ByVal X_Value As Integer)
        x = X_Value
    End Sub

    Public Sub New(ByVal Y_Value As Double)
        y = Y_Value
    End Sub

    Public Sub New(ByVal X_Value As Integer, _
      ByVal Y_Value As Double)

        x = X_Value
        y = Y_Value
    End Sub
End Class
```

```
Dim MP1 As MyPoint = New MyPoint()
Dim MP2 As MyPoint = New MyPoint(5)
Dim MP3 As MyPoint = New MyPoint(3.14159)
Dim MP4 As MyPoint = New MyPoint(2, 6.28318)
```

The first constructor does not accept any parameters and would be called for MP1. The second constructor accepts an X_Value parameter as an Integer and would be called for MP2. The third constructor accepts a Y_Value as a Double and would be called form MP3. The fourth constructor accepts both an X_Value and a Y_Value and would be called for MP4. Visual Basic .NET looks to see what is being supplied and if a constructor exists for the supplied signature. If a constructor exists, it will be called when the object is created and the object will be initialized from the supplied parameters.

STRUCTURED ERROR HANDLING

Visual Basic .NET introduces another form of error handling called Structured Error Handling. This type of error handling is implemented using the new Try...Catch...Finally keywords. The Try...Catch statements are used to capture and handle errors in line instead of jumping to an error handler for the entire procedure. This allows you to predict where an error might occur for any reason and handle it in way that is most appropriate to what the code is doing.

There are several different ways you can implement a Try...Catch block, but if there is a section of code in which you want to catch an exception that might be thrown, then you need to start the code block with a Try statement. After the code that you wanted to trap an error in, you need to have either the Catch or Finally keyword. The Catch will set a block of code that will execute to catch an error that occurs. You write code in this block to handle the error in whatever way you need, such as displaying a message box and logging the error. Code that is in the Finally block will always execute after the Try block if there is no error or will execute after the Catch block if there is an error. The code in this block typically performs any cleanup operations that you may need to do regardless of whether an error occurs or not. An important thing to realize is that you can nest Try...Catch blocks within each other. This allows you to catch an error and try executing code that handles the error. You could even put a nested Try...Catch block inside the Catch or Finally block to catch any errors that might occur on your error handler or your cleanup code.

The following listing shows an example of how to implement Try...Catch error handling:

```
Sub TryCatchExample()
    Dim x As Integer
    Dim y As Integer

    Try
        x \= y
```

```
Catch e As Exception
    MessageBox.Show(e.toString)
    Try
        x \= y
    Catch
        beep()
    Finally
        beep()
    End Try
Finally
    Beep()
End Try
End Sub
```

The first thing that will attempt to execute is the x \= y statement, but this will generate a divide by zero exception, because the y variable is zero. The execution will jump to the first Catch block and will display a message box to the user with a friendly error message. Notice how the line number and the procedure are included for you in the message indicating exactly where the error occurred. Next the code in the nested Try block will execute and generate another exception, so the second Catch block will execute and you'll hear a beep from the speakers. Next, the nested Finally block will execute and you'll hear another beep from the speakers. Finally (pun intended), the code in the original Finally block will execute and you'll hear another beep from the speakers.

Although it may seem a little awkward to use at first, because you're used to the On...Error...Goto statements in previous versions, the advantage comes from being able to handle an error in your error-handling routine. In prior versions, if you had an error while the error handler was executing, you would be thrown out of the routine and it would generate an error in the calling routine. With Try...Catch statements, the code for complex error handling becomes much simpler. When you understand how the Try...Catch code works, it's a lot easier to understand the flow of a program while reading the code, again making the code easier to read and maintain. Microsoft has kept the On...Error...Goto error handling and introduced the Try...Catch exception handling to the language. The choice is yours as to which one you want to use. You can even mix the types of error handling in your project depending on your needs, but you can't mix the two within a single procedure.

FREE THREADING SUPPORT

Visual Basic .NET finally makes it easy for you to run code on different threads. Any code that has the potential of delaying or preventing other tasks from executing can be placed on a separate thread. However, there are limitations to any routine that is to execute on a separate thread. The procedure or method can't have any arguments or return any values. These limitations aren't as restrictive as they may seem — there are workarounds to supplying parameters and getting information back. The basic code to create a thread and have it run a procedure is very simple, as shown in the following listing:

```
Public Sub LaunchThread()
    Dim T As Threading.Thread = New _
            Threading.Thread(AddressOf MyThreadedSub)

    t.Start()
End Sub

Public Sub MyThreadedSub()
    beep()
End Sub
```

Although Visual Basic .NET makes it is easy to run a procedure on a different thread, you now have to understand how threading works and its implications. When using threads, you need to be concerned about how to pass parameters to and from the routines that are running on the separate thread, how to synchronize access to shared resources, how to keep the app responsive, and how to manage the threads you create.

 Threading is discussed in Chapter 12, where you'll see how to create a generic thread manager that you can use to simplify the workarounds and the other code required for supporting free threading.

ASSIGNMENT OPERATORS
Finally, another feature that has been added to Visual Basic .NET is new assignment operators that reduce the amount of typing required. These assignment operators can end up saving you coding time as long as you understand what they are and how to use them. Unless all developers realize what assignment operators are and how they work, they may be confused when looking at code that contains these operators. However, developers will have to understand many new things in .NET in order to read some Visual Basic .NET code, so this may not be an issue. The new assignment operators are:

- ^=: Raises the value of a variable to the power of an exponent and assigns the result back to the variable

- *=: Multiplies the value of a variable by the value of an expression and assigns the result back to the variable

- /=: Divides the value of a variable by the value of an expression and assigns the result to the variable

- ◆ \=: Divides the value of a variable by the value of an expression and assigns the integer results to the variable

- ◆ +=: Adds the value of an expression to the value of a variable and assigns the result to the variable

- ◆ -=: Subtracts the value of an expression from the value of a variable and assigns the result to the variable

- ◆ &=: Concatenates a string expression to a string variable and assigns the result to the variable

It's easier to understand the preceding operations by looking at code that shows an example of each operator:

```
Dim dblExpOp As Double = 2
dblExpOp ^= 3    'Now 2^3 = 8

Dim dblMulOp As Double = 2
dblMulOp *= 5    'Now 2*5 = 10

Dim dblDivOp As Double = 15
dblDivOp /= 5    'Now 15/5 = 3

Dim intDivOp As Integer = 13
intDivOp \= 4    'Now 13\4 = 3

Dim dblAddOp As Double = 7
dblAddOp += 3    'Now 7+3 = 10

Dim dblSubOp As Double = 9
dblSubOp -= 4    'Now 9-4 = 5

Dim strText As String = "Hello "
strText &= "World"   'Now "Hello World"
```

The preceding comments show what the result of each assignment operator is, and you can see how using the assignment operators in your code can save you typing time by not requiring you to type out the variable name twice in the same code statement.

Other Changes to Visual Basic .NET

Up to this point, this chapter has primarily concentrated on the language elements themselves that have changed. Visual Basic .NET also has some general changes that you need to be aware of, the first of which is how projects and solutions are managed in Visual Basic .NET. Visual Basic .NET is built upon and uses the .NET Framework and the Common Language Runtime, just like the other languages in Visual Studio .NET. In order to preserve the functionality of existing applications, the .NET Framework has the capability of interacting with and using COM objects (ADO, ActiveX Controls, and so on) that have already been developed. Although you could use existing versions of ADO for accessing data stores, a .NET version of ADO has been introduced that can be used to simplify and speed up access to the persistent data your applications might need.

Projects and solutions

Visual Basic .NET has changed the project structure that you may be used to. In prior versions, you could create independent projects, and you could create a project group that would group related projects together and be able to view the code for the projects at the same time. Although creating project groups allowed for easier debugging between multiple projects, it had some limitations. If you've used Visual Interdev before, you have a head start on understanding the new structure. Visual Basic .NET introduces several new things to the project structure, including a *solution,* which is a container for everything you would work with for a project. Because all the Visual Studio tools use the same common IDE, the concepts for creating and working with projects had to be merged. Because the IDE is common, you can mix languages at the project level in the solution.

.NET Framework

Visual Basic .NET and the other Visual Studio .NET languages were built upon the .NET Framework. The .NET Framework is a multi-language environment for building, deploying, and running applications and Web services. The framework consists of three main parts: a Common Language Runtime (CLR), unified programming classes, and Active Server Pages .NET (ASP.NET).

The CLR was created to provide both common runtime activities as well as common design-time features. At runtime, the CLR is responsible for managing memory allocation and process and thread management, enforcing security policies, and satisfying any dependencies the component might have on other components (both .NET components and COM objects). The CLR and the .NET Framework will allow the applications you create in Visual Basic .NET to run on other platforms instead of just the Wintel platform. This allows Microsoft or other third parties to provide a framework and CLR for other platforms other then Intel. Plus, your code would be able to run on that platform without recompiling. This is not the same as Java, where the code is interpreted and the byte codes are "compiled on demand" by the virtual machine. The .NET code is compiled to an intermediate language that the common language runtime can communicate with. This is not the same as interpreted pseudocode such as was in Visual Basic prior to version 5.

Unified programming classes are provided by the framework to supply developers with a unified, object-oriented hierarchical, extensible set of class libraries. This object-oriented approach provides the low-level functions that you may relate to using the Windows API. However, it provides other benefits that writing to the Win32 API functions cannot provide, the first of which is portability to other platforms that have a .NET Framework and CLR. Writing any code to the Win32 API immediately limits your code to running on Wintel-based systems. There should be no reason for you to use the somewhat cryptic function calls of the Win32 API, because you should be able to do everything through the CLR and the system classes provided to you. You may not even need to get into the system classes, because you can subclass and inherit from controls and other components in the Visual Basic .NET language. Did you ever call the `SendMessage` function to find a search string in a combo box? Now the combo box has a direct `FindString` method on it. You'll notice this a lot when you start looking at the new controls in Visual Basic .NET.

ASP.NET builds on the .NET Frameworks programming classes providing a Web Application model in the form of a set of Web controls and infrastructure that makes it easier to build Web Applications. Developers have access to a set of controls that wrap the HTML interface elements, but these controls actually run as compiled code on the server and only send down the HTML and client-side scripting that makes the HTML control behave as desired. ASP.NET also provides infrastructure such as session state management that is not dependent on a particular server's memory. The session state information gets sent as text down to the client and back up to the server when the page is submitted, and the developer doesn't have to do anything special to take advantage of this infrastructure. ASP.NET also uses these same concepts to enable developers to deliver software as a Web service. Using the ASP.NET Web services features, developers can focus on writing the business logic, and the infrastructure will be responsible for delivering the service via SOAP.

COM interoperability layer

When Microsoft created the .NET Framework and the CLR, they realized that they had to allow .NET and COM not only to coexist, but that they would have to be able to interoperate with each other for some period of time. Because the .NET Framework and the CLR handle the infrastructure in the .NET world, components created in .NET have to communicate and behave properly with the CLR. COM components don't know anything about the CLR, so there has to be a mediator that allows COM components to access .NET components and for .NET components to access COM components. The interoperability layer makes COM components act as if they're true .NET components. Similarly, the interoperability layer has to make accessing .NET components completely transparent to existing clients using COM.

Microsoft realized that the performance of the .NET to COM interoperability layer is critical to the success of the .NET platform. Due to the complexities involved, marshaling calls between COM and .NET is expected to be slower than marshaling strictly between like components. However, the extra overhead should be offset by performance gains in the .NET runtime. According to Microsoft, the raw overhead of an in-process, direct vtable bound method call between COM and .NET with simple scalar data types for parameters, should be around ten machine instructions. The overhead in COM is a single jump instruction, so the overhead when there is little work done in the method call may be noticeable. However, typical method calls are more complex and the overhead of ten instructions should be negligible compared to the number of instructions executed within such calls.

The bottom line with the interoperability layer is that you may notice a small performance hit when communicating with COM components. This hit can be reduced the same way you reduce the performance hit in dealing with COM components: by reducing the number of calls to the component. This is typically accomplished by creating procedures that accept the arguments they need instead of setting individual properties of an object. Keep in mind that this interoperability layer occurs in all COM components including controls. Therefore, you should try to use the .NET controls in your application whenever possible in order to minimize the effects. If you're dealing completely with .NET components, you don't need to worry about the interoperability layer directly unless there will be COM components that are calling your .NET component. Another point to keep in mind is that if you're using regular ADO and not ADO.NET, you're using COM components and you may experience a small performance hit. There is no way to guarantee whether you will or won't have a small performance hit unless you do some testing. Because a lot of applications will end up making many ADO calls to retrieve and update information in a database, there is a potential here to make your application run slower then it should. This could be solved by migrating your data access technology to ADO.NET.

ADO.NET

ADO.NET was developed to overcome many of the problems that were encountered while using ADO. One of the problems with ADO was that it didn't scale very well when the number of users grew. Traditional client-server applications typically establish a connection to the database and keep the connection open the entire time the application is running. Although this was possible with ADO, it wasn't practical for many types of applications for several reasons. First, open database connections take up valuable system resources, and a typical database can only effectively manage a relatively small number of concurrent connections before performance starts to degrade. As a result, applications that use or require an open database connection are extremely difficult to scale up. The application may perform well for a small number of users but will probably not scale up to a hundred or more users. Web applications need to be easily scalable because the amount of traffic a Web site gets can grow exponentially in a very short amount of time. An application that's based on live connections will make it either difficult or next to impossible to share data between applications or between companies. ADO.NET was built around a disconnected architecture in which applications are only connected to the database long enough to retrieve or update the data. Because the same number of connections on the server can be used to service many more clients, applications that use a disconnected architecture are easier to scale up to large numbers of users. However, not everything should be treated as a disconnected application. Applications that must always have up-to-the-minute data do not fit the disconnected model and may use ADO instead of ADO.NET. These types of applications typically manage a fixed number of physical resources like seats, tickets, or money.

ADO.NET uses XML to persist the disconnected data to files, and it uses XML streams to send the information between components. An *XML stream* is simply a text representation of the data contained within the dataset. This allows ADO.NET to more easily pass data between components because it doesn't have to marshal object data between components like regular ADO does. XML is an industry-standard format for representing data and, as a result, it's more likely that your application can exchange data with other XML-compliant applications. Because XML is text-based, it can be sent via any protocol including HTTP. Because most firewalls block binary information on nonstandard ports, XML is a good candidate for communicating with remote systems, because the XML won't be blocked by firewalls as long as a standard port such as HTTP is used. In fact, Web services use XML and HTTP to communicate with the calling applications and, as a result, their communication channels aren't blocked by firewalls – unlike applications that use DCOM.

Summary

In this chapter, you were introduced to the high-level changes to Visual Basic .NET. Although this chapter presented a lot of information, it wasn't a complete listing of all the changes. This chapter briefly covered the most prominent changes in the language, but entire chapters later in the book talk about the specifics.

The primary reasons for changing features in the language were to make the code more readable and easier to maintain, include features developers have been requesting, help introduce fewer bugs into the code, improve support for debugging, remove redundancies in the language, and make Visual Basic .NET more powerful.

Some of the changes to the language itself eliminated the need to support certain antiquated syntaxes and procedures. A brief overview and introduction was given showing the level of individual customization that can be achieved within the common IDE.

In this chapter, I explained the role the Common Language Runtime and the .NET Framework play in supporting Visual Basic .NET. You were given an overview as to how Visual Basic .NET can call COM components and how COM components can call into components created in .NET.

Chapter 2

A Tour of the Common IDE

IN THIS CHAPTER

- ◆ Common IDE
- ◆ Toolbox changes
- ◆ Code window changes
- ◆ Overview of new and changed windows

The first thing you'll notice when you launch Visual Basic .NET is the new integrated development environment (IDE). Microsoft has said for some time now that it was going to merge the different IDEs into one common development environment. The majority of Visual Basic developers don't work solely in Visual Basic; they may use Visual Interdev, Visual C++, as well as Visual Basic in their programming tasks. As a result, Microsoft wanted to merge the various development environments into a single common development environment, which has now come to fruition with Visual Studio .NET. Visual Interdev is no longer a separate product. You can create and work with HTML and ASP files within Visual Basic .NET. You can also have a solution that mixes development languages at the project level if you have the entire Visual Studio package. The same development environment is used to work with the .NET versions of Visual Basic, Visual C++, Visual C#, and ASP and HTML. This book is about Visual Basic .NET, so I don't cover the other languages. But you should be aware that you could work on a solution that contains other programming languages, even though you may not work with those projects directly.

Although you'll need some time to get comfortable with the new IDE, several features can help you along with the transition. First, the Visual Basic .NET development environment is highly customizable to each individual user's tastes. If you're primarily a Visual Basic developer, several features can be changed to ease your transition to Visual Basic .NET. If you're mainly a Visual Basic developer, many aspects of the common IDE will be new to you, even if they aren't new to the environment itself. This chapter gives you a tour of the basic features and windows of the common integrated development environment and shows you some of the ways that it can be customized.

Getting Started with the New IDE

The first thing you'll see when you launch Visual Basic .NET is the Visual Basic Start Page. If you click on the My Profile option on the left side of the page, you'll see the available options, as shown in Figure 2-1. This page is the first place where you can start to customize the IDE to make it a little friendlier for Visual Basic developers. If you don't see this page, you can bring it up by choosing Help → Show Start Page.

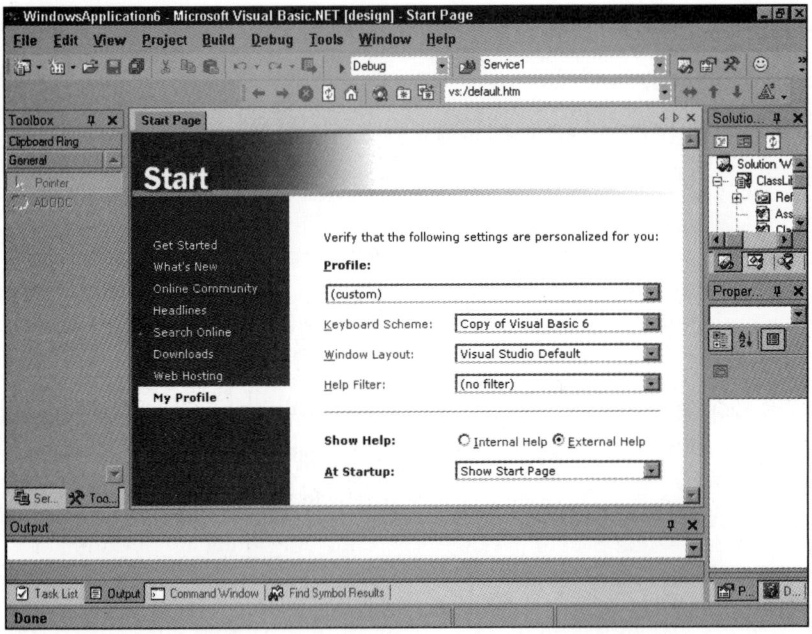

Figure 2-1: The Visual Basic .NET Start Page.

If you're used to Visual Basic, I recommend that you change the profile option to that of a Visual Basic Developer. The content of this book assumes that you've made this change, so if you come across something that doesn't appear to work, check this setting first to make sure it's been changed as suggested. If you change the profile option to Visual Basic Developer, the keyboard scheme, window layout, and help filter all change to Visual Basic defaults. Of these options, the keyboard scheme will probably have the most impact, followed by the window layout option. Setting the keyboard scheme to Visual Basic will allow you to use the familiar keyboard shortcuts for navigating around in the IDE. The window layout option displays the default windows you'd see as if you were in Visual Basic 6. However, this isn't set in stone — you can customize which windows you want displayed, and you can specify the behaviors of certain windows as well. Click on Get Started on the left side of the Start Page, and click on New Project to get started. The New Project dialog box (shown in Figure 2-2) will be displayed, asking what type of project you want to create.

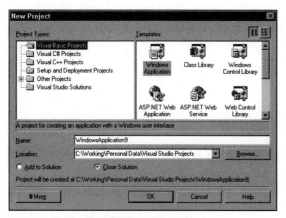

Figure 2-2: The New Project dialog box.

A brief look at Figure 2-2 shows the types of projects that you can create in Visual Basic .NET. As you can see, there are many more templates for different project types than were available to you in prior versions of Visual Basic. The Windows Application, Class Library, and Windows Control Library are the only three that have direct counterparts in prior versions of Visual Basic. The Windows Application maps to the Standard EXE project type in Visual Basic 6; the Class Library maps to the ActiveX DLL project type; and the Windows Control Library maps to the ActiveX Control project type in Visual Basic 6. There are many new project types, and many project types that were available in prior versions of Visual Basic are no longer available in Visual Basic .NET. Take a brief moment to browse the project types in the folder view on the left side of the dialog box to see what other types of projects you can create.

You may notice that there is a project type for setup and deployment projects. In this folder are several different deployment options that you can create for your project. This is a new concept, because within your solution now one or more projects are actually created that handle the distribution and installation of your application. There are also some template projects that create various distributed application architectures and groupings for you. For now, follow these steps:

1. **Click on Windows Application.**

2. **Select the application name and the location where you want the project to be created.**

   By default, it will create the projects in a subdirectory of your My Documents folder called Visual Studio Projects.

3. **Click OK to create the blank windows application project.**

When the new Windows Application project comes up, you'll probably notice that screen real estate is at a premium. The minimum screen resolution requirement listed in the documentation is 800x600, but you'll probably want to have a screen resolution of 1024x768 or better to allow you to keep certain windows open on your desktop. Although Visual Basic .NET can automatically hide some windows for you, the fewer distractions you have with opening and closing various windows, the better your productivity will be.

The Toolbox

Now that the project file is up, the first thing you'll probably notice is that the Toolbox is different. The new Toolbox has each control icon and its class type listed next to it, presented in a vertical fashion. If you see up and down arrows in the tab for the Toolbox, you can scroll through the controls listed there to pick the one you want. Unless you're just learning the controls and getting used to their icons, you'll probably want to display just the icons in the toolbox so you won't have to scroll the toolbar to find a particular control. If you right-click your mouse in the toolbox area, you'll see a pop-up menu. On this menu, there are several options, as shown in Figure 2-3.

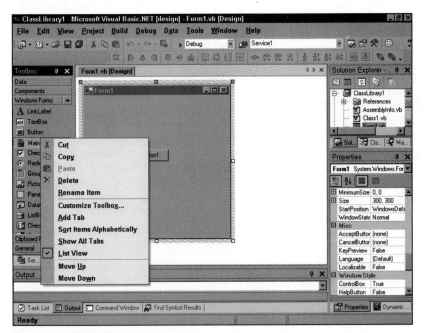

Figure 2-3: The Toolbox context menu.

One of the menu items is called List View, and you'll see there is a check mark next to it. If you were to click on this item, it would clear the check mark, and the controls would revert to the familiar Visual Basic 6 look. Note that each tab in the Toolbox has this setting, and if you want all controls in your Toolbox to appear this way, you'll have to clear this check mark on each tab the first time. Visual Basic will remember your settings and will bring up each tab in the Toolbox according to your preferences. You may also notice a little pushpin in the title bar of the Toolbox. This will automatically hide your Toolbox for you each time you move outside the Toolbox window.

You can see its effect by moving your mouse over the Server Explorer vertical tab at the far left of the screen. The Server Explorer window will slide out over the temporarily fixed Toolbox window and will disappear when you move the mouse outside the window. If you click the pushpin icons in all the visible tool windows, you can increase the amount of screen real estate for the active window tab in the center. Figure 2-4 shows how much screen real estate you can reclaim by setting the auto-hide option on each window.

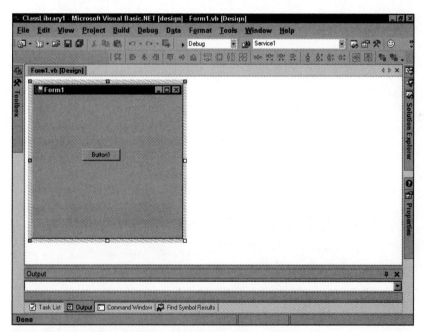

Figure 2-4: All visible windows with the auto-hide option on.

Code Window

Double-click the form to bring up the code for the form, as shown in Figure 2-5. From looking at the figure, you can see that there are already quite a few differences about the code window for the form. The first thing you'll notice is that there is already code in the form that you haven't written. This code is created for you by the Windows Form Designer and is required in order to make things work properly. Prior versions of Visual Basic hid these details from you, and you only saw the code that you had written in the code window. If you were to look at the form file in Notepad, you would realize there are many things in the form file that you don't see as code. If you were to place controls on the form and save the file, you'd still only have one file. Visual Basic had to store the information about the controls on the form along with the code that you may have written. Visual Basic .NET still stores all the information in the form file, but the primary difference is that controls are now described through code. When you place a control on the form, the Windows Form Designer writes the code that creates the control and sets its properties. You may be wondering where this information is located when you look at the code window for the form.

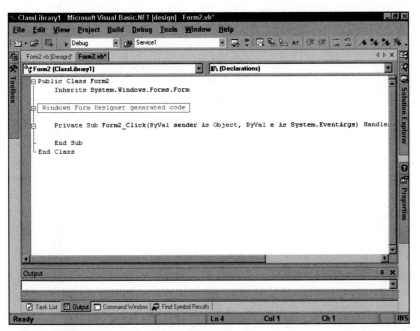

Figure 2–5: The code window for the form click event.

The code windows in Visual Basic .NET have several new features built into them. First, Visual Basic .NET automatically indents your blocks of code for you to your user-defined tab-spacing preference. Second, the code window introduces the ability to collapse functions or blocks of code to hide the details and to make viewing the code easier. With collapsible functions, you could do things like grouping all your property procedures together and then collapsing them so all you see is the property definitions. This is particularly useful when the property procedures don't do anything special with the data and just read or write to the private property storage variable. However, if a property procedure had specific validation code in it, you would probably want to keep that property expanded, so as you're looking at the code you can tell right away that there is something special about the property procedure. Similarly, you could collapse functions that are completed and have been tested so you can concentrate on procedures that relate to completing some piece of functionality. If you look at the far left side of the code window white space, you'll see what appears to be brackets and plus and minus signs. The plus sign will expand a function if it's collapsed and a minus sign will collapse a function that is expanded.

Along with collapsible functions, the Visual Basic .NET IDE introduces the concept of a *region,* which defines a block of code that contains several related functions that can be collapsed and hidden, or expanded and shown as a group. Referring to Figure 2-5, you'll see a line of code that says "Windows Form Designer generated code," with a box drawn around it. This is the symbol for a collapsed region. If you click on the plus sign next to the region, you'll see a group of functions, as shown in Figure 2-6.

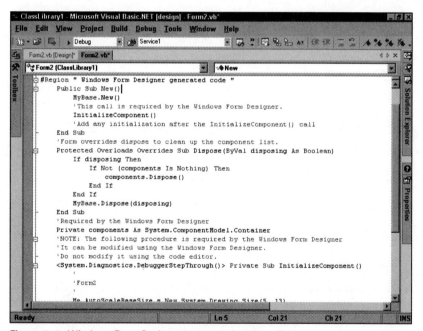

Figure 2–6: Windows Form Designer–generated code region.

You can define your own custom regions of code by following the same syntax that creates the form designer region. Just make sure to include the end region qualifier as shown to close your user-defined region. In the `InitializeComponent` procedure, you'll see a line of code that sets the Text property, which used to be the Caption property in prior versions, to "Form1." Change the line of code to set the Text property to "My Form." and bring back the form designer window by clicking on the "Form1.vb [Design]" tab. Notice how "My Form" is now displayed in the title bar of the form. Even though the comment tells you not to modify the code in the code editor, you can modify it in the code editor. However, you need to be aware that setting properties in the form designer window will overwrite any code that you place here. There may be situations in which you need to control how the form is created, and this is where you would do it. Now that you're back in the forms designer, place a regular button in the middle of the form and set its Text property to "Hello VB .NET." Then click back to the "Form1.vb" tab and look at the code in the Windows Form Designer region.

Figure 2-7 shows the modified Windows Form Designer code that is a result of placing the button on the form. Toward the top of the code, you'll see an event sink that defines Button1 as the source, and `System.Windows.Forms.Button` is the class that you're sinking events from. This is the same as how you would sink events from a control or another class in Visual Basic .NET as well as prior versions. The second line in the `InitializeComponent` procedure establishes the event sink for the button with a new button that it creates. Then you'll see some properties set for the button, and finally you'll see where the button is added to the controls collection. As you can see, the controls on the forms in Visual Basic .NET are now created on the fly at runtime. If you were to duplicate the code that creates Button1 and change all Button1 to Button2 references in the duplicated code, you could create a new button through code yourself. Just make sure you change the location to use different pixel locations so you can see it.

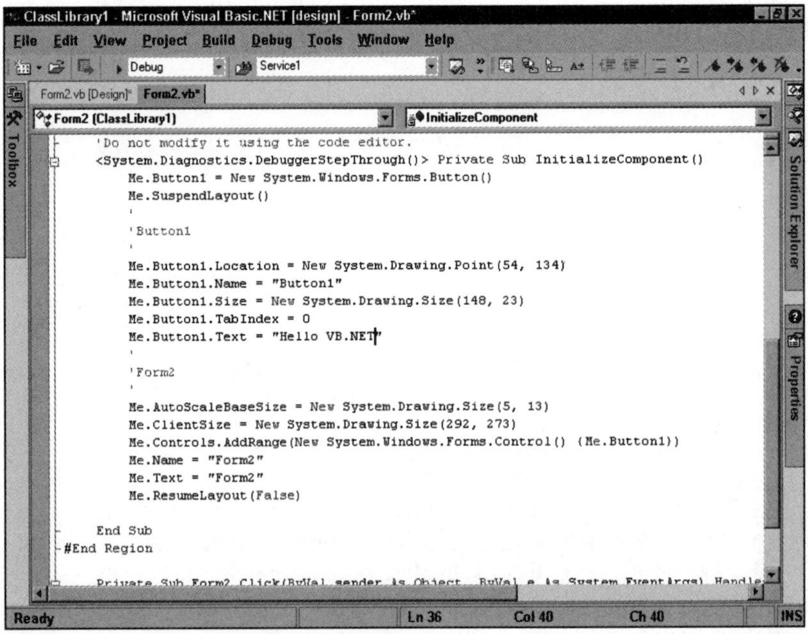

Figure 2-7: Modified Windows Form Designer code.

Task List Window

Visual Basic .NET incorporates a task window that's very helpful when you're writing code. This isn't just an ordinary task window in which you enter things that
you need to do and check them off as you've done them. You can bring up the task
list by going to View → Other Windows → Task List. The task list window appears,
as shown in Figure 2-8.

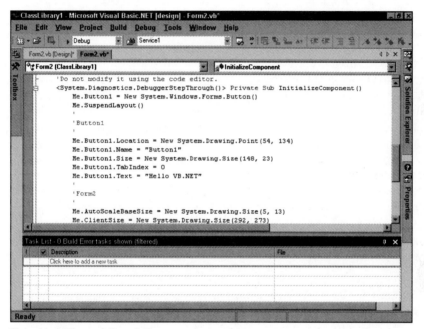

Figure 2-8: The task list window.

The task list currently does not show any tasks, but it says you can click on the
highlighted line to add a new task. Click on the line to add a task, type a description for the task, and click off the line. You'll get the warning dialog box shown in
Figure 2-9.

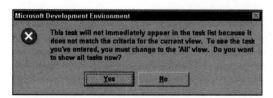

Figure 2-9: Task list warning dialog box.

Click on No for now, because you need to know how to change the filter criteria on your own. If you look at the title bar of the task list window, notice how it says there are no build error tasks shown and that the list is filtered. If you right-click anywhere within the task list items, you'll see a context menu appear with several options. Click on Show Tasks and then All to show all tasks. You'll see the task you entered appear in the task list. The task list window has a handy feature that allows you to define custom tags for comments that will appear automatically in the task list window. A typical use of this feature is when you're stubbing out a procedure and you need to come back and finish some things up with it. If you insert a comment in your code that is prefixed by TODO:, then you'll see that your comment will also appear in the task list window. Visual Basic .NET will automatically show you tasks for comments in your code as long as you prefix the comment with special tags.

Figure 2-10 shows the Options dialog box that appears when you go to Tools → Options. If you select the Task List option from the Environment folder, you'll see the options related to task lists. Here you can add your own comment tokens and adjust the priorities that they'll use. The task list window can sort on any column including the priority column, which is why you would adjust the priority level for a comment token. If you close the dialog box and go back to the task window, you can try clicking on the complete check box in the third column for the comment task, and you'll notice that nothing happens. The comment task lists don't go away unless you remove the comment in the code. If you double-click the comment task, it will display the code window and navigate to the line of code where the comment is located. The task list will also display build errors, and double-clicking on the build errors performs the same action by taking you right to the line of code that's causing the error.

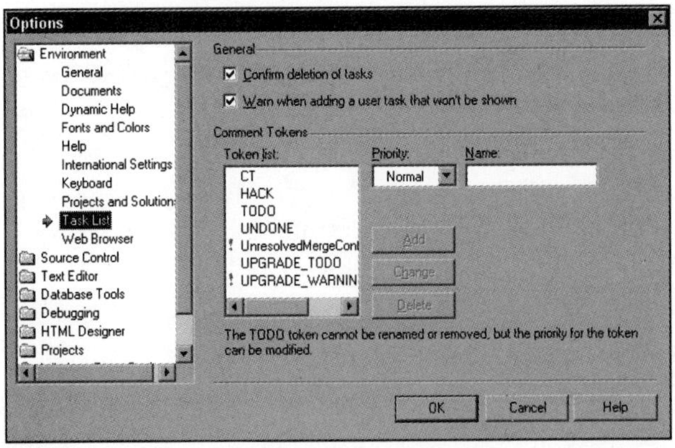

Figure 2-10: The task list Options dialog box.

Solution Explorer

The Solution Explorer window is used to navigate to all the various components in your solution. The Solution Explorer is similar to the Project Explorer in previous versions, but you need to be aware of a few differences between the two. Bring up the Solution Explorer window by moving your mouse over the Solution Explorer tab on the right side of the screen if it's in the auto-hide mode.

Figure 2-11 shows the basic Solution Explorer window. The first difference from prior versions you'll see is that there is a references folder under each project, which conveniently displays all the references for the project. This provides a much easier way of managing dependencies for a project. If you right-click on the References folder, you'll see an option to add a reference to your project. Click the Add Reference menu item, and you'll see the References dialog box, as shown in Figure 2-12.

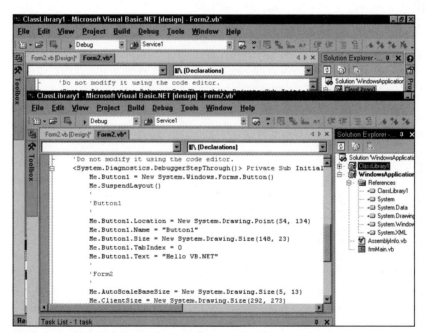

Figure 2-11: The Solution Explorer window.

The Add Reference dialog box breaks out references by their types. The three tabs at the top of the dialog box will allow you to add specific reference types, whether the reference is a .NET reference, a COM reference, or a project within the solution. The behavior of this dialog is a little different in that you must hit the

Select button on the highlighted reference to move it to the bottom list. After you've added all your references, you can click OK, and the selected references in the bottom list will be added to your project and will appear in the References folder for the project. You may be wondering how you remove a reference from the project, since the dialog box is only to add references. The answer is intuitive: You simply select the reference in the References folder for the project and either press the Delete key or right-click and select the Remove option on the menu.

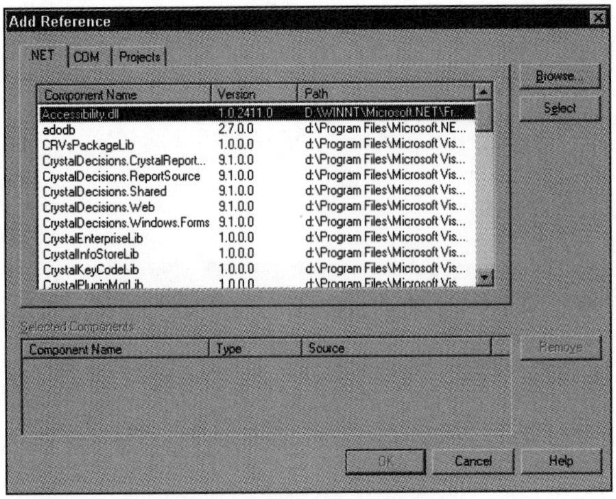

Figure 2-12: The Add Reference dialog box.

The Show All Files icon at the top of the Solution Explorer will display all the files in your project directory. Files and folders that aren't included in the project appear as a dotted outline of a folder or a page icon. Click the Show All Files icon (second from the right) and notice the additional folders and files. If you don't see any additional folders or files appear in the Solution Explorer window, you can build the project from the Build menu and click on the Refresh icon at the top of the Solution Explorer window. Now right-click on the form1.vb file and observe the context menu that appears. Here you can either delete or exclude a file from the project. If you click on Delete, you'll see a warning saying that the file will be deleted permanently. Be careful here, because clicking on the delete option will not only remove the file from your project but it will also delete it from the hard disk. If you simply want to remove the file from the project, you can click the Exclude button and the file will be removed from the project, but it will remain on the hard drive. Click on the exclude item and notice how form1.vb changes icons in the Solution Explorer window. If you right-click on the file again, you'll notice that you can include it back in your project. This feature comes in handy if you add or copy files to the project directory and you want to include them in your project.

You can still browse to a file and add it to the project manually. However, you typically want the file to be located in your project directory so that when you copy a project or retrieve it from Source Safe or other version-control software, all the required files will be included. The context menu that appears also has a couple of handy features that you'll like. If you include other files such as graphics, documentation, data files, and so on in your project directory, you can open the files from within the development environment. You have the option to open it with the default application for the file extension, or you can choose to open it with a different application. For example, if you included a Word document in your project, clicking on the Open option will bring up your document in Word automatically. Many developers weren't aware of this, but prior versions of Visual Basic supported this feature. If you added a file to your project by clicking the Add as Related Document in the Add File dialog box, you could add files to your project; double-clicking on them in the project explorer would open the file in its default editor. This wasn't as intuitive as it is now in Visual Basic .NET. The Open With context menu option is a new feature and brings up the dialog box shown in Figure 2-13.

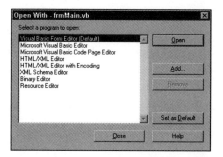

Figure 2-13: Open With dialog box options.

The Open With dialog box has some programs already included in it, but it really comes in handy if you have a particular editor that you want to open up the file in. For example, say you had a bitmap file included in your project and you wanted to open it within your favorite graphics package instead of Paint, which would be the default. This option allows you to add your graphics package editor, and from then on you could open the bitmap file in your graphics editor with just a couple of clicks.

When you realize that the solution explorer can be configured to display the entire contents of the disk directory for the solution and projects, you can take advantage of some other features in the solution explorer to help you maintain a hierarchy of your projects and files. For example, if you want a subdirectory within your project to store any bitmaps, icons, or any other images your project might need, all you'd have to do would be to right-click on the project, click Add and then New Folder from the context menu, select a name for the folder (such as "Images"), and then hit Enter. The folder you added to the Solution Explorer will also be created on the hard drive in the same path.

One of the great features about Visual Basic .NET is that it's highly customizable, by allowing you to create your own templates for just about anything. Bring up a copy of Windows Explorer and navigate to the following directory or wherever you installed Visual Basic .NET: `C:\Program Files\Microsoft Visual Studio.NET\Vb7\VBProjectItems\Local Project Items`. In this folder, you'll see several folders with names such as code, data, UI, and so on. Create a new folder in this directory called "Images." Open up the Images folder you just created and right-click in the file list. Select New and then Bitmap Image from the context menus. You can leave the default name of New Bitmap Image.bmp and hit enter to create an empty bitmap file in this directory. Now go back to Visual Basic .NET and right-click on the Images folder you previously created in your project. From the Context menu that appears, select Add and then Add New Item. Expand the local project items folder and then click on the Images folder in the left categories folder view. The dialog box should look like the dialog box shown in Figure 2-14.

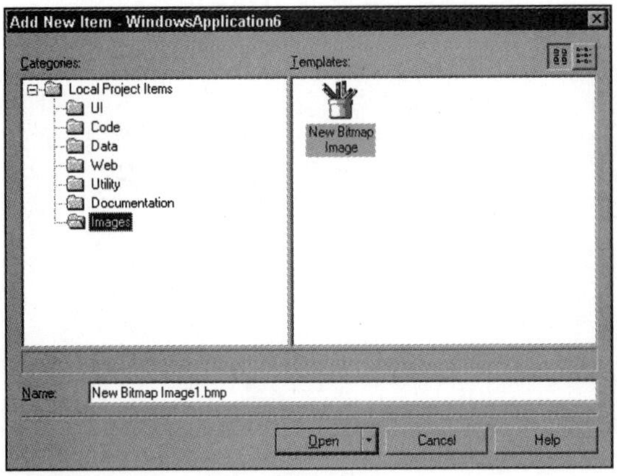

Figure 2–14: The Add New Item dialog box with images.

Click on the new bitmap image template and click the Open button. The bitmap will open up in the IDE. However, there is nothing in the bitmap at this point. Close the bitmap by clicking on the X on the top right of the tab list. In the Solution Explorer, right-click the new bitmap and select Open With and then select the Paint option and click Open. Paint will come up and you'll see a new bitmap image. Paint the image green, save the file, and close Paint. (This step would be skipped if you copied an existing bitmap to the templates directory instead of creating a new bitmap.) Now right-click the bitmap and select the Open option, and you'll see that the bitmap opens up in the resource editor, as shown in Figure 2-15.

You can use the resource editor for viewing and modifying the various images that you may need to include in your application. If you're simply trying to add a new bitmap, icon, or cursor file to your project, it could have been accomplished by simply clicking File and then New File to bring up the New File dialog box. From this dialog box, you have a variety of common accessory template files that you can add to your project. More importantly though, you saw how you could create and use your own templates to reduce the amount of effort when developing applications. Templates can be form files, project files, images, documents, and so on.

Almost anything that you need to use more than once you could create a template for, then create a new item in your project based on your template and make any required modifications.

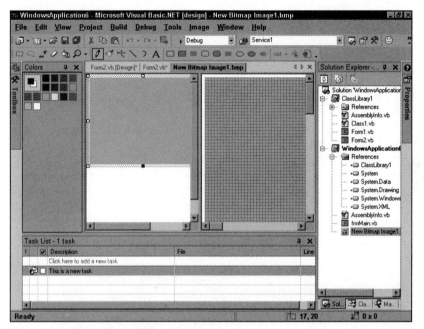

Figure 2-15: Visual Basic .NET resource editor.

Class View Window

The Class View Window is similar to the Object Browser in that it shows a hierarchical view of the various classes in your solution. The Class View provides another way to navigate to the various classes within your project. The Solution Explorer only allows you to see classes that are defined in separate files in your project, but the Class View will show you classes that are defined within other classes or files. Visual Basic .NET allows you to define multiple classes within the same file. These classes can be at the same hierarchy level as the others, or they can be defined within a class itself. The Class View window is used mainly to navigate to the actual class as defined in code. The object browser only displays a hierarchical list of the members, and you cannot jump to the code that defines the class. From context menus within the class browser, you can add classes to your solution; browse the definition of the class using the object browser; jump to the definition of the class in code; sort the list alphabetically, by type, or by access; and group the classes by types.

Server Explorer Window

The Server Explorer window is a new feature in Visual Basic .NET that allows you to see information about a server that you couldn't obtain directly in prior versions of Visual Basic. In addition, the data connections node of the Server Explorer replaces the Data View window that existed in prior versions of Visual Basic. The best way to show you the benefits of the Server Explorer is with a couple of examples.

Figure 2-16 shows the Server Explorer window with the top-level nodes expanded. You'll see how to use the data connections in the data access chapters later in the book. For now, we'll concentrate on the servers node. At first glance, it appears to have similar features as the Administrative tools option off the Start menu. Let's say that you wanted to be able to control the status of a particular service. Keep in mind that you can now write services completely and directly in Visual Basic .NET. This service controller could control one of your own services, or it could control a service that is installed by another application like SQL Server or Exchange Server, or it could control services that are part of the operating system. Expand the services node and scroll down to the messenger service, which is what is used to send and display messages using "net send" at the command prompt. Click on the messenger service and drag it to your form in your project.

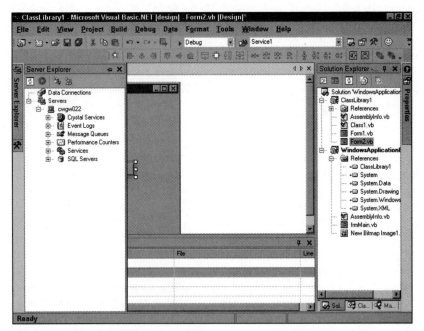

Figure 2-16: The Server Explorer window.

Figure 2-17 shows the development environment after you drag the Messenger Service to the form surface and display the Properties window. Visual Basic .NET stores all controls that don't actually have a user interface in a special section that appears below the Form window. The Properties window that is displayed shows that you created a service controller object, and Visual Basic .NET already populated the machine name and service name properties for you to match the service you selected in the Server Explorer.

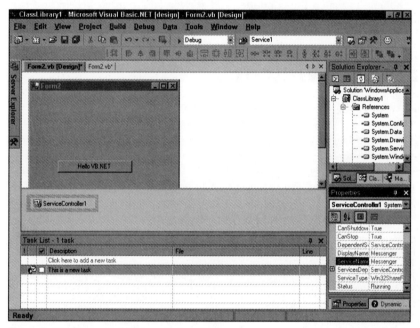

Figure 2-17: The non-visible control container.

Now double-click the button on the form and insert the following code in the click event for the button:

```
If ServiceController1.Status _
  = ServiceProcess.ServiceControllerStatus.Running Then
    ServiceController1.Stop()
ElseIf ServiceController1.Status _
  = ServiceProcess.ServiceControllerStatus.Stopped Then
    ServiceController1.Start()
End If
```

The preceding code will check to see the status of the messenger service and either stop or start the service. Run the project. You can check that the service actually starts and stops by bringing up the services window for the operating system, scrolling down to the messenger service, and viewing its state. Click the button and then refresh the Services window, and you'll see that the service toggles its state. Clicking the button again will restore the service to its original status.

The items that you drag from the Server window are just a shortcut for adding the particular control to the form and setting the properties manually. As a result, you could use one service controller to monitor and control several services even on different machines on the network. You just need to change the machine name and service name to match the computer and service you're interested in and call the refresh method.

Properties Window

The Properties window in Visual Basic .NET is very similar to the Properties window in previous versions. The only real difference is that some properties are grouped together into what could be thought of as a parent property. An example of this concept is the Size property, which you'll see has a plus sign next to it. If you click the plus sign, you'll see two properties called Height and Width, which can be thought of as child properties. In fact, if you're setting these properties through code, you could set them in two different ways, as shown in the following code:

```
Me.Height = 300
Me.Width = 250
```

Or

```
Me.Size = New Size(300, 250)
```

Although the Properties window itself doesn't change much, you may notice that the way certain properties are grouped together or the names of certain properties have changed while others are completely new. The changes, which are covered in later chapters of this book, were required to support the .NET Framework. As the controls, forms, and new or changed properties for each are discussed, you'll understand their purpose and behaviors.

Object Browser

Not much has changed in the Object Browser from previous versions. The Object Browser in Visual Basic .NET is still used to view the class hierarchy and the members on each class for your project or solution and the components that it references. However, due to inheritance, the Object Browser is now required to show the base objects from which the object is inherited. The Object Browser will probably be used heavily at first, as you understand the inheritance hierarchy for the object you'll work with in Visual Basic .NET. It's also useful for browsing the various namespaces that you'll work with to figure out where certain functions are.

Because Visual Basic .NET combines related functions together in a class hierarchy, you may need to search for a particular constant or function in order to figure out where it's located. The concept of namespaces is discussed later, but unless you fully qualify where the constant or function is located, you'll get a compile error stating that the constant or function name isn't declared. The only other change is that you no longer set the properties for the objects in the Object Browser. In prior versions, you set default properties and attributes through the Object Browser, which wasn't intuitive. This type of information is now set through code itself, so it's easier to read the code and understand how things are put together and how they behave.

Command Window

The Command window in Visual Basic .NET serves two purposes. First, one mode of the Command window is called Immediate Mode, and it functions similar to the Immediate Window in prior versions of Visual Basic. The second mode is called Command Mode and is used to type commands to the IDE instead of having to navigate menu structures. By default, the Command Window appears in Command Mode when you display it from View → Other Windows → Command Window.

Figure 2-18 shows the Command window as it appears in its default command mode. The command mode is used to type commands related to the menu structures as well as commands that don't exist on any menu. Let's say that you want to add a class to your project. By starting to type the Project command, you see a list of related things you can do to the project. Hit the down-arrow key once and then hit Enter, and you'll see the Add New Item dialog box with the class template already highlighted. This may not seem like much of a timesaver, but we aren't finished yet. The Command window allows you to define your own aliases for the commands. If you wanted to create an alias "ac," to add a class, you would type in the following command:

```
alias ac Project.AddClass
```

From this point on, you could simply type **ac** in the Command window and the dialog box would appear the same as if you typed out the entire command. There are many predefined aliases that you can use in the Command window, and you can see what their names and commands are by simply typing **alias** and hitting Enter. The alias "immed" is used to switch modes of the Command window to the Immediate Mode.

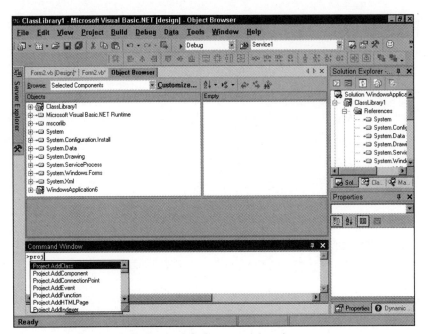

Figure 2-18: Command window in default command mode.

Keyboard Shortcuts

Visual Basic .NET allows you to create your own keyboard shortcuts for executing various commands in the IDE. If you select Tools → Options, you'll see a dialog box that allows you to customize certain aspects of the environment. Click on the keyboard item in the folder view on the left side of the dialog box to view the keyboard mapping schemes.

Figure 2-19 shows the keyboard Options dialog box. In the list on the right side, scroll down and highlight the View.CommandWindow item. Now click in the text box with the Press Shortcut Key above it, press Ctrl+Alt+G, and then click Assign. You'll get a dialog box stating that you can't change the Visual Basic 6 mapping scheme, and it asks if you want to make a copy of it. Select Yes and then select a name for your keyboard scheme. Click the OK button to close the dialog box. Now any time you want to display the Immediate window, you can use the Ctrl+G shortcut as you would in prior versions. If you want the Command Mode, you can use the Ctrl+Alt+G shortcut to switch back to Command Mode.

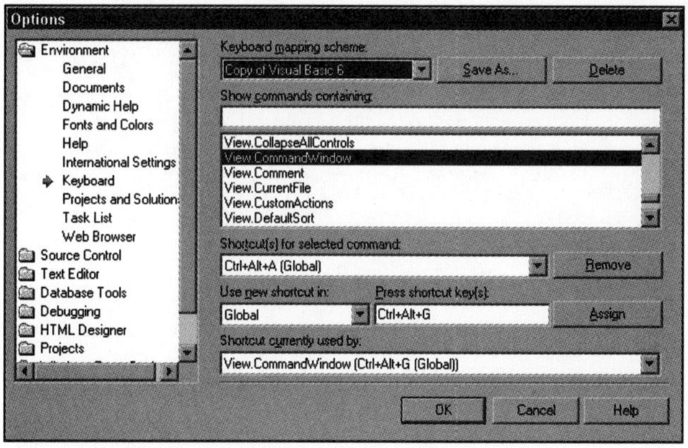

Figure 2-19: The keyboard Options dialog box.

Output Window

The output window in Visual Basic .NET is used to display various status messages while the IDE is performing certain functions like building a project. If you're building a project, it displays its progress and whether any errors occurred. If you're building a solution, it will tell you how many projects were completed, how many were skipped, and how many had errors in them. The output window will automatically appear when information is being written to it, such as a build process, and by default it will appear as another tab in the bottom of the IDE, where the task list and the Command windows appear.

Summary

Visual Basic .NET uses the same common development environment that is used across other products in Visual Studio .NET. This development environment is very customizable to fit the tastes of each developer. Keyboard mappings, window positions and behaviors, colors, fonts, and commands with aliases can all be used to customize the development environment.

The IDE also provides many new windows, behaviors for other windows have changed slightly, and some of the menu choices have changed. Visual Basic .NET provides you with the ability to create and manage templates of various types that can be launched from the development environment. These templates don't have to be forms, classes, or other code elements as in prior versions. You can create templates for documents, images, or just about anything that you use related to the development process.

Chapter 3

Changes to the Language

IN THIS CHAPTER

- ◆ Variables, constants, data types, and type conversions
- ◆ Properties, events, procedures, and optional parameters
- ◆ Use of the Shared keyword
- ◆ Structures, classes, and subclasses
- ◆ Constructors and overloading functions
- ◆ Namespaces

Each time Microsoft has released a new version of Visual Basic, it has changed the language itself. The majority of these changes have involved adding new functionality to the language. Some of the new additions to the language have made other existing features obsolete or outdated. With each version, Microsoft has stated that certain features, keywords, and statements may not be supported in future versions. However, Microsoft has tried to maintain backward compatibility so that code that was written for prior versions would run with minimal, if any, alterations in each new version. Some of the features that were retained were left over from the days when QuickBasic was used.

In order to support certain features that developers have been requesting for many years, Microsoft had to take a step back and rebuild Visual Basic from the ground up. The primary feature that forced this rebuilding was the decision to finally include inheritance in the language. Since version 6 of Visual Basic was released, many things have happened in the computer industry and the information technology field in general. Microsoft introduced the concept of Web Services, which allows you to provide software that can run on remote machines using protocols that allow the required information to pass through firewalls as if you were requesting a Web page. Intel introduced and is now shipping a 64-bit processor. An explosion of software has been created in Visual Basic, which runs on servers to provide information to Active Server Pages as well as traditional Win32 clients.

In order to evolve with the changing demands for Visual Basic, Microsoft has incorporated many features into the language that will make developers more productive. As mentioned in Chapter 1, these changes were made to make the language more consistent and easier to develop, read, and maintain; help developers introduce fewer bugs or errors into their programs; and make applications more robust and easier to debug. The purpose of this chapter is to show you the major changes to declaring and using variables, methods, properties, events, and so on, which are your basic building blocks for creating applications in Visual Basic .NET.

Variables

Variables are used anytime information needs to be stored for later use. When working with variables, there are a few things that you must understand. First, you need to know what the allowable data types are and the class to which the data type belongs. Variables must first be declared and then they must be initialized to a known value before you can use them. In prior versions of Visual Basic, you were required to declare the variable on one line and initialize it on another. Visual Basic .NET allows you to complete these two operations on a single line, making for code that's easier to read and understand. As you work with variables, you also need to be aware of when and where the variable can be used by observing the scope and access modifiers for a variable. Finally, you also need to understand how to convert a variable from one data type into another. This is extremely important if you leave the Option Strict statement turned on in your .NET applications, because you'll be forced to explicitly convert the data from one type to another. This section gives you the information you need to know when working with variables in Visual Basic .NET and lets you know how it has changed from prior versions.

Using reference, value, and default data types

In prior versions of Visual Basic, there were three main classes of data types. There were the value types (Strings, Integer, Long, Double, and so on), object types, and the ugly variant type, which could store both value types and object types. Visual Basic .NET has a reference data type and a value data type. Data types of the value type hold the data within their own memory allocation, whereas reference types contain a pointer to another memory location that contains the data. Value types include all the numeric and binary data types as well as the Char, Date, and enumerated data types. All structures are also a value data type, even if their members are reference data types. Reference data types include all Strings, Arrays, and any data type that's defined by a class.

In prior versions of Visual Basic, the Variant data type was also known as the default data type. The default data type would be used if a variable didn't have a type explicitly defined when the variable was declared. The default data type was also used if the Option Explicit statement wasn't used and if a line of code was executed that contained a variable that wasn't previously declared. In Visual Basic .NET, the default data type is now the Object data type, and the Variant data type has been removed from the language. Any variable that is defined to be of the default Object data type can store either a reference or a value type. However, it's important to keep in mind that any *object variable* (a variable defined based on a defined class) always holds a pointer to the data and never the data itself. As you'll come to understand as you progress through this book, the Object data type is actually an object itself, which exposes four public methods. The inclusion of inheritance in the language means that all data types are derived from this Object data type and, as a result, all data types are objects themselves.

Declaring and initializing at the same time

If you wanted to initialize a variable in prior versions of Visual Basic, you had to declare the variable and then insert a line of code that set the variable to the desired initial state. Visual Basic .NET introduces a new language feature that allows a variable to be declared and initialized at the same time.

Prior versions required the following syntax:

```
Dim intX As Integer
intX = 5
```

Visual Basic .NET allows for the following new syntax:

```
Dim intX As Integer = 5
```

As you can see from the preceding example, the new syntax declares and initializes the variable at the same time. This syntax can also be used to initialize a variable to a parameter that was passed in or to another variable already defined:

```
Private Sub Test(ByVal intInitial As Integer)
    Dim intX As Integer = intInitial
    Dim intY As Integer = intX * 2

    MessageBox.Show (intX)
    MessageBox.Show (intY)
End Sub

Test(3)    'Displays 3 then 6 in message boxes
```

Declaring and initializing a variable on the same line not only saves time, but it makes the code more readable and introduces fewer chances for errors caused by forgetting to initialize the variable. In prior versions, the initialization line of code could easily be lost or deleted, introducing subtle bugs that result from code trying to access a variable that hasn't been initialized yet. As you'll read later, in the section on working with classes, this syntax also works for declaring and initializing object variables.

Working with variable scope and access modifiers

In prior versions of Visual Basic, variables could be declared using the Dim, Public, Private, or Friend keywords. Depending on which keyword was used and the type of module the variable was declared in, access to the variable could be controlled and it would restrict what functions could access the variable. Although Visual Basic .NET retains the previous four declaration keywords, it has introduced a couple more that allow even finer control over the variables. The `Protected` and `Shared` keywords can also be used to declare variables.

When declaring a variable in a procedure, you still declare it using the `Dim` statement, and it's available for use only by the procedure. This hasn't changed from prior versions. However, you need to be aware that Visual Basic .NET introduces the concept of block scope and how it affects your code. Block scope limits where the variable can be used within a procedure. If a variable is declared with the `Dim` statement at the beginning of the routine, then the variable is available anywhere in the routine. However, if a variable is defined within any code that essentially creates a block, it's only available within the block. Examples of blocks are `If...Then` statements, `With` blocks, `loops`, `Select Case` statements, and so on.

The following code shows the concept of block scope:

```
If Something = True Then
    Dim A As Boolean
    A = True
End If

MessageBox.Show (A)
```

Because the variable `A` is declared in an `If...Then` statement, you'll get a compile error on the `Msgbox` line stating that the variable `A` is not declared. You should also be aware that even though the variable is not accessible outside the code block, it's not destroyed until the routine in which it was declared finishes. However, you can declare the same variable in another block in the same procedure and it will work. Block scoping allows you to hide certain variables from the rest of the procedure in order to make the code more readable and maintainable. If a certain block of code needs temporary variables in order to work, but the rest of the procedure doesn't care about those variables, then block scoping allows the variables to be defined and used only within the block. As a result, you can make your code cleaner by only declaring the variables at the beginning of the procedure that are used across multiple blocks in the procedure.

When declaring variables at a module level, you have several options available. You can use the `Dim`, `Public`, `Private`, `Shared`, `Protected`, and `Friend` keywords. When you declare a module level variable using the `Dim` keyword, you're creating a private variable unless you're working with a plain code module. Even though a variable can be declared at the module level with a `Dim` statement, it shouldn't be done. It makes your code much cleaner and easier to read and understand if you explicitly declare it with the `Public` keyword in standard modules and with the `Private` keyword in all other types of modules, if this is the desired behavior.

When you declare a variable to be anything other then `Private`, you're actually creating a read-write property that has no validation to it. Because you're actually creating a property procedure pair for the public variable, you can also use the access modifiers that are available for procedures on a variable. The modifier keywords that can be used on procedures are Public, Private, Protected, Friend, and Protected Friend. The Shared keyword can also be used as a declaring modifier, but unless you explicitly make it public, it defaults to a private shared variable. The use of the Shared keyword and the other procedure modifier are discussed later in this chapter, in the "Procedures" section.

Converting from one data type to another

One of the complaints with prior versions of Visual Basic was how coercion of variables was handled in the language. When possible, Visual Basic would automatically convert variables from one type to another as needed. For example, appending an integer data type to a string variable would force the integer to be converted to a string type, and then it could be appended to the string variable. Critics typically used the phrase *evil type coercion* when explaining the phenomenon. Look at the following code sample that would work in previous versions:

```
'VB6 and Prior
Dim Variable1 As Variant
Dim Variable2 As Variant

Variable1 = "1.5"
Variable2 = 2

Msgbox (Variable1 + Variable2)
```

In the preceding example, what should be displayed in the message box? Prior versions of Visual Basic and other languages would let you concatenate two string variables with the plus sign as well as adding two variables together. The variable types were actually strings, but would Visual Basic attempt to convert the variables to a numeric data type and try adding them together, since the plus sign is supposed to add two variables together? Because the string could be converted to a numeric data type and the other variable was a numeric data type, the displayed result in the message box would be the value of the addition operation on the two variables, which would be 3.5. This demonstrates the problems with automatic type coercion of variables in previous versions of Visual Basic.

Not all automatic type coercions are "evil," as you may have been lead to believe. When converting data types, you can perform either a narrowing or widening operation. An example of a narrowing conversion is one that converts a Double value to an Integer value. With this type of conversion, there is a potential for loss of information in the conversion process. An example of a widening conversion would be the reverse of the narrowing conversion listed above. Converting from an Integer to a Double is a widening conversion, and there is no potential loss of information. Everything that could be stored in an Integer variable can be stored in a Double variable. As you can see, it makes perfect sense for a programming language to perform widening conversions automatically for you. This automatic widening coercion is also referred to as *implicit conversions,* and Visual Basic .NET will perform these types of conversions automatically for you. Again, the common principle for changes in Visual Basic .NET is to make the language easier to code, read, and understand, and to help programmers introduce fewer errors into their code. Because there is a potential loss of data in narrowing conversions and different types of errors can occur as a result, Visual Basic .NET requires you to explicitly define a narrowing type conversion provided that the Option Strict is turned on. Table 3-1 shows the data types and the implicit widening conversions that are allowed in Visual Basic .NET.

TABLE 3-1 IMPLICIT WIDENING DATA TYPE CONVERSIONS ALLOWED

Data Type	Widens to Data Types
Byte	Byte, Short, Integer, Long, Decimal, Single, Double
Short	Short, Integer, Long, Decimal, Single, Double
Integer	Integer, Long, Decimal, Single, Double
Long	Long, Decimal, Single, Double
Decimal	Decimal, Single, Double
Single	Single, Double
Double	Double
Char	String
Any Type	Object, any base type which it is derived or implemented interfaces
Nothing	Any data type or object type

An important thing to realize about the information in Table 3-1 is that Char is the only data type that will widen to a string data type. As a result, any time you need to concatenate a value to String variable, you will need to perform an explicit conversion. You will also need to perform an explicit conversion when you are converting to a narrower data type.

There are several ways to perform explicit conversions, but first we will look at functions that you've probably used in prior versions of Visual Basic. These functions are sometimes referred to as CType functions where *type* is the data type you're trying to convert to. The following are the explicit type conversion functions available for use in Visual Basic .NET.

- ◆ CBool: Boolean
- ◆ CByte: Byte

- ◆ CChar: Character
- ◆ CDate: Date
- ◆ CDbl: Double
- ◆ CDec: Decimal
- ◆ CInt: Integer
- ◆ CLng: Long
- ◆ CObj: Object
- ◆ CShort: Short
- ◆ CSng: Single
- ◆ CStr: String

When working with the CType functions, you need to understand that if the data that you're converting is outside of the range for the data type you're converting to, a runtime error will be generated. For example, if you try to convert a variable that has a value of 256 to a byte data type, an error will occur because the byte data type can only hold values from 0 to 255. In prior versions of Visual Basic, the conversion functions were needed in some places, and in others, they were used to help developers understand what the code was trying to do. However, the conversion functions were actual function calls in the language and, as a result, there was some overhead associated with these calls. In Visual Basic .NET, the CType function calls are compiled inline and, as a result, performance increases because there is no call to a separate function required. The type coercion is compiled into the code that evaluates the expression.

Visual Basic .NET actually introduces another CType function amazingly called CType. This function accepts two parameters of which the first is the expression to be evaluated and the second is the type name for the data type for which you want the expression to be converted. The type name is any legal expression that would be used after the As clause in a Dim statement. This includes any data type, object, class, structure, or interface. Again, if the expression is outside the valid range for the data type you're converting to, a runtime error will be generated. Make sure that you have the Option Strict turned on, otherwise the first conversion will work even though the code says that it won't.

The following code shows a couple of ways to perform an explicit conversion:

```
Dim intA As Integer
Dim strB As String

strB = intA              'Wont work non widening conversion
strB = CType(intA, String) 'Works
strB = intA.ToString     'Works
```

The first way is pretty straightforward and uses the CType function to convert the integer to a string. However, the second way to perform an explicit conversion is shown on the last line of code. As previously mentioned, the standard data types you may be familiar with are actually objects that expose certain methods and properties. Using IntelliSense, if you place a period after the intA variable, you'll see a listing of all the operations and properties the integer object exposes. The ToString method is a method of the integer data type object and returns a string representation for the object. Actually, the ToString method comes from the base "Object" data type. As you'll see later, every object you work with in Visual Basic .NET provides a ToString method on it for converting the data type to a string representation. The Integer object along with the other basic data types expose many different ToType conversion functions that you can use to convert the object's data type to other data types. Some of these are redundant and will be handled automatically for you through implicit widening conversions, but they're provided for you to use should you so desire.

Constants

Visual Basic .NET has also changed the way you're required to declare constants. Prior versions would let you define a constant as in the following:

```
Const MAX_VALUE = 5
```

However, Visual Basic .NET now requires you to explicitly define the data type of a constant when you declare it:

```
Const MAX_VALUE As Integer = 5
```

You can now declare and initialize a variable at the same time by specifying the initial value with an equals sign when the variable is declared. The declaration of constants looks surprisingly similar to this except the Const keyword is used in place of the Dim keyword. Almost everything in Visual Basic .NET is an object, and constants are no exception to this. Placing a period after the constant again shows you a listing of methods and properties of the data type for the constant. The familiar ToString is available along with other type conversion functions.

Properties

Visual Basic .NET changes several things about how procedures are declared and used in your code. The biggest difference is the syntax for declaring a property procedure, and the use of non-indexed default properties is no longer supported in Visual Basic .NET. A public variable is actually treated as a public read-write property, and, as a result, it can use the access modifier keywords associated with functions.

Although using public variables in a module acts like a property procedure, you don't have any control over what data can be placed in the property or perform any other actions that may be required when a property is set like updating other properties that are calculated from the current property. Using property procedures allows you to overcome these limitations and makes your code more manageable and readable by allowing you to eliminate redundant code, encapsulate data better, and limit access to the data to only those that need it.

Procedure within procedure syntax

In prior versions of Visual Basic, you declared a pair of procedures in order to create a read/write property, as in the following:

```
'VB6 and Prior
Private mX As Integer

Public Property Get X() As Integer
    X = mX
End Property

Public Property Let X(vdata As Integer)
    If vdata > 5 And vdata < 20 Then
        mX = vdata
    Else
        Err.Raise 17,"Property:X", "Value out of range"
    End If
End Property
```

You may also have had a property Set procedure if you used default properties, so you could determine whether you were accessing the default property or the object itself. Because Visual Basic .NET no longer supports non-indexed default properties for clarity, the property Let procedure is no longer needed, because everything is an object and the Property Set procedure is used. If you wanted a read-only property, you would omit the Property Let procedure. Similarly, if you wanted a write-only property, you would omit the Property Get procedure. It was also easy to get the property procedures separated from each other in the code, making it harder to read and understand the code. Another problem was that you had to explicitly declare a variable in the Property Let procedure and that if the same variable name was not used in all Property Let procedures, confusion could easily set in. Another thorn is that each Property Get procedure had to have the data returned by specifying the name of the property and then the equals sign and the return value.

In order to provide the same property procedure in Visual Basic .NET, you would write the following code:

```
Private mX As Integer

Public Property X() As Integer
    Get
        Return mX
    End Get

    Set (ByVal Value As Integer)
        If value > 5 And Value < 20 Then
            mx = Value
        Else
            Err.Raise(17, "Property:X", "Value out of range")
        End If
    End Set
End Property
```

The combined property procedure syntax has several advantages and is required for consistency when inheriting properties. The Get and Set are always together in the code and Visual Basic .NET introduces a couple of new keywords that make writing property procedures easier. The first keyword you see that is new is the Return keyword. The Return keyword is used to return a value to either a function or procedure and immediately end execution of the procedure. This is important to realize because no other code after the Return keyword will execute. You can think of the Return keyword as a shortcut that sets the return value for the function or procedure and then immediately issues an Exit Function or Exit Property statement. The Value keyword is the other new keyword and it's used in the property Set statement. The Value keyword is an explicit variable created automatically for you when you create the property procedure and contains the value that's being passed into the property. In Visual Basic .NET, if you want to create a read-only property, you can't just leave out the Set...End Set block. If you do, you'll receive an error stating that a property procedure needs both Set and Get routines. In order to make a property read-only, you qualify the property procedure declaration with the ReadOnly keyword before the Property keyword. Similarly if you want a write-only property, you need to include the WriteOnly keyword in the property declaration. Property procedures that don't specify either the ReadOnly or WriteOnly keywords will default to ReadWrite access and will require both a Set and a Get statement.

Indexed (parameterized) properties

The only way you can have a default property in Visual Basic .NET is if the property procedure is an indexed property. The following code shows how you would create an indexed property:

```
Public Class Test
    Private mX() As Integer
```

```
Public Property X(ByVal Index As Integer) As Integer
    Get
        Return mX(index)
    End Get

    Set (ByVal Value As Integer)
        mx(index) = Value
    End Set
End Property

Public Sub New()
    ReDim mx(5)
End Sub
End Class
```

In order to use the indexed property, you would need to specify an index or parameter value any time you read or write to the property:

```
Dim oTest As New Test()

otest.X(1) = 4
MessageBox.Show (otest.X(1))
```

After you have a parameterized property, you can make the property the default property by including the `Default` keyword before the `Public` keyword in the property declaration. This is much simpler and much more maintainable then having to set the default property through the object browser, as in prior versions. Indexed properties are also referred to as *parameterized properties*. The index can sometimes be misleading because the parameter doesn't have to be a number. The parameter could be textual like Red, Green, or Blue. When you have the default property, you can use the default property by changing the preceding code to read as follows:

```
Dim oTest As New Test()

otest(1) = 4
MessageBox.Show (otest(1))
```

Events

Events are code procedures that are executed at an undetermined time while the program is running. Moving a mouse, clicking on a control, and typing with the keyboard are all events that the user can do and are examples of predefined events of controls and forms. Along with the standard predefined events, you can also create custom event procedures within your applications. Custom event procedures are used to execute code in your application or a listening application when the criteria for firing the event has been met. Visual Basic .NET expands upon the use of events and introduces a new concept called *shared events*. Shared events are events that are defined in a special way and will fire when any objects derived from the class where they're defined raise the event. Shared events are useful for having a common handler for an event, regardless of the number of actual objects that are created.

Predefined events

The controls and forms in Visual Basic .NET still have almost all the events that were available in previous versions. However, it's important to understand that although the controls may look the same as in previous versions, they're completely different controls. This difference in controls was required in order for the controls and forms to work in the .NET Framework in the most efficient manner. You can still add an existing COM control to a .NET application, but keep in mind that in order to do so, you'll be using the COM interoperability layer as described in Chapter 1, and some overhead will be associated with it. Because the controls are completely different controls based on the new .NET Framework architecture, some events may be supported differently. Start a new Windows Application project and place a button on the form. Double-click the button to bring up its click event procedure, which is shown here:

```
Private Sub Button1_Click(ByVal sender As System.Object, _
    ByVal e As System.EventArgs) Handles Button1.Click

End Sub
```

The first thing you should notice is the `Private` keyword. The various access modifiers that can be used on procedures are discussed in the "Procedures" section of this chapter. The `Private` keyword is used by default on all event procedures and, as a result, the event procedure cannot be directly called from outside the object. This will improve the maintainability of your code because it will require a clearly defined interface between two objects. If there is code that needs to run in an event procedure and it needs to be accessible from outside the object that supplied the event, it must be in a separate routine that's exposed.

Right now, you're probably thinking that you'll just change the `Private` keyword to `Public` and be done, right? Wrong. Just changing the keyword to `Public` won't get you where you want to go. If you take another look at the event procedure, you'll notice two arguments that are required in the event procedure. The first one is the sender, which is who is calling the event procedure. The next parameter is the arguments that are required for the particular event procedure. So in order to call the click event of the button, you'd need to call it in the following format:

```
Me.Button1_Click(Me, New System.EventArgs())
```

This may not seem like that big of deal. However, the event procedure we just looked at used the generic `System.EventArgs` argument, which implies that no arguments are actually passed. Other event procedures may require specialized arguments that need to be built and filled in before passing to the event procedure. For example, the `MouseDown` event requires the e parameter to be of a different type:

```
ByVal e As System.Windows.Forms.MouseEventArgs
```

The e parameter in this case, packs a lot of information into one parameter. Information like the x and y position of the mouse and the button that was pushed are all included in one parameter. Even if you could supply all this information, it's much easier to expose a public routine that can be called from either outside or inside the form, such as in the event procedure. Furthermore, the code that you write and expose publicly is probably much easier to understand than `btnSomething_Click`.

Custom events

Visual Basic .NET changes the way custom events are declared and raised from prior versions of Visual Basic. In previous versions, you would define a public event for a form or class module and then somewhere inside the module you would call the `RaiseEvent` function and would specify the event name you're raising. Other objects could initialize an event sink and would be notified if the event was fired. In Visual Basic .NET, you still define a public event, but the way you have to call the event has changed. Every custom event procedure you create will appear as a property with the same name, except the word `Event` is tacked onto the end. The following example shows how you would define and raise a custom event:

```
Public Sub Form1_Click(ByVal sender As System.Object, _
        ByVal e As System.EventArgs) Handles MyBase.Click
    x = New EventClass()
    x.FireEvent()
End Sub


Private WithEvents X As EventClass


Public Sub X_Somethinghappened(ByVal Number As Integer) _
        Handles X.Somethinghappened
    msgbox("Event Was Fired - " & number)
End Sub


Public Class EventClass
```

```
Public Event Somethinghappened(ByVal Number As Integer)

Public Sub FireEvent()
    SomethinghappenedEvent(25)
End Sub
End Class
```

In the preceding listing, there is a class named EventClass, and it exposes a public event and a public method. In the form, the event source is declared using the WithEvents keyword, and the event sink is initialized in the click event of the form. Next, the method is called on the class that will fire the event and then the event sink X_SomethingHappened will fire. The event sink procedure is defined as you would in prior versions. In the code window, you would click the X in the members combo box and the SomethingHappened in the event combo box, and Visual Basic would generate the event procedure as shown in the preceding code.

Simulating control arrays

Visual Basic .NET doesn't support the concept of a control array as prior versions have. However, it still supports a way to have one common routine provide the behavior for many similar controls. If you look at the event procedure in the previous section, you'll see that at the end of the event procedure is a new keyword called Handles and an object dot event name. The handles keyword is used to "hook up" a procedure with an event.

You can take advantage of this in your own code to simulate the functionality of a control array. Start a new Windows Application project and place two buttons on a form. Next, go to the code window of the form and type in the following code:

```
Protected Sub MyEventProc(ByVal Sender As Object, _
    ByVal e As System.EventArgs) Handles button1.Click, _
    button2.Click

    Select Case True
        Case Sender.Equals(Button1)
            msgbox("Button1 Was Clicked")
        Case Sender.Equals(Button2)
            msgbox("Button2 Was Clicked")
    End Select
End Sub
```

Now, run the project, click on the buttons, and observe what happens. As you will see, the appropriate message box is displayed indicating the button you clicked. You now know how to have a common procedure sink the events of other procedures using the Handles keyword. If you're going to do this, you'll need to make the arguments to your event procedure match those for the events you'll be handling. In the above example, you created a brand-new procedure that handled the two events. However, you could also click one of the buttons to bring up the click event for that button and, on the end of the click event, you would insert the `Handles` keyword and the other button name and event you want to handle. It's much easier to get the arguments correct using this method. An important thing to remember about using the handles keyword is that if you supply a routine to handle an event, the original event procedure will still fire.

Creating and using shared events

Visual Basic .NET introduces a very useful concept of shared events. By using the `Shared` procedure modifier, you can create an event that will fire when any objects derived from the class raise the event. This allows you to create any number of objects from a class and create a single object that will be used to trap the event that could be fired from any of the derived objects.

In order to illustrate this concept, let's look at a tire class that raises an event if the tire goes flat. The car class stores four tire objects and needs to know when any of the tire objects goes flat. Start a new Windows Application project, add four buttons on the form (as shown in Figure 3-1), set their text properties as shown, and set their name properties to the same as the text on the button.

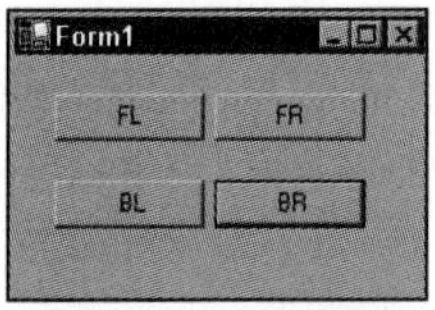

Figure 3-1: A shared event example form layout.

Now, in the code window for the form, insert the following code anywhere within the form class itself:

```
Public Class Tire
    Public Shared Event FlatTire(ByVal BadTire As Tire)
    Public Event DoNothing
    Public TirePosition As String
    Public Sub RunOverNail()
        FlatTireEvent(Me)
    End Sub

    Public Sub new()
        'No special constructor
    End Sub
    Public Sub New(ByVal strTirePosition As String)
        TirePosition = strTirePosition
```

```
        End Sub
    End Class

    Private mcolTires As New Collection()
    Private WithEvents FlatTireMonitor As Tire

    Public Shared Sub FlatTireMonitor_FlatTire(ByVal BadTire _
        As WindowsApplicationX.Form1.Tire) Handles _
        FlatTireMonitor.FlatTire

        msgbox(badtire.TirePosition & " tire is flat!")
    End Sub

    Public Sub FL_Click(ByVal sender As Object, ByVal e As _
        System.EventArgs) Handles FL.Click, fr.Click, bl.Click, _
        br.Click

        Dim TireToFlatten As Tire
        Dim Index As Integer
        Select Case True
            Case Sender.Equals(fl)
                index = 1
            Case Sender.Equals(fr)
                index = 2
            Case Sender.Equals(bl)
                index = 3
            Case Sender.Equals(br)
                index = 4
        End Select
        TireToFlatten = CType(mcolTires(index), tire)
        TireToFlatten.RunOverNail()
    End Sub
```

In the sub new for the form, insert the following code at the end of the routine:

```
    mcoltires.Add(New Tire("FL"))
    mcoltires.Add(New Tire("FR"))
    mcoltires.Add(New Tire("BL"))
    mcoltires.Add(New Tire("BR"))

    FlatTireMonitor = New Tire()
```

The first thing we defined was a tire object that has a shared event called FlatTire. It has a public TirePosition string property; it has a public sub RunOverNail which will raise the event; and it has a couple of constructors, one of which accepts the tire position when it's created to eliminate having to set the tire position property after it's created. Note how the `FlatTire` event has a parameter of the `Tire` type that is set so the event sink can determine exactly which object raised the error. This parameter is not necessary, but in our case we want to know which tire is flat without having to check each one. The next thing we defined was a collection to hold any number of tires. The collection was used to illustrate the point that you don't have to have a predetermined number of objects that you're sinking the events from as you would have had in prior versions of Visual Basic. Next we have an event sink declaration that we'll use to handle the `FlatTire` event from any number of tire classes. The next routine was created by selecting the event sink in the left objects combo box and the `FlatTire` event in the right events combo boxes. All we do in this event is indicate which tire is flat in a message box. The next step is just required to force our event to happen. The event can be raised internally by any defining moment like a property changing, a file appearing on a hard drive, or a time period expiring, or the event can be raised externally in the way we're doing in this example. The code in the click event for the front left tire button handles all four button click events in a common place, and you're able to determine which tire should run over the nail at your discretion. You get a reference to the object in the collection based on the index and then call the `RunOverNail` function to flatten the tire. Finally, the code you placed in the sub `New` for the form creates four tire objects, adds them to the collection, and then hooks up the shared event sink. Run the project and click on the buttons to have the tire run over a nail. You'll see that, through the shared event, we were able to determine what tire has gone flat without having to have a predetermined number of objects for which you're sinking events.

Procedures

A *procedure* is any function, property, event, or sub routine that is used in an application. Visual Basic .NET introduces several new capabilities for controlling how and when procedures are visible to other pieces of code. The new `Shared` and `Protected` modifiers, along with the concept of overloading functions and using constructors, gives you more control over how and when certain pieces of code can execute.

Access modifiers

Whereas prior versions of Visual Basic had the `Public`, `Friend`, and `Private` modifiers for procedures, Visual Basic .NET has those same modifiers as well as `Protected` and `Shared`. `Public` modifiers are used to expose a procedure, property, or event outside the module in which it's declared. Public members on classes and forms can be called outside the project if another application can make calls into the project, as would be the case in a Class Library or Control Library. Similarly, the `Private` modifier allows a procedure to be used only within the object itself. Although private procedures aren't available outside the module in which they're

```
Public Sub OverLoadExample()
Public Sub OverLoadExample(ByVal intP1 As Integer)
Public Sub OverLoadExample(ByVal strTest As String)

OverLoadExample()
OverLoadExample(5)
OverLoadExample("Hello World")
```

In the preceding code snippet, you have three functions defined with the same name except that they each would have a different signature. This allows you to call the same function name with different parameters, and you could have different behaviors based on what was supplied. The first call to the procedure didn't supply any parameters, so the first procedure declaration would be used. The second and third calls to the procedure both pass in a single parameter, but their types are different. As a result, Visual Basic .NET is able to determine that the second call would use the second declaration because the value passed was an Integer. Similarly, the third call would use the third declaration because the parameter that was supplied was a String that matches the declaration signature of the third function.

The concept of overloading a function is used almost all the time when creating constructors for a class. However, its use is not limited just to creating constructors. You can use the concept of overloading procedures anywhere in your code. Earlier in this chapter, you saw an overloaded constructor when the concept of creating shared events was discussed. Overloading functions comes in handy where you typically would have had a method that would've operated on a specific data type and you would have a different named similar method to work on each different data type you would supply to it. Because the concept of overloading functions is used with constructors, another example is given in the "Constructors" section later in this chapter.

Structures

Prior versions of Visual Basic allowed you to create user-defined types that were used to collect related pieces of information. User-defined types allowed you to create a group of related values that could be created and used by declaring a single variable. Although user-defined types had their advantages, they also had some limitations. One such limitation was that the user-defined type could not limit or validate the data that was stored within it. Another limitation was that there was no way to restrict what members were exposed, because all members of a user-defined type had public access. With all the members having public access, there was no way to hide any data or control which members could be changed. Visual Basic .NET has eliminated the user-defined type and has replaced them with structures. In its most basic form, structures duplicate the functionality of user-defined types:

```
Public Structure My3DPoint
    Public X As Integer
    Public Y As Integer
    Public Z As Integer
End Structure
```

However, structures are much more powerful than user-defined types when you understand how to take advantage of them. First, structures now let you control the access to the individual members:

```
Public Structure My3DPoint
    Public X As Integer
    Public Y As Integer
    Public Z As Integer

    Private A As Integer
    Friend B As Integer
End Structure
```

Here we've added a private variable and a friend variable to the structure. The access modifiers that can be used are the same as those listed earlier in this chapter for procedure access modifiers. Although this sounds great, if a member is private, then how can you modify it in the first place? In Visual Basic .NET, a structure can have variable members, but it can also have procedures in it. Earlier in this chapter, you read how any variable declared with anything other than `Private` actually creates a read-write property. So we could rewrite the friend variable as a property procedure:

```
Public Structure My3DPoint
    Public X As Integer
    Public Y As Integer
    Public Z As Integer

    Private A As Integer
    Friend Property B() As Integer
        Get
            b = a
        End Get
        Set (ByVal Value As Integer)
            a = b
        End Set
    End Property
End Structure
```

You can now see how you could use private variables in a structure to store information that may be required by the other members. A structure can have not only variables in it, but it can also have procedures other than properties, like functions and subs, as well:

```
Public Structure My3DPoint
    Public X As Integer
    Public Y As Integer
    Public Z As Integer

    Private A As Integer
    Friend Property B() As Integer
        Get
            b = a
        End Get
        Set (ByVal Value As Integer)
            a = b
        End Set
    End Property

    Public Sub ResetCoordinates()
        x = 0
        y = 0
        z = 0
    End Sub
End Structure
```

Here we've added a sub that will reset the coordinate values to zero. You're probably thinking to yourself that a structure looks very similar to a class, and you're right. The above structure could be changed to a class by simply changing the structure keyword to the class keyword on the top and bottom lines.

Structures are very similar to classes, but there are a few minor differences between the two. Structures don't have to be created before they're used. They're ready for use as soon as they've been declared. Structures can have constructors, but they can't have a constructor that doesn't take any parameters. As mentioned at the beginning of this chapter, any variable that is created from a structure is a value type, whereas any variable created from a class is a reference type. The individual members of a structure cannot have initializers. Finally, one of the biggest differences between structures and classes is that structures cannot be inherited from, whereas classes can.

Classes

When version 4 of Visual Basic was released, developers were given access to classes, which provided many benefits to developers. A class could be created that would do anything that a user-defined type could do (and more). With classes, developers could limit what data was exposed and what data could be stored within it. Classes can be thought of as a user-defined type on steroids. They're much more powerful then a standard user-defined type. Classes can expose public variables or read-write properties, which act just like the members of a user-defined type. However, classes can also have functions and methods that can act upon the data. Typically, developers would write helper functions for using the data within the types and would call these functions when manipulating the data contained within the user-defined types. One of the principles of object-oriented programming is encapsulating the data and the code that operates on the data together into a single unit, which is then called an *object*. When Visual Basic included classes in the language to allow encapsulation of data and functions related to the data, it made its first step towards becoming a full-fledged object-oriented programming language.

With all the benefits that classes can provide over user-defined types, the one thing that has caused the most problems is realizing that a variable created from a class is an object. Although this may seem obvious now, it hasn't always been so to developers. Not every piece of data that you use in a system must or should be represented as an object. Doing so will only increase the complexity of your application, hurt the performance, and make it harder to read, understand, and maintain. Objects provide many benefits, but there are a couple of downsides. First, objects must be created before they can be used by using the New keyword. Contrast this to variables based on user-defined types, which are ready for use as soon as they're declared. Second, an object requires a little more memory than a user-defined type does because of some fundamental differences that have been mentioned. Understanding how and when to use objects properly is the key to reducing the amount of effort required with each application you develop.

Visual Basic .NET expands upon the uses of classes in many ways. At the beginning of this chapter, you learned that almost everything that you work with in Visual Basic .NET is an object. You also learned that every object inherits from the Object data type. Using classes in Visual Basic .NET is the only way that you can take advantage of inheritance in the design of your own applications. The previous section discussed structures and how they're very similar to classes, as well as the major differences between classes and structures. Because classes are very similar to structures and a structure can be converted to a class simply by changing the Structure keyword into a Class keyword, I won't repeat the same information in detail and instead will concentrate on the differences.

Constructors

By now you already know that you can declare and initialize a variable at the same time. In order for this to occur, the variable type you're using has to be based on a class and has to provide a constructor. A constructor is simply one or more sub procedures named New in the class. The concept of overloading a function was discussed earlier (in the "Overloading functions" section), but to simplify things, you have the same named function repeated, but each function has a different parameter signature. Overloading functions is the basis for creating constructors that initialize an object to a known state at the time the object is created. A constructor of the class a variable is based on is used anytime a variable is initialized. The initialization can occur when a variable is declared or it can occur later on. But both times the constructor fires when the object is created:

```
Public Class ConstructorTest
    Public X As Integer
    Public Y As String
    Public Z As Double
End Class

Public Sub Test()
    Dim objConstr As New ConstructorTest()

    With objConstr
       .X = 5
       .Y = "Hello World"
       .Z = 3.14159
    End With
End Sub
```

The preceding code shows how you could define a class, create it, and initialize it. This was your only choice in prior versions of Visual Basic. However, you now have the power of constructors, which can initialize your object for you. In order to define a constructor, you need to have a sub procedure named New in your class:

```
Public Class ConstructorTest
    Public X As Integer
    Public Y As String
    Public Z As Double

    Public Sub New()
        'Basic Constructor
    End Sub
End Class
```

However, the preceding constructor doesn't do anything because we didn't put any code within it. This is called the *base constructor* and is fired when you create the object without any parameters, as we've done. You would put code here that has to run any time you create an object, regardless of what you're going to store in the object. For example, if you need to create collection objects or initialize storage arrays or anything like that, you would put that code here. This is similar to writing code in the class initialize event in prior versions of Visual Basic. This still requires you to set your three properties individually as you've already done, so it doesn't gain you that much. The real benefit of constructors comes in when you override the base constructor and provide custom initialization code:

```
Public Class ConstructorTest
    Public X As Integer
    Public Y As String
    Public Z As Double

    Public Sub New()
        'Basic Constructor
    End Sub

    Public Sub new(ByVal X_Init As Integer, _
        ByVal Y_Init As String, ByVal Z_Init As Double)
        x = X_Init
        y = Y_Init
        z = z_Init
    End Sub

    Public Sub new(ByVal X_Init As Integer)
        x = X_Init
    End Sub

    Public Sub new(ByVal Y_Init As String)
        y = Y_Init
    End Sub

    Public Sub new(ByVal Z_Init As Double)
        z = z_Init
    End Sub
End Class
```

In the preceding code, you have five different constructors that you can use to initialize your object. The first one is the base constructor, which has already been discussed. The next one accepts initial values for all three members. The third, fourth, and fifth constructors each accept a single parameter of different types (Integer, String, and Double).

Now look at how you would utilize the constructors you defined:

```
Dim objConstr As ConstructorTest

objconstr = New ConstructorTest(3.14159)
objConstr = New ConstructorTest(5, "Hello World", 3.14159)
objconstr = New ConstructorTest(5)
objconstr = New ConstructorTest("Hello World")
objconstr = New ConstructorTest()
```

Here you have an object variable and five different ways you could call it. In the first line, you are giving it a decimal number, and the Z_Init constructor is the only constructor that matches the decimal data you have supplied, so the Z_Init constructor is the one that is called. The next line shows how you can supply all three values for the constructor, which will initialize all the members of the class in one line of code. The third constructor uses the integer X_Init constructor and the fourth uses the Y_Init string constructor. The last line uses the base constructor, which in your example doesn't do anything.

With constructors, keep in mind that it's the data types and order of the parameters defined in the constructors that create the signature. If you have two integer member data types and tried to create a single constructor for each one, the compiler would have no way of knowing which method it should call, so you'll get a syntax error stating that there are multiple identical declarations.

Sub classes

One of the new features in Visual Basic .NET is that you no longer have to have a separate file in your project for each class, form, or module. Because classes and forms are actually defined in code with a beginning and an ending statement, you could have one large file that has all the classes, structures, and modules defined within it, but doing so makes it hard to reuse code later or to share the development work with other developers. If you're the developer of a form or another class and you decide that you could do something easier if you used a class, you have several options. First, you could define the class as a separate file as you would have in prior versions of Visual Basic. You could also define the class in the same file but outside the other class declaration. Or you could define the class within the other class declaration:

```
Public Class Class1

End Class

Public Class Class2
    Public Class Class3

    End Class
End Class

Public Class Class4
    Private Class Class5

    End Class
End Class
```

The preceding example shows how you can create multiple classes within the same file and embed classes inside class declarations. If the preceding classes were defined in one class module, classes 1, 2, and 4 would be accessible anywhere within the project. However because classes 3 and 5 are defined within an outer class, they're only available within their parent classes. Because class 3 is public to class 2, an object based on class 3 could be defined by fully qualifying the class as in the following line of code:

```
Dim obj3 As New Class2.Class3()
```

The preceding line of code shows you how the hierarchy of namespaces can be used to collect related classes together. You could use an imports statement on Class2 and then you would be able to create an object of type Class3. However, since Class5 is private to Class4, it can only be created and used within Class4. One reason to encapsulate your classes in this manner would be to have a helper class that's only used by a single form. You could define the class within the form definition, and it would only be available within the form itself.

Namespaces

The concept of namespaces was introduced in Visual Basic .NET to eliminate any confusion as to which function, enum, property, or constant should be used if there would ever be two of the same items accessible at the same time. Prior versions of Visual Basic as well as .NET will prevent this from happening in your own project, but you couldn't prevent this from occurring if you set a reference to one or more external libraries or COM components. Prior versions of Visual Basic would call the function that appeared first in the reference list. By moving the reference order up or down in the References dialog box, you could indicate which function should be called.

Although not its intended purpose, some developers took advantage of this and wrote code that provided the same interface as certain intrinsic Visual Basic functions. One example I've seen of this is writing a message box function that has the same name and parameters as the built-in MsgBox function. They would then move their component ahead of the library where the original function was, and their component would be called instead of the built-in function. They would then do some specific code in their function and then typically call the original function by fully qualifying the name from the library to the class to the function. This allowed developers to do things like logging all message boxes of a certain type to a file before displaying the information to the user.

Visual Basic .NET requires objects and constants to be completely qualified in order to prevent naming conflicts or confusion. For example, two different libraries or components that are referenced might have a constant named orange. There are many different variations of the color orange, but which one should be chosen? Visual Basic .NET solves this by requiring the constant to be fully qualified, as in the following generic example:

```
Form1.BackColor = Component1.Shades.Orange

'or

Form1.BackColor = Component2.Color.Orange
```

As you can see, requiring the complete qualification of functions, properties, constants, and so on eliminates confusion as to which one is being called. However, completely qualifying every call would be a burden to the developer, so Visual Basic .NET supports a shortcut by using the *Imports* statement. The Imports keyword allows you to use names without requiring complete qualification:

```
Imports Component1.Shades

Form1.BackColor = Orange

'or

Form1.BackColor = Component2.Color.Orange
```

By including the Imports statement as shown in the preceding generic example, the constant orange can be used without the complete qualification. However, if you were to use the Imports statement and it brought in conflicting names, you would get a naming conflict and you would still have to specify which one should be used.

Namespaces also have an additional benefit in that any procedures with a shared attribute in the assembly you're importing can be used without requiring an object to be created first. This concept is similar to creating a global multiuse class in prior versions, setting a reference to the library in which the class was defined, and then calling the functions on the object without creating the object first. Visual Basic .NET allows you to use the Imports statement on classes in your own project as well as external projects. So by creating shared methods on classes and importing the namespaces for the classes, you can create helper objects and functions that can be used without explicitly creating the object first. In order to use the Imports statement, the assembly or component must already be referenced in your project. When you type the Imports statement, IntelliSense will display a hierarchical list of namespaces that you can drill down into and use.

The following is another example of why you would use the Imports statement in your code:

```
'VB6 and prior would do the following
Me.BackColor = vbRed     'Does not work in .NET

'VB .NET colors are in System.Drawing.Color
Me.BackColor = System.Drawing.Color.Red
```

```
'However System.Drawing is already in an imports statement
Me.BackColor = Color.Red

'By including Imports System.Drawing.Color statement
Me.BackColor = Red
```

The preceding example points out a couple of things. First, almost all the constants you may be familiar with have changed names and/or locations where they're stored. In prior versions, vbRed was a valid color constant and was available for use anytime. However, Visual Basic .NET organizes the constants and puts them with the classes where they belong. When you're setting the color of something, you're working with an object that's drawn on the screen. System.Drawing is where the drawing functions are grouped and located now. Under System.Drawing, there is a Color class that has all the color constants you can think of for use when drawing objects on the screen. Similarly, if you want to specify a color using the RGB format, you need to use the following function:

```
Me.BackColor = Color.FromARGB(150, 150, 150)
```

Visual Basic .NET also provides another option that you can use to import namespaces. By bringing up the Project Properties dialog box and selecting the Imports item in the folder list, you can set the project level imports that will be available in all modules without having to explicitly set the imports statements in each module. Visual Basic .NET has undergone many changes in order to meet its design goals. The concept of namespaces and organizing the related functions in a hierarchy namespace tree goes a long way toward making code more maintainable and easier to read.

File Structures

You need to be aware of a few changes regarding file structures and extensions in Visual Basic .NET. First, all code files in Visual Basic .NET have a .VB file extension. Because you can mix projects with different languages in a solution, the .VB extension immediately tells you what language the code was written in without having to open it up and look at the code. However, this might cause some problems when you're trying to find a particular file, because you can't group files by their extensions. You can work around this situation by using a consistent naming convention. When you add a form, or class, or any other file to a project, you're given the chance to specify the filename at this point. Because Visual Basic will immediately start saving any changes you make to the file, you should specify the filename you want to use instead of accepting the default filename. When you specify the filename, you should also prefix the filename with an abbreviation for the type of file. For example, you should prefix forms with *frm* so the filenames are saved as frmFileName.VB. Similarly, with classes you should use a *cls* prefix; controls a *ctl* prefix; modules a *mod* prefix; and so on. Doing this now will save you lots of headaches and frustrations when trying to sort through the files. It's true that if you bring it up in the IDE, you'll be able to see what type of file it is. But think about the cases when you don't have the IDE available, as when you're using source safe, copying files from one place to another, sharing files between projects, and so on. Other file extensions that you need to know about are .SLN for a solution, .VBPROJ for a Visual Basic project, .VBPROJ.USER for user settings in the project, .SUO for the user options for the solution, and .PDB for the program debug data.

Another change that you'll get used to is that Visual Basic .NET makes extensive use of XML. Project files are stored and user settings for project files are stored in XML format. XML format is also used to store configuration settings for an application that you can read in at startup to initialize your application. XML is also used to serialize object data so that objects can be marshaled efficiently across component boundaries. ADO.NET uses XML not only to persist data to a stream or a disk, but it also uses XML internally to represent the data being stored.

Summary

Understanding Visual Basic .NET and object-oriented programming will take some discipline and patience, because you need to master or re-master the basics before you can effectively jump into the new and more-advanced features. There are many changes to the language itself, but after you master the basics, the doors will start opening and you'll realize that the changes are beneficial. You will know how best to use the new features to reduce the amount of effort required when developing applications.

Part II

Understanding New Language Features

Chapter 4

Handling Errors in Visual Basic .NET

IN THIS CHAPTER

- Comparing Structured Exception Handling to `On Error` syntax
- Benefits of Structured Exception Handling
- Using exceptions provided by the .NET Framework
- Creating custom exceptions
- `Try...Catch...Finally` syntax and variations

The biggest change to handling errors in Visual Basic .NET is the use of Structured Exception Handling instead of relying on the `On Error Goto` syntax from previous versions. The ability to include Structured Exception Handling in your Visual Basic .NET applications is provided by the .NET Framework and has many benefits over the error-handling capabilities of previous versions. The benefits include:

- The ability to create more robust error handlers
- An easier way of managing or tracking multiple errors
- Flexible handling schemes
- The ability to create and use custom exceptions
- An easier method of reading, understanding, and maintaining the error-handling code

A Structured Exception Handling Primer

The simplest way to describe Structured Exception Handling is that it allows the developer to protect a block of code that may generate a runtime error (exception) and provide the related code to handle the exception, as well as perform any cleanup tasks. You may be thinking that this description describes any generic

85

error handler, which could have been created in prior versions of Visual Basic. Structured Exception Handling is an error handler, but it has a few distinctions that need to be pointed out from the way errors were handled in prior versions.

Error handling in prior versions

Prior versions of Visual Basic provided the On Error statement, which could be used in several different ways. First, it could have been used in an On Error Goto 0 scenario, which effectively turned off the custom error handling capabilities in a procedure and left Visual Basic to provide the default error-handling characteristics for the procedure. The default error handler for Visual Basic will cause the error to be propagated back up the call stack until an error handler is found. If the error was propagated to the top-level routine and it didn't include an error handler, then Visual Basic would simply display the error message on the screen and terminate the program.

The second way the On Error statement could have been used was in an On Error Resume or an On Error Resume Next statement. The plain On Error Resume statement would simply cause the line of code that generated the error to be executed again and again until either the error went away or the application was terminated. The On Error Resume Next statement was used to force the error to be ignored and the next line of code after the one that generated the error would be executed. The On Error Resume Next statement indicates that the author of the code knows that at least one line of code following the statement may generate an error. If you were lucky, you would see an explanation in the code comments that explained why the Resume Next statement was used. The code that the developer knows may generate the error may be followed by a check for a specific error number, or another error-handling directive would be used to either turn off the custom error handling or to resume with a different error handler. Using the On Error Resume Next statement with a test for a specific error was the best way to trap and handle errors where they occurred in the procedure. However, testing for an error after each line of code is an unnecessary burden to the developer.

The third way the On Error statement could have been used was in an On Error Goto statement, which forces the execution flow of the procedure to jump to the line of code that's indicated in the Goto statement. This method of error handling makes it impossible to create clean, concise, easily understandable error handling code that traps for and handles the errors as they occur in the code. However, the On Error Goto syntax did prevent developers from having to test for every possible error. The Goto statement forced the execution flow of the procedure to jump all over the place if a single error handler were placed in each routine to handle and recover from all the possible errors that could occur. As a result, procedures with an On Error Goto handler in them typically did something simple with the error, like just logging it and raising it up to the calling procedure.

When working with error handlers in prior versions of Visual Basic, errors were raised by calling the Raise method of the error object and supplying a specific error number. An error number by itself could not convey all the information about the error that occurred. As a result, developers had to have prior knowledge of the mappings between the error numbers and the definitions. Granted, the mappings were specified in the documentation, but it wasn't an integral part of the language. When code was written to trap and test for a certain error, the resulting code had to check for a specific number. Although developers had the ability to use unallocated error numbers for raising custom errors, there was no way to guarantee that the error number wouldn't be used by another component. Even if named constants or enumerations were used for specifying the error numbers, the resulting error-handling code was awkward at best and often hard to read and understand.

The error-handling capabilities in prior versions of Visual Basic were cumbersome and easily led to situations where the error-handling capability was separated from the code providing the functionality. If the code that contained the functionality was moved to a different procedure, the error-handling code had to be adjusted as well by either re-creating the proper error handler in the new procedure, or trying to break out the specific error-handling code for the desired piece of functionality from the complex error handler. Either way you look at it, you can begin to see how more bugs could be introduced into the application when making these types of modifications.

Comparing error handling in Visual Basic .NET to prior versions

Visual Basic .NET still supports handling errors using the On Error syntax, but it's only for compatibility with existing Visual Basic applications that are upgraded to run in the .NET Framework environment. The .NET Framework provides for Structured Exception Handling and should be used instead of the On Error syntax from prior versions of Visual Basic. Because Structured Exception Handling is a product of the .NET Framework, error handlers that use this technique are compatible with the other languages that support the .NET Framework. Using the On Error syntax in Visual Basic .NET immediately prevents your code from being used in other languages that support the .NET Framework. As you progress through this chapter and after a few comparisons between the old On Error syntax and the new Structured Exception Handling techniques, you'll realize how Structured Exception Handling can provide the many benefits highlighted at the beginning of this chapter.

The easiest way to get started with exceptions is with a quick example. The following code shows a procedure with an error handler using the old On Error syntax:

```
Private Function TestA(ByVal A As Integer, _
    Optional ByVal B As Integer = 0) As Integer

    Dim intDivResult As Integer

    On Error Goto EH

    If A < 0 Then Err.Raise(12345, "TestA", _
        "A Can Not Be Negative")
```

```
        intDivResult = A \ B

        Return intDivResult

        Exit Function
EH:
        If Not Err.Number = 11 Then
            If Err.Number = 12345 Then
                With Err()
                    .Raise(.Number, .Source, .Description)
                End With
            End If
            MessageBox.Show(Err.Number & " " & Err.Description)
            Return -1
        End If
    End Function
```

From looking at the preceding code, what do you think would happen if the function were called by the following code:

```
MessageBox.Show(TestA(3).ToString)
```

In order to figure out what would happen, you would first have to check to see if the value of the A variable was less than zero. In this case, it's not, so you would proceed and realize that the code would encounter an error when the intDivResult variable was calculated, because the value of the B variable was zero and dividing by zero generates an error. At this point, the code would jump to the bottom of the procedure where the error handler was located and the error handler checks to see if the error number for the error that was generated was anything other than 11. If the error number was neither 11 nor 12345, then it would display a message with the error number and description and then return a –1 to the calling function.

From experience, you may already know what error number 11 indicates. But if not, you would have to look it up in the documentation before you could understand what the function was trying to accomplish. If you didn't have access to the documentation at the time you were reviewing the code, you'd be stuck. As you can see, developing error handlers using the On Error syntax can produce code that's hard to read and understand, especially if you're not looking at the code from within the development environment. The preceding code also has another problem in that it relies on the calling routine to check the return value to see if the function worked properly in some cases, and in other cases an error would be raised that would have to be accounted for. Furthermore, returning an error code in the return value is not a good programming practice – it can cause other hard-to-find bugs later on because the calling routine doesn't have to check the return value of a function.

Now take a look at the same function rewritten to take advantage of Structured Exception Handling provided by the .NET Framework:

```
Private Function TestB(ByVal A As Integer, _
Optional ByVal B As Integer = 0) As Integer

    Dim intDivResult As Integer

    If A < 0 Then
        Throw New ArgumentOutOfRangeException("A", _
            "A Can Not Be Negative")
    End If

    Try
        intDivResult = A \ B
    Catch e As DivideByZeroException
        intDivResult = 0
    Catch e As Exception
        MessageBox.Show(e.ToString)
        intDivResult = -1
    End Try

    Return intDivResult
End Function
```

The preceding code uses Structured Exception Handling and produces the same results as the On Error syntax function, including using the return value of the function to indicate an error, which again is not a good programming practice.

Now look at the preceding function to understand how Structured Exception Handling works. In the .NET Framework, an Exception is a class that is instantiated as an object when a runtime error occurs and contains detailed information about the error. Through the use of inheritance, the .NET Framework provides numerous classes that inherit from the Exception class. A quick search in the Object Browser matching the substring "Exception" will display a listing of the various named exceptions that are built in to the .NET Framework. Exceptions are generated by using the Throw keyword, as shown in the preceding code when the ArgumentOutOfRangeException was used to indicate that the A variable cannot contain negative values. Structured Exception Handling places the code to handle an error with the code that actually generated the error. The code and the error handler are combined together by a Try...Catch...End Try block. The code that's in the Try block is executed, and if an exception (error) occurs, then the execution point will immediately jump to the Catch block(s). A Catch block is where the exception is handled and can be used to trap for specific as well as generic exceptions, as shown in the preceding code. The first `Catch` block is used to trap and handle exceptions that occur when a number is divided by zero. There is no limit to the number of specific exceptions that could be trapped in a single `Try...Catch...End Try` block. You simply need to insert additional `Catch` blocks before the `End Try` statement in the code. The preceding code also shows how to trap for a generic exception after all the specific exceptions have been trapped. If no specific `Catch` block is executed, then the `Catch` block for the generic handler will execute. By using Structured Exception Handling, you can see how easy it is to create and understand the execution flow of the procedure.

Defining and using custom exceptions

The .NET Framework provides many predefined exceptions that are thrown when an error occurs. When you need to manually throw an exception, you should first look to see if there is a predefined exception that can be used like the `ArgumentOutOfRangeException` that was used in the example in the previous section. If there is not a suitable predefined exception in the .NET Framework that will work, you should create and use your own exception. Through inheritance, it's easy to create your own custom exception, as shown in the following code:

```
Public Class MyCustomException
    Inherits ApplicationException
End Class
```

The simplest of custom exceptions is a class that inherits from the `ApplicationException` class. In order to throw an exception of the type `MyCustomException`, you only need to throw an instance of the custom exception, as shown in the following code:

```
Try
    Throw New MyCustomException()
Catch ex As MyCustomException
    MessageBox.Show("My Custom Exception Thrown")
End Try
```

As you're creating applications in Visual Basic .NET, you may only need to know that an exception occurred and you don't need to know any details about the context of the exception. In this case, you simply need to define your working set of empty custom exception classes and make sure they're available to the local namespace of both the throwing and calling procedures.

There may also be times when it would be beneficial to know more about the context of the exception. For example, the `ArgumentOutOfRangeException` that has been used exposed a property that indicated which argument was out of range and it also exposed a property that allowed you to give a more meaningful description as to why the argument was out of the allowed range. When you want to provide additional information to the calling routine about the exception that occurred, you need to add the additional property procedures and private variables to the class to store this information. However, if you don't provide a constructor or set of constructors that allows the properties to be specified when the object is created, you won't be able to use the Throw New syntax as previously shown. Add a description property, local variable, and constructor to the MyCustomException class as follows:

```
Public Class MyCustomException
    Inherits ApplicationException

    Private mstrDescription As String

    Public Property Description() As String
        Get
            Return mstrDescription
        End Get
        Set(ByVal Value As String)
            mstrDescription = Value
        End Set
    End Property

    Public Sub New()
        'Default constructor
    End Sub

    Public Sub New(ByVal Description As String)
        mstrDescription = Description
    End Sub
End Class
```

Now when you need to specify the information that will be available in the Description property of the exception, you can throw the error as follows:

```
Try
    Throw New MyCustomException("Hello")
Catch ex As MyCustomException
    MessageBox.Show(ex.Description)
End Try
```

As you can see, it's easy to define and use custom exceptions in your Visual Basic .NET applications. Besides being easy to use, custom exceptions can improve the readability and maintainability of your code.

Using Try...Catch...Finally Blocks

By now you have a basic understanding of how Structured Exception Handling is used in Visual Basic .NET. This section of the chapter goes beyond the basics and demonstrates the flexibility of Structured Exception Handling and lets you know how the basic technique can be adapted and extended upon to allow you to create robust error-handling code as you develop your application.

This previous statement cannot be emphasized enough. In order for an application to have robust error-handling capabilities, the error-handling mechanism is an integral part of the application and needs to be incorporated into the application from the beginning as it's developed. Trying to insert error- or exception-handling into the application after it's almost complete would be like trying to run the electrical wiring and plumbing in a house after the insulation and drywall are already in place. Although it could be done, it would be a lot harder to accomplish and would require a lot of unnecessary patchwork to the walls as opposed to if it had been placed in the walls before they were closed up.

Variations on the Try...Catch structure

Up to this point, the examples have only used a Try block with one or more Catch blocks. The .NET Framework allows for several different variations of Structured Exception Handling to be used based on the individual requirements of each block of code that needs to be protected. In addition to the Try and Catch blocks, there is also a Finally block that can be used as well. By now, you know that the code that's placed within a Try block will attempt to execute first. If an exception is generated anywhere within the Try block, then the execution pointer will immediately jump to the first Catch statement. If the exception is being filtered by specific exceptions in each Catch statement, then each statement will be examined to see if it should handle the exception.

The order in which the Catch statements are listed is important, because only one Catch statement will execute if there are multiple Catch statements that could handle the exception. For example, if the Catch statement for the generic Exception class were placed before the specific derived exception class, then only the generic handler would execute.

If there are no Catch blocks that match the thrown exception, a Finally block (if present) will begin to execute. However, after the Finally block executes, the exception will begin to bubble up the call stack until another Catch block or the application exception handler catches it. If the application-level handler catches the exception, you'll be presented with a dialog box stating that an unhandled exception has occurred, and the user will be given a choice of either continuing or quitting the application immediately. This is a benefit of exception handling that wasn't available with the On Error syntax in prior versions. If an error occurred in prior versions and wasn't trapped, then it too would travel up the call stack until it reached the application-level handler. But in this scenario you aren't given the choice of continuing, because the application would be terminated unconditionally.

The Finally block, as its name implies, will always execute after a successful Try or after the Catch block in an unsuccessful Try. As a result, the code in a Finally block is the ideal place to put any cleanup code that may be required, because it will always execute. The Finally block provides a great benefit over the old On Error syntax when you need to make sure certain things happen before the procedure exits, regardless of whether an error occurred. With the On Error syntax, you had to either duplicate code in the error handler to account for the abnormal exiting, or you had to use a line Label with another Goto statement to jump to the cleanup section. With the Finally block of a Try...Catch...Finally structure, you place all your cleanup code in a single place, and you can be assured that it will always execute before the procedure exits:

```
Public Sub TestC()
    On Error Goto EH
    'Do something
    Goto Cleanup
EH:
    'Handle the error
Cleanup:
    'Do any cleanup here
End Sub


Public Sub TestD()
    Try
        'Do something
    Catch
        'Account for error
    Finally
        'Always execute cleanup code
    End Try
End Sub
```

Each of the preceding routines would accomplish the goal of always executing any cleanup code but the Try...Catch...Finally syntax, as shown in TestD, is much cleaner and easier to follow.

When using the Try...Catch...Finally syntax, there are three basic variations, as shown in the following code:

```
Try
    'Do something
Catch
    'Catch the exception
End Try


Try
    'Do something
Finally
    'Dont catch exception
    'Perform cleanup
    'Exception thrown in calling routine
End Try


Try
    'Do something
Catch
    'Catch exception
Finally
    'Perform cleanup
End Try
```

Each variation has a unique purpose, as described in the comments, and is one of the reasons why the `Try...Catch...Finally` syntax of Structured Exception Handling is easy to use and is so powerful. Even though it's called Structured Exception Handling, the way it's implemented is not set in stone. It's structured, but it remains flexible enough to meet the ever-changing needs in the applications you develop.

Nesting of Try...Catch blocks

Structured Exception Handling has another benefit in that the `Try...Catch...Finally` blocks can be nested within each other. Structured Exception Handling can only "handle" one exception at a time. However, nested `Try...Catch` blocks have the ability to catch and track exceptions within exceptions, as shown in the following code:

```
Try
    'Do something
Catch
    'Catch exception
    Try
```

```
            'Try to handle first exception
        Catch
            'Catch second exception
        Finally
            'Perform cleanup for second exception
        End Try
    Finally
        'Perform cleanup for first exception
    End Try
```

There is no limit to the number of layers of nesting that you can create to handle the most complex scenarios. Even though you could have several layers of nesting, through the automatic indention of the blocks, you can easily determine where the point of execution is currently and which line of code will be executed next. If you're using nested exception handlers, you can also throw what's called a *chained exception.*

Chained exceptions allow you to throw exceptions from within a Catch block of another exception while preserving the original exception. Although this may seem a little confusing at first, the purpose of a chained exception is to provide the calling routines with a linked list of Exception objects. The previous exception is accessed through the InnerException property of each exception. The InnerException property of the first exception that was thrown will be Nothing. Chained exceptions are similar to a call stack trace and can be used to diagnose where the original exception occurred and why.

The following code shows how to use chained exceptions in your applications:

```
Try
    Try
        Throw New ArgumentOutOfRangeException()
    Catch ex As Exception
        Throw New DivideByZeroException("DVZ", ex)
    End Try
Catch ex As Exception
    MessageBox.Show(ex.InnerException.ToString)
    MessageBox.Show(ex.ToString)
End Try
```

In the preceding code, the nested exception block simply throws the ArgumentOutOfRangeException, and in the Catch block, the Divide_ ByZeroException is thrown and passes the original ex Exception object. In the outer Catch block, the first message box will display the Argument_ OutOfRangeException information, while the second message box will display the DivideByZeroException information.

Using filtered handlers on structured exception handlers

Visual Basic .NET provides an extension to the Structured Exception Handling capabilities provided in the .NET Framework. Visual Basic .NET allows you to specify a When clause on a Catch statement. The following code shows how this could be used to streamline exception handling in Visual Basic .NET:

```
Dim A As Integer
Dim B As Integer
Dim C As Integer

Try
    C = 1 \ A
    C = 1 \ B
Catch ex As DivideByZeroException When A = 0
    MessageBox.Show("Divide By Zero On A")
Catch ex As DivideByZeroException When B = 0
    MessageBox.Show("Divide By Zero On B")
End Try
```

In the preceding code, there are two separate DivideByZeroException Catch statements, but each one has a different filter used in the When clause. The first one will be executed only when the A variable is zero, and the second one will be executed only when the B variable is zero. Filters allow you to wrap multiple similar statements within a single Try block but still be able to know the exact reason why the exception occurred.

Visual Basic .NET also supports another extension that allows you to exit a Try...Catch...Finally block in a structured manner. The Exit Try statement can be used to exit the block from within the Try or the Catch blocks. If the code is in the Finally block, then it will have to complete the block or provide another way to short-circuit the execution.

Summary

The purpose of this chapter was to introduce you to the concept of Structured Exception Handling and how to implement it in Visual Basic .NET. In the documentation on Structured Exception Handling, there is a topic that discusses some recommendations to follow in order to get the most value out of using exceptions. The following is a quick summary of the recommended practices for using exceptions:

◆ When naming exception classes, make sure to end the name in "exception."

◆ When creating custom exception classes, make sure to provide a default (empty) constructor, a constructor that accepts just a message, and a constructor that accepts a message and an inner exception object.

◆ If there is a preexisting exception, use it instead of creating another custom exception.

◆ Don't derive exceptions from the base Exception class. Instead create a new base exception for each namespace, and derive it from the base Exception class. All other exceptions created in the namespace should then be derived from the namespace's newly created base exception.

◆ If possible, design the default flow of a procedure so that an exception isn't thrown. An exception by definition is something out of the normal flow of the procedure.

◆ Exceptions should be thrown outside the calling procedure only if the calling procedure can do something as a result of the exception being thrown.

◆ If you catch the generic exception, you should either handle it completely or throw the exception in the calling routine using chained exceptions where appropriate.

◆ Before throwing an exception, all intermediate results, variables, handles, and so on should be cleaned up. The calling routine should always assume that there are no internal side effects as a result of the thrown exception.

Structured Exception Handling is a huge improvement over the old On Error syntax in prior versions. When you understand how to use exceptions and the many benefits they provide, you won't want to use another On Error statement again. As you've seen in this chapter, Structured Exception Handling can make your code more robust, easier to read and follow, more maintainable, and also compatible with other languages that support the .NET Framework.

Chapter 5

Understanding Inheritance in Visual Basic .NET

IN THIS CHAPTER

◆ Inheritance basics

◆ Inheritance with data types

◆ Overriding base methods

◆ Using interfaces

◆ Visual inheritance

Although there are many changes to Visual Basic .NET from prior versions, the addition of inheritance to the language is probably the most drastic and most beneficial change to the Visual Basic language. If you make the commitment and put forth the effort to understand inheritance, your reward will be a key that will unlock a series of doors in your quest for understanding Visual Basic .NET and increase long-term productivity and reduce code-maintenance requirements. As you progress through each door, you'll gain a better understanding of inheritance and the pervasive role it plays in Visual Basic .NET.

It's important to understand that inheritance is just another tool that you can add to your programming toolbox. With any tool, there is both a proper way and an improper way to use the tool for the task at hand. Think about how you could use a sledgehammer to smash a brick. You could use the sledgehammer to hit the brick with the handle, or you could hit the brick with the head of the hammer. Although both approaches may work to smash the brick, if you don't use the tool properly, you'll have to expend a lot more effort to get the job done.

A lot of work in programming deals with picking and properly using the right tool for the job at hand. In this chapter, you discover how inheritance is incorporated in the Visual Basic language and how to take advantage of it in your applications. Visual Basic .NET includes more then one type of inheritance. The first type of inheritance is used as you write code, and it's important to understand this type of inheritance first. When you understand the topic of inheritance in writing code, you'll then be able to understand how Visual Basic .NET implements visual inheritance for objects that display a user interface. Think of the material in this chapter as an instruction manual for the new inheritance tool you just acquired.

When you read and understand your instruction manual, you'll be amazed at how it can reduce the amount of programming effort required as you create applications with Visual Basic .NET.

Code Inheritance

With the release of .NET, Visual Basic has finally become a complete object-oriented programming language. Developers have requested that Microsoft incorporate support for inheritance in Visual Basic for some time now, and with Visual Basic .NET, they've finally gotten their wish. However, support for inheritance wasn't just tacked on at the end — it was designed into the language at the lowest level with the release of the .NET Framework. With the .NET Framework and the Common Language Runtime, Visual Basic has the same inheritance capabilities as any of the other languages in the Visual Studio .NET product. When you start looking at Visual Basic .NET, you'll be surprised at the level for which inheritance is used in the language. Everything in Visual Basic .NET is an object and everything else is eventually derived from this base object. When you understand the basics of inheritance and how it's used in Visual Basic .NET, you'll have a better understanding of how you can directly use inheritance in your own applications to reduce the amount of programming effort required.

Door 1: Everything is an object

The first step to understanding inheritance is realizing that every variable, form, and control is an object in Visual Basic .NET. In prior versions of the language, a variable could be one of three main classes of data types:

- The intrinsic or value data types, such as String, Integer, Long, Boolean, and so on

- The object data types, such as object or any specific object type defined by a class either internally or externally

- The ugly Variant data type, which would allow virtually anything to be stored in it, including intrinsic data types and object data types

Although the Variant data type had some advantages in prior versions, the disadvantages by far outweighed the advantages. Because Visual Basic .NET is now finally a true object-oriented programming language, it has incorporated new features in the language that make the Variant data type obsolete, so Microsoft has removed it and the other intrinsic data types from the language. You may be wondering how, when the intrinsic data types were removed, you're going to work with simple information. The answer is that even though the intrinsic data types are removed, they've been replaced by objects for which the majority have the same names as the intrinsic data types. The languages that have been created to use the .NET Framework all use the same underlying cross-language data types. The data type names you're familiar with in Visual Basic, like Integer, actually use the Int32 data type located in the `System` namespace.

Now, through inheritance, Visual Basic .NET includes a new object data type, which in itself is an object that exposes four public functions. This object data type is the base type for every other object in the language. The intrinsic data types have been replaced with objects that inherit from and expand upon the base object type. The names of these objects should be very familiar to you, because they're named the same as the intrinsic data types they replaced. To illustrate this point, if you declare a variable as a String and in code place a dot after the variable name, in the IntelliSense pop-up window you'll see a list of properties and methods that you can use, such as `Length`, `Insert`, `Remove`, and so on. If you select the String object in the Object Browser and look at the detail pane (mscorlib.System.String), you will see that the Object Browser has an entry for bases and interfaces. For the String object, you'll see that there is only one base class it derives from, which is the Object class. Take a minute to browse some of the other objects and look at their base classes to get a feel for what's happening.

TIP If you're trying to find a method on a particular object, don't give up at the top level. You may need to drill down through the base classes to find the particular function you're looking for. Even though the object in question doesn't directly expose something, one of its base classes from which it's derived can expose the functionality, and it will be available for you to use in the object in question.

Because everything in Visual Basic .NET derives from the Object class or data type and, hence, supports the same four functions that are exposed on the base class, you should understand what the four functions are, how they're used, and how you can change the default behavior of these functions. The four functions the Object class exposes are `Equals`, `GetHashCode`, `GetType`, and `ToString`.

The `Equals` function is used to determine if the specified object is the same instance as the current object. The function is called by passing the object to be compared against as a parameter of the function and returning a Boolean, which indicates whether the references are identical:

```
Public Sub Test()
    Dim objA As Object = "Hello World"
    Dim objB As Object = "Hello World"
    Dim objC As Object = "hello world"
    Dim objD As Object
```

```
MessageBox.Show (objA.Equals(objC))
MessageBox.Show (objA.Equals(objB))
MessageBox.Show (objA.Equals(objD))

objD = objA
MessageBox.Show (objA.Equals(objD))
End Sub
```

In the preceding code, the first message box displays False, because the objects are not identical due to the lowercase letters in objC. The third message box displays a False as expected, because the objects are clearly not equal. The fourth message box displays a True, because the two objects were set equal to each other in the line preceding the message box function.

The second message box displays a True, even though they're two different objects. The String object type inherits from the base object class, and this is what is assigned to objA, objB, and objC. Inheritance allows derived classes to let the base class provide the default behavior, or the derived class can provide its own behavior for functions in the base class. The default behavior for the Equals function in the Object class only checks for reference equality. Reference equality was demonstrated in the third and fourth message boxes. However, the String object overrides the reference equality check provided in the Object class and provides its own implementation of the Equals function. The String object checks for value equality and, as a result, it returns true in the second message box, because both strings are equal.

The GetHashCode function returns an integer that can be used as a key when using certain hashing algorithms and hash tables. The hash code is dependent on at least one of the instance fields and must return the same hash code for the same inputs. This function can be overridden by derived classes to provide a hash key that is unique to the derived object.

The GetType function returns the type of the object in question. If you were just to display the result of objA.GetType in a message box, you'd get an error, because the value that's returned is an object of the type class. If you want to display the type, you need to convert the information in the Type object into a string. The easiest way to convert any object to a string is to use the ToString function on the object itself. By displaying objA.GetType.ToString in a message box, you would see the textual description of the type of object, which in this case would be System.String.

The ToString function will probably be one of the most used functions because of the strict type conversions you'll encounter and because it's also used for displaying data to the user. Any class that you define on your own will probably override the default behavior of the ToString function to make it return exactly what you want. The purpose of the ToString function is to return a textual description of your object. The objects in Visual Basic .NET that replaced the intrinsic data types override the ToString function provided in the base object class so that you can work with the data contained in those objects as a string instead of having to explicitly perform type conversions on each variable.

Door 2: Inheritance basics

The concept of inheritance allows you to change the behavior of the implementation of the base class. One way that you can change the behavior of the derived class is to extend the class by adding new functions to the derived class. When you inherit from a base class, all the public, as well as all the private and friend, functions, methods, and properties come along for the ride. Private functions can be helper functions that are required only by the class that they are contained within and cannot be called directly from classes that inherit from it. However, a public function exposed in the base class can call its private members without any additional work. As you can see, when a class inherits from another class, it's inheriting the behavior of the class with which it can modify as needed and allowed.

If you're the designer of a base class, you have complete control as to how it can be used. Visual Basic .NET provides several keywords that can be used to allow or not allow a derived class to override one of its functions. You can also require that an inherited class must override a particular function. Or you can require that in order to use the class you're defining, it must be inherited, which prevents instances of your base class from being created directly.

By default, a public class can be inherited from unless the NotInheritable keyword is used when defining the class. If you want to force that the only way to use your base class is to inherit from it, you would use the MustInherit keyword when you define your class. If you want to inherit behavior from another class, you would use the Inherits keyword immediately after the class declaration. The following example shows the various modifiers that can be placed on a definition of a class:

```
Public Class X
    'Inheritable
End Class

Public NotInheritable Class Y
    'No classes can inherit from this class
End Class

Public MustInherit Class Z
    'Can not create an instance directly
End Class

Public Class W
    Inherits X
End Class
```

The class-level modifiers indicate how the base class can be used when another class inherits from it. There are also function-level modifiers that are used to determine how the functions can be used as they relate to inheritance. The keywords

Overridable, NotOverridable, and MustOverride determine how the functions can be used. By default, public methods are NotOverridable, so you must explicitly indicate that the function can be overridden by using the Overridable keyword.

```
Public Function Test() As Integer
    'Same as Public NotOverridable Function Test() As Integer
End Function

Public Overridable Function Test2() As Integer
    'Allows derived class to override this function
End Function
```

The MustOverride keyword uses a different syntax when declaring the functions. Because the use of this keyword forces the derived class to provide an implementation of the function or method, there is no need to put or even allow any code in the base class function. As a result, when declaring functions with the MustOverride keyword, there is only the initial method declaration. No other statements are allowed, not even the End Sub or End Function statements. Furthermore, if any statements contain this keyword, then the MustInherit keyword is required when defining the base class, as in the following example:

```
Public MustInherit Class X
    'Can not create an instance directly

    Public MustOverride Function Test() As Integer
    Public MustOverride Sub DoSomething()

End Class
```

Door 3: Base methods can be overridden

The purpose of being able to override a function in the base class is to allow the derived class to provide a different implementation from what the base class provides. One such use for this behavior is required when you're adding items to a combo box. In prior versions of Visual Basic, you could add an item, which is displayed to the user, and an ItemData property for each item. The ItemData is typically a key value, so you don't have to perform a search for the textual value that was selected to get the key. This is no longer the case in Visual Basic .NET. The new combo box (as well as other controls) only supports adding objects to the combo box through the Add method of the Items collection. You could add strings or numbers, but if you do this then you don't have any way of storing the associated keys. However, because the combo box wants to add an object, you can define your own custom object to add instead. In this example, we'll add a few states to the combo box and retrieve the StateID for the selected state.

For this example, put a combo box and two buttons on the form. On the property sheet for the combo box, clear out the ComboBox1 entry in the text property.

The first button will load the combo box with the data, and the second button will display the StateID of the selected state in the combo box. You'll need to define a class that will be used as your object, so place the following code anywhere within the class declaration of the form:

```
Public Class CBStateItem
    Public StateName As String
    Public StateID As String

    Public Sub New(ByVal strStateID As String, _
        ByVal strStateName As String)
        StateID = strStateID
        StateName = strStateName
    End Sub
End Class
```

Now you need to create some objects and add them to your combo box. Place the following code in the click event of the first command button:

```
ComboBox1.Items.Add(New CBStateItem("IN", "Indiana"))
ComboBox1.Items.Add(New CBStateItem("OH", "Ohio"))
ComboBox1.Items.Add(New CBStateItem("TN", "Tennessee"))
```

Now in the click event of the second command button, place the following code to display the StateID of the selected item:

```
Dim CBItem As CBStateItem

CBItem = CType(ComboBox1.SelectedItem, CBStateItem)
MessageBox.Show (CBItem.StateID)
```

Now run your project, click on the first command button, and observe what happens to the combo box. Click on an entry in the combo box, click on the second command button, and observe what happens. The StateID comes back okay, but the combo box does not display the correct information. If you look at the class we defined, we didn't give the combo box any way of knowing what we wanted it to display. Where did the information in the combo box come from? It came from the default implementation of the ToString function, which came from the base object class. Now add the following lines to the class, run the project again, and observe what happens:

```
Public Overrides Function ToString() As String
    Return StateName
End Function
```

As you can see, by overriding the ToString function from the base object class and providing your own implementation of it, you can get the combo box to display the names of the states in the combo box. The advantage of this comes when the requirements change and you need to display the StateID in the combo box as well. All you have to do is change the ToString function to return the state name; you could also append the StateID to the return value. You could also define a new class that inherits from the CBStateItem class and override its ToString function to provide the information you need. The only difference is that you would just add and work with objects of the new derived type instead of the base CBStateItem type. The concept of overriding functions is useful when you need to change the behavior of one or more functions in the base class. This allows you to still use the functionality provided in the base class as needed, and it also allows you the flexibility to change the behavior as needed.

Door 4: Using interfaces

Implementing an interface is an alternative to inheriting from a base class if all you need is a predefined set of functions, methods, and properties. Using interfaces is almost the same as creating and inheriting from a base class that doesn't provide any public or private functionality on its own. An interface is simply a set of properties, methods, and events that don't provide their own implementation. Prior versions of Visual Basic allowed you to consume interfaces, but you couldn't create them directly. A workaround existed that allowed you to define stub functions in a class module and then implement the class module like an interface, but this was awkward and you risked accidental implementation of the interface class. Visual Basic .NET allows you to define true interfaces within the language and use them through the improved Implements keyword. When using inheritance, a class can only inherit from one base class. However, a class can implement any number of interfaces. This is the primary reason why you would use interfaces instead of inheritance on base classes that contain many MustInherit members.

The best way to describe how to define and use interfaces in Visual Basic .NET is with an example. We'll define a couple of interfaces that a wheel assembly object on a car would use. Place the following code inside the class declaration for form1 in a new Windows Application project:

```
Public Interface Tire
    Property Diameter() As Integer
End Interface

Public Enum RimTypes
    Steel = 0
    Chrome = 1
    Aluminum = 2
End Enum
```

```vbnet
Public Interface Rim
    Property RimType() As RimTypes
End Interface

Public Enum BrakeTypes
    Disc = 10
    Drum = 11
    Regenerative = 12
End Enum

Public Interface Brake
    Property BrakeType() As BrakeTypes
    Sub ApplyBrakePressure(ByVal PressurePercentage As Integer)
End Interface

Public Class Wheel
    Implements Tire
    Implements Brake
    Implements Rim

    Private mDiameter As Integer
    Private mBrakeType As BrakeTypes
    Private mRimType As RimTypes

    'Implementation of the Tire Interface
    Public Property Diameter() As Integer _
      Implements WindowsApplication1.Form1.Tire.Diameter
        Get
            Return mDiameter
        End Get
        Set
            mDiameter = value
        End Set
    End Property

    'Implementation of the brake interface
    Public Sub ApplyBrakePressure(ByVal PressurePercentage _
      As Integer) Implements _
      WindowsApplication1.Form1.Brake.ApplyBrakePressure
        'Provide the brake pressure to the wheel based on
        'the pressure percentage and the brake type
    End Sub

    Public Property BrakeType() As _
      WindowsApplication1.Form1.BrakeTypes Implements _
```

```
          WindowsApplication1.Form1.Brake.BrakeType
             Get
                 Return mBrakeType
             End Get
             Set
                 mBrakeType = value
             End Set
          End Property

          'Implementation of the Rim interface
          Public Property RimType() As _
             WindowsApplication1.Form1.RimTypes Implements _
             WindowsApplication1.Form1.Rim.RimType
             Get
                 Return mRimType
             End Get
             Set
                 mRimType = value
             End Set
          End Property
       End Class

       Protected Sub Form1_Click(ByVal sender As Object, _
          ByVal e As System.EventArgs)
          Dim oWheel As wheel = New wheel()
          Dim oWheel2 As Wheel = New Wheel()
          Dim iRim As Rim

          oWheel.BrakeType = BrakeTypes.Disc
          oWheel.RimType = RimTypes.Aluminum

          oWheel2.RimType = RimTypes.Chrome
          irim = CType(oWheel2, Rim)
          MessageBox.Show (irim.RimType)
       End Sub
```

Before attempting to run the project, you need to make sure you change the
WindowsApplication1 prefixes in the code to match whatever you named the
application when you created it. Run the project, click on the form, and notice what
happens. You defined the Tire, Brake, and Rim interfaces, and you defined a wheel
class that implemented the three interfaces you defined to make a wheel assembly.
Notice that when you implement an interface, you have to provide the entire implementation, including any property procedures, private variables for the properties,
and methods that are defined in the interface. In the click event of the form, you're
creating two new wheel objects and setting a couple of properties. The properties
are part of the wheel object because you implemented the interfaces.

Notice what you did on the second wheel object. First, you set the rim type of the second wheel to the Chrome enum wheel type. Next, you obtained a direct reference to the interface by converting the wheel into a rim object and stored a reference to the rim interface on the wheel object. The message box indicated that the RimType of the rim object was a 1, which is the correct enum for the chrome wheel type. If you were to set the iRim.RimType property to a different rim type and checked the value of the RimType property of the wheel object, you would see that the wheel object reflects the changes you made.

Door 5: Understanding when to use class inheritance and when to implement interfaces

Now that you've seen how to use inheritance and interfaces, you may be wondering when you should use one over the other. Using interfaces and inheritance is very similar, but there are advantages and disadvantages to each one. Understanding when to use one over the other will only come from experience, but I've included some suggestions that may help you to decide.

INTERFACE IMPLEMENTATION

Interfaces should be used when you need to have a defined set of functions and methods on an object but when you can put the implementation code in each class that supports the interface. Although interfaces are similar to inheriting from a class that has the MustOverride keyword on every function, method, and property, a class can implement any number of interfaces, whereas inheritance can only inherit from one base class. Interfaces flatten out the hierarchy of classes to some extent. However, interfaces can inherit from another interface just as classes can inherit from another class. Interfaces are very useful when using polymorphism or when converting one object to another as was shown in the "Door 4: Using interfaces" section.

CLASS INHERITANCE

You should probably use inheritance when you encounter any of the following circumstances:

- You want to simplify a lower-level API that doesn't use classes.

- You can reuse code from the base classes.

- You need to apply the same class and methods to different data types.

- The class hierarchy is relatively small.

- You need to be able to make global changes to child classes by changing the base class.

Creating a class that hides the implementation of low-level calls is a good reason to use inheritance. Often this is called a *wrapper class,* because it wraps the low-level calls, places a layer of abstraction between the underlying complexities, and makes it easier to use a particular piece of code. An example could be creating a class that handles the low-level communications calls to a piece of hardware. You can think of this approach as creating a driver that talks to a particular piece of hardware and exposes methods and other functionality in an object-based approach to make the task of communicating with the hardware easier. After you create the driver, other components can inherit from your base class and can communicate with the hardware without having to rewrite the same code in different places. If any of the protocols change for communicating with the hardware, you only have to change the behavior in the base class and the derived components will have the changes.

Any time you have code or functionality you want to reuse, inheritance is a good candidate for this. Inheritance allows you to reuse the functionality provided in the base class and doesn't require you to place the code in more than one place. Think about how many times you've re-created the same functionality for working with queues, stacks, or lists. You could have a stack for managing the mouse pointer, managing activities, or managing other tracing activities. Although they handle different things, the underlying behavior is the same. The Object data type and how everything is derived from the Object type is one example of inheritance. Another example would be to look at a control that is placed on a form. In the Object Browser look at the `System.Windows.Forms` namespace in the `System.Windows.Forms` assembly and look at the `RichTextBox` object. If you expand the base classes of the `RichTextBox` object, you will see that it inherits from `TextBoxBase`, which inherits from `Control`, which inherits from `Component`, which inherits from `MarshalByRefObject`, which finally inherits from `Object`.

If you have a situation in which several different data types need to perform the same function but each implementation is a little different, then it's a good candidate for inheritance. Take, for example, several different types of shape objects that need to draw themselves on the screen. You could have a base object that defines the X and Y coordinates for the screen and a draw method:

```
Public MustInherit Class Shape
    Public X As Integer
    Public Y As Integer

    Public MustOverride Sub Draw()
End Class

Public Class Circle
    Inherits Shape

    Public Radius As Integer

    Public Overrides Sub Draw()
        DrawCircle(MyBase.X, MyBase.Y, Radius)
```

```
        End Sub
    End Class

    Public Class Rectangle
        Inherits Shape

        Public Width As Integer
        Public Height As Integer

        Public Overrides Sub Draw()
            DrawRect(MyBase.X, MyBase.Y, Width, Height)
        End Sub
    End Class
```

As you can see from the preceding listing, you defined a base Shape class that contained the coordinates for a drawing point and the draw method, which must be overridden by the derived class in order to provide the actual drawing of the shape on the screen. Note that because we were required to put the MustInherit keyword in the declaration of the base class, an object cannot be created based on the Shape class. The Circle and Rectangle classes both inherit from the base Shape class and extend it to provide other required information that makes the object unique. The circle needs the radius as an additional parameter in order to draw a circle from the X and Y coordinates defined in the base class. Similarly, the rectangle needed additional Width and Height parameters before it could draw a rectangle.

Although it isn't a physical limitation, the number of classes in the hierarchy should be relatively small. The reason for this is if you get too many layers of classes in the hierarchy, understanding where the implementation actually occurs can be difficult. The implementation could be at the base class, the final child class, or any child class in between. If you have an application in which you have many layers in the child class hierarchy, then you may need to rethink your design, because you may be using classes that are too granular in nature.

One of the most powerful features when using inheritance comes from its basic design. Items in derived classes can take advantage of functionality in the base classes without having to explicitly code them. This allows code to be centralized, and if the base code is changed, then all the child classes will pick up the change without having to be modified. However, this can be a double-edged sword, because changing the base class may cause undesirable effects in the derived classes. Changing the base classes should be approached with caution if you allow any of your exposed classes to be inherited from by anyone outside your control. If you're working on classes that aren't exposed to the world, as would be the case if you were creating a reusable component, then you may not want to do this because you don't have control over the end users of your component. If you always know how your class is used, as would be the case if it's never exposed publicly outside your application, then you could change the behavior in the base class. But changing the behavior in the base class should be approached with caution, to ensure that it won't have adverse effects on the rest of your application.

Visual Inheritance

Now that you understand the basics of inheritance through code, we'll look at another use of inheritance in Visual Basic .NET. Visual inheritance allows you to define the look and feel of a particular form and then inherit the behavior as well as the visual interface of the form. This approach allows you to create a standard framework type form in an application and then have other forms inherit from this form and extend upon it, providing functionality that's unique to each form without worrying about plumbing or user interface standards defined for your department or company.

Door 6: Understanding visual inheritance

Although the concept of visual inheritance may seem magical or mysterious at first, when you look at how it's done, it will fall into place because you understand how Visual Basic .NET implements inheritance through code.

Start a new Windows Application project and go to the code window for the form. Look at the structure of how a form is defined. The first line defining the form is as follows:

```
Public Class Form1
    Inherits System.Windows.Forms.Form
    .
    .
    .
End Class
```

In prior versions of Visual Basic, forms were classes with a visual interface, although it wasn't intuitive. Forms could expose public properties, methods, and events just as a class module could. In Visual Basic .NET, it's now blatantly obvious that a form is in fact a class module. You already know that classes can inherit from other classes, so it shouldn't be that hard to think that forms could inherit from other forms. In fact, even a new form already inherits from an existing form defined in the System.Windows.Forms.Form class. Now expand the region that is defined by Windows Form Designer–generated code to see the code that's hidden in this collapsed region. Here you can see how the form's components container is initialized and how the form's events are hooked up and exposed to you as a developer. Now go back to the design-time visual form and place a command button and a label anywhere on the form. Go back to the code window and look at what has changed just by adding the button and the label on the surface of the form. The Windows Form Designer automatically generates code that dynamically creates the controls on the form and sets their properties and positions. So all you're doing when you place controls on a Windows form is telling the Windows Form Designer what control you want to be created on the form and where you want the control to be positioned, as well as any other properties you set for the control. As a result, the visual part of the form actually comes from code in the form itself. A form is simply a class with code that provides a default behavior of drawing the form at runtime.

From here, it shouldn't be hard to understand that when you inherit from another form, you're inheriting its default behavior. If your base form class allows you to override a function, then you can change the default behavior. If the form doesn't expose public methods, properties, or controls, then the derived form cannot do anything with base form. Controls have a Modifiers property that allows you to choose between Private, Protected, and Public. This is how you can allow or disallow derived forms to modify controls on the base form. The same rules apply for defining the modifiers for functions that give you complete control over the behavior of your form when it's inherited.

Door 7: Using visual inheritance

Although the underlying code is the same, a couple of extra steps are required to inherit from a form:

1. Start a new Windows Application project.

2. On Form1, place two command buttons in the bottom-right corner of the screen (as shown in Figure 5-1), and set their text properties as shown.

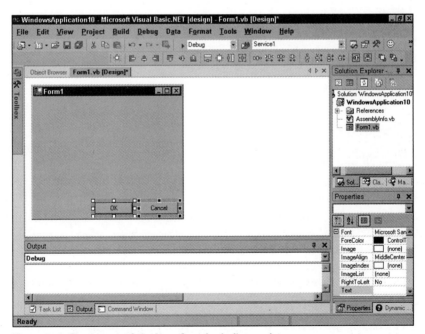

Figure 5-1: The layout of the base form in design mode.

3. Set the Anchor property to `Bottom Right` for both buttons.

4. Set the DialogResult property for the OK button to OK.

5. Set the DialogResult property for the Cancel button to Cancel.

6. Name the OK and Cancel buttons `cmdOK` and `cmdCancel`, respectively.

7. Set the Text properties of the buttons to OK and Cancel, appropriately.

Now you will inherit another form from this form, but before you do, you must build the project first. After you've built the project, you can add an inherited form by selecting Project → Add Inherited Form. The Add New Item dialog box appears. You'll notice that the dialog box has the inherited form template already selected for you. This is where you can change the name of the new form that you're creating, but for now just leave it and click the Open button. You'll then see the Inheritance Picker dialog box, as shown in Figure 5-2.

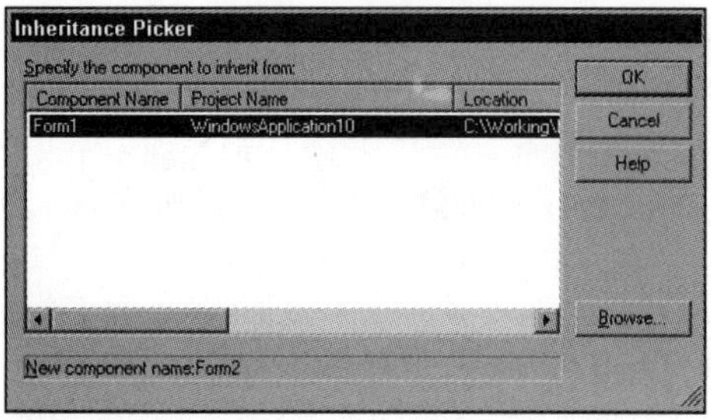

Figure 5-2: The Inheritance Picker dialog box.

Click on Form1 in the list view to inherit from this form. Click the OK button, and the inherited Form2 will be added to your project. Open up Form2 in design mode, and you'll see the form, as shown in Figure 5-3. Notice how the OK and Cancel buttons have a small graphic in their top-left corners (and that they cannot be moved), and how there are no modifiable properties in the Properties window. This is because the default value for all controls' Modifiers property is Assembly.

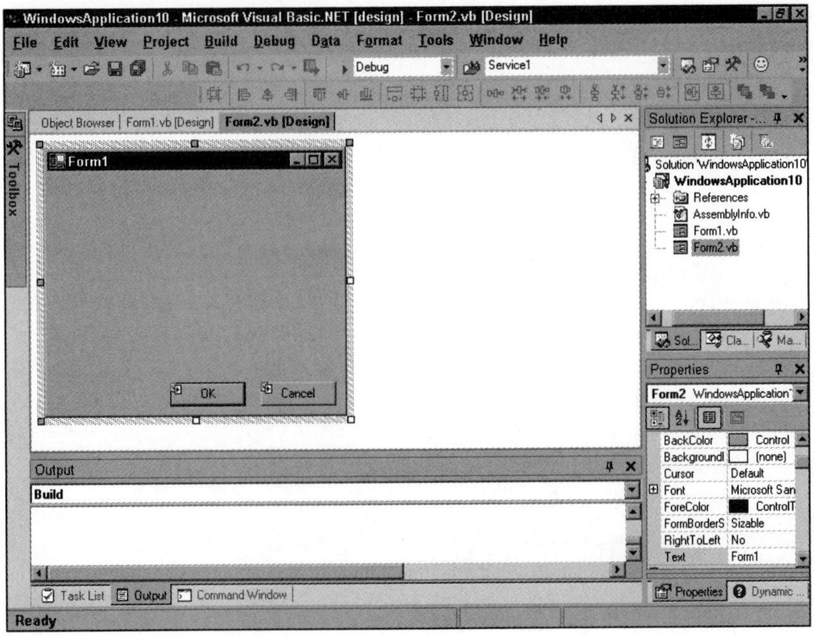

Figure 5-3: The inherited form in design mode.

Change the Modifiers property on the buttons to Family and rebuild the project. Now change the Text property of the inherited form to Dialog Box and resize the form. Notice how the OK and Cancel buttons retain their bottom-right anchor property and adjust their positions as the form is resized. Now add another form to the project, and place a command button on the form. In the click event of the command button, insert the following code:

```
Dim frmDialog As Form2 = New Form2()

Select Case frmDialog.ShowDialog
    Case Windows.Forms.DialogResult.OK
        MessageBox.Show ("OK Button Pressed")
    Case Windows.Forms.DialogResult.Cancel
        MessageBox.Show ("Cancel Button Pressed")
End Select

frmDialog = Nothing
```

Because you set the dialog result properties for both command buttons in the base form, if the form is shown as a dialog box, then clicking on either button will close the window and set the dialog result property so the calling form will know which button was pressed to close the form. Now, in the Solution Explorer window, right-click on the project and select Properties. In the Properties dialog box (shown in Figure 5-4), select Form3 as the startup object and click OK.

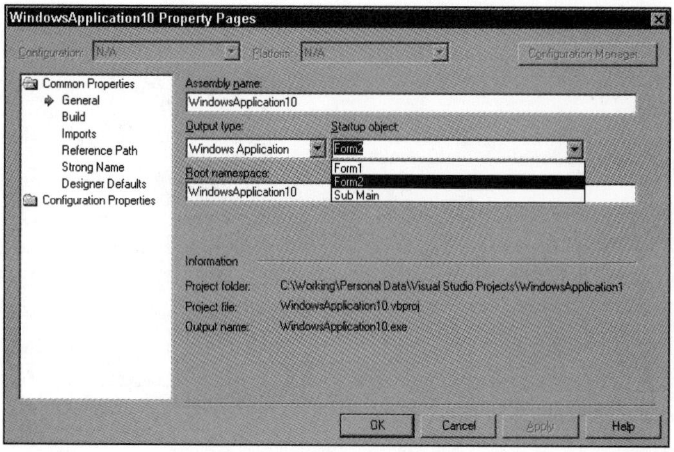

Figure 5-4: Setting the startup object in the Project Properties dialog box.

Run the project and click on the button on Form3, and the inherited dialog box will appear. Notice how you can resize the form and the buttons retain their bottom-right anchor. Click on one of the buttons and notice that the form is automatically unloaded, and the button you clicked is displayed in a message box. Click OK on the message box, and close the form to stop debugging.

Bring back up Form1 in the design mode and place a label in the upper-left corner of the form. Set the Modifiers property of the label to Family, run the project again, and click on the button to bring up the dialog box again. Notice how the label appears in the inherited form when you added it to the base form. Stop the debugger and bring up Form2, which is the inherited form in the designer. The label on the form has the same graphic as the buttons. Check the Properties window for the label and change the text property of the label to "Hello World." Because the label was marked as Assembly in the Modifiers property, it's accessible in the base form and any derived form. Run the project again and observe the results. You have now overridden the default behavior of the label by changing what it displays to the end user. If you want to extend the inherited form, place any number of controls on the designer of Form2. The controls that you placed on the design surface of the inherited form don't have the graphic on them, and you have complete control over the behavior of those controls.

Whenever you change the base form, you need to rebuild the project so the changes to the visual inheritance on the forms are reflected in the inherited forms.

Summary

In this chapter, you discovered the basic concepts of inheritance and found out several ways that you can use inheritance in your projects. Visual Basic supports inheriting classes from base classes and gives you complete control to decide how your class should and can be used when it's inherited.

You discovered how to inherit from other classes and how to override default behavior from the base classes to provide a different implementation from what the base class provides. You also found out about the concept of interfaces and when to use inheritance versus when to use interfaces. You discovered how to extend inherited objects to provide additional functionality that isn't provided in the base class.

You discovered how Visual Basic supports visual inheritance with forms, which are just classes that create a user interface at runtime. You observed how you can change the behavior of the base class or form and see the changes propagated through the inherited forms.

Inheritance is a powerful tool that you've added to your toolbox and that can reduce the amount of programming effort required when developing applications. An important thing to note is that, although inheritance is a useful concept for programming, it can get you into trouble if you don't take the time required to properly design your application. Inheritance can only reduce your programming effort if you take the time to understand how it should be used and to do proper design work upfront, which will indicate areas of functionality in your application that can benefit from the use of inheritance.

Chapter 6

Using the New Controls in Visual Basic .NET

IN THIS CHAPTER

- ◆ Windows form designer controls
- ◆ Visual and non-visual controls
- ◆ Provider controls
- ◆ Server-side controls

When creating applications with Visual Basic .NET, you'll most likely use the controls that are provided even when you're developing server-side applications, because there are new controls that were created primarily for this purpose.

It's important to realize that the controls in Visual Basic .NET are all new controls. Although many of the controls have versions similar to controls in prior versions, they aren't the same controls. Visual Basic .NET provides a set of controls designed to take advantage of the .NET Framework. However, you can still use an ActiveX control from prior versions or from a third-party vendor, but you need to remember that the COM interoperability layer imposes a small performance penalty when using COM objects in the .NET Framework.

Although many of the controls in the toolbox may be familiar, there are several new controls as well that you'll need to understand. This chapter covers the basic tools in your toolbox and will give you a basic understanding of how they're used and how the familiar controls may be different from their counterparts in prior versions.

Windows Form Designer Controls

The controls used with the Windows Form Designer will probably be the most-used controls, so I'll start with them. These controls are used in applications based on the Windows Application project template and have three main types: regular visible controls, design-time controls, and provider controls. You're probably already familiar with regular and design-time controls, but the concept of provider controls is new to Visual Basic .NET.

Regular visible controls

The regular visible controls are those that are placed on a form and provide a user interface to the user at runtime. Each control will be discussed as you progress through this chapter, but you'll need to understand some of the new common properties that apply to all visible controls.

COMMON PROPERTIES

The Locked property is a new feature to Visual Basic .NET and is not like the Locked property of a text box as in prior versions. The Locked property allows individual controls to be locked in place on a form. This feature is similar to the lock controls command in prior versions except that now it's used at the control level instead of the form level. This property is used to prevent accidental movements or resizing of a control after it's properly placed. The Locked property of text boxes in prior versions is now implemented through the ReadOnly property of the .NET framework TextBox object.

The Anchor property is also new to Visual Basic .NET. It allows controls that are placed on a form to retain their position relative to the edges of a form. The Anchor property is set to Top-Left by default for controls that are placed on a form. This matches the behavior in prior versions where the controls were fixed by their Top and Left properties and didn't move when the form was resized. If you were to change the Anchor property to Top-Right and drag the right side of the form to make it bigger, the control would slide to the right as the right side of the form was moved. If you set the Anchor property to Top-Left-Right, the control would keep its left, top, and right edges the same distance from where they were set at design-time. As a result, the width of the control would increase as the right side of the form was moved to the right. If you take some time to understand how controls behave when you set the Anchor property, the majority of all resizing code that you had to write in prior versions can be eliminated. There will always be exceptions, but using this property will allow your forms to take advantage of changing screen real estate sizes and provide the same look to the user regardless of the form dimensions.

The Dock property allows you to dock any visible control to one edge of the form or parent container control. Or you can have the control automatically fill the form or container in which it's placed. Although the Dock property can be handy in some situations, it can be a little difficult to use when trying to dock multiple controls. If you were to dock a control to either a container control or a form, it would dock as you would expect. If you set the Dock property on another control to the same as the first control, the second control will not dock to the edge of the container as the first control did. Instead, it will dock to the edge of the first control. In order to use the new splitter control, you have to understand how the various Dock property settings affect the behavior of the control.

The Text property, although not on every control, is a common property for setting the text that's displayed for the control. In prior versions of Visual Basic, the controls weren't consistent — some used the Caption property, while others used the Text property. Visual Basic .NET has changed the controls to make them more consistent, and the controls will use the Text property if they display textual information on the screen. Even forms themselves use this property to set the text of the title bar.

The Cursor property allows you to automatically set the mouse pointer icon when it's over the control. The property box lets you see what the actual choices are along with their names, which makes picking the desired cursor easier.

 TIP Clicking on a control and then clicking on the form will draw the control with its default size at the location of the mouse cursor.

LABEL
The Label control in Visual Basic .NET has several new properties that you should be aware of. The new Label control supports standalone images or images that are stored in an ImageList control. The Image property allows you to specify an image that will be displayed in the Label control. The ImageAlign property allows you to specify where the image should be placed in the label. The ImageList property allows you to specify the ImageList control where the images are stored. The ImageIndex property allows you to see the images as you pick an image index from the ImageList control. Not much else has changed with the basic Label control from prior versions.

LINK LABEL
The LinkLabel control is a control that is new to Visual Basic .NET. It allows you to create a label within your Windows Application that behaves like a hyperlink in a Web page would. The control automatically handles setting the colors and mouse cursor when the cursor is over the control, when the link has been visited, when it's disabled, and so on. The LinkLabel control allows you to set the properties for the cursor style and the various colors that correspond to the different statuses and events of the control.

BUTTON
In Visual Basic .NET, the Button now is just of type Button, as opposed to prior versions in which the type was CommandButton. The behavior of the button control hasn't changed from prior versions. However, the Button control does introduce a new property called DialogResult. This property is used when you're displaying forms as dialogs, and you need to know what type of action caused the form to close. Setting this property allows you to assign a standard dialog result to a button, which will be returned to the calling function that displayed the form as a dialog. OK, Cancel, Abort, Retry, Ignore, Yes, No, and None are the standard dialog result behaviors that can be assigned to a button. If this property is set and the form is displayed using the ShowDialog method, clicking on this button will automatically close the window and set the return value to indicate how the user closed the form. It's important to realize that this behavior is only present if the form is shown as a dialog box. This allows a single form to behave differently depending on whether it is a standard form or a dialog requesting user input.

TEXT BOX

The Text Box control in Visual Basic .NET is your basic control for accepting and displaying information to users. There are several new properties on the Text Box that you should know about. The AutoSize property allows the text box to expand automatically in order to display the entire contents. The AcceptsReturn and AcceptsTab properties are used with multiline text boxes and indicate that the text box will allow the Return or the Tab character within the text string stored in the text box. The Lines property allows you to define what text will be on each line at design-time. This property will also allow you to manipulate the individual lines of a text box at runtime. The new CharacterCasing property allows you to automatically control whether the text should be normal (mixed), uppercase, or lowercase. If you set the property to upper or lower, all text entered into the text box through typing or pasting data will be cased according to the option you've selected. As mentioned earlier, the Locked property of prior versions is replaced with the ReadOnly property in Visual Basic .NET.

MAIN MENU

The Main Menu control will probably cause a lot of developers to jump for joy because it allows menus to be designed visually on the form. This control is much easier to use and is far more intuitive than the menu builder in prior versions of Visual Basic. As soon as you place a Main Menu control on a form, you'll see a box at the top of the form telling you to "Type Here." Click on this message and start typing to create your menu controls. Anywhere you see a "Type Here" message, you can insert new menu items. If you get out of place and need to insert a menu item, simply type the menu item at the end or bottom and then drag it to the proper place in the menu. If you need a separation between menu items, simply place a hyphen for the menu text and a horizontal separator bar will be displayed.

When you're done creating the text for your menu system, you can right-click anywhere in the menu structure and click the Edit Names item from the context menu that appears. Now the names of your menus are displayed and clicking on a menu item and typing will now set the name for the control. At the same time the names are shown, the actual menu text is shown as well, which helps you to know what the name of a particular menu item is for when you need to insert an event handler. Clicking on a menu item allows you to set properties for it through the standard Properties window. The RadioCheck property allows you to use a circle in the menu structure representing that the menu item works with several mutually exclusive menu items.

CHECK BOX

The Check Box control has been revamped to make it easier and more flexible to use in applications. The CheckAlign property allows you to position the physical check box in any one of nine allowable positions. These positions are defined by a grid that has left, middle, and right positions horizontally, and top, middle, and bottom positions vertically. The Checked property has been added to allow developers to easily use the checked status. In prior versions, you had to check the value property against vbChecked or vbUnchecked constants. Because the Checked property is a Boolean property, it allows you to set it or use the value in equations and conditional statements. The CheckState property works in tandem with the Checked property and allows you to check for the new indeterminate state, which is how the checkbox is grayed out. The ThreeState property determines whether the user can change the checkbox if it's in an undetermined state. The AutoCheck property allows the automatic toggle of the check box checked property to be turned on or off. By default, it's on, and clicking the check box will allow the check box to toggle its Checked property. By turning this property off, you can validate whether you want the checked property to be toggled before it's changed. These properties combined together give you much more control over the behavior of the check box and can eliminate some of the code that you had to previously write for toggling check boxes and using the value within code.

RADIO BUTTON

The Windows documentation as well as other languages always referred to this control as a Radio Button, but Visual Basic used the Option Button syntax, which led to some obvious confusion. In order to make Visual Basic consistent with the Windows documentation as well as other programming languages, the Option Button has been renamed to Radio Button.

The Radio Button has some of the same properties as the Check Box, as you will see. The Radio Button has the CheckAlign property, which behaves the same way as it does for check boxes. It also uses the checked property, which is a Boolean value indicating whether the Radio Button is selected. The Radio Button also shares the same AutoCheck property as the CheckBox control. However, although the AutoCheck property is present, it doesn't behave the same way as it does with the CheckBox control. By default, this property is true, and when you select a radio button, it's automatically "Checked" and the other radio buttons within the same container are automatically "Unchecked." This behavior allows you to perform some validation before setting the Checked property of the Radio Button that was clicked. The default for this property is true, which forces it to behave like the option button of prior versions. However, if you decide to change this property and then decide to set the Checked property through code, you must write the code to set the Checked property of the other Radio Buttons in the group to false. Otherwise you can have multiple Radio Buttons within a group that are checked. Typically, if this is the behavior you're intending, then you should use the Check Box control instead of the Radio Button control.

GROUP BOX

The Frame control in prior versions has been renamed to Group Box in Visual Basic .NET. Not much has changed to the Group Box since prior versions. However, the BorderStyle property that was available in previous versions is no longer supported. If you use the Group Box control, you'll always have a border drawn around it. If you want a group box that doesn't display a border, then you'll need to use the new Panel control.

PICTURE BOX

Visual Basic .NET no longer has both an Image control and a Picture Box control. The Picture Box control is used to display images of all types. The basic control that all other controls inherit from provides a BackgroundImage property. Setting an image to this property will display an image in the control, and if the image is smaller than the control, the image will be tiled to fit the control. If the control were to be resized, the BackgroundImage would automatically tile to fill the space of the control. The Picture Box also supports an Image property, which will display one image in the upper-left corner of the picture box. Although the Picture Box control itself does not have an Autosize property as previous versions did, the Picture Box can still be set to the same size as the picture by using the Height and Width properties of the Image property of the picture box. Another difference between the new Picture Box and prior versions is that the Picture Box is no longer a container for other controls. If you need a container, you have a couple of options. You could use either the Group Box or the new Panel control. With these controls, you could set the BackgroundImage property to the desired image, or you could use a picture box within these containers to display the image while the other controls "float" on top of the picture box.

PANEL

The new Panel control is a generic container control that behaves similar to the Picture Box in prior versions except that it doesn't support an Image property. But it does support the BackgroundImage property as previously mentioned. The Panel control, like the Group Box control, is used to group controls together. Groups are important for Radio Buttons because, by default, all the Radio Buttons within a single group are mutually exclusive. The Panel control would be used when you want either a fixed single line or a sunken panel look to a group of controls. Because you can't change the look of the border on a Group Box, you use the Panel control any time you want a border different from the standard Group Box.

 TIP If you want the panel to have a raised look, place a button within the panel, clear its text property, and set the enabled property to false. Next, set the Dock property of the button to fill, and then right-click on the button and send it to the back of the control order. As an alternative, you could use the Tab Control without any tabs on it and obtain the same results.

DATA GRID

The Data Grid control is a very flexible tool used to display data from ADO.NET data sources. Discussion of this control will be postponed until Chapter 7. You need to understand the basics of ADO.NET first before you can understand how the control works. An example of how to use the control to display data from databases as well as data from any other source is shown in Chapter 7.

LIST BOX AND CHECKED LIST BOX

The ListBox control in prior versions is now two separate controls. The List Box control implements normal list box behavior, whereas the Checked List Box control is used for displaying check boxes in the list. The Checked List Box control is just like the regular list box except it allows the user to check each item individually, similar to selecting multiple lines in a multi-select list box. In fact, the Checked List Box inherits from and extends the regular List Box control. In order to add an item to the list box, you use the Add method of the Items property. Because almost everything in Visual Basic .NET is an object (including strings and numeric data), the Add method of the items collection accepts an object as its only parameter. If you simply want to display a list of data and retrieve whatever the user selected, you can just add strings to the list box. The selected item will return the string or numeric data that the user selected. However, most of the time it's beneficial to store extra information with the displayed text such as a lookup code that matches an ID in a database. In this case, all you need to do is define your own object that stores all the related information as properties on the object. You only need to override the default ToString method that is present on every object and return the information you want displayed in the list box. The selected item will return the object that was added to the list box with all properties defined. Because the selected item actually returns an Object type, you only need to convert the object to the type that was added using the CType function and you could retrieve all the related information. In fact, you'll see that this method of defining and adding your own objects to controls can be used in the Combo Box and Domain Up Down controls as well.

COMBO BOX

The new Combo Box control is very similar to the Combo Box control that was in prior versions of Visual Basic. However the way of adding and retrieving items is done the same way as list boxes. You define your own display objects and set their values and then add the display objects to the Combo Box. There are a couple of new properties that give you more control over how the data is displayed. The DropDownWidth property allows you to specify the width of the drop-down data, which can even extend past the edges of the form. The MaxDropDownItems property defines the maximum number of line items that are displayed when the box is dropped down. These two properties give you more control over the runtime behavior of the combo box as it displays the information to the user. In addition to the new properties of the controls, most of the controls provide other runtime properties and methods that reduce the effort required when programming with them. For example, the Combo Box control has methods on it to FindString and FindStringExact. These methods allow you to make one call to determine the index of the item that matches a particular string. When you have the index, you can display the correct item. This is much quicker than trying to loop through the items in a combo box one at a time, comparing the values. In prior versions of Visual Basic, you may have used the SendMessage API call to do this same thing, but now you can do it with a method of the combo box. Visual Basic .NET is built on the common language runtime, and as soon as you write a Windows API call, you no longer can port it to other platforms that support the common language runtime. As a result, you'll notice that there should be a .NET Framework call into the common language runtime for every API call that you've had to use.

LIST VIEW

The List View control in Visual Basic .NET is very similar to the List View control that was provided in the Windows Common Controls library. The List View control provides four different view modes: list, details, large icon, and small icon. One of the differences from prior versions is that there are several different ways to add items and subitems to the List View control. Each ListViewItem object represents a new item, and if you're working in the details view mode, adding a ListViewSubItem object to the SubItems collection of the ListViewItem object will display the data in multiple columns. The List View control allows you to add items and you can manipulate the ForeColor, BackColor, and Font properties of each item. This would allow you to create a colorful alarm or status list that could show an alarm item with a red background and when the alarm was acknowledged, the background could be changed to another color. Prior versions of Visual Basic allowed you to set the color of the text on each List View item but not the background or the subitems for each item.

TREE VIEW

The Tree View control in Visual Basic .NET has many improvements that make it easier to work with. In prior versions, the syntax of adding parent and child nodes was convoluted and was not easy to understand. The branches in a Tree View control are simply a collection of TreeNode objects accessed through the Nodes property. If you want sublevel nodes under any node object, you simply add them to the nodes collection of the parent node. If you think of the Tree View control as the root node, you will realize that each time you add a node to the nodes collection, you're creating top-level root nodes that will be visible even if everything is collapsed. If you want a single root node, then you would need to add this node and then traverse the hierarchy as you add all the other nodes underneath this node.

TAB CONTROL

The Tab control in Visual Basic .NET has finally got things right. The tabs are managed through the TabPages Collection Manager. As you add tabs to the TabPages collection, you can set all the properties for each tab page in one place. In previous versions, you could use either the Tab Strip control from the common controls library or you could use the SSTab control from the tabbed dialog control. The Tab Strip control forced you to create containers for the controls for each tab and manually size and display the container that corresponded to each tab that was clicked. If you used the SSTab control, you didn't have to manage the display of each individual tab page, but you did have to realize that each tab page was not a container in and of itself. If you placed two option buttons on two different tab pages, clicking one would clear the other unless you created and placed the option buttons on each tab page in their own containers. Each individual tab page in the Visual Basic .NET Tab control is an individual container and can be flipped through at design-time, and controls can be dropped right on each page container.

DATE TIME PICKER

The Date Time Picker control in Visual Basic doesn't appear to have changed from the DTPicker control in prior versions. If you've used this control before, it should act the same way in Visual Basic .NET. If it worked fine for your previous projects, then it should be fine in .NET. However, the same poor usability issues that were in the previous control are still in the .NET version.

MONTH CALENDAR

The Month Calendar control in Visual Basic .NET appears to have the same functionality as the Month View control in prior versions. The Value property has been replaced by the Text property, but that is the extent of the modifications.

SCROLL BARS

The horizontal and vertical scroll bars have not changed from prior versions.

SPLITTER

The Splitter control is a new control to Visual Basic .NET and allows you to create regions that can be adjusted by the user. When the Splitter control is placed on a form, the value of its Dock property (defaults to Left) is used to place the control next in line to any other controls that have their Dock property set to the same value. To see how the Splitter control works, place two panels on a form. Set the background image properties of the panels to different images on your system. Place a Splitter control on the form, and then set the Dock property of the second panel to fill (center, middle position). Run the project and click on the Splitter control between the two images. Drag it left and right, and observe what happens to the images in each panel. As you drag the splitter from left to right, the width of the left panel increases and the left position of the right panel travels to the right. Similarly when you drag the splitter from the right to the left, the width of the left panel decreases, while the left position of the right panel travels to the left.

DOMAIN UP DOWN

The Domain Up Down control is used to provide the user a scrollable list of choices. Although a user could use the arrow keys on a keyboard to scroll through items in a combo box, it's not very easy or intuitive to the users. The Domain Up Down control would be best used when there are only a few choices that the user can choose among. You can add a list of strings through the item collection and the user would be able to scroll through the items to select the desired information. However, the Domain Up Down control is another control that will accept any object in the items collection.

NUMERIC UP DOWN

The Numeric Up Down control is similar to the Domain Up Down control, except it is intended to allow the user to select only numeric values and provide the user an easy way of scrolling through the available values at a predetermined increment. The Numeric Up Down control allows you to define a minimum, maximum, increment, and number of decimal places. As an example, assume that you need to allow a user to choose a percentage rate and you only wanted increments of one-eighth of a percent from 0 to 3 percent. You would set the minimum to 0, the maximum to 3, the decimal places to 3 and the increment to one-eighth (0.125). The user would then be able to scroll through the allowable values with each increment being one-eighth of a percent.

TRACK BAR

The Track Bar control in Visual Basic .NET is based on the Slider control in previous versions. The new Track Bar control doesn't support selecting a range as the previous versions did. Otherwise, the Track Bar has the same functionality as in prior versions.

PROGRESS BAR

The Progress Bar control in Visual Basic .NET has changed a little from prior versions. The new Progress Bar control doesn't support the smooth scrolling option as prior versions did. The new control does add a new property called Step that lets you define an increment by which the current value is incremented each time you call the PerformStep method.

RICH TEXT BOX

The Rich Text Box control in Visual Basic .NET has some added features that you should know about. First, the new control allows you to get access to each line of text through the lines collection. The new control also supports zooming in and out through the ZoomFactor property. In addition, you can set properties on the control to allow it to accept the Tab character within the document and some other nice features.

TOOL BAR

The Tool Bar control in Visual Basic .NET is very similar to the Tool Bar control in prior versions. However, with the new control you add buttons to the buttons collection using the Collection Property Manager. You still add buttons to the collection and assign their images to an image from one or more Image List controls.

STATUS BAR

The Status Bar control hasn't changed from prior versions.

Non-visual controls

Along with controls that provide a user interface at runtime, there are also non-visual controls that don't provide a user interface at runtime on the form on which they're placed. However, some of these controls can display information to the user through an icon in the task tray or through a specialized dialog box. In prior versions of Visual Basic, you had to find a place on the form where the non-visual control could be placed without interfering with the layout of the regular controls. Visual Basic .NET creates a new window at the bottom of each form designer window that provides a convenient container where the non-visual controls are automatically placed. This section talks about these non-visual controls on the Windows Forms tab of the toolbox.

IMAGE LIST

The Image List control in Visual Basic .NET differs in several ways from the control in prior versions. First, the new control allows you to set the desired color depth when displaying a picture from the image list. You can choose 4-, 8-, 16-, 24-, and 32-bit color depth levels. The new control also gives you detailed information about the images it contains, such as the file type, color resolution, image size, and so on. However, the new control is limited to displaying images in a maximum size of 256 by 256 pixels.

TIMER

The timer control in Visual Basic .NET has a couple of welcome changes from prior versions. First, the interval property is an Int32 data type, which means that you can now have an interval of almost 25 days instead of a little over a minute. The only way to turn the timer on or off now is to set the enabled property to true or false. As a result, the interval property must now be at least one millisecond; otherwise, an exception will be raised.

NOTIFY ICON

The Notify Icon control is a new control in Visual Basic .NET. It provides an easy way for your application to display simple status information from the system tray in the task bar. After you display an icon in the task tray, you can respond to events that occur on the icon. You can display a status message, a tooltip, or a context menu, or perform any other action you may want within your application. The control handles all the plumbing required for displaying the information in the system tray and responding to user events and fires these events within your application for you to use. Because you can now write Windows Services directly within Visual Basic, you could have a service monitor program that runs when a user logs in and displays information to the user about the status of your service.

COMMON DIALOG CONTROLS

Visual Basic .NET has simplified using the Common Dialog control that was in prior versions. The prior version required you to set several flags and properties and then call upon the correct method to display the dialog box. Visual Basic .NET has separated the functionality of the Common Dialog control into five different controls, each with a specific and obvious purpose. The new controls are the Open, Save, Font, Color, and Print dialog controls. In order to allow the user to select a file that your program will use, you simply have to put the Open File Dialog control on a form and call the ShowDialog method of the control. The next line simply needs to check the FileName property of the control to retrieve the file the user selected. The Save, Font, and Color dialog controls are as straightforward to use as the Open File Dialog control.

PRINT CONTROLS

Using the printing dialog controls allows your application to interact with the installed printers to change layouts, paper sources, printers, and so on, and to preview and print a document. The easiest way to work with the print controls is to place a print document control on a form. The PrintPage event of the print document control is where the code is placed to draw the information on the print page. Before the ShowDialog method can be called on any of the other controls, the document object must first be set to a PrintDocument object. The PageSetup dialog allows you to choose the paper sizes, margins, orientation, and paper sources for the document. The dialog box for the PrintDialog control allows you to set the print range, number of copies, printer, and printer properties.

Visual Basic .NET provides a Print Preview control and a Print Preview Dialog control. The Print Preview Dialog control will automatically handle multiple pages, zooming, printing, and so on. The dialog control displays a standard dialog that handles all the paging and zooming. If you want to have the print preview displayed within a form, then you need to implement all the layout and paging controls on your form and call the methods on the Print Preview control. The Print Preview and the Print Preview Dialog controls will retrieve the information that has been set by default or by the other dialog boxes for the PrintDocument and will cause the print document to be printed. Instead of going to paper, the Print Preview control will display what the document would look like if it were to be printed.

Provider controls

Visual Basic .NET introduces a new class of controls; when one of these controls is placed on the form, additional properties will show up on the property page of the other controls on the form. When the properties are present, you can set them, and the provider controls will perform the actual implementation for you.

TOOLTIP

If you place a control on a form and look at the property page for it, you may notice that there is not a ToolTip property as there was in prior versions of Visual Basic. Visual Basic .NET still supports tooltips; it just supports them in a different way. As soon as you place a ToolTip control on the form, you'll notice that there is a property called "Tooltip On Tooltip1." You can set this property to display the tooltip information automatically. You can also set the tooltip for any control at runtime by calling the SetTooltip method on the ToolTip control and supply a control name and the text for the tooltip. When the tooltip is set for a control, it will retain the information until it's cleared.

CONTEXT MENU

The Context Menu is a new control that lets you create individual pop-up menus that will automatically appear when you right-click on a control. The Context Menu control uses the same menu designer as the Main Menu control. After you create the context menu, you'll see it listed as a choice for the context menu properties of other controls. Any context menu you create will override any default context menu that may normally appear with a control. For example, a text box has a default context menu that displays the options to Undo, Cut, Copy, Paste, Delete, and Select All. In prior versions of Visual Basic, if you didn't want the default context menu to appear, you had to disable the text box, call the PopUpMenu method to display the custom context menu, and then enable the control again. In Visual Basic .NET if you set the context menu property to a context menu control, the default context menus will no longer appear, and you don't have to write any code to make your context menu appear. If you want to provide clipboard support, then you'll need to include these items on your custom context menu.

TIP If you don't want any context menu to be displayed at all, you can simply place a context menu on the form without creating any menu items and set the context menu property to this menu. Visual Basic .NET will not display a menu if there are no menu items to be displayed.

ERROR PROVIDER

The Error Provider control is a new addition to Visual Basic .NET. By placing an error provider on your form, you'll see a new property appear called Error On ErrorProvider1. This property can be set at design-time or it can be set at run-time. If you set it at design-time, then all controls that have something in this property will display an error icon next to the control. You could use this feature to indicate required fields, and as fields were validated or filled in, you could clear this information and the icon would disappear. If you set it at runtime, then you would set it when you perform validation for a control. If the data within the control is invalid, then you would set the error text and the icon would appear next to the control. The error text appears as a tooltip when the mouse is hovered over the error icon. The error icon by default is a red circle with a white exclamation point in it. This can be changed to display any icon you want. In fact, you could place two Error Provider controls on the form and one could be a red X indicating that there is an error and the other could be a green check mark indicating that everything is okay. In order to set the information at runtime, you call the SetError method on the Error Provider control. If you supply any text, then it will place the icon next to the control. If you supply an empty string, it will clear the icon from the control. You can even indicate how and when the icon should blink to grab the user's attention. Also, if you set the information at runtime, you can even specify where the icon should be displayed around the control and the padding between the icon and the control. The Error Provider control doesn't just have to display error information. There are many uses for the control but they all typically get the user's attention and display information at a glance so the user can immediately know that something needs attention.

HELP PROVIDER

The new Help Provider control in Visual Basic .NET allows you to link up controls with information in a help file and it allows you to display a special type of tooltip that you've probably seen when working with Windows dialogs. In prior versions, you could only specify the HelpContextID for the default help file associated with the project. When you place a Help Provider control on a form, four new properties appear on controls that can receive focus. The HelpKeyword On HelpProvider1 property allows you to specify a keyword that will be used to search for the related topics in the help file. The HelpNavigator On HelpProvider1 property allows you to specify how the help file should be displayed and used. The choices available for this property are Topic, Table Of Contents, Index, Find, Associate Index, and Keyword Index. The HelpString On HelpProvider1 property allows you to enter free-form text that will be displayed in a special window that resembles a tooltip window. This help tooltip window appears when the user presses the F1 key when a control has the focus. The help tooltip windows don't automatically disappear when the mouse is moved off the tooltip window. The user must click a mouse button when they want the window to be closed. Another key difference is that the window is actually deactivated when the Help window appears. If there is code that is written to execute when the window is deactivated, then it will fire while the Help window is displayed. The Help Provider control also allows you to set the properties on any control similar to the other provider controls by calling methods on the Help Provider control.

Components Tab

The Components tab includes many new controls that would typically be used on an application written to run on a server. However, there is nothing that prevents you from using these controls anywhere in your applications. The controls expose various properties, methods, and events that can make certain programming tasks much easier. None of these controls directly provides an interface for the user to see.

File System Watcher

The File System Watcher control allows you to set a few properties that indicate the path, file filters, and event filters, and it will watch for the specified event to occur and raise an event to your application. This control is best suited for when you need to know that a file system operation has occurred in a directory. Your event filter choices are file name, directory name, attributes, size, last write, last access, creation time, and security. When the change event occurs, you can get the full path to the file or directory by using the e.FullPath syntax where *e* is the event arguments parameter to the change event. The File System Watcher could be configured and used when your application needs to know when files are created in a certain "handoff" directory and then needs to perform some operation on the file, such as importing data into a database or refreshing parameters in the application. The File System Watcher prevents you from having to write the code and waste the processor time of constantly polling the directory for the file.

Event Log

In prior versions of Visual Basic, you could log an event to the event log through the App object, but there were some problems with this approach. First, it wouldn't log to the event log while the application was running in the development environment. Furthermore, you had no control over the source and other parameters, so you were limited as to what you could do with the event log. There was a way to use some low-level API calls to get more control over the event log, but it required direct memory manipulation, and all the parameters had to be safeguarded to prevent access violations from occurring. It was almost impossible to read the information in the event log, even using the API calls, due to the structures that were required.

The new Event Log control not only allows you to write events to the event log, but it also allows you to read and watch for events in the application, system, and security logs, not only on your local machine, but also on other machines across a network as well. Although it's a little harder to read an event log directly, it's easy to write events to the logs or to watch for events to occur in a log. The EnableRaisingEvents, Log, MachineName, and Source are the four main properties that you'll need to set. The EnableRaisingEvents property allows the control to raise events that can be trapped when the specified entry is placed in the log the control is set to monitor. The Log property indicates whether the control will use the Application, System, or Security logs. The MachineName property allows you to specify a computer that the control will use. If you place a period in the MachineName property, the control will use the local computer. The source property is typically the name of the application or service. If the control is set up to monitor the events of a certain log, then the EntryWritten event will fire. In order to write events to the specified event log, you simply need to call the WriteEntry method of the control. The WriteEntry method has many different signatures that can be used to specify the details of the log entry. You have almost complete control over the information that will be written to the log, including the raw data, message, severity, event ID, source, and category of the entry.

Message Queue

The Message Queue control allows you to create, send, and receive messages through message queuing. A message queue might be used by an application for several reasons, such as workflow routing and processing, dividing processing power among multiple machines for scalability, guaranteed message delivery, and disconnected applications that are required to communicate with each other. In order to use the control, message queuing needs to be configured on the server and the connectivity to it needs to be established on the client machine.

Performance Counter

Microsoft has always stated that enterprise systems should use the event logs and the performance counters so that the health of the system could be determined or monitored and notifications or alerts could be created to inform administrators that there is a problem. However, you couldn't create and use performance counters directly from Visual Basic. The performance counter hooks typically required a DLL to be created in C that would expose the required interfaces and hooks.

The new Performance Counter control now allows Visual Basic developers to create, read, and write to the performance counters on the local computer. It also allows you to read performance counters on other computers on the network. It exposes methods that allow you to read the value of a counter, increment the counter by a specified amount, decrement the counter by one, or to set the counter to any value directly. You can either specify a counter that's already provided by the operating system and installed applications, or you can create a custom counter that's for use by your application. Unless you create a custom counter, the counter will be read-only. You must specify a custom counter in order to be able to write information to the counter object. The category name, counter name, instance name, machine name, and read-only are the five main properties that need to be set in order to work with the performance counters. A *category* is a grouping of one or more related counters. Examples of categories are processor, server, memory, process, and so on. The category and counter objects provided by the system are not custom counters and, as a result, you cannot write to any of them. In order to write to a counter, you must create a custom category and counter. This can be accomplished through code, but it's much easier to do using the Server Explorer. If you expand the local computer in the Server Explorer, you'll see performance counters as one of the branches. Expand the performance counters branch and you'll see all the categories that are installed on your local machine. If you right-click on the top node of the performance counters branch, you can create a new category. Fill out the dialog box as shown in Figure 6-1, and click OK.

This will create a performance counter on your local system and will be displayed in the Server Explorer window. The easiest way to use your performance counter is to drag the newly created counter (not the category) from the Server Explorer onto your form. It will create and configure a performance counter control for you. If you change the read-only property to false, you can now write to your performance counter through the Increment, IncrementBy, and Decrement methods as well as the RawValue property. Now that you have a full-fledged performance counter object, you can use the performance monitor application to add your counter and set alerts, just as you could with any other performance counter. Just add a couple of buttons on the form and perform an increment operation on the counter in the first button and perform a decrement operation on the counter in the second button.

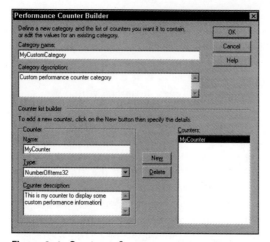

Figure 6-1: Create performance counter category.

Process

The Process control encapsulates all the details for working with processes into one control. The Process control is used to launch other processes and be notified when other processes are shut down. Although prior versions had the ability to shell out to another program, this approach had its limitations. If you wanted to know when the other application terminated, you had to write code that used the Windows API in order to monitor that process status. The new control allows you to retrieve all running processes, hook up to a particular process, and even kill the process if so desired. The control can be set up to raise an event when the process exits. This event could be used to retrieve any files and perform any cleanup operations that may be required.

Service Controller

The Service Controller control allows Visual Basic developers to start, stop, pause, and resume any service (including custom services created in Visual Basic) on the local computer as well as other machines on a network. It also allows you to check the status of the specified service to see whether it's running. Using the Service Controller is pretty straightforward. There is a MachineName and a ServiceName property that you set, and then you can call the methods Start, Stop, Pause, and Continue. You should note that the calls operate asynchronously and will return immediately. If you need to ensure that the service has completed the specified command, then you should immediately call the WaitForStatus method in which you specify the desired state and an optional timeout. The timeout period is of the System.Timespan type and can be supplied by using the New System.Timespan() constructor and supplying the proper values within the parentheses. The Status property allows you to monitor the status of the service and will return the value indicating the various stages the status can be in.

Timer

The Timer control that's included on this tab isn't the same timer that was included on the Windows Forms tab. The timer on the Windows Forms tab was of the type System.Windows.Forms.Timer, while this timer is of the type System.Timers.Timer. There are some key differences between these two types of timers, which you need to be aware of.

Both timers have an Enabled and an Interval property, but the system timer exposes an AutoReset and SynchronizingObject properties. The AutoReset indicates whether the timer should automatically start counting again when the event was fired. When the timer event occurs, the Enabled property of the timer will be tripped to false. If the AutoReset property is true, the Enabled property will be set back to true, which will start the timer again. Whenever the Enabled property is changed from false to true, the ElapsedInterval property will be reset to zero and the timer will start counting again from zero. The combination of the AutoReset and the Enabled properties allow the system timer to be used as a "One Shot" timer. This ensures that your application will not keep getting timer events until the first timer event could be processed. By setting the Enabled property back to true when the code in the tick event of the timer fires, the timing of the process that is guarded by the timer now more closely fires at the predetermined intervals. Without the "One Shot" timer, several tick events could be backed up before your application could get a chance to process them.

Summary

Although some of the controls in Visual Basic .NET have not changed or have changed very little, there are many new controls and changes to existing controls that you'll need to be familiar with. Visual Basic .NET introduces a host of new controls that allows your application to do things that were either impossible or very difficult to do in prior versions.

Visual Basic .NET provides several controls that can be used to monitor the health of your application or other applications. Whether they're used on the client or server doesn't really matter. However, using the controls in general can reduce the amount of coding required by your application and can enhance its functionality and maintainability.

Part III

Data Access in Visual Basic .NET

CHAPTER 7
ADO.NET

CHAPTER 8
XML Support in .NET

Chapter 7

ADO.NET

IN THIS CHAPTER

- Using the SQL Server .NET Data Provider
- Using the OLE DB .NET Data Provider
- Reusing existing code among providers
- Using the `DataReader` object
- Using the database wizards to make connections and datasets
- Creating SQL statements with the Query Builder

In this chapter, I show you two distinct types of data adapters. I'll create sample programs to retrieve records from both types of data sources and even jump into porting code from one adapter to another.

ADO versus ADO.NET

ADO.NET represents a dramatic improvement over standard ADO. To begin, we'll explore some of the advancements of ADO.NET and compare them to the functionality contained within ADO.

Data representation

ADO uses a `RecordSet` object, which looks like a single table. To define relationships between multiple tables, you must include a `JOIN` query to assemble data from multiple tables into a single result table. ADO.NET on the other hand, can contain one or more tables represented by `DataTable` objects. Relationships in ADO.NET are accomplished by using the `DataRelation` object, which can associate rows in one `DataTable` object with rows in another `DataTable` object.

Data visitation and access

ADO uses a `RecordSet` object to scan rows sequentially. The `RecordSet` object typically supports connected access, through the use of the `Connection` object. When you communicate with a database, the calls are routed through an OLE DB provider. ADO.NET navigates databases using nonsequential access to rows in a table. Much like a tree diagram of a database, or nodes in an XML file, ADO.NET follows relationships and is able to navigate from rows in one table to corresponding rows in another table. Because ADO.NET uses disconnected access, cursors are not needed; standard ADO uses both client-side and server side cursors with limited disconnected access.

Sharing data

ADO uses COM marshalling to send disconnected record sets. This is a serious drawback, because only the data types allowed by the COM standard can be used. To get around this limitation, many type conversions could be needed, which is exhaustive on system resources. ADO.NET transmits all data as XML DataSets. Because XML has no restrictions on data types, no conversions are required. Because these DataSets are represented by XML, sending this information through firewalls is also made very simple. Many firewalls are typically configured to prevent low-level system calls such as COM marshalling. Therefore, transmitting ADO record sets through firewalls was often very troublesome.

Scalability

ADO uses database locks and database connections. If these connections and locks are used for long periods of time, valuable database resources are consumed. ADO.NET uses disconnected database access without database locks. This frees up the resources of the database and allows for greater speed.

Using ADO.NET

In this section, I outline the different features of ADO.NET as well as ways of using the different features. For most of these examples, you'll need Microsoft SQL Server 2000.

SQL Server .NET Data Provider

The SQL Server .NET Data Provider employs its own protocol to communicate with SQL Server. For this reason, it increases performance by communicating directly with the database server and has no need for an OLE DB or ODBC layer.

There are two distinct ways of using this provider: through code only and through the use of SqlDataAdapters and other .NET components. It's actually recommended, when accessing SQL Server, that you use the .NET integrated components to establish the connect and build DataSets because it increases performance. But I cover both methods here.

CODING THE SQL SERVER DATA PROVIDER

A connection to SQL Server can be accomplished in as little as five lines of code. Following is code that will return the first name of every employee in the Pubs database:

```
Dim myConnection As New SqlConnection("data source=DEVELOPMENT;initial " & _
    "catalog=pubs;integrated security=SSPI;persist security info=False;" & _
    "workstation id=POWERHOUSE;packet size=4096")
myConnection.Open()
Dim mycommand As IDbCommand = myConnection.CreateCommand()
mycommand.CommandText = "SELECT * from EMPLOYEE"
Dim myreader As IDataReader = mycommand.ExecuteReader()
Do While myreader.Read()
  Console.WriteLine("{0}", myreader.GetString(1))
Loop
myConnection.Close()
```

Before attempting to run this code, keep in mind that two separate namespaces can be used for database access. The System.Data.OleDb is used for all OLE DB .NET Data Providers, while System.Data.SqlClient is used for accessing SQL Server 7.0 and greater. To try this code, insert Imports System.Data.SqlClient at the top of your code window.

The first thing that must be established when connecting to a database is a database connection string, as seen in the following line:

```
Dim myConnection As New SqlConnection("data source=DEVELOPMENT;initial " & _
    "catalog=pubs;integrated security=SSPI;persist security info=False;" & _
    "workstation id=POWERHOUSE;packet size=4096")
```

That data source argument in this connection string contains the location of our database server. In this particular example, the server happens to reside on a machine by the name of DEVELOPMENT.

Next, you encounter the initial catalog, which is the name of the database you want to connect to. The word *initial* in initial catalog is very important here, because it clues you in to the fact that your catalog can change during this connection without having to create an entirely new connection. The integrated security setting simply tells SQL Server that you'll be using its security measures. In this example, SQL Server is configured to allow LAN IDs with access or internal SQL Server Logons. The workstation id is the name of the computer that is accessing SQL Server. This is generally used for logging purposes on SQL Server so the Database Administrator can see who's currently connected to the system.

Last but not least, you have the packet size. The packet size describes just how big each packet of data can be that it returns to the client. On a busy network, it may be a good idea to reduce this number so as to prevent packet overruns and collisions. I've stuck with the 4,096 bytes because .NET-provided components use this size as a default.

After you've defined your connection string, you can open the data source with the following command:

```
myConnection.Open()
```

This becomes very import later when you learn that data can be returned from a database, the data can be updated, and then a connection can be reestablished and sent back to the server to update the database.

After the database is open, we create a database command object and call the CreateCommand method of our connection object. You're now free to insert a SQL statement that is sent to SQL Server, as seen here:

```
Dim mycommand As IDbCommand = myConnection.CreateCommand()
mycommand.CommandText = "SELECT * from EMPLOYEE"
```

After the SQL statement has been built and sent to the database server, we must now prepare for the data return. Accepting the data returned from the database can be handled in one of two ways. The DataReader will accept the data but it's a forward-only, read-only source. This means that you can read the data but not update it, and you can move backward in the records that were sent. The alternative method would be to populate a DataSet. The DataSet allows you to move freely around the data and perform updates. In this example, you're using a DataReader as seen in these last few lines of the previous example:

```
Dim myreader As IDataReader = mycommand.ExecuteReader()
Do While myreader.Read()
    Console.WriteLine("{0}", myreader.GetString(1))
Loop
myConnection.Close()
```

Here you've created a DataReader and loop while the reader is currently returning data. Using the Console.WriteLine command, you dump out the second item in our array of returned information. When you run this code, your output window in the .NET IDE should look similar to that shown in Figure 7-1.

LEVERAGING THE DATABASE CONNECTION WIZARDS

Using the database connection wizards is generally a much easier task than attempting to code everything yourself. Not only do these wizards build your connection, but they also allow you to build very complex SQL statements using a visual interface. You'll now use the database wizards to retrieve a list of employee first names within our SQL Server database, just as you did in the previous example.

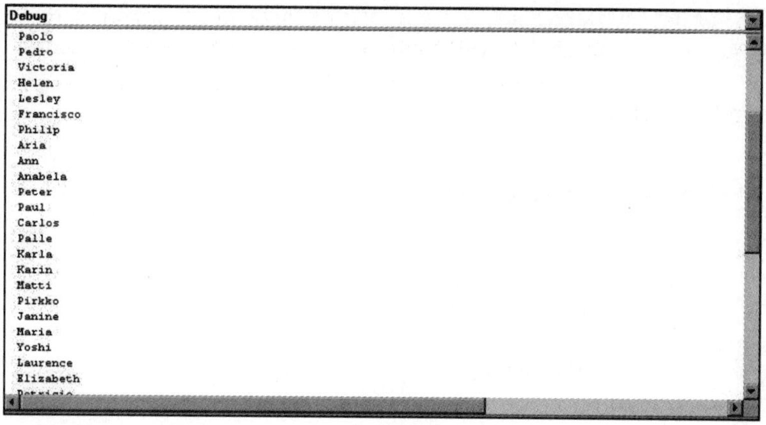

Debug
Paolo
Pedro
Victoria
Helen
Lesley
Francisco
Philip
Aria
Ann
Anabela
Peter
Paul
Carlos
Palle
Karla
Karin
Matti
Pirkko
Janine
Maria
Yoshi
Laurence
Elizabeth

Figure 7-1: DataReader returns the requested rows.

Start a new Visual Basic .NET project and name it Employee. When the form of this application appears in the form designer, move to your toolbox and add a ListBox to the form. The size and location of this ListBox is unimportant at this point, just as long as you can see several rows within it.

Move back to your Toolbox as you click on your Data tab, as shown in Figure 7-2.

Toolbox
Data
Pointer
DataSet
OleDbDataAdapter
OleDbConnection
OleDbCommand
SqlDataAdapter
SqlConnection
SqlCommand
DataView
Components
Windows Forms
Clipboard Ring
General

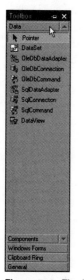

Figure 7-2: The Data tab contains .NET components for database access.

After you've clicked the Data tab, you'll see two distinct sets of controls, those for OLE connections and those for Microsoft SQL Server. Double-click on the SqlDataAdapter. After a brief moment, you should be greeted by the Data Adapter Configuration Wizard, as shown in Figure 7-3.

Figure 7-3: The Data Adapter Configuration Wizard.

Click Next on the first screen. The wizard now needs to know what data connection you want to use. Click the New Connection button. The Data Link Properties window will open and allow you to specify the location of SQL Server and login information. Item 1 on this form is the name of your SQL Server machine. If you have SQL Server running locally, type **localhost** into the server name box. If this is a remote machine, enter in the name of the PC, as I've done in Figure 7-4.

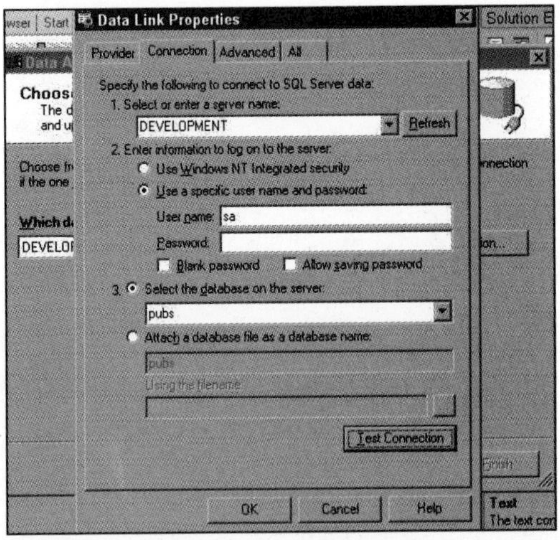

Figure 7-4: Configure the MS SQL Server connection properties.

Enter the login name into Item 2 on this window, and select the database from Item 3. After you've selected the Pubs database, click the Test Connection. If this test is successful, we're ready to move on, so click the OK button. You'll be returned to step 2 of the Data Connection Wizard. In the combo box on the screen, you should see the connection you just built. Click the Next button.

The Wizard now needs to know if you plan to retrieve data based on a SQL statement or an existing stored procedure, or if you want to create a stored procedure to manipulate data. Select Use SQL statements, and click the Next button.

From this Wizard window, you can type in a SQL statement for the data you want to retrieve, or you can click the Query Builder button for a visual interface of building a SQL statement. Click the Query Builder button. You must now add tables to your SQL statement. Locate the employee table, and double-click it. The employee table has now been added to your SQL statement. Click the Close button.

At the top of the Query Builder window in the employee box, put a check mark next to fname by clicking on it, as shown in Figure 7-5.

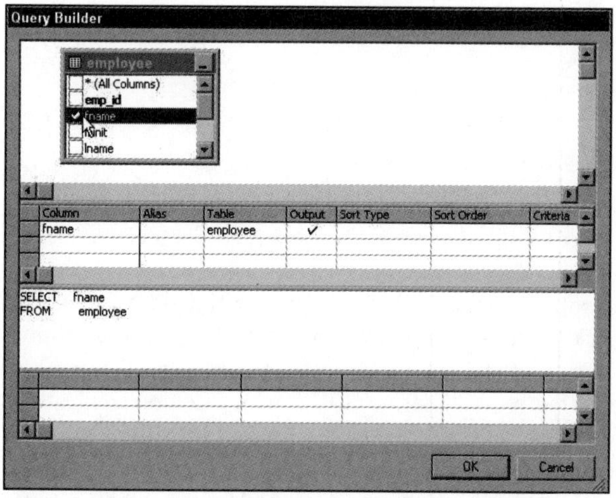

Figure 7-5: Build queries with a simple point and click.

You should now see a query toward the bottom of this window that reads as follows:

```
SELECT   fname
FROM     employee
```

You can now click the OK button in the Query Builder to return to the Data Adapter Wizard. When you're back at the Wizard, click the Next button. The Wizard will now generate code to select data from the database, as well as update and delete records. Click the Finish button in the Wizard to wrap things up.

When you return to the Form Designer, you'll notice two new items that have been added to your project, `SqlDataAdapter1` and `SqlConnection1`. This is everything you need to connect to SQL Server. At this point however, you still haven't created a DataSet to store the data once it has returned from our database. To create a DataSet, right click on `SqlDataAdapter1` object and select Generate DataSet, as shown in Figure 7-6.

☒	View **C**ode
	Configure Data Adapter...
	Generate Dataset...
	Preview Data...
✄	Cu**t**
⎙	**C**opy
▦	**P**aste
✕	**D**elete
⌖	P**r**operties

Figure 7-6: DataSets can be
generated automatically.

TIP   You can preview the data that a DataSet will contain by right-clicking on
the `DataAdapter` object and selecting Preview Data.

When the DataSet window appears, ensure that the New option is selected and name this DataSet dsfName. Click OK to generate this DataSet and add it to your project. When the DataSet has been added to your project, you can bind it to your ListBox control to show the resulting recordset from SQL Server. Click on the ListBox and go to the Properties window. Change the `DataSource` property for the Listbox to dsfName1 by clicking the dropdown arrow box next to the property. After your data source has been defined for this control, you can define what field actually returns the data to be displayed. Click the dropdown arrow box next to the `DisplayMember` property. The property window will display a treeview control of the database table. Expand the Employee table and click on fname, as shown in Figure 7-7.

Be sure not to click on the icon next to fname. Doing so will result in an error.

The Wizards and shortcuts built into the Visual Studio .NET IDE perform many helpful tasks, but they can't do everything. At this point, you need to add some code to finish things up. It's not so bad though — it's only one line of code.

Double-click on your form in the Form Designer to be taken to the `Form1_Load` event handler in a code window. In here, you'll need to fill our DataSet, so the database records populate our ListBox when the application runs. Add the following line of code to the Form Load event:

```
SqlDataAdapter1.Fill(DsfName1)
```

Figure 7-7: DisplayMember allows us
to select our data population source.

By calling the `Fill` method of our `SqlDataAdapter` object and passing in the
DataSet name, all our records are returned from the database and display in the
data bound ListBox control. Figure 7-8 is the outcome of all your (and Visual
Studio's) hard work.

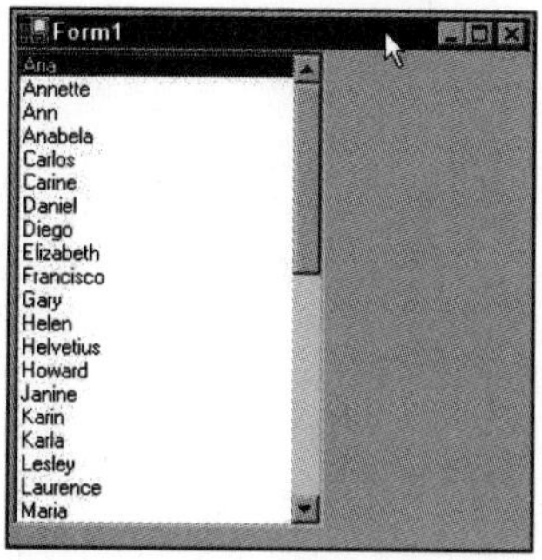

Figure 7-8: Resulting records from SQL Server
with one line of code.

ADO OLE DB Managed Provider

The OLE DB Data Providers use COM interop for database access. If you want to use
the database access through a firewall, your access may be inherently impaired
without some modifications to your firewall's permissions. It's recommended that
under some circumstances, you use this provider rather than the SQL Server
Managed Provider:

- ◆ If you're writing middle-tier applications using Oracle or Microsoft SQL
  Server 6.5 or earlier, use the OLE DB .NET Data Provider.

- ◆ If you're writing a single-tier application that uses Microsoft Access as the
  database, you're encouraged to use the OLE DB Managed Provider.

◆ If you're writing a middle-tier application that uses Microsoft Access as the database, it isn't recommended that you use the OLE DB .NET Data Provider.

PORTABILITY

ADO.NET provides a common programming model for the .NET Data Providers. This means that code written for a SQL Server .NET Data Provider will work with the OLE DB .NET Data Provider as well. You can examine an example of this by building a routine that retrieves all Authors listed in the Pubs database and returns the records as an XML DataSet.

OLE DB .NET DATA PROVIDER

Create a new Project and name it Portability. Place a TextBox on your project's Form. Change the MultiLine property of the TextBox to TRUE and set the ScrollBars property to Vertical. You shouldn't be able to resize your TextBox both horizontally and vertically. Resize the TextBox so it takes up the upper portion of your form, and move your button to the bottom of the form, as shown in Figure 7-9.

Figure 7-9: The Portability interface.

Double-click on the button you added to go to a code window. When you're there, scroll to the very top of the window and add the following line of code:

```
Imports System.Data.OleDb
```

As you may recall, different namespaces are required to access the OLE DB Data Providers and the SQL Server Data Providers. First, you'll test the OLE DB Data Adapter against your SQL Server Database.

Insert the following code into the Click event of the button that you added previously:

```
Dim myDataSet As New DataSet()
Dim myConnection As New OleDbConnection("Provider=SQLOLEDB;data source=" & _
    "DEVELOPMENT;initial catalog=pubs;integrated security=SSPI;persist security" & _
```

```
" info=False;workstation id=POWERHOUSE;packet size=4096")
myConnection.Open()
Dim myDataAdapter As New OleDbDataAdapter("SELECT * FROM AUTHORS", myConnection)
myDataAdapter.Fill(myDataSet)
TextBox1.Text = myDataSet.GetXml
myConnection.Close()
```

Here you create a `DataSet` object and establish a connection to the database server by defining several connection properties, as you did before in the previous section of this chapter. One thing that should stick out is your `Provider` parameter. The `Provider` parameter accepts the name of the OLE DB Provider you're connecting to. In this example, you'll be connecting to a Microsoft SQL Server, so you pass `SQLOLEDB` as your Provider parameter.

After your connection information has been established, you create an `OleDbDataAdapter` object and pass it the SQL statement you want to retrieve records with, and you pass in your Connection object. You're then free to call the `Fill` method of the `DataAdapter` and pass in the Dataset that is to be populated.

After a few moments, your DataSet is populated and you can then insert the results of the `GetXml` method to the Text Property of your TextBox. The `GetXml` method of the DataSet will return an XML representation of all data that is currently stored within our DataSet.

Before running this application, you'll need to modify the connection string by replacing the data source and workstation id with the names of the computers you're using. When you've done this, press F5 to run this application. When the application opens, click the button at the bottom of our form to begin. After a few moments, you'll see a large amount of XML populate the TextBox, as shown in Figure 7-10.

Figure 7-10: A DataSet populates the TextBox
with an XML representation of the data.

This was a very simplistic example, which you'll now convert to a SQL Server .NET Data Provider to examine just how little code you must change.

SQL SERVER .NET DATA PROVIDER

Proceed back into the code editor for our Portability project. At the very top of this window, you'll need to reference a different namespace, because you are now dealing with SQL Server. Change the Imports statement at the top of the code window to the following:

```
Imports System.Data.SqlClient
```

When the SQL Server namespace has been defined, scroll back down the Code window to the Button click event handler. You need to modify two lines of code here to get things back up and working with this data provider.

On the second line of this method, you'll need to change the connection type from an OleDbConnection to a SqlConnection and remove your Provider parameter. The resulting line should now look like this:

```
Dim myConnection As New SqlConnection("data source=" & _
"DEVELOPMENT;initial catalog=pubs;integrated security=SSPI;persist security" & _
" info=False;workstation id=POWERHOUSE;packet size=4096")
```

Again, you'll have to change the data source, and workstation id to match the computers you're using. Because you now have a SqlConnection object, your DataAdapter that you're currently using will have to be changed because it references an OleDbDataAdapter object. Change the declaration for myDataAdapter from OleDbDataAdapter to SqlDataAdapter. This modified line of code should now be as follows:

```
Dim myDataAdapter As New SqlDataAdapter("SELECT * FROM AUTHORS", myConnection)
```

You can now run this application as you did before. You should see the same results as you saw in the OLE DB example.

Porting Data Provider code from one provider to another is extremely painless and requires very little effort. In this particular example, you had to change two lines of code. This would be rather troublesome in a large application with many connections and data adapters, but under those circumstances it would be best to create a function that handled the actual data and just accepted a DataAdapter as a function parameter. Then you would only need to change the type of data adapter in one place, because the proposed function doesn't care what type of data adapter it uses.

Summary

ADO.NET represents a giant leap forward in database access. Not only are the components extremely lightweight, but they utilize the same methods and properties, so porting code from one provider to another is extremely painless.

Chapter 8

XML Support in .NET

IN THIS CHAPTER

- ◆ Understanding the structure of XML
- ◆ Learning to create well-formed XML
- ◆ Understanding stream-level XML parsing
- ◆ Understanding the Document Object Model (DOM)
- ◆ Understanding XML document fragments
- ◆ Understanding XML validation with Schemas
- ◆ Navigating XML with Xpath
- ◆ Understanding and creating XML DataSets

In this chapter, I explain some of the exciting new XML features contained within the .NET Framework. While examining these features, you also learn to leverage the power of the XML capabilities to create datasets, transform XML into HTML, and modify XML streams on the fly.

A Brief Introduction to XML

The power of eXtensible Markup Language (XML) is widely known for its ability to represent data in a structured, text-based format. XML also supports validation and transformation, which helps make it one of the best data transports available today.

XML, much like a database, stores data in a predefined format that makes it quite easy for the programmer to deal with. Unlike HTML, which uses predefined tags, XML uses no predefined tag sets and leaves the tag definitions and relationships between them up to the author of the document. Consider the following XML:

```
<?xml version="1.0" encoding="UTF-8"?>
<AddressBook>
    <Family>
        <FirstName>Aimee</FirstName>
        <LastName>Patterson</LastName>
        <PhoneNumber>3095558187</PhoneNumber>
    </Family>
```

```
<CoWorker>
        <FirstName>Stuart</FirstName>
        <LastName>Laughlin</LastName>
        <PhoneNumber>3095554289</PhoneNumber>
</CoWorker>
</AddressBook>
```

The first thing you see in this example is a processing instruction: `<?xml...>`. This is an XML declaration that details what version of XML the document was authored in, as well as the character set that was used. As you can see by looking at the rest of the example, this XML represents data contained within an address book. This particular address book contains records for family members and coworkers. Within each section of the address book, we have elements (columns, for the database savvy) that contain the first name, last name, and phone number for each contact.

.NET-Supported Features

.NET currently supports all the major standards of XML with the exception of Simple API for XML (SAX). The reason for this is that SAX isn't currently supported by any standards body, such as the World Wide Web Consortium. It originated from a joint development project started on the XML-Dev mailing list, and it likely won't be supported until a standards body decides to take responsibility for it. This is of little concern to most of us, however, because there are many other methods of reading and writing XML.

In the following sections, I discuss the standards supported in .NET, as well as several applications that utilize these standards.

XML namespaces

XML namespaces are a form of qualifying attribute and element names. This is done within XML documents by associating them with namespaces that are identified with Universal Resource Indicators (URIs). The following is an example of using a namespace declaration, which associates the namespace prefix bdp with the namespace `http://www.testwebsite.org/nmspc`.

```
<x xmlns:bdp='http://www.testwebsite.org/nmspc'>
```

After we've added this line to our XML file, we can then take advantage of this qualified name as an element type in the following section of XML:

```
<x xmlns:bdp='http://www.testwebsite.org/nmspc'>
  <bdp:weight units='LBS'>1500</bdp:weight>
</x>
```

As you delve into XML, this will be of little use to you. It won't be useful, in fact, until you get into creating interactive XML Web pages for the Web, and even perhaps Web pages that must follow very strict guidelines for transporting data.

Stream level

The stream-level interface provided by .NET is much like that of SAX in that they both use a stream. The difference though is that SAX is event-driven and this implementation is not. When I say *event-driven,* I mean that events are fired as the parser reads through the XML file and encounters tags, attributes, processing instructions, and so forth.

The stream-level interface is forward-reading only, but it provides many advantages over non–stream-based methods – like the Document Object Model (DOM), for example. Because a stream interface reads an XML file in piece by piece, there is very low memory overhead. A drawback to this method is that you, the programmer, must watch for all appropriate tags after each read of the file. Stream-level interfaces are also forward-reading only. This means that after you've read the first record, you can't go back in the file and read it again without starting all over. Stream levels also make file modification on the fly much harder than it would be with an interface such as DOM.

To illustrate how easy it is to use the stream interface (the XmlReader), we'll build an address book application that stores names and phone numbers in an XML file and then displays that information on the screen.

ADDRESS BOOK EXAMPLE
Begin a new Visual Basic .NET Windows Application by selecting File → New. From here, select Windows Application and name it AddressBook. When a blank project opens up, you'll need to add three controls. They are:

- ListBox
- Button
- OpenFileDialog

Place your ListBox in the upper left-hand corner of the form, and extend it across the form to the opposite side and down to the bottom, leaving enough room at the bottom for your button. Change the Anchor property of the ListBox to Top,Bottom,Left,Right. Now move your button to the lower right-hand corner of the form, and change its Anchor property to Bottom, Right. All that's left is to change the caption of the form to Address Book and the Text property of the button to Load XML. For aesthetic reasons, you may also want to change the font type and size of your ListBox to something a bit more readable – I chose Courier New as my font with a font size of 12.

Our address book now contains a ListBox and button that will resize with the form in a layout similar to that shown in Figure 8-1.

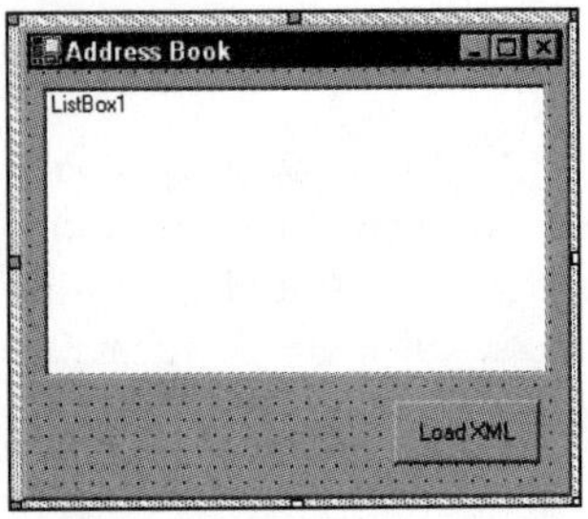

Figure 8-1: The completed address book interface.

With the user interface complete, it's now time to start adding some code to the application to open an XML file and parse out the necessary information. While in the form designer, double-click on the Load XML button to go to the code window. At the top of this window, just before the class declaration, we need to insert an Import statement for the XML namespace as seen here:

```
Imports System.Xml
```

> **TIP** You can view the code window of a form by selecting the form in the Solution Explorer and then clicking the View Code icon in the Solution Explorers toolbar.

The address book application will utilize constants to store the names of tags we'll be looking for while parsing the XML file. These constants should be placed within the Form1 class just below the statement that says Inherits System.Windows.Forms.Form. The following lines of code are the five tags we will be looking for:

```
Const FirstNameTag As String = "FirstName"
Const LastNameTag As String = "LastName"
Const PhoneNumberTag As String = "PhoneNumber"
Const FamilyTag As String = "Family"
Const CoWorkerTag As String = "CoWorker"
```

With that code in place, we can now place some functionality behind our button click event to load the XML file. Add the following lines of code to your Button1_Click event that was created when you double-clicked the Load XML button on your form:

```
Dim XMLTR As XmlTextReader
Dim FirstName As String
Dim LastName As String
Dim PhoneNumber As Long
```

In this section of code, you've declared a variable as your XmlTextReader that will then later assign to the XML file that you want to open. You've also created three temporary variables to store the data that you retrieve from the XML file.

You previously added an OpenFileDialog control for selecting the XML data file that we want to read. This is generally the preferred method, because not everyone will place the XML file at the same location on their computers. To ensure that the OpenFileDialog control only shows XML files, you need to add a filter to the control and then show the dialog. Add the two lines of code to your button click event just below the variable declarations that were just added:

```
OpenFileDialog1.Filter = "XML File (*.xml)|*.xml"
OpenFileDialog1.ShowDialog()
```

Within the filter you provided the file description to the user, XML File (*.xml) followed by a pipe symbol and then the actual wildcard string used to locate the appropriate file types. This format has not changed from the previous version of Visual Basic, so if you're making the transition, rest assured that all your previous filters will work fine with .NET. With your filter in place, you call the ShowDialog method of the OpenFileDialog control, which opens a modal dialog box and lets the user search for an XML file to open, as shown in Figure 8-2.

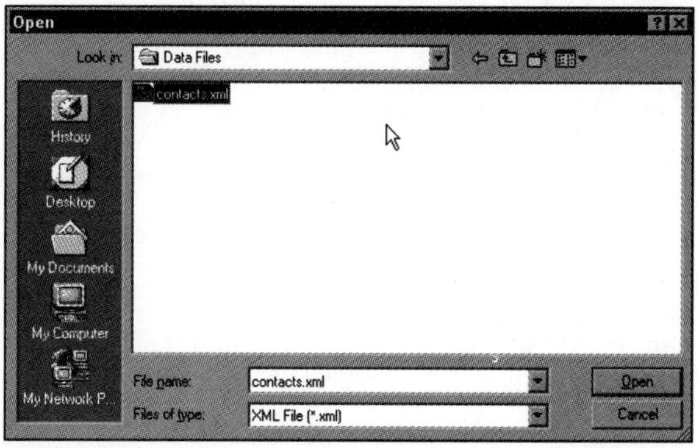

Figure 8-2: Browse for an XML file using OpenFileDialog.

When a filename has been selected in the `OpenFileDialog` control, you can open the file and retrieve all the relevant information needed by our address book. Insert the following code into the click event of the Load XML button to finish things up:

```
If OpenFileDialog1.FileName <> "" Then
ListBox1.Items.Clear()
XMLTR = New XmlTextReader(OpenFileDialog1.FileName)
  While (XMLTR.Read())
    If XMLTR.LocalName = FirstNameTag Then
      FirstName = XMLTR.ReadInnerXml
    End If
    If XMLTR.LocalName = LastNameTag Then
      LastName = XMLTR.ReadInnerXml
    End If
    If XMLTR.LocalName = PhoneNumberTag Then
      PhoneNumber = XMLTR.ReadInnerXml
    End If

    If XMLTR.NodeType = XmlNodeType.EndElement Then
      If XMLTR.LocalName = FamilyTag Or _
        XMLTR.LocalName = CoWorkerTag Then
        ListBox1.Items.Add(FirstName & " " & LastName)
        ListBox1.Items.Add(Format(PhoneNumber, "(####) ###-####"))
        ListBox1.Items.Add("--------------------")
      End If
    End If
End While
XMLTR.Close()
End If
```

Now take a closer look at this code. The first thing you must do in this routine is make sure a filename was selected in our `OpenFileDialog` control. This is done by enclosing most of your code with an `If...Then` statement. If the user decided to press Cancel in the `OpenFileDialog`, no filename would be returned, so you should just ignore their request to process a file.

You then call the `Clear` method of our `ListBox` items collection. This will ensure that any data previously in the control will be removed before you add it again. (This, in fact, leads up to the next section, where I show you how to add XML data to a file using DOM.)

With the form ready to go, you instantiate a new `XmlTextReader` and assign it to our `XMLTR` variable that you previously declared, as shown in this line of code:

```
XMLTR = New XmlTextReader(OpenFileDialog1.FileName)
```

As you can see, the only thing you need to pass the XmlTextReader is the path and filename of the XML file that you want to open. In this particular example, you're simply passing it the value of our OpenFileDialog filename property. Your XML file is now open and you can call the Read method of XMLTR to stream the data in. This is done within a While loop, so you can watch for an End Of File marker. Simply looping constantly through the file will cause an IO Exception, which you really want to avoid.

Within the While block, you must now be on the lookout for our tags denoting that you've encountered one of the three data items you are in search of: First Name, Last Name, and Phone Number. This is done by viewing the LocalName property of your XmlTextReader variable, XMLTR, which contains the streaming data. The following is a code snippet that you've already placed into your project:

```
While (XMLTR.Read())
   If XMLTR.LocalName = FirstNameTag Then
     FirstName = XMLTR.ReadInnerXml
   End If
   If XMLTR.LocalName = LastNameTag Then
     LastName = XMLTR.ReadInnerXml
   End If
   If XMLTR.LocalName = PhoneNumberTag Then
     PhoneNumber = XMLTR.ReadInnerXml
   End If
```

You have one If...Then statement for each of the data items that you're looking for. Each time a tag is encountered within your XML file, you check the name of that tag against your constants that you previously placed at the top of the source file. If a match is made on any of these tags, you've found the appropriate tag and are now well aware that your actual data will follow. To retrieve the data contained within the start and end tags, you must use the ReadInnerXml method. This method takes an XML string, looks between the first and last tag, and returns that data that is between the two. For example:

```
<FavoriteBeverage>Caffeine</FavoriteBeverage>
```

Given the preceding XML string, a call to ReadInnerXml would simply return "Caffeine."

If you're curious how this method would react to a more complex XML string, take a look at another example:

```
<Contents>
   <Ingred>Carbonated Water</Ingred>
   <Ingred>High Fructose Corn Syrup</Ingred>
</Contents>
```

As you may have guessed, a call to the ReadInnerXml method on this XML string would return simply:

```
<Ingred>Carbonated Water</Ingred><Ingred>High Fructose Corn Syrup</Ingred>
```

You may then take this result and make additional calls and drill down even farther. After you've located all the data and stored it within the temporary variables, you must now be on the lookout for the closing element of Family or CoWorker (for example, </Family> and </CoWorker>), because they both represent the end of a record. When one of these is encountered, you take the data you have and add it to your ListBox, as shown in the following snippet:

```
If XMLTR.NodeType = XmlNodeType.EndElement Then
  If XMLTR.LocalName = FamilyTag Or XMLTR.LocalName = CoWorkerTag Then
    ListBox1.Items.Add(FirstName & " " & LastName)
    ListBox1.Items.Add(Format(PhoneNumber, "(###) ###-####"))
    ListBox1.Items.Add("--------------------")
  End If
End If
```

In this section of code, you're first checking the type of node that was returned from the XML file. If the node happens to be of type XmlNodeType.EndElement, it could possibly be the Family or CoWorker end elements. You then check for those two tags and, if you find them, simply add the data to your ListBox, followed by a separator line.

When your Read method has completed reading the XML file, it'll drop out of the While loop. It's important to remember that while using the XmlTextReader, it's a stream reader, which means that it's treated the same as if you opened a regular file. This being the case, you must close the file, as seen in this line of code:

```
XMLTR.Close()
```

If the file is not closed, any attempt at adding data to the file will fail because the file is already open.

TESTING THE ADDRESS BOOK

To test your application, take the XML data located at the beginning of this chapter and type it into Notepad. Now save this file to disk with any name just as long as it ends with .xml. You can now run the Address Book program and click the Load XML button. You'll be greeted with an Open File dialog, so you'll need to navigate your drive until you find the XML file that you just saved with Notepad. When you've located the file, either double-click on it or select the file and click the Open button. The Address Book program will parse the file, and the results you see should look like that shown in Figure 8-3.

Figure 8-3: XML data successfully parsed and displayed.

Document Object Model (DOM)

The Document Object Model (DOM) presents documents (typically XML and HTML) as a hierarchy of node objects, much like that of a tree. Each node in a DOM can have child objects of various types, or they could be what are considered leaf nodes that can't contain any child items. To illustrate this, take a look at the following XML file:

```
<AddressBook>
  <Person>
    <FullName>Bob Smith</FullName>
    <PhoneNumber>
      <Home>3095551212</Home>
      <Work>3095552323</Work>
      <Pager>3095553434</Pager>
    </PhoneNumber>
  </Person>
</AddressBook>
```

This XML code represents an address record that also contains two sub-items within the Person node. Figure 8-4 shows a graphical representation of the tree structure, denoting just how this is viewed by DOM.

As you can see from this representation, Person is a child node of AddressBook; FullName and PhoneNumber are children of Person; and Home, Work, and Pager are child nodes of PhoneNumber. All the items under PhoneNumber are considered *leaf nodes*. These nodes may contain data, but you can plainly see that they can't contain any child nodes.

In actuality, this is only partially true. You haven't set up any validation on this XML file, so it's very possible to create child nodes under Pager, Work, and Home. (I get into validation a bit later in the chapter.)

To illustrate just how easy it is to use DOM, you're going to take the sample application from the previous section and extend it to allow you to add records to your XML data file. We'll add these records using the DOM interface.

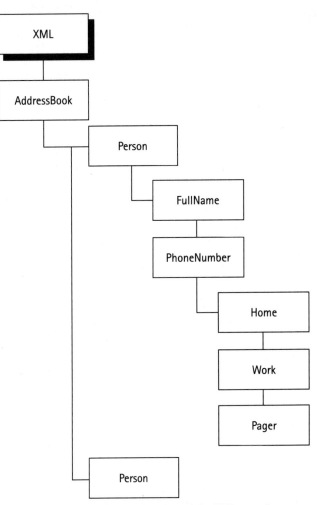

Figure 8-4: A graphical representation of the XML record.

APPENDING DATA WITH DOM

To add data to your Address Book application, you'll need another button on the main form just beside the Load XML button. Add the button to your form and change the text property to Add Contact. Set the Anchor property of this button to Bottom, Right so it remains at the bottom when the form is resized. Your main form should now look like that shown in Figure 8-5.

Figure 8-5: The Address Book with
a button to add contacts.

Your application will also need an additional form to allow data entry. To add an additional form, click on the Project menu and then select Add Windows Form. From the Add New Item window, simply select Windows Form and click Open. When the new form opens up in the designer, you may want to change the Text property of the form to Add Contact. Now that the form is ready, you need to add several controls to it (see Table 8-1).

TABLE 8-1 CONTROL NAMES AND PROPERTIES FOR THE ADD CONTACT WINDOW

Control Type	Control Name	Text Property	Checked Property
Text Box	txtFirstName	Empty	N/A
Text Box	txtLastName	Empty	N/A
Text Box	txtPhoneNumber	Empty	N/A
Label	Label1	First Name	N/A
Label	Label2	Last Name	N/A
Label	Label3	Phone Number	N/A
Label	Label4	Contact Type	N/A
Button	btnOK	OK	N/A
Button	btnCancel	Cancel	N/A
Radio Button	rbFamily	Family	True
Radio Button	rbCoWorker	Co-Worker	False

When you've added all the controls to the form and set the properties accordingly, they need to be arranged similar to what's shown in Figure 8-6.

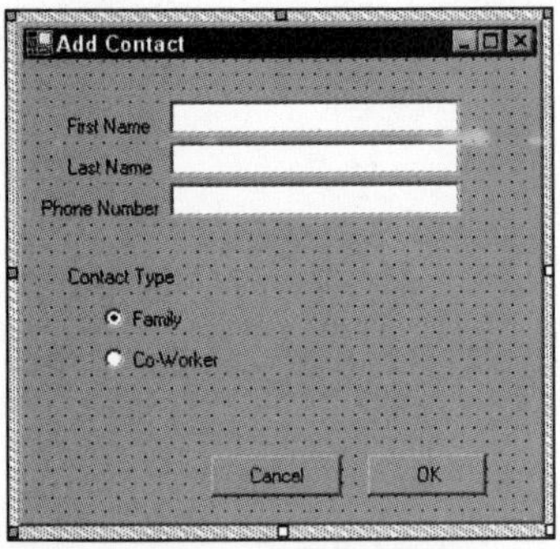

Figure 8-6: The Add Contact form with all the necessary controls.

Our Add Contact form will require a few public members within its class. Double-click either of the buttons on the form to get to a code window. Once in the code window, you'll need the following lines of code placed at the top just under the statement that says Inherits System.Windows.Forms.Form:

```
Public FirstName As String
Public LastName As String
Public PhoneNumber As String
Public ContactType As String
```

When adding data to your XML file from this screen, all the information will be stored in these variables so it can be retrieved easily from the main interface. You can now add code to the buttons and finish up this form.

Return to the form designer by double-clicking on the form in the Solution Explorer. Once there, double-click on the OK button that you placed on the form. This will take you to the Click event handler. The following code needs to be added to this event handler:

```
Me.FirstName = txtFirstName.Text
Me.LastName = txtLastName.Text
Me.PhoneNumber = txtPhoneNumber.Text
If rbFamily.Checked = True Then
  Me.ContactType = "Family"
Else
  Me.ContactType = "CoWorker"
End If
Me.Hide()
```

The steps you take in this section of code are very straightforward. You assign all the data to your public members that you previously declared. You also check to see which radio button was selected and assign the ContactType accordingly. After you've assigned all the data, you call the form Hide method, which will take the user back to the main interface. Return to the form designer and double-click the Cancel button. Add the following code to the Cancel button's Click event:

```
Me.FirstName = ""
Me.LastName = ""
Me.PhoneNumber = ""
Me.ContactType = ""
Me.Hide()
```

If the user clicks the Cancel button, you simply want to clear out all the public members and hide the form. This ensures that when you return to the main form of the application you don't mistakenly add residual data to the XML file.

XML DOCUMENT FRAGMENTS

Now that the data entry form is ready to go, you add the code that will save your XML out to the data file. You're going to add data to your XML file using DOM to load the file and the XmlDocumentFragment to build the node you want to save.

From the form designer of your main form, double-click on the Add Contact button. It's within this event that you'll add the code necessary to open your data entry form and save the information to your data file. Add the following code to the click event of the Add Contact button:

```
Dim addContact As New Form2()
Dim XD As XmlDocument = New XmlDocument()
Dim XDF As XmlDocumentFragment
addContact.ShowDialog()
```

In this section of code, you must create a new instance of your Add Contact form so you have access to the methods and properties of this form (for example, First Name, Last Name, and so on). You now declare XD as a new XmlDocument, which is where your XML data file will reside when you read it in. The XmlDocumentFragment variable that you're declaring is a wonderful tool to have at your disposal. A *document fragment* is essentially one or many parts of an XML document that you want to build. After you've built all the necessary components into this XmlDocumentFragment, you can then append this fragment onto another XML document. In this example, you'll create a node containing the contact information and then append it to the end of our existing XML file. With all the variables declared, you add a call to the ShowDialog method of your Add Contact form to open the form up. You're using ShowDialog rather than Show because you want the form to be modal when it appears.

Add the following code to your event handler just below the code you previously added. You can then examine the code and find out just how you accomplish adding content to an XML document.

```
If addContact.FirstName <> "" Then
  XD.Load(OpenFileDialog1.FileName)
  XDF = XD.CreateDocumentFragment
  XDF.InnerXml = "<" & addContact.ContactType _
    & "><FirstName>" & addContact.FirstName _
    & "</FirstName><LastName>" _
    & addContact.LastName _
    & "</LastName><PhoneNumber>" _
    & addContact.PhoneNumber _
    & "</PhoneNumber>" _
    & "</" & addContact.ContactType & ">"
  XD.DocumentElement.AppendChild(XDF)
  XD.Save(OpenFileDialog1.FileName)
End If
```

The first thing you must accomplish within this code is to check for the existence of data in your `FirstName` variable that the `Add Contact` form exposes. If no data exists, you know that the user has canceled out of the form and you should not attempt to do anything, which is why you've wrapped this entire block of code with an `If...Then` statement.

By calling the `Load` method of our `XmlDocument` object and passing the path to the XML file (or even a URL to an XML file), the XML file is loaded into memory in its entirety. You can then create a document fragment based on our XmlDocument as seen in the following line.

```
XDF = XD.CreateDocumentFragment
```

In the previous section, I explained the `InnerXml` property. You use that again here to assign the appropriate XML to your document fragment. As you look at the preceding code, you may be wondering why I'm stringing all the XML tags together. There are more sophisticated ways of creating these elements, but it's a bit much for such a simple task. Some of the more advanced ways of creating tags would be best used when dynamically adding large amounts of XML at unknown points in a document — such as an XML representation of a large database.

TIP

The use of `InnerXml` allows you to directly insert XML text into a document or document fragment. Using `InnerText` will only allow you to insert non-XML strings. If you attempt to insert XML text into this property, the text will be converted as if it were a leaf node or value of a node within the XML document.

Once our XML has been added to the DocumentFragment, you can append it to the original XML data file with the following code, which you added earlier:

```
XD.DocumentElement.AppendChild(XDF)
```

You've created the necessary XML and appended it to your XML file. It's now time to save the XML back out to the drive. You can now call the Save method of your XML document and pass it a filename or stream (such as Console.Out). In our Stream example, I made it very clear that you must specifically close the data file or you would run into problems. This is one of those circumstances. If the XML file had not been closed, you could obviously not have written back out to it and would then encounter an IO Exception.

TESTING THE ADDRESS BOOK

To begin testing the application, press F5 or select Start from the Debug menu. When the application starts, you'll need to click the Load XML button and find your test file that was previously created in this chapter. After the file has been loaded and displayed on the screen, you can click the Add Contact button. It's necessary to load the XML file first, because when you create the DocumentFragments, you're referencing the XML file by the FileOpenDialog.Filename property, which must contain the name of the file.

At this point, your Add Contact screen should open up. Enter in the contact's information, as shown in Figure 8-7.

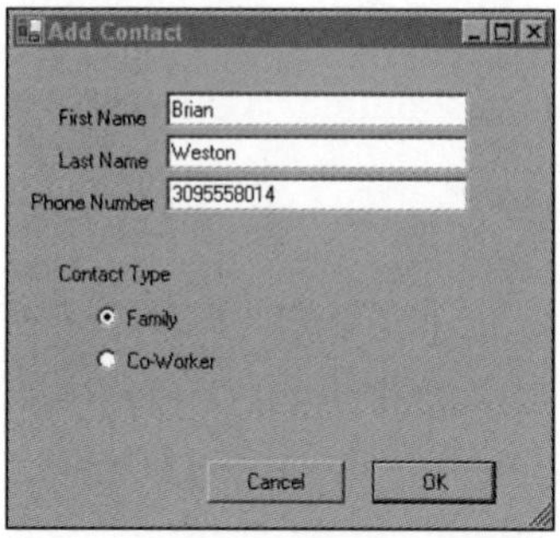

Figure 8-7: Add contact information into the data entry screen.

After you've entered in all the information, click OK. The Add Contact screen will disappear, and you will be back at the main interface. Don't worry when your contact doesn't appear in the list. As you may recall, you didn't include code to refresh your display. Simply click the Load XML button again and reload the XML file. You should now see your contact at the bottom of the list.

If you're so inclined, open up the XML file with Notepad. You'll notice that the newly added fragment is properly formatted and structured. When documents are saved back out using DOM, they're automatically indented and formatted with a predefined standard that make them pleasant to view with the human eye.

TAKING DOM FURTHER

The DOM interface provides many methods for navigating and viewing data. Not only can a DOM tree be completely enumerated, but methods such as GetElementsByTagName allow the values of specific tags to be returned. This particular method even allows the use of wildcards! Consider the following code:

```
Dim XD As XmlDocument = New XmlDocument()
Dim XNL As XmlNodeList
Dim x As Integer

XD.Load("c:\contacts.xml")
XNL = XD.GetElementsByTagName("FirstName")
For x = 0 To XNL.Count - 1
  MsgBox(XNL(x).InnerXml)
Next
```

In this example, I've hard-coded in the name and path of your test XML file. Here you are experimenting with the GetElementsByTagName method, which returns a XmlNodeList object. When you run this code, a message box will appear with each First Name that is encountered in your file. To view this information, you must loop through the NodeListCollection, which is zero based, and display the InnerXml of each item. If you were to specify the Family tag in this routine, you would see an entire XML record for each Family record listed within the file.

The XmlDocument class contains many methods and properties for navigating and viewing data contained within an XML file. For more information, you may want to check a list of the XmlDocument Class member.

XML Schemas

An *XML Schema* is a method used to describe XML attributes and elements. This method for describing the XML file is actually written using XML, which provides many benefits over other validation techniques, such as Document Type Definition (DTD). These benefits include the following:

◆ Because the Schema is written in XML, you don't have to know an archaic language to describe your document. You already know XML — what could be better?

◆ The same engines to parse XML documents can also be used to parse Schemas.

◆ Just as you can parse Schemas in the same fashion as XML, you can also add nodes, attributes, and elements to Schemas in the same manner.

◆ Schemas are widely accepted by most major parsing engines.

◆ Schemas allow you to data type with many different types. DTD only allows type content to be a string.

If you consider the test XML file we created at the beginning of this chapter, a valid Schema would be as follows:

```xml
<?xml version="1.0" encoding="UTF-8"?>
<xs:schema xmlns:xs="http://www.w3.org/2001/XMLSchema"
elementFormDefault="qualified">
  <xs:element name="AddressBook">
    <xs:complexType>
      <xs:sequence>
        <xs:element ref="Family"/>
        <xs:element ref="CoWorker"/>
      </xs:sequence>
    </xs:complexType>
  </xs:element>
  <xs:element name="CoWorker">
    <xs:complexType>
      <xs:sequence>
        <xs:element ref="FirstName"/>
        <xs:element ref="LastName"/>
        <xs:element ref="PhoneNumber"/>
      </xs:sequence>
    </xs:complexType>
  </xs:element>
  <xs:element name="Family">
    <xs:complexType>
      <xs:sequence>
        <xs:element ref="FirstName"/>
        <xs:element ref="LastName"/>
        <xs:element ref="PhoneNumber"/>
      </xs:sequence>
    </xs:complexType>
  </xs:element>
  <xs:element name="FirstName" type="xs:string"/>
  <xs:element name="LastName" type="xs:string"/>
  <xs:element name="PhoneNumber" type="xs:string"/>
</xs:schema>
```

At a casual glance, you can see that references are made to Family and CoWorker elements. Within these elements, you make references to FirstName, LastName, and `PhoneNumber`. These are the elements that are allowed to appear within each of the `Family` and `CoWorker` nodes. At the end of your Schema, you've actually defined what variable types each of these items can or must contain (that is, `String`). This is a very simple example, and you could delve in deeper and add constraints on the maximum number of records and so forth.

Many parsing engines allow you to specify Schemas for validation. Not only can you do this, but you can also include references to the Schema within the original XML file. To accomplish this, you could simply change line 2 of your XML file as follows:

```
<AddressBook xmlns:xsi="http://www.w3.org/2001/XMLSchema-instance"
xsi:noNamespaceSchemaLocation="C:\ContactSchema.xsd">
```

This tells your XML parser that the current file has a Schema associated with it and that the following XML should abide by the rules contained within that Schema.

XPath expressions

XPath is a method for searching an XML document based on node objects. XPath was developed to behave very similarly to that of a URL. By specifying a hierarchical path, information subsets can be returned from that XML. Not only can XPath expressions return subsets of information, they can perform mathematical functions on the data, much like Excel, and return totals, for example.

EXTENDING THE ADDRESS BOOK

To demonstrate the easy of use of XPath, you're going to add some functionality to your Address Book application. Open up the Address Book with the Form Designer by double-clicking Form1 in the Solution Explorer. Once you're there, double-click on Form1 because you'll need to add an additional button. Next to your Add Contact button, add a button and change the Text property to Last Names. Set the `Anchor` property for this button to `Bottom, Right`. Figure 8-8 contains your interface with the new button.

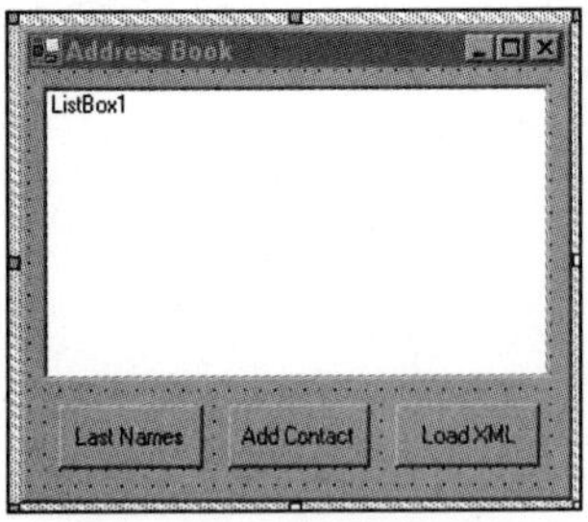

Figure 8-8: Last Names allows us to search using XPath.

Now that your visual interface is complete, you can start writing some code. Double-click on the Last Names button to get to a code window. Add the following declarations to the top of your Button3 click event:

```
Dim XD As XmlDocument = New XmlDocument()
Dim XNL As XmlNodeList
Dim XRE As XmlElement
Dim LastNames As XmlNode
```

You are first declaring a new XML document to hold the file that you're opening via your OpenFileDialog. The XmlNodeList that you declare will hold the list of items that are returned from our XPath expression. XRE is the root element of your XML document and the starting point of your search. You declare an XmlNode variable for iterating through all your search items once XPath has done its magic.

As you did in our Add Contact routines, this will rely on the user first loading the XML file with the Load XML button first. After the user has loaded the XML file, this routine can then retrieve the name of the XML file from the OpenFileDialog control. Insert the following code into the event handler just below the declarations:

```
XD.Load(OpenFileDialog1.FileName)
XRE = XD.DocumentElement
XNL = XRE.SelectNodes("/AddressBook/Family")
```

Using the Load method of your XmlDocument class, you load the document previously referenced by the Load XML button. Your XRE variable must contain the root element of your XML file, which is used as a starting point for our search. To retrieve the root element, you immediately set XRE to the DocumentElement property of your XmlDocument class. The SelectNodes method is where we actually pass in the XPath expression that you wish to use.

If you open the Address Book XML file with Notepad, you'll notice that the document root is called AddressBook. When using XPath expressions, you must abide by the hierarchy of the document. Therefore, you're telling our SelectNodes method that you're looking for all Family records under the AddressBook node. If you wanted to look up CoWorker information, you would pass in the following XPath expression:

```
/AddressBook/CoWorker
```

Alternatively, you could view all data within the file by just passing in /AddressBook as your expression. Also keep in mind that you're allowed to use wildcards within this expression, which makes it extremely versatile. The expression you're currently passing in is just for demonstration purposes and you'll return to this statement to change it in a bit.

After you've selected the correct nodes using XPath, you'll want to clear out your `ListBox` on the main form and populate it with the names that you've retrieved. Insert the following code into the event handler just below the line containing the XPath expression:

```
ListBox1.Items.Clear()
For Each LastNames In XNL
   ListBox1.Items.Add(LastNames.InnerText)
Next
```

Using a `For...Each` statement, you can loop through all items within your XNL collection and display them in our `ListBox`.

TESTING THE XPATH FUNCTIONALITY

Run the Address Book application and click the Load XML button. After you've selected the data file and the names and phone numbers have been displayed, click the Last Names button. The results you see will vary depending on whether you've added any information into your address book. Figure 8-9 shows the results.

Figure 8-9: XPath has returned all text
items from our XML files Family node.

Your address book has returned a list of everyone under your `Family` node and displayed their First Name, Last Name, and Phone Number concatenated together. There are ways to avoid this type of behavior, and this was done simply to demonstrate the behavior of your expression.

For example, let's say you want to know how many last names make up your family tree. If you've entered in everyone from you mother's side of the family, your father's, and even your spouse's, you would undoubtedly see a very large list of last names. To do this, you need to modify our expression to just include last names and disregard the first name and phone number. Change your XPath expression to `/AddressBook/Family/LastName`. The actual code should now read as follows:

```
XNL = XRE.SelectNodes("/AddressBook/Family/LastName")
```

Once you've changed the line of code, try your application again. You'll notice that only the last names of everyone under your `Family` node have been returned from the XML file.

You may want to think of XPath expressions much like `Select` statements in the database world. They allow you to search and define sets of data, perform calculations on those sets, as well as take only the selected data, manipulate it, and feed it back out to the XML file.

XML DataSets

The `DataSet` is a brand-new item to .NET. Though this item is technically part of ADO.NET, I cover it here because of its importance to XML and database programming. The `DataSet` is a representation of data that's stored entirely in memory of the computer. It contains tables, columns, constraints, and relationships among the tables. `DataSets` were created with a goal of adding an unprecedented level of XML support. This was done by designing it hand-in-hand with the XML Framework.

`DataSets` can read and write XML. This is done either behind the scenes using the XML Framework parser or by passing in a `XmlTextReader`. For XML writing tasks, the XML Framework well-formed writer is used. The `DataSet` is not only capable of writing out its data in XML, but also the Schema so the data can be validated. The Schema is encoded using W3C standards, also known as *XSD,* and the data is stored as XML that conforms to that Schema.

The `DataSet` uses XML as its primary means of serialization, which makes it an excellent choice for moving data between tiers in a disconnected fashion. Because it's disconnected, you won't have to worry about using up Database connections while the data is transported and perhaps even manipulated. When you're done with the data, it's returned to the `DataSet`, where it can be merged back into the database and all changes committed.

USING DATASETS

To demonstrate the power of `DataSets`, you're going to build an application that stores snippets of code. This application should allow the user to enter in a name for the snippet and Rich Text for the actual code so it can be properly formatted. The main interface should display the name of all stored code snippets, and when a name is clicked, the actual code should be displayed.

To begin, create a new Windows Application project and name it `CodeSnippets`. When the project opens, add a `MainMenu`, `SaveFileDialog`, and an `OpenFileDialog` to the project. You'll also need to add a `ListBox` and a `RichTextBox` to the project. The properties for the controls are shown in Table 8-2.

TABLE 8-2   CONTROLS NEEDED FOR THE CODE SNIPPET INTERFACE

Control	Name	Text	Anchor
ListBox	lstSnipList	Empty	Top,Left,Right
RichTextBox	rtbCodeSnipDetail	Empty	Top,Botton,Left,Right
Menu	mnuFile	&File	N/A
Menu	mnuOpen	&Open	N/A
Menu	mnuNew	&New	N/A
Menu	mnuExit	E&xit	N/A
Menu	mnuOptions	&Options	N/A
Menu	mnuAddSnippet	&Add Snippet	N/A

When you've completed this step, ensure that the controls are arranged similar to those in Figure 8-10. Ensure that the menu items Open, Save, and Exit are all submenu items of File and that the Add Snippet menu item is a subitem of the Options menu.

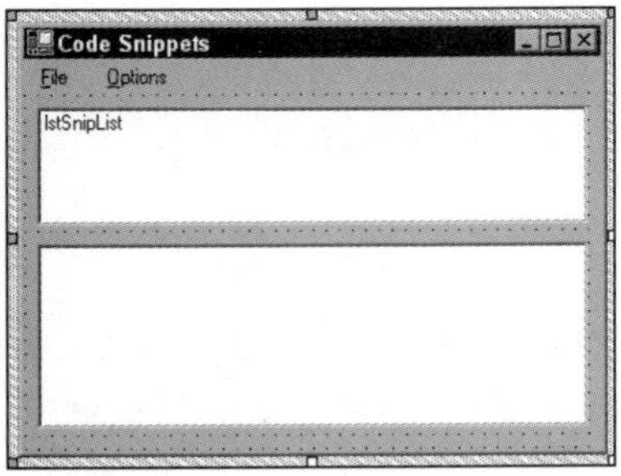

Figure 8-10: The code snippet interface takes shape.

Your snippet application will also need a form in which the user can enter new records. Click the Project menu and then select Add Windows Form. On the Add New Item window, select Windows Form and click Open. On this form, you'll need to add two labels, a text box, a rich text box, and two buttons. The buttons on this form should be called btnCancel and btnOK, with their Text properties set to Cancel and OK, respectively. The text box on this form should have a name of txtSnippetName, and the RichTextBox should be named rtbCode. Set the Text properties for the Labels to Name and Code Snippet. Arrange the items on this form to that shown in Figure 8-11.

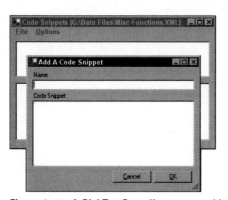

Figure 8-11: A RichTextBox allows us to add
formatted and highlighted code.

Finally, you should set the Anchor Property of the TextBox to Top,Left,Right
and the Anchor Property of the RichTextBox to Top,Bottom,Left,Right. You
want the RichTextBox to expand with the window so the code you place here can
be viewed at a presentable size; the TextBox for the snippet name should only
expand horizontally with the form. Set the Anchor properties for your two buttons
to Bottom,Right and then you can begin coding.

This form will have to contain two public member variables. These variables are
used to pass the snippet name and the actual code back to the main interface for
processing. Double-click on the OK button to get to a code window. At the top of
the code listing just below the statement that begins with Inherits.System.
Windows.Forms.Form, place the following lines of code:

```
Public SnippetName As String
Public SnippetCode As String
```

With that in place, you're ready to place some functionality behind your OK button. Scroll back down the code window until you reach the event handler that was
created when you double-clicked your OK button. Add the appropriate lines of code
to this handler, as shown here:

```
Private Sub btnOK_Click(ByVal sender As System.Object, ByVal e As
System.EventArgs ) Handles btnOK.Click
    Me.SnippetName = txtSnippetName.Text
    Me.SnippetCode = rtbCode.Rtf
    Me.Hide()
End Sub
```

Here you simply assign the values of the TextBox and the RichTextBox into your
public member variables. As you can see, instead of returning the Text property of
your RichTextBox, you're returning the Rtf property. This is actually the raw Rich

Text representing the content of the control. You're using rich text because the code can be stored formatted, in multiple fonts and with color. Don't be fooled as you're typing because IntelliSense will not show you that Rtf is a valid property for the control, but rest assured that it is.

Return to your Form Designer by double-clicking Form2 in the Solution Explorer. When your form appears, double-click on the Cancel button. This will take you to the Click event handler of that button. Here you want to accomplish almost exactly what you did with the OK button, except that you want to make sure all the member variables are cleared out. This will ensure that when you return to the main form, you don't add any leftover data to your DataSet. Add the following code to this event handler:

```
Private Sub btnCancel_Click(ByVal sender As System.Object, ByVal e As
System.EventArgs) Handles btnCancel.Click
    Me.SnippetName = ""
    Me.SnippetCode = ""
    Me.Hide()
End Sub
```

You can now begin to add code to your main interface. Double-click on Form1 in the Solution Explorer to open that form in the Form Designer. When you're in the Form Designer, then click on the File menu you added to this application. When the menu drops down, double-click on the New menu item that was added.

When the code window opens up, you'll need to create several public variables that are available to the entire Form1 class. Scroll to the top of the code window and add the following code just below the statement that says Inherits System.Windows.Forms.Form:

```
Dim dsCodeDataSet As New DataSet()
Dim drCodeDataRow As DataRow
Dim dtCodeTable As DataTable
Dim DataFile As String
```

You'll cover each of these variables as you encounter them throughout the rest of this project. For now, scroll back down to the event handler that was created when you double-clicked the New menu item.

The New menu item will allow you to create a new DataSet file, and a file containing the Schema for this DataSet. The first thing you must do is set the properties of your SaveFileDialog. Add the following code to the mnuNew_Click event handler:

```
SaveFileDialog1.Title = "Create a New Snippet DataSet"
SaveFileDialog1.DefaultExt = ".XML"
SaveFileDialog1.Filter = "XML DataSets (*.XML)|*.xml"
SaveFileDialog1.ShowDialog()
```

As you can see, you set the Title of your SaveFileDialog, a default extension to use in the event that the user doesn't type one in with the filename, and a filter to show only XML files. After you've done all this, you show the dialog. The user can now type in a filename that code snippets will be saved to. You're taking this approach and allowing different data files to be created and opened rather than creating one file, because you may want to separate out code snippets into what operations they perform (that is, Data Related, String Manipulation, and so on).

You now need to make sure a name was entered and then create the DataSet and save both files out to disk. Add the following code just below what you already added to this event handler:

```
If SaveFileDialog1.FileName <> "" Then
  dtCodeTable = New DataTable("Snippets")
  dtCodeTable.Columns.Add("Name", GetType(String))
  dtCodeTable.Columns.Add("Code", GetType(String))
  dsCodeDataSet.Tables.Add(dtCodeTable)
  dsCodeDataSet.WriteXmlSchema(SchemaName( SaveFileDialog1.FileName ))
  dsCodeDataSet.WriteXml(SaveFileDialog1.FileName)
  Me.Text = "Code Snippets (" & SaveFileDialog1.FileName & ")"
  DataFile = SaveFileDialog1.FileName
End If
```

After you've verified the existence of a filename, you must create a new table in this DataSet. You're going to call your table Snippets. After your table has been created, you're free to add columns to this table. Your table need only have two columns: Name and Code. You add these columns with the following lines of code, that were just added to your application:

```
dtCodeTable.Columns.Add("Name", GetType(String))
dtCodeTable.Columns.Add("Code", GetType(String))
```

The syntax here is obvious. You call the Add method of our Columns collection and pass the name of the column and the type of column. In this particular example, they are both Strings. After both of the columns have been added, you must call the Add method of your Tables collection to add your new table and columns to the DataSet.

Your DataSet now contains a table and columns, everything you need to start storing data. Now you must write this DataSet and its corresponding Schema out to disk so you can begin using it, as seen here:

```
dsCodeDataSet.WriteXmlSchema(SchemaName( SaveFileDialog1.FileName ))
dsCodeDataSet.WriteXml(SaveFileDialog1.FileName)
```

The first line of this code calls the `WriteXmlSchema` method of your `DataSet` object. As you may have already noticed when you typed this code in, the function `SchemaName` is not recognized. This function simply takes the name of your `DataSet` XML file, trims off the extension (.XML), and appends on DataSet.xsd. We're using this function because we want both filenames to correspond to each other and you remove the XML extension so when the user is browsing for a data file, they won't see the Schema as well as the actual data. Scroll down to the bottom of your code window and add the following function just before the line that says `End Class`:

```
Private Function SchemaName(ByVal Filename As String) As String
   Dim PartialName As String
   PartialName = Filename.Remove(Len(Filename) - 4, 4)
   Return PartialName & "DataSet.xsd"
End Function
```

Now that you have the `SchemaName` function taken care of, your New menu item will work. But before you test it out, there are a few other lines of code that you didn't cover in that section of code. After both the `Schema` and `DataSet` have been closed, you're taking the name of the file and changing the `Text` property of your main interface to show the name of this data file. This is to remind the users which file they're actually using. After you've set that `Text` property, you assign the data filename to a public variable called `DataFile` that you created earlier. The reasoning for this will become evident very shortly.

You're now able to create a `DataSet` XML file. Press F5 to start your application. When the program runs, click on the File menu and select New. Find an appropriate spot for your data file and give it a name. When you click the Save button, you will be back at your main interface and you'll notice that the filename and path for the `DataSet` appears in the title bar of the application, as shown in Figure 8-12.

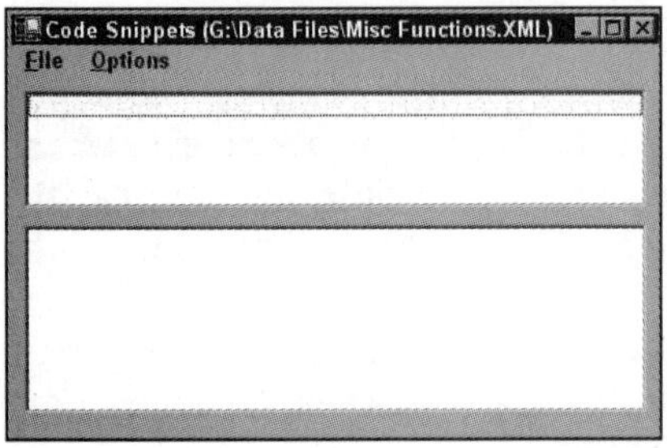

Figure 8-12: The XML DataSet appears in the title bar as a reminder.

EXAMINING OUR DATASET

Before we move on, let's take a look at what exactly we just accomplished. Using Notepad, open up the Schema file that was just created by your application. This file will have an extension of .XSD and will be located in the same place you created the XML `DataSet` file. Here are the contents of that Schema file:

```
<?xml version="1.0" standalone="yes"?>
<xsd:schema id="NewDataSet" targetNamespace="" xmlns=""
xmlns:xsd="http://www.w3.org/2001/XMLSchema" xmlns:msdata="urn:schemas-
microsoft-com:xml-msdata">
  <xsd:element name="NewDataSet" msdata:IsDataSet="true">
    <xsd:complexType>
      <xsd:choice maxOccurs="unbounded">
        <xsd:element name="Snippets">
          <xsd:complexType>
            <xsd:sequence>
              <xsd:element name="Name" type="xsd:string" minOccurs="0" />
              <xsd:element name="Code" type="xsd:string" minOccurs="0" />
            </xsd:sequence>
          </xsd:complexType>
        </xsd:element>
      </xsd:choice>
    </xsd:complexType>
  </xsd:element>
</xsd:schema>
```

Toward the center of this Schema file, you'll see definitions for your columns. They define the column names, the column types, and the minimum number of occurrences that are allowed within our XML file. Just above those two lines, you'll see the name of your Table as well. This is a very straightforward Schema definition and would be much more complex if you would've added multiple tables or even constraints.

You're free to open up the actual `DataSet` XML file in Notepad as well, but at this point there are only a few lines, because you haven't actually added any data.

OPENING DATASETS

You could very well add data to your `DataSet` immediately after you use it, but then there would be no way of viewing that data once you closed the application. To solve this, you must now add some logic to your Open menu item. Return to the Form Designer by double-clicking on Form1 in the Solution Explorer. Now double-click on the Open menu item to return to a code window, in the event handler for this menu item.

Your Open menu item is almost identical to the New menu item with three exceptions:

♦ You don't have to define the table name and column names, because they already exist.

♦ You don't have to save any XML out to disk, because the file already exists, when it was created with the New menu item.

♦ At the end of this method, you must assume there is data in the file and therefore attempt to load that data and show it in your ListBox.

Add the following code to the mnuOpen_Click event handler:

```
OpenFileDialog1.Title = "Open a Snippet Dataset"
OpenFileDialog1.Filter = "XML DataSets (*.XML)|*.xml"
OpenFileDialog1.ShowDialog()
If Openfiledialog1.filename <> "" Then
  dsCodeDataSet.ReadXmlSchema(SchemaName(OpenFileDialog1.FileName))
  dsCodeDataSet.ReadXml(OpenFileDialog1.FileName)
  Me.Text = "Code Snippets (" & OpenFileDialog1.FileName & ")"
  DataFile = OpenFileDialog1.FileName
  LoadSnippetNames()
End If
```

As you experienced before, you're referencing a method that doesn't yet exist — LoadSnippetNames. Scroll to the bottom of your code window and add the following method just below the SchemaName function:

```
Private Sub LoadSnippetNames()
  lstSnipList.Items.Clear()
  dtCodeTable = dsCodeDataSet.Tables!Snippets
  For Each drCodeDataRow In dtCodeTable.Rows
    lstSnipList.Items.Add(drCodeDataRow!Name)
  Next
End Sub
```

This method serves one purpose and one purpose only: to look at all records in your DataSet and add the name of every code snippet to your ListBox. You're doing this because you want to present the user with a list of all available snippets. They can then click on a snippet name in the list and your application will then present the actual code within the RichTextBox.

As you can see, you first clear out the contents of the ListBox using the Clear method of your Items collection. Then, using the following code, you define out DataTable by using the Tables collection of your DataSet and passing in the Table name.

```
dtCodeTable = dsCodeDataSet.Tables!Snippets
```

The For...Each command will loop through all items contained within the Rows collection and return every piece of data. At this point, you're only interested in the Name column, so you add only that to the ListBox.

Your Code Snippet application can now save, open, and search DataSet files. You still haven't provided the functionality to actually view code once a Snippet Name has been selected. To do this, return to the Form Designer by double-clicking Form1 in the Solution Explorer. Once in the form designer, double-click on the ListBox you added to the top of the form. Double-clicking on the list box will take you to the SelectedIndexChanged event handler. This event is fired every time a user clicks on an item in the list box. It's from here that you can look at the item selected and search your DataSet for the corresponding code to display on the screen. Add the following code for this event:

```
dtCodeTable = dsCodeDataSet.Tables!Snippets
For Each drCodeDataRow In dtCodeTable.Rows
   If drCodeDataRow!Name = lstSnipList.SelectedItem Then
     rtbCodeSnipDetail.Rtf = drCodeDataRow!Code
   End If
Next
```

This is very similar to the LoadSnippetName that you created earlier. You define your table and then use a For...Each control statement to loop through the rows of information. Now, though, you're comparing the name of each code snippet with that which was selected in your ListBox. When a match is found, you assign the value of the Code column to your RichTextBox Rtf property. This will show the code snippet with all the proper formatting as when it was originally saved.

Some enhancements could be made to this method because after a match is found, it continues to search all rows. If the DataSet is very large, you may notice a bit of a lag in the program. It would be best to jump out of this routine once a match was located, but the current implementation will serve your purposes for now.

That just leaves some code to actually open your Add a Code Snippet window. Return to the Form Designer of Form1 and double-click the Add Snippet menu item. Here you must create an instance of Form2 and then display it modally. To do this, add the following code to this event:

```
Dim AddWin As New Form2()
AddWin.ShowDialog()
```

Once the user has opened the form, added some data and clicked either OK or Cancel, you'll need to check one of the member variables of that class — you'll check the `SnippetName` variable. If you recall, you added code to the Cancel button to clear out all variables. This would prevent the application from saving data when the user actually wanted to Cancel out of the form. Add the rest of this code to the event handler as well:

```
If AddWin.SnippetName <> "" Then
    dtCodeTable = dsCodeDataSet.Tables!Snippets
    drCodeDataRow = dtCodeTable.NewRow()
    drCodeDataRow!name = AddWin.SnippetName
    drCodeDataRow!code = AddWin.SnippetCode
    dtCodeTable.Rows.Add(drCodeDataRow)
    dsCodeDataSet.WriteXml(DataFile)
    LoadSnippetNames()
End If
```

You've ensured that data is being returned so you can define the table you want to use with the `Tables` collection, which you're already familiar with. In the following lines, which you just added, you call the `NewRow` method indicating that you wish to add data, and then you assign the values of those public variables to the Name and Code columns.

```
drCodeDataRow = dtCodeTable.NewRow()
drCodeDataRow!name = AddWin.SnippetName
drCodeDataRow!code = AddWin.SnippetCode
```

You can now add the row to your `DataTable` and then write the XML out to file using the `WriteXml` method of the `DataSet` object. Earlier, you assigned the name and path of your data file to a public variable, which you use here. You had to make that assignment, because at this point in your program, you don't know if the user just created the `DataSet` using the New menu item or if they opened an existing one. Without this information, you wouldn't know to look to the `SaveFileDialog` or the `OpenFileDialog` control for the appropriate filename and path.

After the XML has been written out, you need to refresh the `ListBox` to update any code snippets that have been added. To do this, you call `LoadSnippetNames`. You can now press F5 to give the program a test run.

TESTING THE CODE SNIPPETS APPLICATION

If you didn't create a `DataSet` file earlier during testing, do so now with the New menu item. If you already have one, simply use the Open menu item and locate the file. When you've located a file or created one and the name is displayed in the title bar, click on the Options menu and select Add Snippet. When the window appears, give your code snippet a name and either cut and paste some code from Visual Basic .NET into the `RichTextBox` or enter some in, as shown in Figure 8-13.

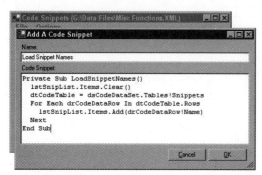

Figure 8-13: Give this snippet a name and use Rich Text to store it.

I've entered in a function that you used within this program. When you have the name and code in, click OK. When you return to the main interface, you'll see your code snippet listed at the top of the window. Click on the name and the code will appear in the RichTextBox at the bottom, as shown in Figure 8-14.

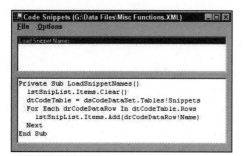

Figure 8-14: Search and display XML items when clicking in the ListBox.

Summary

The example provided in this chapter is just a basic overview of DataSets. They are not only very flexible, but they are also powerful and easy to use. XML makes up the transport mechanism for DataSets, which makes building other tiers, such as Web interfaces, very easy. When you've acquired knowledge on the new ASP.NET, test yourself by building a Web front-end to this application.

Part IV

Tying It All Together

Chapter 9

Developing Applications in Visual Basic .NET

IN THIS CHAPTER

- ◆ Working with projects and solutions
- ◆ Creating reusable class libraries
- ◆ Creating Windows applications
- ◆ Creating Web applications
- ◆ Creating console applications
- ◆ Creating Windows controls
- ◆ Creating Windows services
- ◆ Creating Web Services
- ◆ Using the registry

In this chapter, I help you understand how to create applications based on the various project types in Visual Basic .NET. Along the way, you'll gain some insights as to when to use the various project types and how you can combine multiple project types into a single application. You'll also discover how to use some of the new tools in the development environment to make your programming tasks easier.

In this chapter, I walk you through a series of examples that are combined together to form a working sample application suite. This same application suite will be used in Chapters 10 and 11, which discuss debugging and deploying Visual Basic .NET applications.

Laying the Groundwork

When you create a new project in Visual Basic .NET, you're given many different choices and templates for project types. If these templates don't match what you need, you're free to create and use your own templates (see Chapter 15). Figures 9-1 and 9-2 show the standard Visual Basic .NET project templates that are available to you.

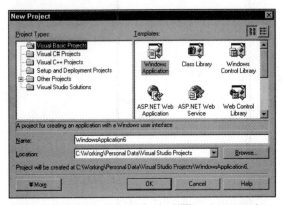

Figure 9-1: Standard Visual Basic .NET project templates.

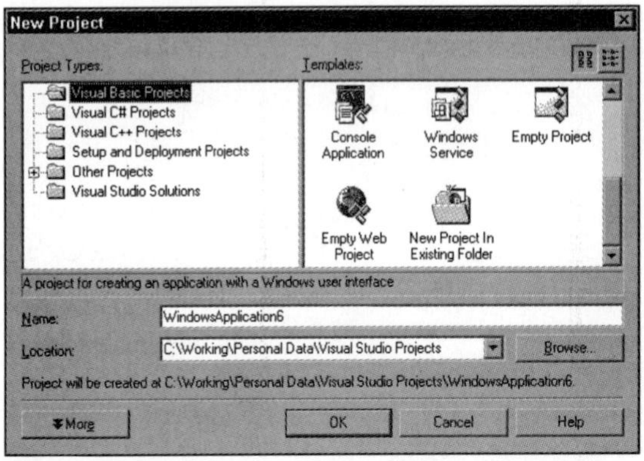

Figure 9-2: Standard Visual Basic .NET project templates.

The Windows Application, Class Library, and Windows Control Library project templates correspond to the Standard EXE, ActiveX DLL, and ActiveX Control projects respectively, in prior versions of Visual Basic. These three project types are the only ones that have a direct ancestor in prior versions. The ASP.NET Web Application is similar to an IIS Application type in Visual Basic 6, but it's much more powerful and easier to use. The ASP.NET Web Service creates a Web service similar to creating Web services with the SOAP toolkit that was available for version 6. The Console Application and Windows Service are welcome additions to the project templates in the Visual Basic language. These types of applications weren't possible in prior versions of Visual Basic without the use of third-party tools. A console application is used from the command prompt and is used for character-based user input and output when a graphical interface isn't desirable. The Windows Service project template allows you to create full-fledged native services that can run in the background and don't require a user to be logged into the machine.

Windows Application

Select the Windows Application template, change the name to `MigratingExample`, and then click the OK button. Visual Basic .NET will create a solution file of the same name and add the new project to this solution. If you look at the Solution Explorer window, you'll see two files. The first one is the standard blank form, and the second one contains information for the assembly. Open up the `AssemblyInfo.vb` file to view the contents of it. The information in this file allows you to set resource information for the assembly, which was located in the Project Properties dialog box in prior versions. You can change the information in the attributes for the assembly if you want by changing the strings associated with each attribute. You can close this file and go back to the Solution Explorer window.

In the Solution Explorer, you'll see that the form included in the project is named `Form1.vb`, which you'll want to change. However, you can't simply change the `Name` property of the form because it doesn't exist in Visual Basic .NET. Forms and classes are given the name you specify for them in the Add Item dialog boxes, but you weren't given a chance to change the name when you created the project. At this point, you have two options that will change the name of the form after it's been created. The first and easiest way to do this is to remove the form from the project and then add a new form back to the project, giving it the correct name. However, this isn't practical if you've already made changes to the form. In this case, you have to open up the code window for the form, perform a search and replace on the existing form name in the current module, and change all instances of the form name to the new name. After this is complete, you need to rename the form in the Solution Explorer by right-clicking on the form and selecting the `Rename` item from the context menu. When you rename a form in the Solutions Explorer, it automatically renames the persisted file.

The Solution Explorer in Visual Basic .NET has more capabilities for managing solutions and projects than previous versions have had. The Solution Explorer organizes and displays its contents based on the underlying directory structure of the hard drive where the files are stored. If you click the Show All Files icon at the top of the Solution Explorer, you'll see all the files located in the directory structure where the project is located. Files that aren't part of the current project file will appear as ghosted icons in the Solution Explorer window. This feature allows you to include a new file in the project by right-clicking on the file and selecting the Include In Project item from the context menu. As long as the files are located within the directory structure for the project, as they should be, it's easier to add and remove files from the project as needed by toggling the Include or Exclude menu items for the file.

In this case, you haven't made any changes to the form yet, so you can simply delete the form from the project by right-clicking on it in the Solution Explorer and selecting the Delete item from the context menu that appears. You can then add a new form back into the project by selecting the Add Windows Form item from the Project menu. Give the form the name `frmMain.vb`, and click the Open button. The form will be added to the project and will appear in the root level of the project file. If you were to try to run the project, you'd get an error stating that the startup object is invalid. This was originally set to `Form1`, but when we removed that form from the project, the startup object became invalid. You can fix this by selecting `frmMain` from the startup object combo box in the Project Properties dialog box, as shown in Figure 9-3.

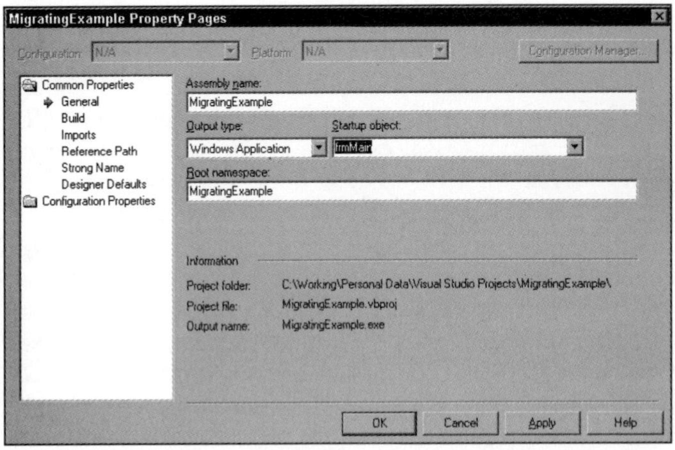

MigratingExample Property Pages

Configuration: N/A   Platform: N/A   Configuration Manager...

Common Properties
  General
  Build
  Imports
  Reference Path
  Strong Name
  Designer Defaults
Configuration Properties

Assembly name:
MigratingExample

Output type: Startup object:
Windows Application   frmMain

Root namespace:
MigratingExample

Information
Project folder: C:\Working\Personal Data\Visual Studio Projects\MigratingExample\
Project file: MigratingExample.vbproj
Output name: MigratingExample.exe

OK   Cancel   Apply   Help

Figure 9–3: Changing the startup object in the Project Properties dialog box.

Visual Basic .NET doesn't automatically organize and group the related file types for you as prior versions of Visual Basic have done. If you want to group your files by type, then you need to create folders on your hard drive in the project path that will contain the specified types of project items. After you create the folders on your hard drive and have the Show All Files option selected in the Solution Explorer, you can drag and drop the files from one location to another within the project directory.

TIP You can copy or move files between projects in a solution the same way you would if you were using Windows Explorer to manage files.

On the `frmMain` form, change the `IsMdiContainer` property to true. Any form can be an MDI container by setting this property either at design time or runtime. In Visual Basic .NET, you can have more than one MDI container form in any given project, unlike prior versions where you could only have a single MDI container form in a project.

Class Library

The next component of this application is a class library, which we will add by clicking the New Project icon on the toolbar. You'll see a dialog box that looks like the one shown in Figure 9-4.

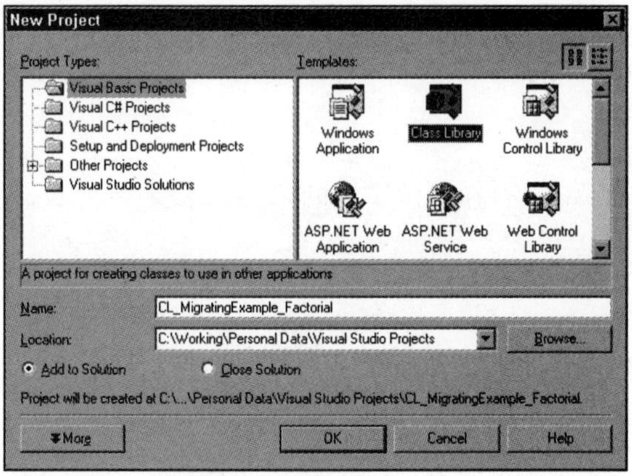

Figure 9-4: New Project dialog box.

In this dialog box, you pick the project type, give it a name, and have the option of adding the project to the current solution or closing the current solution and adding the project to a new solution. Select a class library template, give the project the name `CL_MigratingExample_Factorial`, and make sure to select the Add To Existing Solution option. Then click OK. This will add the class library to the solution file. Rename `Class1.vb` to `clsFactorial.vb` in the Solution Explorer and to `clsFactorial` in the code window. As you can see, renaming simple class files is a lot easier than renaming a form. Within the code for the class, insert the following code to return a factorial for a supplied integer value:

```
Public Function GetFactorial(ByVal Value As Integer) As Long
    If Value = 1 Then
        Return Value
    Else
        Return GetFactorial(Value - 1) * Value
    End If
End Function
```

The preceding function is a recursive function that keeps calling itself with a value of 1 less than the supplied value. When the supplied value equals 1, the function returns a value of 1, the recursion stops, and all the return values are multiplied together to calculate the factorial for the supplied number.

Now that you have the factorial function created, you need to add some controls to test it out, as shown in Figure 9-5:

1. Add a new form to the class library project and name it `frmFactorial.vb`.

2. Add two Text Boxes to the form and clear their Text properties.

3. Add a Button to the form and set its Text property to "Generate Factorial."

4. Add two Labels to the form, and set the Text properties to "Number" and "Factorial Result."

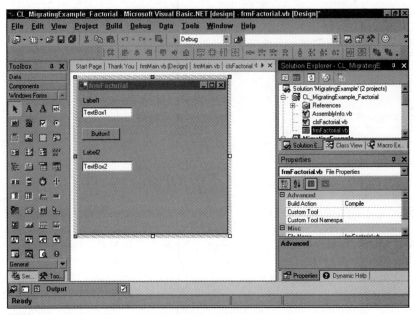

Figure 9-5: Layout of controls added to frmFactorial.

When you place controls on a form, their tab order is initially set to the order in which they're added. Visual Basic .NET makes it much easier to set the correct tab order of a form than prior versions did. If you select the Tab Order item from the View menu, you'll see numbers appear in the upper-left corner of each control, as shown in Figure 9-6.

Each time you click on the number, it cycles between the available tab order positions based on the number of controls on the form. If you start at the control that will be first in the tab order and click on each control in the correct tab order, the tab order will be correctly set for all the controls on the form. Set the tab order for the controls on this form so that it's in sequence from top to bottom. When you're done setting the tab order, click on the menu item again to turn it off.

Next, insert the following code into the click event of the button so that the factorial is calculated and displayed in the second text box:

```
Dim Factorial As New clsFactorial()

TextBox2.Text = Factorial.GetFactorial(CInt(TextBox1.Text))
```

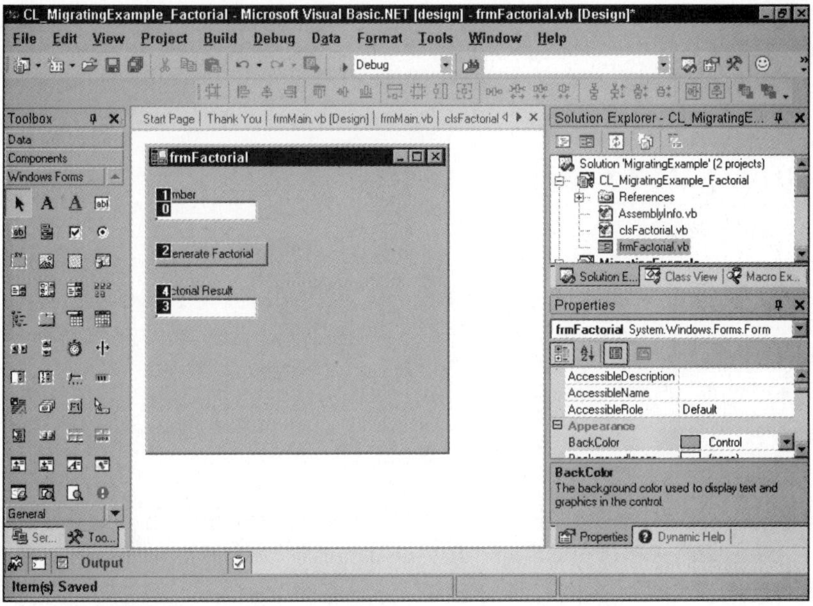

Figure 9-6: Using the tab order designer.

At this point, you have a class library that has a public class and a public form within it. The form makes a call into the class to perform the actual factorial calculation and then displays it within the second text box. Removing the functionality from the form and placing it within the class module allows it to be encapsulated and called from many different sources, as illustrated in the rest of this chapter.

Tying It Together

This section contains some ancillary information that you'll probably use when developing applications in Visual Basic .NET. When working with multiple projects in a solution, you'll need to be able to set references to the other projects so you can debug the entire application at one time. This section also describes how to work with menus and access the registry from within your application.

Referencing other projects

Switch to the Windows Application project and add a reference to the class library project by right-clicking the references folder in the Solution Explorer and selecting Add Reference. In the dialog box that appears, select the Projects tab and then select the class library containing the factorial form and class. On the frmMain MDI form, add a button to the form surface. Unlike prior versions of Visual Basic, you can now add any control to the surface of an MDI form. These controls will appear to float over the top of any forms that are placed within the MDI container at runtime. In

Visual Basic .NET, MDI forms are just like any other forms and can do anything that can be done with a regular form. Within the Click event of the button on the MDI form, insert the following code to display the factorial form that is located within the class library.

```
Dim frmFactorial As New CL_MigratingExample_Factorial.frmFactorial()

frmFactorial.Show()
```

If you run the project and click on the button on the MDI form, you'll see the factorial form displayed outside the MDI container form, fully functional. If you want to place the form within the MDI container, you simply need to insert the following line of code after you show the form:

```
frmFactorial.MdiParent = Me
```

If you were to run the project now, you would see forms similar to that shown in Figure 9-7. You can see from the figure that the factorial form is, indeed, within the MDI container and operates just like any other MDI child would operate, except that this form was created and displayed from an external reference. This type of scenario could be used to create a framework container application and then other optional features could be installed and used if they're present. This also allows an application to be split up and organized into components that contain logical groupings and separations, which would make the application more maintainable.

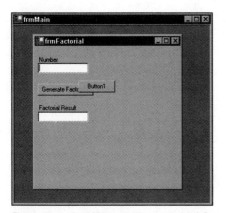

Figure 9-7: An MDI container and child form created from a class library.

Working with menus

Next you add a menu that provides some basic functionality to the application. Place a main menu control on the frmMain form and create a File menu with an

Exit submenu item on it. Right-click on the menu control and select the `Edit Names` item from the context menu. Name the menus as shown in Figure 9-8, and then clear the `Edit Names` menu selection.

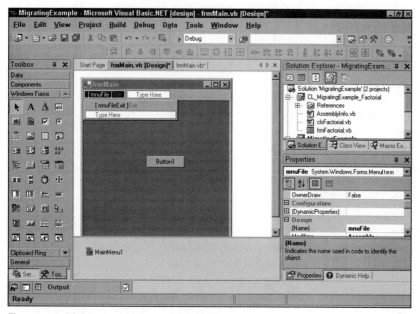

Figure 9-8: Main menu settings on frmMain.

The properties for each menu item allow you to have your menu item exhibit various behaviors such as a window list, radio check or regular checked styles, shortcuts, and so on. The menu items also have a special property called `OwnerDraw`, which when set to True, indicates that the menu will paint itself instead of allowing Windows to paint it. This allows you to create custom menu displays with special colors, fonts, and graphics. You'll learn about graphics programming in detail in Chapter 14, but the following code will show you how you can create a custom graphic for the exit menu item. Set the `OwnerDraw` property of the `mnuFileExit` menu item to True and then bring up the code window for `frmMain`. Drawing custom graphics in a menu control is a two-step process, which involves telling the system how big your menu item is going to be and then drawing the item itself. Before a menu control is drawn, the `MeasureItem` event is fired, which allows you to set the width and height of the menu item. Insert the following code into the `MeasureItem` event for the `mnuFileExit` menu item:

```
e.ItemHeight = 17
e.ItemWidth = 100
```

This tells the system that the size of your menu needs to be 17 pixels high by 100 pixels wide. These events will fire for all owner-drawn menu items and the system will automatically size the overall menu tree based on the item requiring the largest size. Next, the DrawItem event will fire, which contains an initialized graphics object that you can use to draw upon. This graphics object has its origin located at the top-left corner of the menu grouping. Top-level menus each have their own graphics containers and as a result, the origin of the File menu item and the origin of another top-level menu item such as Help would not be identical. When working with submenus, such as the menu that contains the mnuFileExit menu item, the graphics container is the same container for all the menu items in the particular submenu. As a result of this, these submenu items must have some way of knowing where they should paint their menu. This is accomplished by checking the Bounds object argument, which gives a Rectangle object that supplies this information. Insert the following code into the DrawItem event for the mnuFileExit menu item:

```
Dim GB As Drawing2D.LinearGradientBrush
GB = New Drawing2D.LinearGradientBrush(e.Bounds.Location, New _
        Point (e.Bounds.X + e.Bounds.Size.Width, _
        e.Bounds.Y), Color.Red, Color.Green)

e.Graphics.FillEllipse(GB, e.Bounds)

e.Graphics.DrawString("E X I T", New Font(Me.Font, _
        FontStyle.Bold + FontStyle.Italic), _
        New Pen(Color.White).Brush, e.Bounds.Size.Width / 2 - 23, _
        e.Bounds.Location.Y + 3)
```

You will understand what the preceding code is doing and how to expand upon this to customize the way menus are drawn when you read through Chapter 14, but for now just run the project and click on the File menu, and you should see your Custom menu displayed (see Figure 9-9).

Figure 9-9: Owner-drawn menu with custom graphics.

The next thing you do is write code to end the program when the `mnuFileExit` menu item is clicked. Open up the `Click` event for the menu item that was added and insert the following code:

```
Me.Close()
```

Using the registry

Now that you have the Windows Application running, you're going to save the position and sizes of the forms to the registry when a form closes and then restore the values from the registry the next time the form is displayed. You'll create a class that handles this behavior, because it's obviously common to any form that needs to save and restore these settings. Add a class to the Windows Application project and name the class `clsFormSettings`. The registry functions are located within the `Microsoft.Win32` namespace, so at the beginning of the class insert the following line of code to import the namespace for use within the class:

```
Imports Microsoft.Win32
```

This class is going to automatically detect when the form it's watching has been loaded and closed. In order to do this, you need to sink the events of a form object. So insert the following line of code toward the top of the class definition:

```
Private WithEvents frm As Form
```

Because the class is going to save the information to the registry, it will need to know where to save and retrieve the settings from. So add the following line of code to store this information:

```
Private strBaseRegistryKey As String
```

Next, you need to make sure that these variables are set properly in order to use the class, so you're going to create a constructor with the required parameters:

```
Public Sub New(ByVal BaseRegistryKey As String, _
    ByVal FormObject As Form)
   strBaseRegistryKey = BaseRegistryKey
   frm = FormObject
End Sub
```

The preceding constructor will establish the event sink and store the path to the registry hive when an object based on this class is created. Next you're going to add a shared read-only property to the class, which can be used to retrieve the default location of the settings in the registry. This will allow this default path to be supplied in the constructor if so desired, but it doesn't have to be and could be overridden by supplying a different registry key path.

```
Public Shared ReadOnly Property FormSettingsBaseRegKey()
    Get
        Return "Software\MigratingToVBDotNet\Example\Settings"
    End Get
End Property
```

In order to keep the registry functions together, you'll create a single function that will save and restore the settings for the form and use a directional enumerator to indicate which operation should be used. Insert the following enum after the private variable declarations at the beginning of the class definition:

```
Private Enum SaveOrRestoreOptions
    Save = 0
    Restore = 1
End Enum
```

Next, you have to create the function that will save and restore the values to the registry for the form object that the class will sink the events from.

```
Private Sub SaveOrRestoreFormSettings(ByVal SaveOrRestore As _
        SaveOrRestoreOptions)
    Dim RegKey As Microsoft.Win32.RegistryKey

    Try
        RegKey = Registry.CurrentUser.OpenSubKey(strBaseRegistryKey _
                & "\" & frm.Name, True)
        RegKey.GetValue("X", "")
    Catch
        Registry.CurrentUser.CreateSubKey(strBaseRegistryKey _
                & "\" & frm.Name)
        RegKey = Registry.CurrentUser.OpenSubKey(strBaseRegistryKey _
                & "\" & frm.Name, True)
    End Try

    Select Case SaveOrRestore
        Case SaveOrRestoreOptions.Save
            RegKey.SetValue("X", frm.Location.X)
            RegKey.SetValue("Y", frm.Location.Y)
            RegKey.SetValue("W", frm.Size.Width)
            RegKey.SetValue("H", frm.Size.Height)
        Case SaveOrRestoreOptions.Restore
```

```
            frm.Location = New Point _
                (RegKey.GetValue("X",frm.Location.X), _
                RegKey.GetValue("Y", frm.Location.Y))
            frm.Size = New Size _
                (RegKey.GetValue("W", frm.Size.Width), _
                RegKey.GetValue("H", frm.Size.Height))
    End Select
End Sub
```

The first thing the preceding function attempts to do is to open the key and read in a value. If the key isn't present, then the exception will be caught and the key will be created and then opened. Next, the function checks to see whether it should save the settings or restore them, and then performs the desired operation. Finally, the Load and Closed events have to be trapped for the form and call the SaveOrRestoreFormSettings method with the correct direction:

```
Private Sub frm_Load(ByVal sender As Object, _
        ByVal e As System.EventArgs) Handles frm.Load
    SaveOrRestoreFormSettings(SaveOrRestoreOptions.Restore)
End Sub

Private Sub frm_Closed(ByVal sender As Object, _
        ByVal e As System.EventArgs) Handles frm.Closed
    SaveOrRestoreFormSettings(SaveOrRestoreOptions.Save)
End Sub
```

At this point, the class is complete and the only thing left is to put it into operation for the forms that should exhibit this behavior. In the declarations section for frmMain, insert the following line of code to hook up the clsFormSettings object to the form:

```
Private FormSettings As clsFormSettings = New _
    clsFormSettings(clsFormSettings.FormSettingsBaseRegKey, Me)
```

Now if you were to run the project and move the frmMain form to a different position on the screen, change the size, and then close the form and run the project again, you would see that the form returns to previous size and position.

The preceding code showed you how to use the Registry to persist the size and location of a form. Although it's important to know how to use the Registry in Visual Basic .NET, you should also know that applications created in Visual Basic .NET can make use of a configuration file to persist information that isn't necessarily machine dependent. The configuration file is an XML file that can be used to persist certain information about the application and read this information when the application is launched. Chapter 11 shows you how you can use this file to your advantage when deploying applications, so the application doesn't rely on hard-coded parameters when it's compiled.

Creating Web applications

Next, you'll see how easy it is to convert your application to run as a Web application instead of a Windows application. Add a new Web Application project to your solution and give it the name `MigratingExampleWebApp`. An ASP.NET Web Application is created in basically the same manner as a regular Windows Application except that you use Web controls instead of Windows controls, and a few other programming elements such as form navigation require some changes.

When a new Web application is created, it will have a default Web form called `Webform1.aspx` just as a regular Windows application would have a default form of `Form1.vb`. Delete the default Web form and add a new Web form back to the project and name it `frmFactorial`. On this new Web form, add the same two labels, two text boxes, and a button just as you did in the Windows form. Figure 9-10 shows the `frmFactorial` form converted to a Web form with the same controls placed on it, except the controls are now Web controls.

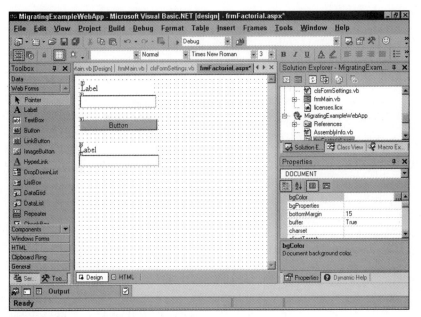

Figure 9-10: Factorial form converted to Web form.

Change the text properties of the controls using the properties window as you normally would, so they're the same as those in the `frmFactorial` Windows form. Next we need to add a reference to the class library where the factorial calculation routine is located. This is done the same way you added a reference to the class library from the Windows application. Figure 9-11 shows the references for the Web application with the Class Library project selected.

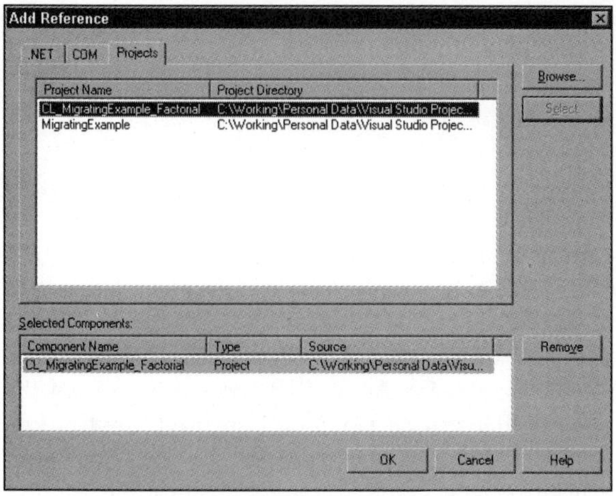

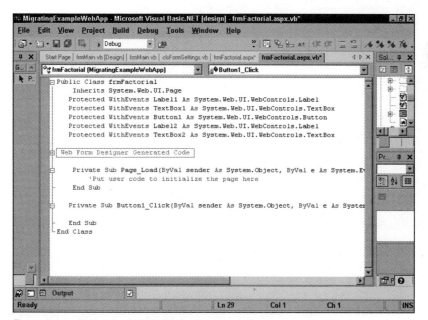

Figure 9-11: Adding reference to the Class Library project in the Web application.

Now that we have established a reference to the Class Library, we can write the code to tie the Web Form to the Class Library and generate the factorial number. If you double-click on the button on the Web form, you'll be brought into a Visual Basic code window, and its contents will look similar to what you see in Figure 9-12.

Figure 9-12: Contents of the Web form code window.

As you can see, the contents look similar to that of the code in the regular Windows form except that the base class inherits from a basic Web page object and the controls that are used come from the WebControls namespace. Insert the following code into the Click event of the button:

```
Dim Factorial As New CL_MigratingExample_Factorial.clsFactorial()

TextBox2.Text = Factorial.GetFactorial(CInt(TextBox1.Text))
```

This is the same code that was placed in the Click event of the button for the Windows form. Make the Web Application the startup project by right-clicking on it in the Solution Explorer and selecting the Set As StartUp Project item from the Context menu. The next step is to define the start page for the Web application. Right-click on the frmFactorial.aspx file and select the Set As Start Page item from the context menu. Run the project and you'll see the Web form come up in Internet Explorer; it will look like the Windows form in the Windows Application project. If you enter a number in the first text box and then click on the button, you'll see that the factorial is calculated and displayed in the second text box, as shown in Figure 9-13.

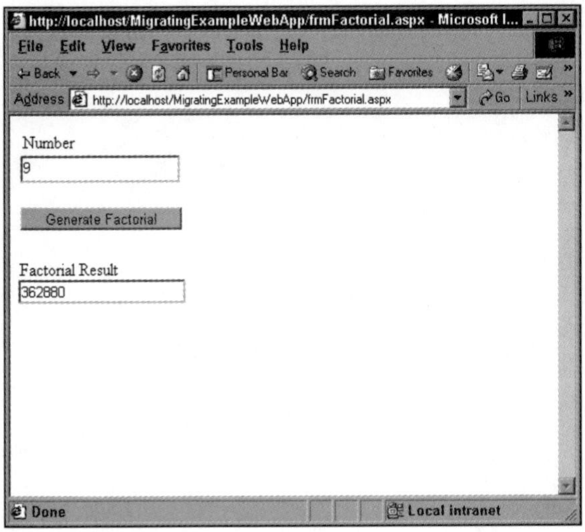

Figure 9-13: Results of running the Web form project.

The code that is displayed in the browser is pure HTML and can be verified by viewing the source for the Web page that was displayed. The Web controls are server-side controls that generate pure HTML for delivery to the client. Any code that you write in the Web form itself is actually executed on the server. You can now start to see the benefits of encapsulating the business logic for an application in class libraries. By doing this, you were able to create two different user interfaces very easily, which support the underlying business logic.

Creating console applications

At this point, you have a class library that is called from both a Windows client and a Web client, which are the two main types of user interfaces that are used to create applications today. You're going to reuse your business logic in yet another type of application that is new to Visual Basic .NET. You're going to create a command console style application that will do the same thing.

Add a new Console Application project to the solution and give it the name MigratingExampleConsoleApp. Next, add a reference to the factorial class library project as you've done in the other projects. A standard console application uses information either by using parameters supplied on the command line or by displaying and retrieving information from the user in a series of questions and answers. You're going to do both in this example, but first insert the following helper functions within the code module to eliminate duplicate code that would have to be created:

```
Private Sub DisplayFactorial(ByVal Number As Integer)
    Dim Factorial As New _
CL_MigratingExample_Factorial.clsFactorial()

    Try
        Console.WriteLine("The factorial of " & Number & _
            " is " & Factorial.GetFactorial(Number))
    Catch
        Console.WriteLine("An error occurred while trying " & _
            "to calculate the factorial of " & Number)
    Finally
        Console.WriteLine()
    End Try
End Sub

Private Sub GetEnterKey()
    Console.WriteLine("Press enter to continue...")
    Console.ReadLine()
End Sub
```

Next, insert the following code into the Sub Main procedure, which is the heart of the application:

```
Dim strCommandLine As String = Command()
```

```
If Len(Trim(strCommandLine)) > 0 Then
    Dim strCommandLineArray() As String
    Dim AnyArg As String

    strCommandLineArray = Split(strCommandLine)
    For Each AnyArg In strCommandLineArray
        Try
            DisplayFactorial(AnyArg)
        Catch
            Console.WriteLine("The supplied parameter (" & _
                AnyArg & ") was incorrect")
            Console.WriteLine()
        End Try
    Next
    GetEnterKey()

Else


    Do
     Console.Write("Enter a number to get the factorial" & _
            " or N to quit -> ")
        strCommandLine = Console.ReadLine
        If Not UCase(Trim(strCommandLine)) = "N" Then
            Try
                DisplayFactorial(CInt(strCommandLine))
            Catch
                Console.WriteLine("The supplied parameter (" & _
                    strCommandLine & ") was incorrect")
                Console.WriteLine()
            End Try
        End If
    Loop Until UCase(strCommandLine) = "N"

End If
```

The preceding code will first check to see if any command line parameters were supplied. If so, then it will use a space character as a delimiter and break out the individual factorial requests. It will then loop through each request and attempt to calculate and display the factorial for each one. When all the requests have been processed, the application will wait for the Enter key to be pressed and will then terminate because the code that is executing will have completed. You can specify command line parameters that will be used when the application is run in the development environment by opening the Project Properties dialog box, selecting the Configuration Properties folder, and clicking on the Debugging item. Enter the following parameters as command line arguments, click OK, and then run the program after setting the Console Application as the startup project:

```
9 5 7 x 4
```

You will see the familiar command prompt window appear and it will look like the command window shown in Figure 9-14. As you can see, each factorial was calculated and the results were written out to the command window.

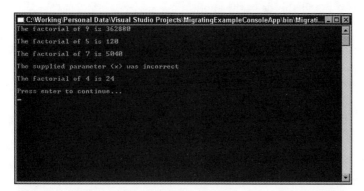

Figure 9-14: Factorial console application using command line parameters.

If there are no command line parameters supplied, then the application will request a number from the user and then attempt to display the factorial of the number. This process will continue until the user enters an N and then presses the Enter key. The command window results for running the application in this mode are shown in Figure 9-15.

Figure 9-15: Factorial console application with no command line parameters.

In prior versions of Visual Basic, you couldn't create applications that displayed results or information in the command window. You could create applications that didn't show any user interface but accepted command line parameters. But this method didn't give any feedback that the application worked or if there were any errors. With a console application, you'll see a familiar flash of the command window and then it'll go away, letting you know that everything was successful. If an error occurs, you could catch the exception and display an error message in the command window and wait for the user to acknowledge the error before exiting. In this example, the Console Application created an external object and called a function on the object so there is really no limitation as to the power that you can provide in a Console Application if it fits the needs of the application.

Creating Windows controls

When you understand the basics of inheritance and how it's used in the controls in Visual Basic .NET, you'll be able to create your own controls easier than you could in prior versions. Up until now, if you were creating an ActiveX control in Visual Basic, you either had to manually write the code for each property and then delegate the property value to the underlying control, or you could run the Interface Wizard, which would create a lot of these for you. This was true even for simple things like background and foreground colors. When creating Windows controls in Visual Basic .NET, the properties are inherited from the base control automatically. The majority of the time this will be sufficient, and you will not have to do anything more with the property. However, there may be a few times where you need to change the behavior that the base class provides. In this case, you would simply override the individual property and supply the correct behavior.

When developing Windows controls, the object browser will be invaluable to you as you figure out where each property and control are inherited from. The Windows controls in Visual Basic .NET may actually have several layers of inheritance, and you will need to at least be familiar with the base classes. Figure 9-16 shows the inheritance hierarchy for the simple text box control.

As you can see from the Figure 9-16, the text box control has five layers of inheritance before it eventually inherits from the object data type. You learned at the beginning of this book that everything in Visual Basic .NET is an object and the base data type is the object data type. You know that a text box control has a background color property, but where do you think this property originates? The answer is that it's located in the Control object. After looking at the object browser, you may also be wondering why the text box control inherits first from a TextBoxBase object. Think about what other control behaves like a text box control. Now look at the RichTextBox object and, if you expand its bases, you'll see that it also inherits from the TextBoxBase object. If you look at the VScrollBar and HScrollBar objects, you'll see that they both inherit from the ScrollBar object. Each one simply changes how the scrollbar is displayed on the form, but the behaviors and other properties are exactly the same.

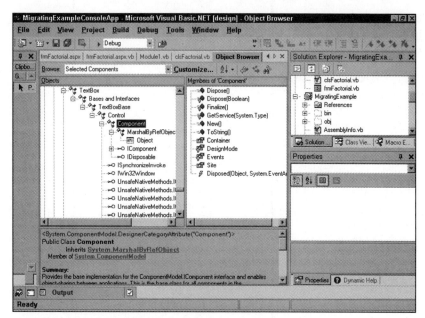

Figure 9-16: Inheritance hierarchy for text box control.

The point of the quick lesson on control inheritance is that you always need to be aware of inheritance and understand how it can be used in your own controls that you create. The example presented in this chapter walks you through creating a specialized user control that you may be able to modify and use within your applications. In this scenario, there is a requirement that all text boxes must automatically select the entire contents of the text box when the control receives focus.

With this scenario, there are three basic approaches that will satisfy the requirement. The first approach would be to write code in each text box to select the entire contents of the text box when it receives focus from tabbing to the control:

```
TextBox1.SelectAll()
```

The first thing you should notice is that this can now be accomplished in one line of code in Visual Basic .NET. You no longer need to set the start position and then the select length based on the length of the contents of the text box as in prior versions of Visual Basic. If there were only a couple of text boxes in the form or application that needed to exhibit this behavior, then this would be the most efficient approach, because it would meet the requirement in the least amount of time and effort. However, if there were an additional requirement that the solution would be used in other applications with more than a couple text box controls, this approach would not work very well, because it would require a lot of code with duplicate functionality to be written.

The next approach would be to create a class that handles these functions automatically, and this class would then be linked to the form and text box controls at runtime:

```
Public Class clsAutoSelectTextBoxes

    Private Class clsTextAutoSelect
        Private WithEvents txt As TextBox

        Public Sub New(ByVal txtBoxControl As TextBox)
            txt = txtBoxControl
        End Sub

        Private Sub txt_GotFocus(ByVal sender As Object, _
          ByVal e As System.EventArgs) Handles txt.GotFocus
            txt.SelectAll()
        End Sub
    End Class

    Private mcolTextAutoSelect As New Collection()
    Public Sub New(ByVal frm As Form)
        Dim AnyControl As Control

        For Each AnyControl In frm.Controls
            If TypeOf (AnyControl) Is TextBox Then
                mcolTextAutoSelect.Add(New _
                    clsTextAutoSelect(AnyControl))
            End If
        Next
    End Sub
End Class
```

Then, in order to establish the link at runtime, you would need to declare a module-level object variable of the clsAutoSelectTextBoxes type and then initialize it after the controls have been added to the form, which will be after the call to the InitializeComponent method in the constructor for the form:

```
Private mAutoSelectTextBoxes As clsAutoSelectTextBoxes


'Add any initialization after the InitializeComponent() call
mAutoSelectTextBoxes = New clsAutoSelectTextBoxes(Me)
```

This approach is better than the first but still requires a module-level object variable and a call to initialize the object variable in each form in the project.

The last approach would be to create a control that inherits from the text box control and provides this behavior automatically. This control would then be added to the toolbox of any project that requires it and would be used instead of the standard text box control. Because the control would inherit from the original text box control, any changes or updates to the normal text box control would also automatically appear in the new auto-select text box control. Because this section is about creating Windows controls, let's get down to business and create this specialized control that will meet the specified requirements.

The first thing you need to do is to add a Windows Control Library project to the current solution, giving it a name of MigratingExampleControlLibrary. By now, this should be of no surprise to you, but go ahead and delete the user control from the project and add a new user control to the Control Library project, giving it a name of MigratingExampleControlLibrary.vb. Next, you're going to inherit the behavior of a standard text box control, so you need to change the base class inherits statement so that it reads as follows:

```
Inherits System.Windows.Forms.TextBox
```

This will immediately change the control behavior from a generic user control to a text box control. You'll also notice that you no longer have a generic user control surface on which you can place controls. This should be obvious, but when you change the control to inherit from a text box, we lose the support for placing other visual controls on the designer surface because a text box control is not a container. You can, however, add other designer controls that don't have a user interface such as timer controls, context menus, and so on. Now in order to write the code that will fire when the control receives focus, you need to select the Base Class Events object in the top-left object combo box and then select the GotFocus event in the top-right event combo box in the code window. Insert the following line of code in this event procedure in order to have the underlying text box select its entire contents:

```
MyBase.SelectAll()
```

Next, you need to build the Windows Control Library project so that it can be added to the toolbox. After the solution has been built, bring up the Windows Application project and make it the Startup Project. Next, you'll need to add the control to the toolbox for the project. However, you won't see the MigratingExampleControlLibrary component in the listing on the .NET Framework Components tab. You'll have to first browse to the Control Library, which will be located under the Bin directory for the Windows Control Library project. After you select the library in the Browse dialog box, you'll then see the Control Library listed with the other .NET framework components, as shown in Figure 9-17. Make sure to click the check box to select the component and then click OK.

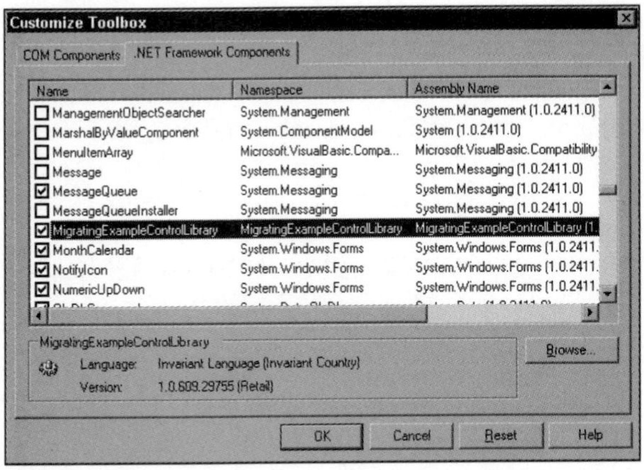

Figure 9-17: Selecting the Windows Control Library and adding it to the toolbox.

You can now bring up frmMain and if you look in the toolbox, you'll see the control appear in the toolbox with the standard user control bitmap because you didn't specify a toolbox bitmap to use. Place a couple of these controls on the surface of the frmMain form and watch how they behave. The controls look and behave just like any other text box would at design time. This is because you didn't change any of the behavior that was inherited from the text box control. You can also look at the Properties dialog box and notice that all the properties that are present in a text box control are present in the Custom Windows control you created, and you didn't have to write any code to achieve this. If you were to run the application, you'd see that these text boxes automatically select the entire contents as they receive focus, which was the intended behavior. In order to achieve this behavior in this method, only one line of code had to be created in the custom windows control. Simply placing these on the form instead of the standard text box was all that was required to implement this new behavior yet still retain all the properties and behavior of a standard text box control.

In the previous example, you just assumed that if the control was used, then it would always automatically select the contents of the text box and there was no way to disable this feature. As you're creating custom windows controls, it's always a good idea to provide a way to turn a custom feature on or off. This makes the control easier to use and doesn't limit its acceptance by other developers. So instead of just assuming that the auto-select feature will be on all the time, you should include a property that can be set to turn this feature on or off. In the code for the windows control you just created, add the following code to create and expose a property that will be used to turn the auto-select feature on or off:

```
Private mblnAutoSelectAll As Boolean

Public Property AutoSelectAll () As Boolean
    Get
```

```
        Return mblnAutoSelectAll
    End Get
    Set(ByVal Value As Boolean)
        mblnAutoSelectAll = Value
    End Set
End Property
```

Next, in the GotFocus event of the text box, change the code to read as follows, in order to check the status of this property before assuming that the contents should be selected:

```
If mblnAutoSelectAll Then MyBase.SelectAll()
```

Now build the Windows Control project and then switch back to the frmMain MDI form in the Windows Application project. Select one of the custom text box controls that are placed on the form and look at the Properties window. If you scroll to the bottom, you'll see the property located under a Misc category. In Visual Basic .NET, you can control where the property should be displayed by supplying a category attribute. Attributes are used to describe information about a piece of code and are placed before the declaration of the property or procedure. An *attribute* is a specialized class that is used to relay important information to designers and can also be read while the code is running. You're going to use a couple of attributes in the System.ComponentModel namespace, so it will be easier if you import this namespace into your code:

```
Imports System.ComponentModel
```

After the namespace has been imported, you'll add a couple of attributes to the property procedure as follows:

```
<Browsable(True), _
Description("Sets whether or not the control will automatically" & _
    " select the contents when it recieves focus"), _
Category("Behavior")> _
Public Property AutoSelectAll() As Boolean
```

Attributes are separated by commas, and in the preceding example, we defined three attributes for the property procedure. The Category attribute determines what category the property will be placed in when viewed in the object browser. The Description attribute sets the text that will be displayed at the bottom of the Properties window when the property is clicked on. This helps the developer know what the property is used for at a glance and would be the same as if you set the description in the object browser Properties dialog in prior versions. Finally, there is a browsable attribute, which determines whether the property will be visible in the

Properties window. If you were to rebuild the control library and then click on one of the controls on the main form, you'd see the Properties window, as shown in Figure 9-18.

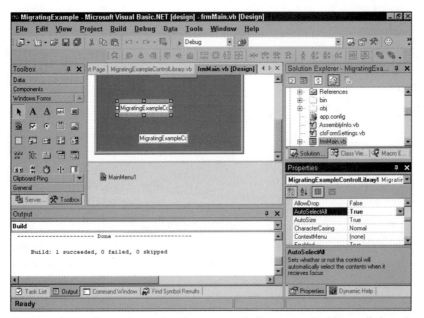

Figure 9-18: The Properties window for custom windows control with supplied attributes.

Along with the attributes, there are also a couple of other behaviors that properties will exhibit in the Properties window. First, if you right-click on a property, the majority of properties in Visual Basic .NET will have a reset item that sets the property back to its original state. You can implement this feature for the AutoSelectAll property by inserting the following code in the control:

```
Public Sub ResetAutoSelectAll()
    mblnAutoSelectAll = False
End Sub
```

For any property for which you want to implement this feature, simply create a procedure that is prefixed with the word Reset followed by the name of the property, as in the preceding example.

You may also want to serialize your property values for persistence so that any changes made in design mode are stored and then retrieved at runtime. This is similar to reading and writing the properties to a property bag object as in prior versions of Visual Basic. In order to do this, the class must be able to be serialized and the property must have a matching `ShouldSerialize` procedure similar to the reset method:

```
Public Function ShouldSerializeAutoSelectAll() As Boolean
    If mblnAutoSelectAll Then
        Return True
    Else
        Return False
    End If
End Function
```

This will only serialize and persist the property if it isn't the default value. Another nice feature in the Properties window is that you can specify a default value for a property, and if the value is not the default value, then the Properties window will display the value in bold, which lets you tell at a glance all properties that have been changed. This is accomplished by adding a `DefaultValue` attribute to the property procedure. Keep in mind that a default attribute and the default keyword are two different things. You already know that Visual Basic .NET doesn't support non-indexed default properties. The `DefaultValue` attribute simply is read and used by the Properties window to display the value in a bold or in a regular font. You can accomplish this by adding the following attribute to the end of the list of current attributes for the property:

```
DefaultValue(False)
```

If you look at the `Size` or `Location` properties, you'll see that properties in Visual Basic .NET can also be compound properties that contain other values. A `Size` property has both a `Width` and a `Height` property underneath it. If you need to create a compound property, then a few more steps are required. For this example, we're going to create a compound property called `MyCompoundProperty` and this property will have a `Color1` and a `Color2` property underneath it. The first step to creating a compound property is to create a class within the same code module for the control but outside the class definition for the control that contains the private variables, public property procedures, and the reset and serialize functions for each of the sub-properties:

```
Public Class CompoundProperty
    Private mColor1 As Color
    Private mColor2 As Color

    Public Sub New()
        mColor1 = Color.White
        mColor2 = Color.Black
    End Sub
```

```
        Public Property Color1() As Color
            Get
                Return mColor1
            End Get
            Set(ByVal Value As Color)
                mColor1 = Value
            End Set
        End Property

        Public Function ShouldSerializeColor1()
            Return True
        End Function

        Public Sub ResetColor1()
            mColor1 = Color.White
        End Sub

        Public Property Color2() As Color
            Get
                Return mColor2
            End Get
            Set(ByVal Value As Color)
                mColor2 = Value
            End Set
        End Property

        Public Function ShouldSerializeColor2()
            Return True
        End Function

        Public Sub ResetColor2()
            mColor2 = Color.Black
        End Sub
End Class
```

After the compound property class is defined, an object variable must be created in the parent class, which in this case is the class you've been working with that defines the custom windows control and the properties that we're trying to expose:

```
Private mMyCompoundProperty As CompoundProperty = New
CompoundProperty()

Public Property MyCompoundProperty() As CompoundProperty
    Get
```

```
            Return mMyCompoundProperty
        End Get
        Set(ByVal Value As CompoundProperty)
            mMyCompoundProperty = Value
        End Set
End Property

Public Function ShouldSerializeMyCompoundProperty()
        Return True
End Function

Public Sub ResetMyCompoundProperty()
        mMyCompoundProperty = New CompoundProperty()
End Sub
```

This will create the compound property called MyCompoundProperty. However, there is a small problem at this point. If you were to build the control project and then look at the properties for the control on the main form, you wouldn't get the desired results. You'd see the property name but you wouldn't see the compound sub-properties, as shown in Figure 9-19.

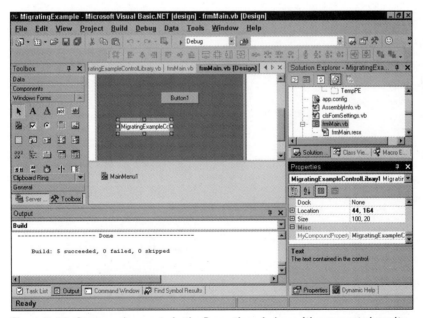

Figure 9-19: Compound property in the Properties window with unexpected results.

Why did the compound property not appear correctly? The class that was created from the compound property has to be somehow different than the control class, because normal properties appear fine in the Properties window. After several tries and some thorough research into the documentation for the .NET Framework, the light came. When you created the control class in the first place, you changed it so that it would inherit from a text box instead of a user control. I tried the concept with just using a user control and again, a normal property appeared fine in the Properties window. So there had to be something in common with these two objects and a quick look at the Object Browser proves the point. If you drill down to the base classes, you'll eventually see that each of these objects inherits from the `Component` object. After looking at the documentation for the `Component` object, the answer became obvious, because it finally stated that the `Component` provides design-time support. Open up the code for the custom control and in the `CompoundProperty` class, insert the following line of code at the top of the class and rebuild the control project:

```
Inherits Component
```

If you go back to the main form and look at the properties of the control, you'll see that the compound property now behaves as expected, as shown in Figure 9-20.

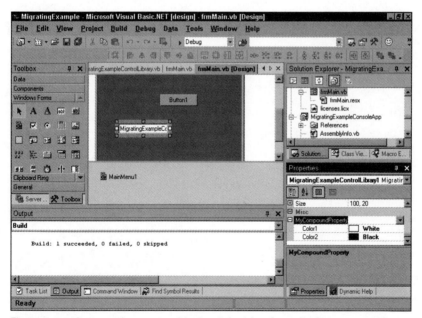

Figure 9-20: Compound property with class inheriting from the Component object.

From the previous examples, you should now know how to create custom windows controls that interact with the Properties window just like other properties on forms and controls in the .NET Framework. You can also make your property fit in any category displayed in the Properties window. If you want a new category, you simply need to specify the new category name you intend to use. Using attributes will allow you to supply specialized information about your class and procedures that can be used by the development environment as well as code that is executing at runtime. Compound properties can be used to further group related properties together in the Properties window. Compound properties not only reduce the number of properties that are displayed, they can also organize various properties into a hierarchical approach that can help other developers understand the purpose that each property is intended to be used for.

Creating Windows services

Visual Basic .NET now allows you to create native services that will run in the background without requiring a user to be logged into the computer. This wasn't possible in prior versions of Visual Basic without resorting to using specialized third-party controls or hacks. When you understand the power of services and how they can be used independently or in concert with each other, you can create applications that run as part of the operating system just like SQL Server, Exchange Server, IIS, and so on. Although there are other benefits and uses of services, the most important one is that you can now create server-side applications that can work like any of the above commercial server products.

The ability to create services completely in Visual Basic is a great feature. However, along with this capability also comes more responsibility and challenges. Services are designed to run without any user interaction, and after they're running, they should continue to operate until the operating system instructs them to quit. Because they're intended to run without any user interaction or user interface, you must follow some simple guidelines, outlined below, so your service will be reliable and maintainable:

◆ Services must have robust error handling.

◆ Services must manage resources effectively.

◆ Services should never try to interact directly with a user.

◆ Services need to use the Event Log to communicate their status.

◆ Services should make use of Performance Counters.

◆ Services that are configurable should have a separate maintenance applet.

Each of the preceding items will be discussed in turn, but they all share a common purpose, which is to make the service reliable and easy to use. The first two items in the list are the most important features that need to be included when creating a service application. Services must account for unknowns by including robust error handling. Without robust error handling, an error could cause the service to crash or stop responding. You've probably come across a few services in your work that weren't as stable as they should've been. Servers and server software are intended to run uninterrupted, 24 hours a day, 365 days a year. For some companies, every minute a server is down costs them a certain amount of revenue. These companies demand that everything on the server is as robust as possible so they minimize the server downtime. In order for a service to be reliable, there must be provisions to catch and gracefully handle any errors that may occur.

Although services also run on workstations, the majority of them are intended to run on a server. As such, services must play nicely in the sandbox with the other services. If a service that you create consumes so much memory that the operating system is forced to start swapping applications in and out of the page file, the entire server will come to a crawl. Other resources that your application must manage effectively are disk and CPU activity. The reason your application was created was to perform some unit of work on the server, so you can't eliminate CPU activity. If your service reads anything from persistent storage, you can't eliminate disk activity either. When developing services, you must constantly think about the consequences on the three main resources of memory, CPU utilization, and hard-disk activity. Balancing these resource usages is the key to creating services that perform well on their own and also work well with other services. A single server may service hundreds of clients, and if your application causes the performance of the server to suffer, you are affecting all these clients as well. Contrast this to a single desktop application where if the application ties up the computer, it only affects the current user.

The next thing to realize when designing services is that they never should try to interact directly with the user. Services start when the operating system starts, even if there is no user logged on. Services are also typically run on a server, which is locked up in a server room and probably doesn't have someone sitting in front of it to respond to any prompts, even if they were to appear on the screen. Services typically run under the system account unless otherwise specified. As a result, you need to be aware of any permissions issues that may arise when accessing resources on the local server or across the network, such as trying to log onto a database server using NT authentication. Because services aren't intended to interact directly with a user, you must rely on other means to convey information about the status and performance of your service. The best way to convey status information about your service, including any errors that have occurred, is to log this status information to the Event Log. On well-managed servers, a network administrator will either review the logs regularly or use tools that monitor the logs on several computers and notify them if an error occurs. Up until now, using the Event Log within Visual Basic was limited unless you used a third-party tool or wrote a component that handled the memory allocation and management required to log events to the Event Log. Visual Basic

.NET introduces event log controls and objects that can be used to read and write to the event logs maintaining complete control over all the information that is supplied to the log. Along with the Event Log, which is used to primarily indicate status information, services typically use performance counters to communicate performance information about the service. Performance information could include number of items processed, time to complete processing, number of users, or just about any other performance metric you could think of. Again, Visual Basic .NET provides controls and objects that let you create and manage performance counters specific to your application.

Some services may need to be configurable while others do not. You may need to control the number of threads, workers, or other variables that can be used to fine-tune your application to obtain the best performance for the computer on which it's running. The easiest way to accomplish this is to have the service read its configuration information in on startup from the registry, an external file, or an external database server. For performance reasons, you would typically read this file in when the service starts and cache any required information for the life of the service. This configuration information doesn't typically change and it would be a waste of resources to constantly read the information in while the service is running. Most services require that they be stopped and restarted when changing configuration information. Depending on the requirements, you could write a separate application that handles the configuration information, or you could simply rely on a standard editor to change the information in its native format. Along with the configuration information, you may need to create a custom monitor application that could be used to display status and performance information about your service by reading the performance counters, service status, or other information specific to your service. For this application, you may create an application that runs in the system tray and displays at a glance information for the status of the service. This application could be either on the same computer as the service is installed on, or it could be installed on a remote computer and be used to communicate with the service remotely so it isn't required to physically be at the computer where the service is running.

Now that you understand some of the requirements for services, you can create a simple service application that ties in to the other projects in our solution. You'll create a service that accepts and processes requests from a client application that you'll create as well. The service will use the Event Log and performance counters to relay information back to the same client for simplicity about the status of the service. As you've probably already guessed, the service will accept requests for factorial calculations and return the results back to the client.

The first step is to add a new Windows Service project to your solution and name it `MigratingFactorialService`. You'll see a designer surface for `Service1`. This isn't your desired name, so from previous experience, you'd be tempted to remove this from the project and add it back in with the correct name. However, you don't have a choice to add a service to the project, so in this case you'll need to rename the file in the Solution Explorer to `FactorialService.vb` and then open up the code window and perform a search and replace changing `Service1` to `FactorialService`. You also need to update the startup object for this project to reflect the change. If you look at the code, you'll see some initialization code and an `OnStart` and `OnStop` events. These two events are where you place code to get the service working and then complete any cleanup tasks when the service ends. If you look at the `OnStart` event, you'll see that it provides a string array of any arguments that are passed into the service. If you look at the properties for a service that isn't started, you'll see that you can supply startup parameters to the service. These parameters will then be supplied in the arguments array. The majority of services don't have any startup parameters but use configuration files or registry settings that will supply any information that's needed.

The first thing you want to do in your service is log information to the Event Log that the service has started. Insert the following code in the `OnStart` event for the service to indicate that the service started:

```
Dim Log As EventLog = New EventLog("Application")
Log.Source = "Migrating Factorial Service"
Log.WriteEntry("Factorial Service Starting", _
        EventLogEntryType.Information, 1234)
```

You also want to know when the service was stopped, so insert the following code — which is almost the same as the preceding code, except the message and event ID have changed — into the `OnStop` event:

```
Dim Log As EventLog = New EventLog("Application")
Log.Source = "Migrating Factorial Service"
Log.WriteEntry("Factorial Service Stopping", _
        EventLogEntryType.Information, 1234)
```

If you were to set the service project as the startup project and run the application, you would see a message box appear with error information, as shown in Figure 9-21.

Figure 9-21: Service start failure message.

A service cannot be run from within a debugger, so it must be compiled and then installed. The `InstallUtil.exe` is located in the .NET Framework folder in the operating system directory; a search will locate it for you. Copy this to the binary folder for the service project, so you can install the service without having to specify the entire path for either the installer or the assembly. If you were to run the installer on the assembly, you'd see that the install did not complete because there were no public installers in the project. Installers are required for certain components such as event logs, performance monitors, services, and so on. In order to add the installer for the service, switch to the designer view and right-click on the designer surface and select the Add Installer item from the context menu that appears. This will add a couple of installers onto the designer surface, as shown in Figure 9-22.

If you select the `ServiceInstaller1` component in the designer surface and view the Properties window, you'll see several parameters that can be set for the service including the display name, service dependencies, and start type. You'll also see a `ServiceProcessInstaller` component on the designer surface. You need to click on this and then, in the Properties window, make sure to change the `Account` property so that it reads `LocalSystem`. If you were to build the project and then run the `InstallUtil.exe` executable from the command line and give it the name of the `MigratingFactorialService.exe` assembly, the service would be installed. You can verify this by opening up the services applet and browsing for the service, as shown in Figure 9-23.

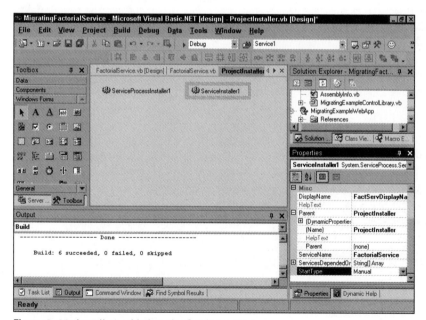

Figure 9-22: Installers added to the Service project.

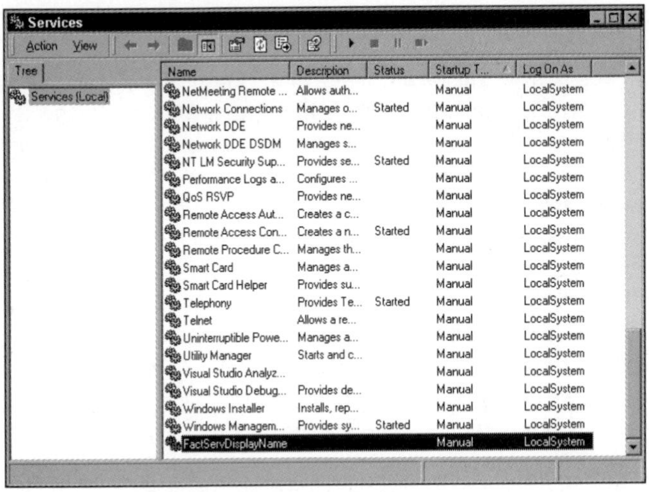

Figure 9-23: Verifying service was installed.

If you start the service from the service control manager and then stop it, you'll see that it behaves like a normal service even though it doesn't do anything. If you were to look at the event log, you'd see four events were logged letting you know that the service was starting, started successfully, stopping, and stopped successfully. Now that we've verified that the service is working properly, we can add the functionality that makes the service unique.

The service is going to listen on port 1357 for factorial requests. When it receives a request on this port, it will then calculate the factorial and send back the response. First, insert the following code into the service module, which contains the code that listens for the request and returns the result:

```
Private Sub ServiceWorker()
    Dim WSL As Net.Sockets.TcpListener
    Dim WSS As Net.Sockets.Socket
    Dim NetStream As System.Net.Sockets.NetworkStream
    Dim StreamReceive As System.IO.StreamReader
    Dim StreamSend As System.IO.StreamWriter
    Dim strData As String
    Dim CharBuffer() As Char
    Dim Fact As CL_MigratingExample_Factorial.clsFactorial = New _
            CL_MigratingExample_Factorial.clsFactorial()
    Dim lngFactResult As Long

    Const DataSize = 1024
    Do
        WSL = New Net.Sockets.TcpListener(1357)
        WSL.Start()
```

```
        WSS = WSL.AcceptSocket

        NetStream = New System.Net.Sockets.NetworkStream(WSS)
        StreamReceive = New System.IO.StreamReader(NetStream)
        StreamSend = New System.IO.StreamWriter(NetStream)

        ReDim CharBuffer(DataSize)
        StreamReceive.Read(CharBuffer, 0, DataSize)
        strData = CharBuffer

        lngFactResult = Fact.GetFactorial(CInt(strData))
        strData = lngFactResult

        StreamSend.Write(strData)
        StreamSend.Flush()

        StreamSend.Close()
        NetStream.Close()

        WSL.Stop()
    Loop
End Sub
```

Next, you're going to run this code on a separate thread, so you need to have a thread object declared at the module level:

```
Private thrServiceWorker As Threading.Thread
```

In the `OnStart` event for the service, the thread needs to be initialized and started, so add the following code to accomplish this:

```
thrServiceWorker = New Threading.Thread(AddressOf ServiceWorker)
thrServiceWorker.Start()
```

Also, when a request to stop the service has been received, the worker thread needs to be aborted so the service can stop:

```
thrServiceWorker.Abort()
```

This is all the code that's required in your service, so you need to create the client that will communicate with your service. On the `frmMain.vb` form, add a text box, a button, and another text box. The first text box will contain the number you want to get the factorial for; the second text box will contain the factorial as it's retrieved from the service. The button will establish a TCP/IP session with the service and request the factorial of a number through the service. Insert the following code in the Click event of the second button:

```
Dim TCPC As Net.Sockets.TcpClient
Dim NetStream As Net.Sockets.NetworkStream
Dim StreamSend As System.IO.StreamWriter
Dim charBuffer() As Char

Const DataSize = 1024

TCPC = New Net.Sockets.TcpClient("localhost", 1357)

NetStream = TCPC.GetStream
StreamSend = New System.IO.StreamWriter(NetStream)
StreamSend.Write(CInt(TextBox1.Text))
StreamSend.Flush()

Dim SR As System.IO.StreamReader = New
System.IO.StreamReader(NetStream)
ReDim charBuffer(DataSize)
SR.Read(charBuffer, 0, DataSize)
TextBox2.Text = charBuffer

NetStream.Close()
TCPC.Close()
```

Now if you were to build the project and run it, you could start the service using the service controller or the Net Start command from the command line, and the client would return the result as calculated by the service. However, there are a couple of things you need to be aware of. First, when a service is running, you can't compile the service because the file is in use. The service needs to be stopped using the service control manager or using the Net Stop command before you can run the project, and you have to wait for the service executable to be released from the operating system. This process can become very time-consuming as you're debugging the service. As an alternative, you could add a ServiceController control to the form, and then start the service when the form is loaded and stop the service when the form is closed:

```
Try
    ServiceController1.ServiceName = "FactorialService"
    ServiceController1.Start()
Finally
```

```
ServiceController1.WaitForStatus( _
        ServiceProcess.ServiceControllerStatus.Running)
End Try
```

```
ServiceController1.Stop()
```

Even after placing the control on the form, situations or errors may still arise as you are developing the service, and you'll need to be able to stop the service manually before trying to compile the service. So you should become familiar with the command line parameters for starting and stopping services. The samples shown here were only for demonstration purposes and lacked some of the very things I discussed earlier that services should have. In addition, the example using the sockets approach lacked many of the requirements that a normal socket-based application would typically have. Our service can only accept one client at a time and only passes a small parameter back and forth. Real services would need to launch multiple threads to handle the requests from the different clients and would need a way of passing more information back and forth. This additional information may exceed the buffer sizes that were allocated, and loops would have to be created to read the remaining contents. There are other ways to communicate with a service in addition to socket-based programming. However, sockets have the benefit of being easily configurable, and the ports that are used can be documented or restricted to cooperate with firewalls and other network protection schemes. As long as the communication protocols are defined and documented, a socket-based approach would allow you to create a service in .NET and could allow clients written in other languages (including prior versions of Visual Basic) to communicate with and use the service you created.

Creating Web Services

Visual Basic .NET also allows you to easily create another type of service called a Web Service. A *Web Service* runs under a web server and communicates with clients using the HTTP protocol. The contents of the packages traveling between the server and client are wrapped up in an XML stream. Using the HTTP protocol and XML-based text streams, a Web Service can communicate through most firewalls because most firewalls allow HTTP traffic to flow through. Any type of client that can send and receive the properly formatted packets can use a Web Service, including other Web Services.

The best way to understand how Web Services can be used is to start with an example. Again, no surprise here: You will create a Web Service that will communicate with clients to return a factorial result for a number. Start by adding an ASP.NET Web Service application to the current solution, and give it a name of FactorialWebService. Next, add a reference to the Factorial Class Library project as you've previously done.

Insert the following code to create the public function for the Web Service that will return the factorial result:

```
<WebMethod()> Public Function GetFactorialWS(ByVal Number As
Integer) As Long
    Dim Fact As CL_MigratingExample_Factorial.clsFactorial
    Fact = New CL_MigratingExample_Factorial.clsFactorial()

    Return Fact.GetFactorial(Number)
End Function
```

As you can see, the function looks like any other function we would create in Visual Basic .NET, with the exception of the WebMethod attribute. The function simply accepts a number, creates the factorial class library, calls the routine in the class library, and returns the factorial for the number. This is all you're going to include in the Web Service.

There are several options that you can use to debug the Web Service, but the easiest is as follows. First, set the Web Service project as the startup project in the solution and then set the Service1.asmx page as the start up page as you did in the ASP.NET Web application. If you build and run the project, you'll see the browser displayed and it will navigate to the page, which contains information about the Web Service, as shown in Figure 9-24.

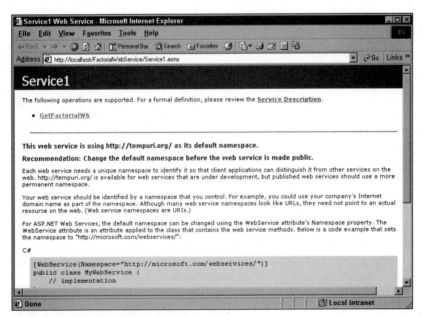

Figure 9-24: The Web Service description page.

This page contains information that describes the Web Service by the supported methods and contains links that can be used to view the actual details of the service description, as well as links to pages that will display and allow you to test the individual methods. If you click on the service description hyperlink, you'll see a new Web page appear that contains the XML text that describes the service, as shown in Figure 9-25.

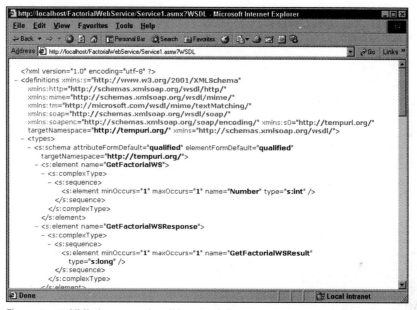

Figure 9-25: XML document describing the definition and implementation of the Web Service.

The only method that was included in the Web Service was the `GetFactorialWS` function. If you were to click on the hyperlink for the description, as shown in Figure 9-24, you would see a sample page appear, as shown in Figure 9-26. This page lists the sample SOAP requests and responses for the Web Service and provides a convenient way to test the Web Service without having to create a custom client application. This is especially beneficial if the service is going to be called from another service or a client outside your control. If you were to enter value for the `Number` parameter, and clicked the `Invoke` button, you'd see the result returned, as shown in Figure 9-27.

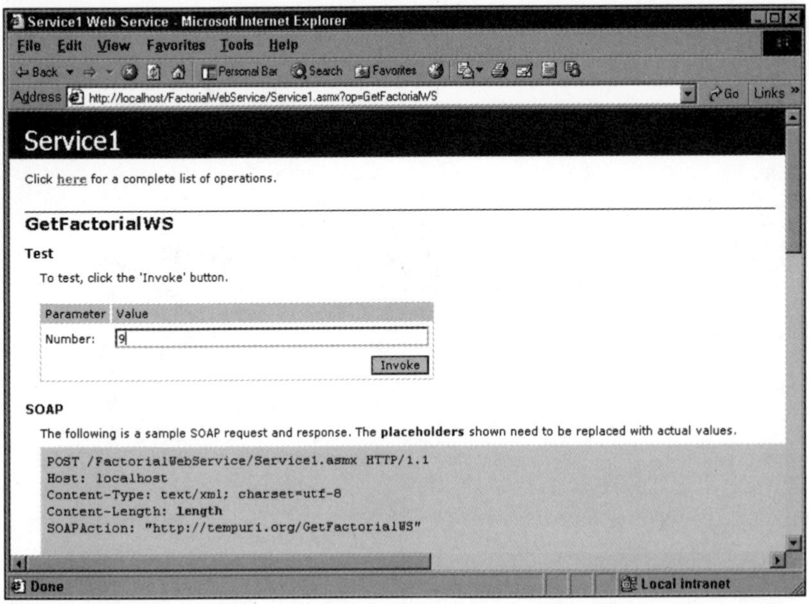

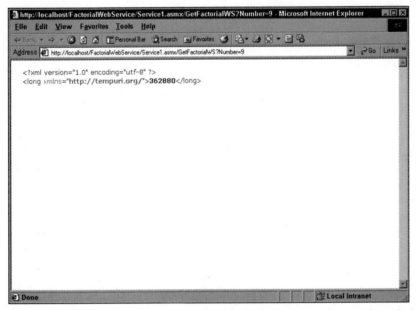

Figure 9-26: Test page for the supplied Web methods with parameter lists and invoke method.

Figure 9-27: Results of the invoke method on the Web Service proving that it worked.

Now that you have verified that your Web Service works, you can write a custom client that can call the methods on this service or any other Web Service. Reset the startup project to the Windows Application, and then right-click on the references for the Windows Application project. Select Add Web Reference from the context menu that appears, and you'll see the dialog box, as shown in Figure 9-28.

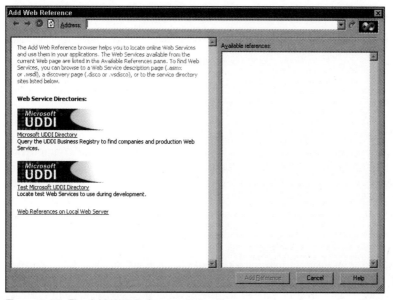

Figure 9-28: The Add Web Reference dialog box.

If you select the hyperlink for the Web References on Local Web Server, you'll see the two ASP.NET applications you've created. Both the service and the Web app will be shown, but click on the FactorialWebService link. You'll now see the information for the Web Service that was created. You can view the contract and you can also view the documentation for the Web Service, which will allow you to bring up the same invoke sample page that allows you to test the service and the results from within the dialog box. Here you're accessing the same information and proving your Web Service works without debugging it from within the development environment. After the service has been selected, click the Add Reference button at the bottom of the dialog box.

In the Solution Explorer window, you'll see a new Web References folder appear in the folder list. If you expand this folder, you'll see a reference named LocalHost, and the Service1 Web Service that was created will be under this Web reference.

Rename the Web Service reference from localhost to MyWebService. This is how you specify the namespace for accessing the components in the Web Service. Add another button on the main form, and insert the following code in the click event:

```
Dim MyWeb As New MyWebService.Service1()
MsgBox(MyWeb.GetFactorialWS(InputBox("Enter a number")))
```

If you were to run the project and click on the button that was just added to the main form, you'd see that the factorial result is calculated and displayed for the number you specify.

Summary

Visual Basic .NET introduces several new project types, which this chapter briefly discussed. By properly breaking out your applications into reusable components, you can create applications that take advantage of these reusable components in many ways. This chapter showed you how you could create a single class library that can be consumed by the various project types in Visual Basic .NET. The underlying business logic was encapsulated into a reusable component and was called from a Windows Application, a Web Application, a Console Application, a Windows Service, and also a Web Service.

In this chapter, you also learned the basics of creating custom windows controls that exhibit the various behaviors that other controls display in the Properties window. You also were shown a couple of different ways that you can communicate with remote components that aren't platform- and language-specific. You created a true Windows service and responded to network requests from clients using the TCP/IP protocol as the communications channel.

Visual Basic has raised the bar once again, as you can now create just about any application that's needed to fulfill the requirements. These applications can be as simple or as complex as need be to get the job done. With .NET, Visual Basic has indeed grown up from a hard-working teenager to a harder- and smarter-working adult that can work well with others. This chapter has really only scratched the surface on the types of applications that can be created now with Visual Basic .NET. As time goes by, applications will be developed in Visual Basic .NET that most people would never have imagined could be done in Visual Basic .NET.

Chapter 10

Debugging Applications in Visual Basic .NET

IN THIS CHAPTER

- ◆ Debugging windows available in the IDE
- ◆ Using the Build Configuration Manager
- ◆ Using the Event Log for debugging applications
- ◆ Using code attributes
- ◆ Using the available stack trace object
- ◆ Debugging the various project types available in .NET

As you're developing applications in Visual Basic .NET, you'll spend a fair amount of time debugging these applications. As you probably know, there is no single key or punch list that you can use when debugging an application that isn't working properly. Debugging an application is a process that involves four main steps:

- ◆ Correcting syntax errors
- ◆ Correcting runtime errors and exceptions
- ◆ Correcting logical errors
- ◆ Verifying that the application is producing the correct results

Developers who've used prior versions of Visual Basic have had the luxury of a pretty good set of tools to assist them in the debugging process. Visual Basic .NET is able to extend upon the previous debugging toolset for a couple of reasons – the first and foremost of which is the common integrated development environment that's shared among all the products in the Visual Studio .NET family. As a result, Visual Basic developers now have the same tools available to them as C++ and C# developers. Of course, some of these tools will probably never be used by a Visual Basic developer. The Registers window is probably the best example of this. The majority of all Visual Basic developers will probably never look at the Registers window, but it's there if you ever need to use it. Similar debugging tools include the Threads, Memory, and Module windows.

The other primary reason why Visual Basic has improved support for debugging applications is because it's built upon the .NET Framework. The .NET Framework introduces several things that can be used when trying to debug an application — from class and procedure attributes to specialized controls that provide the capability to log messages to the Event Log or that can use performance counters to display information about the application while it's running.

Regardless of what you've used in the past, you'll probably have to learn how to use some additional debugging tools in order to effectively debug applications in Visual Basic .NET. Some types of projects that you can now create in Visual Basic .NET can't be debugged within the development environment, so you'll have to rely on other methods if you create these types of applications.

Understanding the Debugging Windows

Before you get into the new debugging tools, it's worth the effort to quickly review the tools that have existed in prior versions of Visual Basic and note any changes that have been made in Visual Basic .NET. A change that's common to the various debug windows is that the majority of them are only available to view if the development environment is running in debug mode. If the window isn't visible initially, it can be added from the Debug menu. The debug windows form their own tab group, which is automatically hidden when the application stops executing in the development environment.

Breakpoints

A *breakpoint* is the simplest debugging tool you have available in your toolbox. Placing a breakpoint on a line will cause the program to stop executing normally and enter debug mode. In prior versions of Visual Basic, you could add or remove a breakpoint, but that was about it. In Visual Basic .NET, after you add a breakpoint to a line of code, you can right-click on the breakpoint and select the Breakpoint Properties item from the context menu, and you'll see a dialog box like the one shown in Figure 10-1.

Looking at the Properties dialog box, you'll see that a couple of buttons will bring up more options about the breakpoint. The Condition Options dialog box (shown in Figure 10-2) allows you to set a condition on the breakpoint similar to adding a watch statement in prior versions and selecting one of the different watch type options when the watch is created.

Along with the breakpoint conditions, you can also set the breakpoint to only enter debug mode after the line has been executed a specified number of times. You can set the number of hits that are required before breaking to be an absolute number, a multiple of a number, or when the hit count is greater than or equal to a specified number. You can also reset the hit count at any time by bringing up the Hit Count dialog box (shown in Figure 10-3) and explicitly resetting the number.

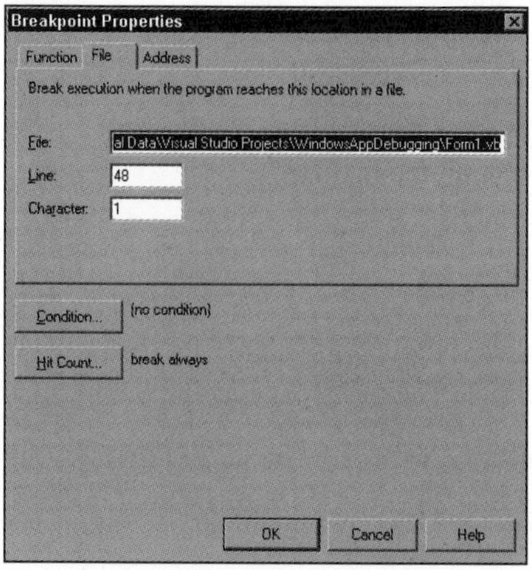

Figure 10-1: The Breakpoint Properties dialog box.

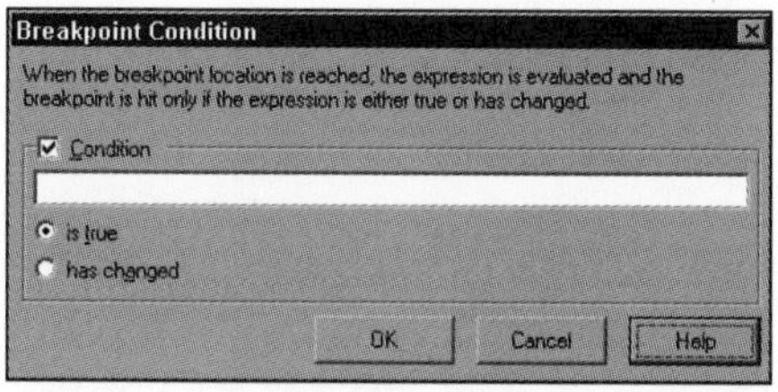

Figure 10-2: The Breakpoint Condition dialog box.

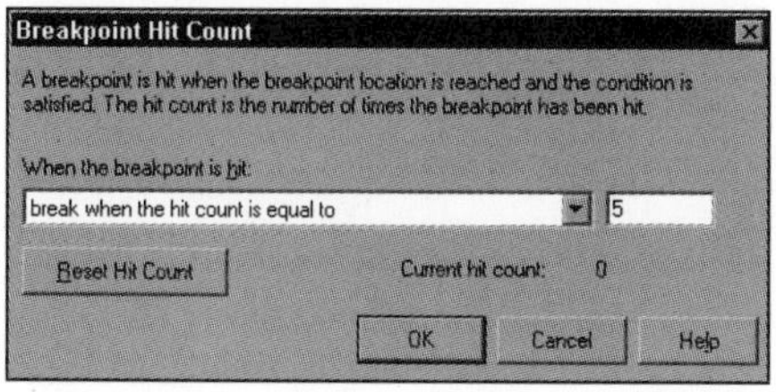

Figure 10-3: Breakpoint hit count options.

The best place for using the hit count option for a breakpoint is when the line of code is within a loop and you need to check the values at a certain point. For example, if you need to check the last cycle of the loop, you could break in the first cycle, see how many more times you need to let it execute, set the hit count option, and then let it run normally until you reach the last item in the loop, and it will automatically go back into break mode for you on the last element. This feature will end up saving you a lot of time when you're debugging code that's executing within a loop. It keeps you from having to insert special code that includes a `Stop` statement when a certain condition is True in the loop, and eliminates the possibility that you'll forget to remove the code that created the stop condition.

Another new feature of breakpoints is that they're now persistent. When you set a breakpoint, it remains until you clear it or clear all the breakpoints. If you close the project and then open it back up, you'll notice that all the breakpoints are still enabled.

Immediate window

The next tool that's typically used after the application is in debug mode is the Immediate window. The Immediate window can be used to execute code, assign values to variables, and display the values of variables. It's pretty much a one-stop shop — just about anything can be done in the Immediate window after the application has entered break mode. However, the Immediate window is now accessed by using the Command window in immediate mode.

The Immediate window in Visual Basic .NET exhibits behavior that's a little different from prior versions. In prior versions, you could use the Immediate window to test routines that you'd coded by simply calling the functions from the Immediate window while the application was still in design mode. This is no longer the case in Visual Basic .NET. The application has to be running before anything can be evaluated in the Immediate window.

Another behavior change is the way the arrow keys function in the new Immediate window. Pressing the up and down arrow keys cycles through the list of previously entered commands. If you want to move the cursor up and down, you'll need to hold down the Control key when pressing the arrow keys. Furthermore, the only line that will execute is the last line in the Immediate window. If you were to position the cursor to a previously entered command and press the Enter key, the command would not be executed. Instead, the command would be copied to the last line in the Immediate window. If you pressed the Enter key again, it would then execute.

Locals window

The Locals window is still present and is used to display the names, values, and data types of the variables that are in the current scope. The only changes to the Locals window from prior versions appear to be cosmetic in nature (see Figure 10-4).

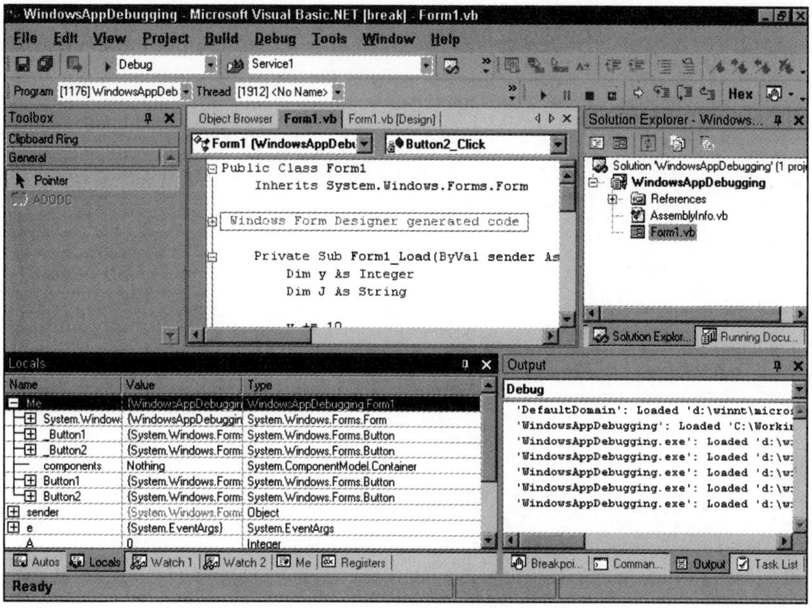

Figure 10–4: The Locals window in Visual Basic .NET.

Watch window

The Watch window is used to display the contents of a variable. The break options that existed in prior versions are now managed under breakpoint properties. Visual Basic .NET has multiple Watch windows that can be used to group related variables to watch together for easier viewing. Another feature of the new Watch window is that you simply type in the variable name or expression, similar to typing in a task in the Task List, in order to add a Watch. As soon as you tab off the name column, the other columns will be filled with the appropriate data.

Autos window

This new window will display all the variables and values that appear in the previous and current statements. The Autos window is useful when there are many variables combined together in a single statement. Using the Autos window allows you to determine easily what the result of the line should be without having to print each variable in the Immediate window or hover the mouse over each variable and view the results individually.

Exceptions window

You'll use the Exceptions window quite extensively as you work with the new structured error-handling techniques in Visual Basic .NET. The Exceptions window, as shown in Figure 10-5, shows the various exceptions that are defined and allows you to change the debugging behavior for when the exception is thrown and if it's not handled. If you define your own exceptions in your application, you can also add them to this list and specify the behavior that should occur for them as well.

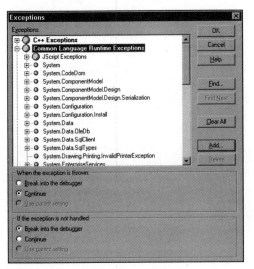

Figure 10–5: The Exceptions window.

Understanding the Debugging Tools

Visual Basic .NET provides you with various windows that can assist you when you're trying to debug an application. Along with these windows, there are also various tools that can be used to aid in the debugging process.

Build Configuration Manager

The Build Configuration Manager can be used to selectively compile projects into Debug or Release modes. When compiled into Debug mode, the symbolic debugging files are created so that the development environment can attach to the process as it's running and display meaningful information about the project while it's being debugged. Attaching to a running process is probably new to most Visual Basic developers, but it allows the application to be run and manipulated from within the development environment even though it wasn't started from the development environment. The Build Configuration Manager by default includes a Debug and a Release configuration, but others can be added to support any custom configuration needs you may have.

Conditional compilation constants

Conditional compilation statements can be used to selectively turn on or off certain features when the application is compiled. Visual Basic .NET uses two predefined conditional compilation constants that can be used anywhere in the code. The DEBUG and TRACE constants are defined and can be selected in the Project Properties dialog box. The conditional compilation constants are still accessed the same way they were in prior versions, using the #If statements. However, there is a new feature in Visual Basic .NET where the conditional compilation constants show up through IntelliSense, so you can see the constants that have been defined.

Trace and Debug Objects

Prior versions of Visual Basic have had the Debug statement that can be inserted into code to aid the developer in debugging the application. In Visual Basic .NET, the Debug statement can be used to display information to the Output window and can also be used to validate assumptions in the code. When the application is compiled, the Debug statements are not included and do not add any overhead to the compiled executable when it's running.

Visual Basic .NET introduces a Trace object that can be used like the Debug object, except that the code remains in the final executable. If an assertion fails on a trace statement, a warning dialog box appears, similar to the one shown in Figure 10-6.

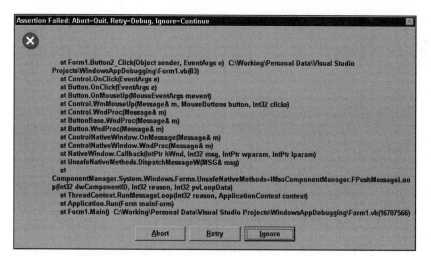

Figure 10-6: The Assertion Failed dialog box in a compiled executable.

The user then automatically has the options of choosing to abort and end the application, try to execute again the line of code that failed the assertion, or ignore the assertion and continue. All this is accomplished for you automatically by using the Trace.Assert method. When used properly, traces can be invaluable when debugging an application – especially when you're trying to diagnose problems that only occur in a compiled executable and not in the development environment. However, if you use traces, you must realize that there is a small amount of overhead that's added in the compiled executable in order to provide the features that an assert call from a trace object can provide.

Another feature of the Trace object is that you can create a custom listener for the trace assertion and display an alternate dialog box, or you can log information to the Event Log instead of displaying a message box. This allows you to use the trace methods on applications that don't have a user interface or that are running on a different computer.

When using the Trace object, you must make sure you have selected the `Define Trace Option` in the Project Properties window. The Trace object will not be compiled in unless the definition was included in the project.

Logging to the Event Log

Using the Event Log to write out status messages is another invaluable tool that can track the flow of a program to aid in debugging. In Chapter 9, you created a Windows Service, so you know that Windows Services can't interact with the desktop and can't run in the debugger. The Event Log can be used to write out status messages so that errors can be diagnosed more easily. Errors can be homed in on by checking the last message that was logged to the Event Log, finding the message in the source code, and then looking for the next message that should've been logged but wasn't. You then know that the error occurred between those two lines of code.

If you're going to use event logging to aid in diagnosing errors and debugging an application, you should have some way of turning the logging on or off without having to recompile the application. If you don't turn off the logging, then you'll fill up the Event Logs with unnecessary information and be incurring overhead that isn't necessary when everything in the application is running fine. You can turn on and off logging in several ways, but the two easiest ways would be to have a Registry key that sets the logging status or to use a command line parameter to the application.

Fortunately, Visual Basic .NET makes it easy to log messages to the Event Log, giving you complete control over the information and how it's logged. In order to log a message to the Event Log, you simply need to create an `Event Log` object, set the source, and then write an entry to the log:

```
Dim EvtLog As EventLog = New EventLog("Application")

EvtLog.Source = "MyEventLogSource"

EvtLog.WriteEntry("This is a test of the event log",__
    EventLogEntryType.Warning, 12345)
```

The preceding code would create the Event Log entry, as shown in Figures 10-7 and 10-8.

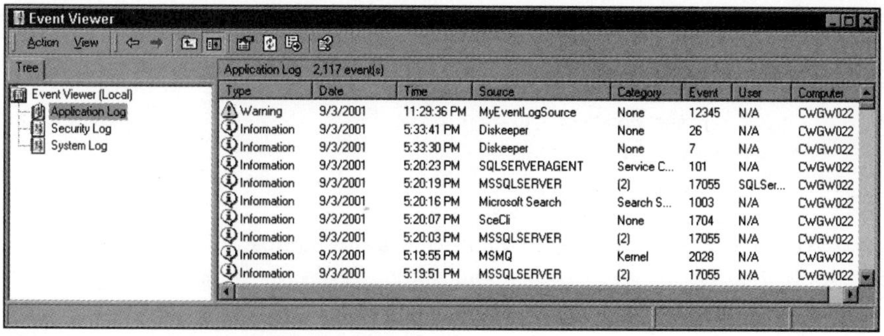

Figure 10-7: An application Event Log entry.

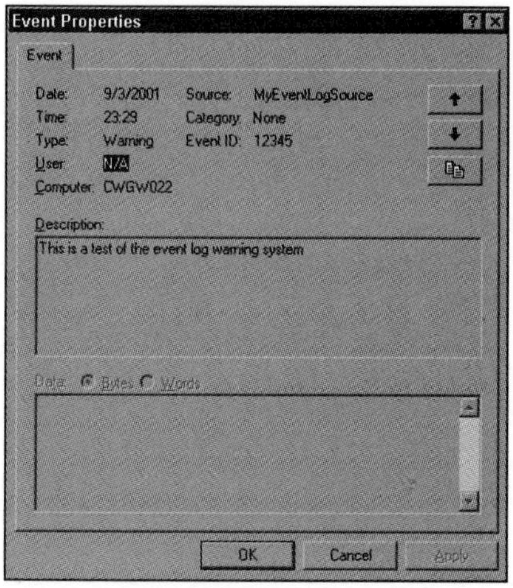

Figure 10-8: An application Event Log message.

Using code attributes

Visual Basic .NET allows certain attributes to be applied to functions that can be used for various debugging features. The first attribute that you may find beneficial is the DebuggerStepThrough attribute. This attribute can be applied to procedures and will cause the debugger to step through instead of stepping into a procedure when single stepping through code.

```
<System.Diagnostics.DebuggerStepThrough()> Private Function __
    Test() As Integer
        Dim X As Integer
        Dim Y As Integer
```

```
    X = 5
    Y = 6
    Y += X

    Return Y
End Function
```

In the preceding code example, the function will automatically be stepped through as you're debugging an application. You should use this procedure attribute on functions that have already been debugged, tested, and verified that they work properly. The best use of this attribute is on small helper functions that are placed inline to other lines of code, as in the following example:

```
B = Test() * Test() + 5
```

The debugger will behave as if the Test function is in a compiled module that can't be stepped into even though the code is present. If the function contains a breakpoint and also contains this attribute, the debugger will stop execution at the breakpoint if it's encountered, just as it would at any other breakpoint. If you look at the code for the InitializeComponent method in a Windows form, you'll see that it contains this attribute so you don't have to step through all the code that's in the routine when the form is created.

The next attribute that can be used is the DebuggerHidden attribute:

```
<System.Diagnostics.DebuggerHidden()> Public Function Test() _
As Integer
```

This attribute works similar to the step through attribute except that if you were to place a breakpoint within the procedure with this attribute, it wouldn't enter break mode. It would simply step right through it:

Finally, there is also a Conditional attribute that can be used on procedures.

```
<System.Diagnostics.Conditional("EnableTest")>  Public Function _
Test() As Integer
```

This attribute allows you to define a procedure and only have it included if the conditional compilation constant is set. At this point, you may be thinking that you could do this in prior versions of Visual Basic by wrapping the entire procedure around a conditional compilation constant #If statement. Indeed, this would work. But if you called the function from anywhere in the project, you would also have to wrap the calls around a conditional as well; otherwise it would try to execute a procedure that isn't present. Visual Basic .NET will allow you to define a procedure with this conditional attribute and will automatically strip out any calls to the function in the entire project. This works in debug mode and in compiled executables.

Stack trace

You now have a built-in `StackTrace` object in Visual Basic .NET. This feature is long overdue in Visual Basic. In prior versions of Visual Basic, if you wanted a stack trace, you had to create a stack-management object and push and pop the procedure names to the stack manager. To make matters worse, there was no way to retrieve the function or procedure name that the execution pointer was in, so you had to duplicate the procedure name. Also, if any routine encountered an error that wasn't handled, then the execution pointer would jump out to the calling routine, which could make the call stack list unreliable.

If you simply want to know the entire stack trace, you could accomplish this with the following code:

```
Dim ST As New StackTrace()

MsgBox(ST.ToString)
```

Insert the preceding code into the click event of a button and you'll see a stack trace, as shown in Figure 10-9.

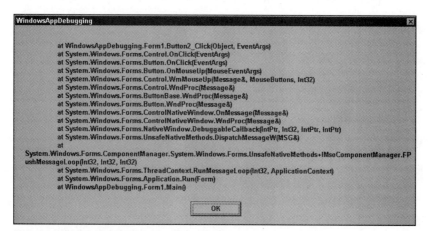

Figure 10-9: Displaying the stack trace through code.

Compare Figure 10-9 with Figure 10-6, and you'll see that the `Trace` object uses the `StackTrace` object to display the majority of its information. The stack trace shows everything all the way down to and past the Windows message loop that triggered the click event in the first place.

The `StackTrace` object contains a listing of individual `StackFrame` objects, which can be retrieved through the `StackTrace.GetFrame` method. Each `StackFrame` object has its own set of properties that can be queried to get more information, such as the file name, line number, and so on.

Debugging the Various Project Types

Each project type in Visual Basic .NET has different debugging requirements that vary from one to another. This section covers the basic requirements for debugging each project type that can be created in Visual Basic .NET.

Windows applications

Windows applications are the easiest to bring up in the debugger. All you need to do is to open the project in the development environment and set a breakpoint at the appropriate place. When the execution pointer reaches the breakpoint, the debugger will be activated.

Class libraries

Because a class library is a DLL, it can't be debugged directly. You must first create a client application that will create the DLL and call into the appropriate method. If you add the client project to the class library solution, you can set the client project as the startup project and then set the appropriate breakpoints in the class library and run the project. When the breakpoint is reached, the debugger will be activated.

Windows controls

A Windows control library is another type of class library and is debugged in a similar manner. Add a client project to the control library solution and set the appropriate breakpoints in the code for the control. The only difference between the Windows control and class library is that you have to place the control on a Windows form in a Windows application project. When the project is run and the breakpoint is reached in the control, the debugger will be activated.

ASP.NET Web Applications

Debugging ASP.NET Web Applications is actually a relatively simple process, because all the code that executes is executed on the server. When you set a startup page for the Web Application project and run the project, Visual Basic will launch the Web browser and display the Web page. If you place breakpoints in the project, when the program flow reaches a breakpoint, the debugger will be activated allowing you to debug the application. The ASP.NET Framework handles the persistence and translation of code to HTML controls and events and back to standard Visual Basic Web Forms, Web Form Controls, and events.

ASP.NET Web Services

There are a couple of different ways to debug an ASP.NET Web Service. If you simply need to test individual methods, you can set the startup page for the project to the page containing the Web Service and run the project. You'll see the detail information about the service appear. You can click on the individual methods and supply the required parameters within the Web page that's displayed and invoke the Web Service method directly. You'll see the results of the method appear as XML in a new Web page.

If you need to have a more sophisticated client, then you'll need to supply a suitable client project such as a Windows Application to the solution. You then need to go through the process of adding a Web reference to the client project pointing to the Web Service that needs to be debugged. After the Web Service reference is created and the namespace is specified, the client can create Web Service objects and call the methods on them using the same code that would be used to call methods on the object if it wasn't a Web Service. One of the best features for debugging Web Services in the Visual Studio development environment is the fact that after the Web Service reference is established, the methods and procedures on the service are available through IntelliSense.

Windows Services

Windows Services are probably the most difficult to debug because they cannot run inside the Visual Studio development environment. They must run under the operating system's service control manager. As such, the debugging options are extremely limited, because you must resort to debugging the service primarily using the Event Log and optionally performance counters. When debugging a service, you need to write to the Event Log often enough so that you can determine where any errors may be occurring.

When creating the service, you may want to incorporate a feature such as a registry key or startup parameter that can be used to determine the level of logging that's done in the service. This way, you could simply flip a switch and have more detailed logging be completed on an as-needed basis. Another tip that you can use when debugging and diagnosing services is to keep track of the number or frequency of errors that are occurring. When the number exceeds a predetermined threshold, you have the option to suppress further error messages of the same type, or you could put the service thread to sleep to try to wait for the errors to correct themselves.

Services also have another catch that you may encounter when trying to debug them. In order to test the service, you need to run the service under the service control manager. In order to run the service under the service control manager, it must be a compiled executable. Also, you must install the service into the service control manager using the `InstallUtil.exe` command line utility. The command line utility will not install the service unless you have added and properly configured the installers to the project for the service. When you have the service installed in the service control manager, you'll need to be able to start and stop it. You'll have to start the service and then test it or any clients that need to connect to the service.

As you're testing and debugging the service, you'll need to make changes to the code for the service, which will work fine until you try to compile the service. If the service is still running, then you'll get a permission denied error because the compiler can't copy the new executable onto the old one because it's in use. If you stop the service at this point and immediately try compiling again, you'll probably get the same error. If this happens, relax, take a deep breath, count to ten, and then try again.

It typically takes a few seconds for the service to stop after the stop request has been made. After the service stops, it takes another couple seconds for the service control manager to release the service. After a few times of this, you'll learn that if you get in the habit of stopping the service before you start making any changes to the code, you should be fine. You'll also become very familiar with the command line shortcuts for starting and stopping your service using the `Net Start` and `Net Stop` commands – because it'll save you time as you're debugging your service.

Console Applications

A Console Application is pretty straightforward to debug. The majority of the time, you'll simply need to set the breakpoints in the code and then run the project. The command window will be displayed and you can interact with it as you're stepping through the code. There may be times when you can't debug the Console Application in this manner, in which case you would need to launch the Console Application from the command line, supplying any required parameters, and then attach to the running application from within the Visual Basic development environment.

Summary

Visual Basic .NET has a variety of tools that you can use when debugging the applications you create. The various debugging tools each have their own purpose, and the majority of Visual Basic developers will probably never use some of them.

Each of the project types in Visual Basic .NET has its own debugging requirements, and you need to know how you can debug each one. The Windows Application project is probably the simplest of projects to work with when debugging, and the Windows Services are probably the most difficult to work with when trying to debug.

Chapter 11

Deploying Applications in Visual Basic .NET

IN THIS CHAPTER

- ◆ Windows Installer
- ◆ Setup projects
- ◆ Deploying applications
- ◆ Dynamic properties
- ◆ Using the configuration file

So far in this book, any samples and walkthroughs that I've included have had you run the project within the development environment. The development environment is used to develop and debug applications, but when the application is complete, you need a way of deploying it to the target machine. In prior versions, this involved creating a setup or installation program that would copy all the files to the target computer, register any COM components, create Start menu groups, and any required program shortcuts. For simple all-or-nothing deployment applications, the Package and Deployment Wizard that was included with Visual Basic was typically sufficient. It didn't have a lot of glitz, but it got the job done most of the time. However, sometimes the setup program needs to have more functionality than the Package and Deployment Wizard could provide. In scenarios like this, a third-party install program application would be used to fulfill the requirements that the Package and Deployment Wizard couldn't accomplish.

Installation programs and the installation project could easily become their own projects that needed to be managed and completed in parallel to the application that they were being created for. Later in this book, you read about different application development scenarios, particularly about incremental versioned releases. Before the application is completely finished, it needs to be installed on various machines throughout the development process as it moves from development to testing to final deployment. If the install program is developed and tested in parallel with the application it's created for, it can save precious time in the testing and bug-fixing phases. You've probably worked with some people who think that the development and use of the installation program should only be used in final deployment. These people typically think that any components that are used should be manually copied and registered either by hand or by a batch file, because they don't trust the installation program.

Look at a common deployment scenario with which you probably have had a similar experience. The application is a client-server workflow application that has several specialized user interfaces. The application uses one or more servers, in which each server can have specialized capabilities depending on the components of the application that are installed on each server. The development team creates some core features and utilities that are used by the individual components that are being created. The application is designed to easily scale out based on the demands placed upon it. In the minimal configuration, all the functionality areas are installed on a single server. The application scales out by adding more servers to reduce the workload on any one server. As more servers are added, the functional areas of the application can be partitioned out against the available servers to distribute the workload more efficiently. In the middle of the spectrum, each functionality area could be on a separate server. On the highly scaleable end, multiple servers can be assigned for a single functionality area. Now think about the deployment scenarios required of this application. The core server-side utility features need to be installed on each server; the core client features need to be installed when the rich client is installed. When a functionality area is installed on a server, only the related and dependent files should be installed. Now, as the application is being developed, binary compatibility is often broken, and files are added to and removed from the project, requiring changes to the final set of files that will be deployed. In order to have and maintain a clean and working environment on the server, the application needs to be completely removed and the server brought to a known state before installing the next version. In order to have a clean environment, all files, registry entries, program groups, and shortcuts must be removed from the server.

In the preceding scenario, how long do you think it would take to install the application by manually copying, registering all components in the proper order, and creating any necessary folders and shortcuts? What about the manual uninstall process? How thorough and accurate is the documentation outlining all the required steps? What are the chances of missing a required file or accidentally skipping a step? What if an older version of a file were used instead of the most recent? Finally, and probably most importantly, how repeatable is the process? Installation programs were created to save time, reduce the complexities, and improve the reliability of installing and removing applications from computers.

The purpose of this chapter is to discuss the sweeping changes that are involved with deploying applications in Visual Basic .NET. These changes make the tasks of building, deploying, and maintaining applications created in Visual Basic .NET much easier than in prior versions.

Windows Installer

After version 6 of Visual Basic was released, Microsoft came out with a new product called Windows Installer to solve many of the problems that could occur when deploying applications. The Windows Installer is either available with or included in the various operating systems that Microsoft supports. You probably first saw the Windows Installer used in Microsoft Office 2000, but as new versions of Microsoft products have been released, these products have been using the installer as well. The Windows Installer is a service that concerns itself with what should be installed — not how it should be installed, as in traditional installation programs. Each application installed by the installer maintains a database that's used to install it. The installation database contains information about what files and registry keys are required in order for the application to run.

The Windows Installer has many advantages over traditional installation programs, including the following:

♦ It uses a transactional installation process.

♦ It creates self-repairable applications.

♦ It performs clean uninstalls.

♦ It provides better support for corporate deployment of applications.

♦ It has the ability to advertise features and install on demand.

♦ It offers support for application service packs or patches.

♦ It allows end users to create customized installations based on desired features.

♦ It allows reusable installation components (merge modules) to be created and used.

Out of the preceding list, the two advantages that are most beneficial are the transactional install process and the self-repairable applications. If an error occurred in a traditional installation program, the computer was left in an unknown state from which it may or may not have been able to recover. The installation program might rely on certain assumptions about the state of the files and registry keys that aren't valid if an error occurs during the middle of the process and might not be able to restore the operating system to the previous state or resume from the point of the error. The Windows Installer is a transactional installation engine, so if an error occurs during the installation for any reason, all changes are rolled back. Another benefit of the transactional install process is that when the application needs to be removed, the installer can use the database to cleanly uninstall the entire application or just an individual feature. Because the Windows Installer keeps a requirements database for each application it installs, it can use the database to repair an application if the user deletes any files or registry keys required by the application.

The Windows Installer uses a published, documented database format, which allows third parties to create installation databases for their applications, if they want to. However, even though the database format is documented, it's pretty complex, and manually creating the database is discouraged. It's better to use a tool that creates the database and all the entries in it. After the Windows Installer was released, Microsoft, as well as a couple of the third-party installation program software vendors, developed and released a program that creates the installation database required by the Windows Installer for Visual Basic 6 applications. If you want to understand more about the Windows Installer, you can review the documentation in MSDN. Not surprisingly, the Windows Installer technology is used to install applications created in Visual Studio .NET, but just understanding the installer is not enough. There are more options available to you when you need to install a .NET application along with the new project types that are available.

Deploying Applications

In this section, I walk you through the steps required to deploy an application created in Visual Basic .NET. The examples here assume you have created the various projects in Chapter 9 and will extend upon the information previously presented. That said, if you created and tested the Windows Service Application, you already have some understanding of the different requirements for installing applications that have special requirements. The Service Application required that you add a special control called an *installer* to the service, build it, and then install it into the service control manager using a command line utility before it could be tested.

Installer controls are used to provide certain required configuration information about another control or a project itself that is used when the application is installed. If you look at the installers that were added for the service, you'll see that they provide a means of setting the service account user name and password, dependent services, service description, and service display name. If you've ever had to manually install a service into the service control manager and set the dependent services, you'll appreciate all the work that the installers will do for you.

To get started, you'll need to add a new project to the solution. When the Project dialog box comes up, you'll need to select the Setup and Deployment Projects folder in the Project Types tree view. You'll then see a listing of the related project templates, as shown in Figure 11-1.

As you can see, there are four basic deployment project types, which are used for different types of applications. The Cab Project template is used to create a cabinet file that is used to download controls to a Web browser similar to prior versions of Visual Basic.

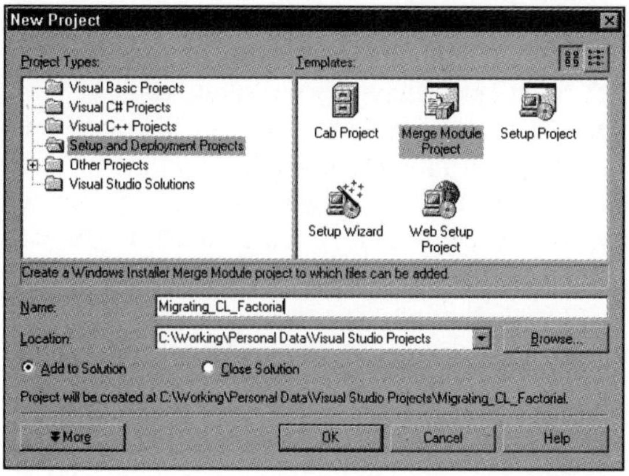

Figure 11-1: Setup and deployment project templates.

The Merge Module Project template is used to create a reusable merge module installation file for components that could be shared between applications. A merge module should be created for each version of your component, and after it's created it should never be changed. The merge module contains all the dependencies and installation information for the component that it contains. Merge modules can contain other merge modules, so as you build a merge module for a particular version of a component, you can simply include the dependent merge modules for the dependent components. The functionality of a merge module can be compared to the functionality of a COM component that you may have created in prior versions of Visual Basic.

The Setup Project template creates an installer for a Windows-based application. The wording of this may be a little misleading because one of the Visual Basic project types is Windows Application. A Windows-based application includes applications based on the Windows Application template, but it also includes Console Application, and Windows Service application types. A Class Library and a Windows Control Library are not stand-alone applications, because they require a container or client application that will create them. Therefore, a Merge Module Project template should be used to create installers for these applications, because they have the potential to be used by other applications.

The last template, Web Setup Project, is used to create an installer for a Web application. For Web applications that don't use other components, simply copying all the required files to the Web server could deploy them. However, this isn't recommended, because the installer for Web projects also has the capability to set the required application settings in Internet Information Server.

Creating the basic installation package

In the development examples, you created a Class Library for the factorial calculation, which was used by almost all the other project types that you created.

Therefore, you'll need to create a Merge Module deployment project for the Class Library. In the New Project dialog box, make sure you add the project to the solution option, name the project MM_Migrating_CL_Factorial, and click OK. An empty merge module project will be added to the solution. Select the merge module project and right-click on it in the Solution Explorer. From the context menu that appears, select Add and you'll see there are four things you can add to a merge module. You can add an individual file, a project output, another merge module, or an assembly. In order to add the outputs of a project, the project must be in the solution, so you can see why the merge module project was added to the overall solution. Select the Project Output option and you'll see a dialog box appear, as shown in Figure 11-2.

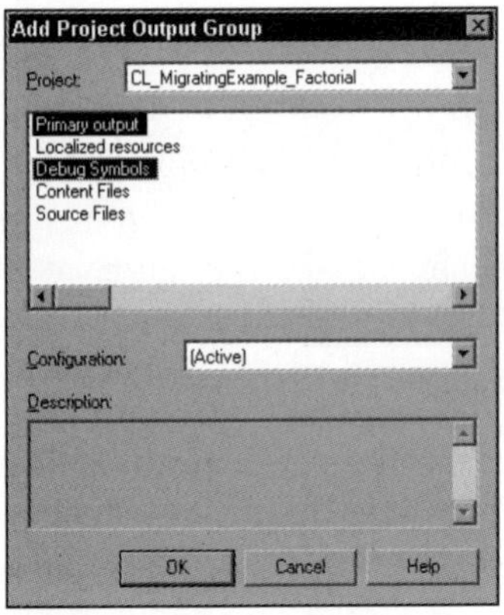

Figure 11-2: The merge module Add Project Output Group dialog box.

This dialog box allows you to select the project and the desired output files that should be included in the merge module. Select the Primary Output and Debug Symbols in the list and click OK. If you look at the merge module project, you'll see two files added to the merge module, which are the Class Library DLL and the PDB files. The next step you need to take is to right-click on the merge module project and select the build option so the merge module is compiled.

Now that you've created the reusable merge module for the Class Library, you can add the merge module into another setup project that will install all the pieces of the main application. Add another project to the solution, except this time select the standard Setup Project template and give it the name Migrating_Setup and click OK. The editor for the target machine file system appears, as shown in Figure 11-3.

This editor is used to define the files that will be installed on the target machine and where they'll be installed. The basic installation folders are shown by default, but as you can see from the Figure 11-3, you can add a special folder and install files on the target machine in these special folders. In order to add a file to one of the folders, right-click on the folder in the File System Editor and select Add from the context menu. Then select the appropriate item to add, as shown in Figure 11-4.

Figure 11-3: Target machine file system editor for the setup project.

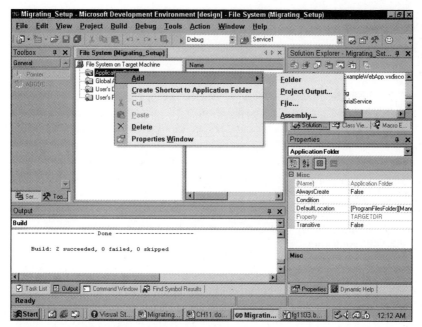

Figure 11-4: Adding files to the target folders.

The first thing that we need to add to the main setup project is the merge module we created for the Class Library. In order to do this, select the Application Folder and then Add, Project Output. You see the same dialog box as shown in Figure 11-2, except this time select the merge module project you added and built, select the project, and click OK. Next, follow the same steps to add the outputs from the Windows Application and Console Application to the same folder. When you add the Windows Application project, you should notice that the output from the Windows Control Library was also added automatically, because the Windows Application used the sample Windows Control that was created.

Next, we need to be able to run the programs from the Start menu by clicking on shortcuts. In order to create a shortcut, you first right-click on the file wherever it was added to the target folders and select the Create Shortcut option from the menu. You then change the name of the shortcut that was created to something meaningful, and then drag it to the desired target folder. Create a shortcut for the "Primary Output from MigratingExample" and rename it to "Run Windows App" and then drag it to the Users Programs Folder. This will place the shortcut to the Windows Application in the root of the programs folder on the Start menu, which is where the Microsoft Office shortcuts are placed. Under the Users Programs folder, create a new folder and name it "Migrating to VB .NET." Then place another shortcut to the "Primary Output from MigratingExample" here.

You can't copy the shortcut from one location to another. You must create a new shortcut to the same physical file and then drag it to the desired location.

Next, in the subfolder that was just created, also create a shortcut to the console application in the same manner as above, naming the shortcut "Factorial Console App Standard." Create another shortcut, except change the name to "Factorial Console App With Parms." Select the shortcut with parameters and in the Properties window and add 5 6 7 8 9 x 1 to the arguments property. Here you can see how easy it is to add customizations, such as command line parameters, to the shortcuts that will be created for your application.

Finally, add the outputs of the Windows Service project to the application folder. Your target file system should appear, as shown in Figures 11-5 and 11-6.

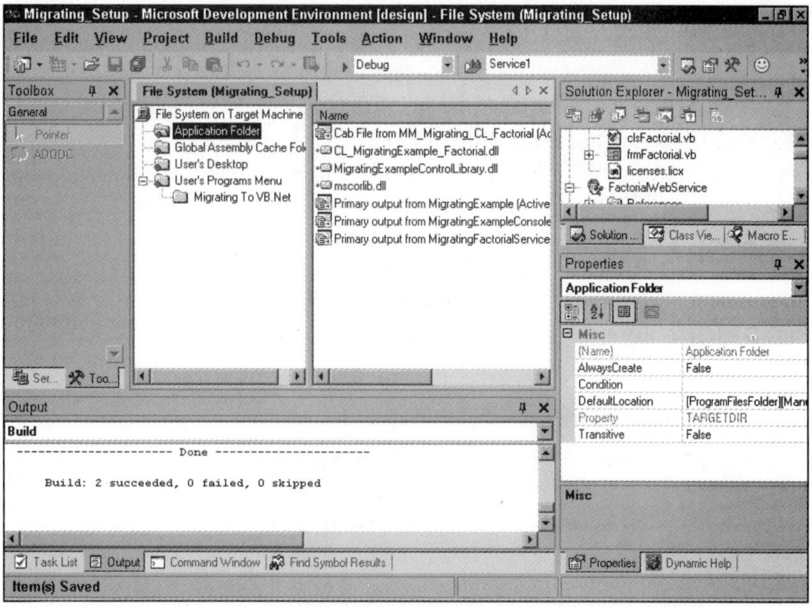

Figure 11-5: The target file system application folder.

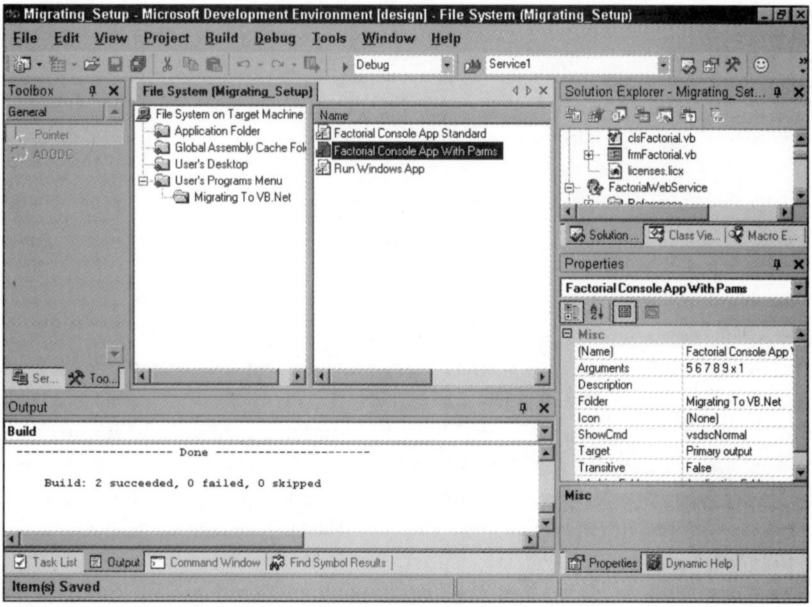

Figure 11-6: The target file system program folder.

If you right-click on the setup project and select Build, the development environment will build the Windows Installer file for the project, which has an extension of .msi. If you watch as the installer database is created, you see that all the required Framework files are processed, not just the files you selected. This should make some sense, because in order to run applications created on Visual Basic .NET, the user needs to have the .NET Framework installed on their machine. The installer file is also a compressed file so the actual size requirements for deploying the application to the target computer's hard drive will be a little bigger. The installer file is located under the Setup Project folder on the hard drive where the rest of your project and output files were saved. If you run the `Migrating_Setup.msi` file, you see the Welcome dialog box for the setup application, as shown in Figure 11-7.

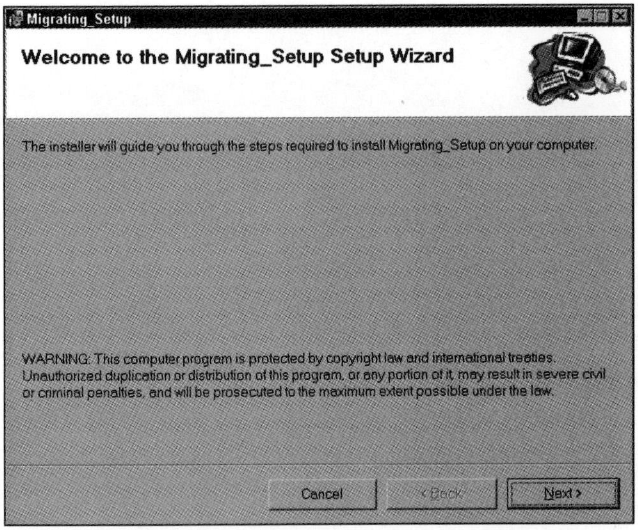

Figure 11-7: The Welcome screen on the Windows installer setup file.

Figure 11-8 is the next dialog in the installation sequence. It allows you to change where the application is installed, who can use the application, and how much disk space the installation of the application requires.

If you click the Disk Cost button, you'll see how much space will be required to install the application. Figure 11-9 shows that the application will be installed completely on the system drive and will require 35 MB of disk space in order to do so.

If you click the Next button, you're at the last dialog box, which will start the actual installation process. The Windows Installer will then complete the installation of the application and all the required supporting files in the .NET Framework.

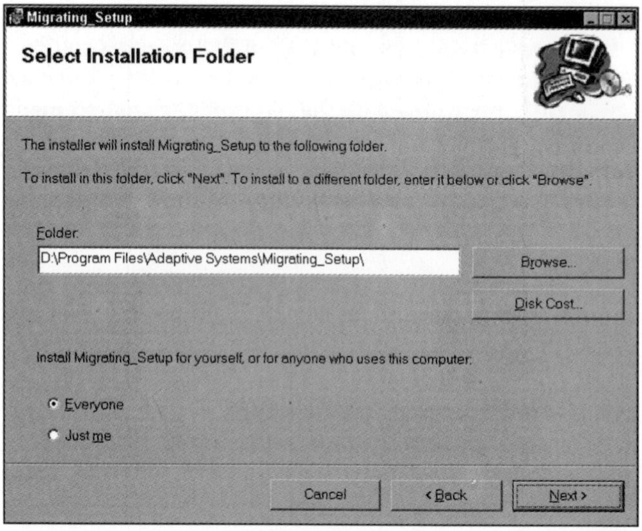

Figure 11-8: The installer directory selection.

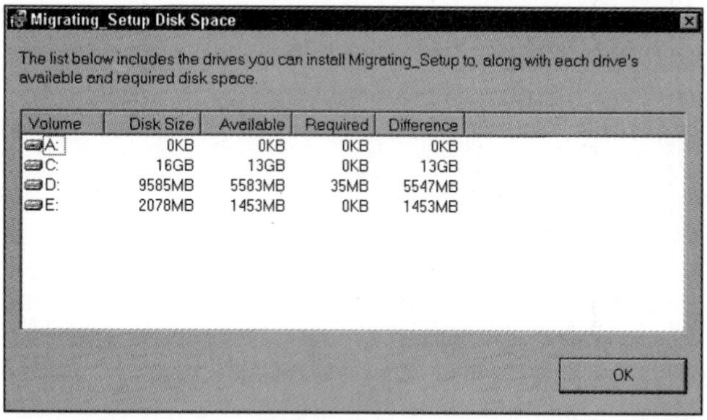

Figure 11-9: The installer Disk Space Cost dialog box.

Customizing the installation package

Now that you've seen the installation dialogs, look at some of the options you have available for customizing the appearance and behavior of the setup project. If you click on the setup project in the Solution Explorer, you'll see that the icons at the top of the Solution Explorer are different. The icons that appear allow you to bring up the various setup project editors like the File System Editor, which you have already used to specify the locations of the files on the target machine. The other icons allow you to create custom registry entries and custom file type associations. The file type associations allow you to specify a program file that will be launched and the associated actions that can be performed on the file from the context menu that appears for the specified file types. The User Interface Editor allows you to choose the dialogs that will appear in the setup program and the appearance of those dialog boxes. There are several standard dialogs that can be added to the various installation stages and launch types, as shown in Figure 11-10.

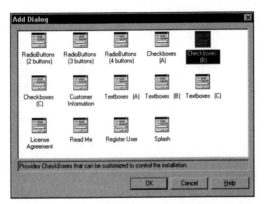

Figure 11-10: The available installer dialog templates.

If you want to include a custom Read Me file that will be displayed during the setup process, you would bring up the User Interface Editor, select one of the dialog groups, right-click on the group and select Add Dialog. Here you can add the Read Me dialog to the setup project. Each dialog box has properties that can be set, and the Read Me dialog allows you to specify a file that contains the contents you want to display. You could also add a custom License Agreement dialog box in the same manner as the Read Me dialog. In addition, you can also choose not to include certain dialogs in the installation program by simply deleting them, or you can move them up and down in the display order by using the User Interface Editor.

If you need the setup package to create certain registry entries for you, then click on the icon in the Solution Explorer to bring up the target machine Registry Editor. Here you can create any hives and entries that your application needs and they'll be created on the target machine. For each entry you create, you can also use the Properties window to specify any special requirements of the entry. You can specify whether the entry should be created, whether the entry is deleted on an uninstall, any conditions that have to be met before creating the entry and whether those conditions are reevaluated each time the application is installed or reinstalled.

The other icons allow you to define launch conditions and custom actions. Launch conditions are applied to the installation program to check for prerequisites of the application, including operating system, installed applications, and so on. The Custom Actions Editor allows you to define custom actions and the conditions that will launch these actions. Custom actions run executable files and allow you to supply arguments to these files when the installation program reaches the action point. There is a lot of information in the documentation about how to create and customize the installation process; review this information if you need to customize the installation process.

By now you should realize that through the various editors that are included to use with the installation packages, you can easily customize the most common features of the installation process to suit the needs of your application. Furthermore, the third-party installation-program software vendors will probably have their own tools that will allow you to customize the installation process more than you can from within the development environment.

Verifying the installation

After the installation process completes, you can verify that everything was installed properly. Figure 11-11 shows the Start menu after the installation process has completed. Here you can see that the proper shortcuts and folders were created. If you click on the Factorial Console App With Parms menu item, you see the outputs, as shown in Figure 11-12. As you can see, the Console Application is running correctly, which also means that the Class Library is installed and functional.

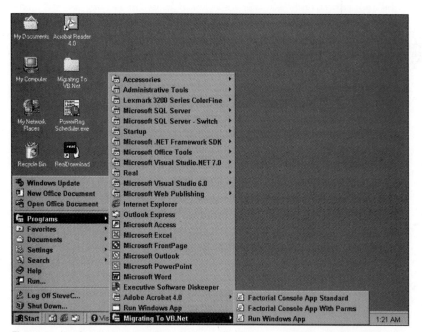

Figure 11-11: Start menu program shortcuts that were created by the installer.

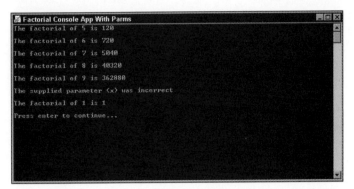

Figure 11-12: Testing install with the console application with the parameters shortcut.

Figure 11-13 shows the Service Control Manager with the service installed in it. Notice how you didn't have to do anything special, because the installation of the service was handled properly from the installers that were added to the service. The installers for the service were called automatically when the installer for the main application was run. You can start and stop the service from the Service Control Manager to verify that it functions properly. If you run the main Windows program and enter a number in the input text box associated with Button2, you'll see that the service is started automatically, and the result is displayed in the second text box. If you refresh the Service Control Manager, you'll see that the service started, and when the application ends, another refresh will show the service has stopped.

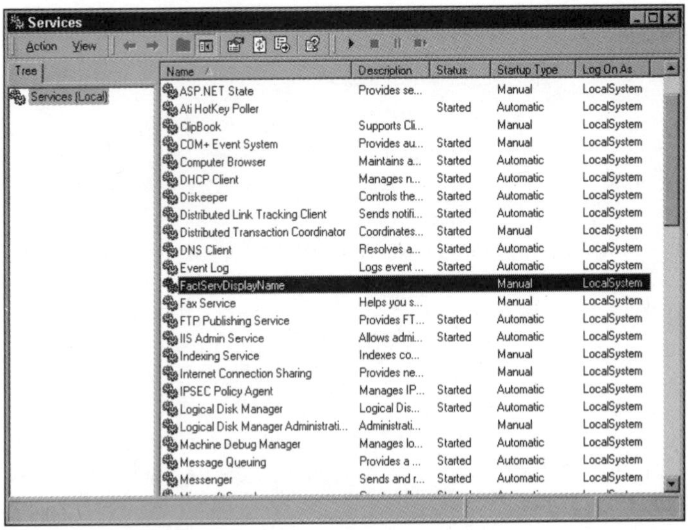

Figure 11-13: The Service Control Manager with factorial service installed.

Finally, you can look at the Add or Remove Programs dialog box and see that the application was installed and how you can either remove or repair the installation of the application, as shown in Figure 11-14.

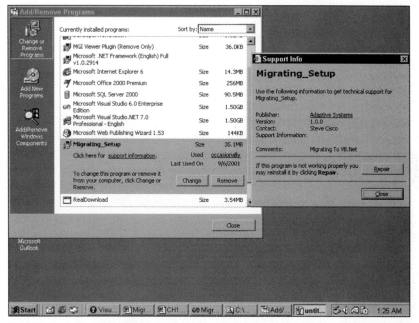

Figure 11-14: The Add or Remove Programs dialog box with support information displayed.

Dynamic Properties

Visual Basic .NET introduces a dynamic properties feature that is used to store configuration information about the application in an external XML file. As you're working with forms and controls, you'll see that there is a `DynamicProperties` item in the Properties window. Open up the main form on the Windows Application project in design mode, and make sure the Show All Files option is selected for the project in the Solution Explorer. At this time, you won't see the configuration file because you haven't specified any dynamic properties. In the Properties Window for the main form, select the `Advanced` item underneath the `DynamicProperties` item and you see the dialog box shown in Figure 11-15.

This dialog box allows you to define the dynamic properties that are stored and retrieved in the configuration file automatically. At this time, don't click any properties, but do click on the OK button. When you click on the OK button, a file called App.Config will be added to the project. If you double-click on this file, it opens up for editing in XML mode, as shown in Figure 11-16.

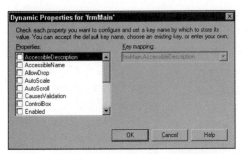

Figure 11-15: Dynamic Properties Configuration dialog box.

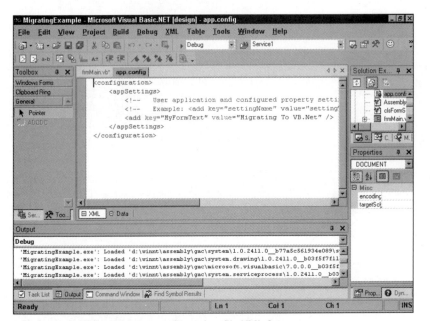

Figure 11-16: The application configuration file XML format.

Add the following key to the file as described in the XML comments:

```
<add key="MyFormText" value="Migrating To VB.NET" />
```

When the key is added, you can switch over to the Data View tab for the configuration file, and you can drill down to see the data in a grid type format. Figure 11-17 shows the data view of the XML designer for the configuration file where you can add new key value pairs as you would when adding records to a table.

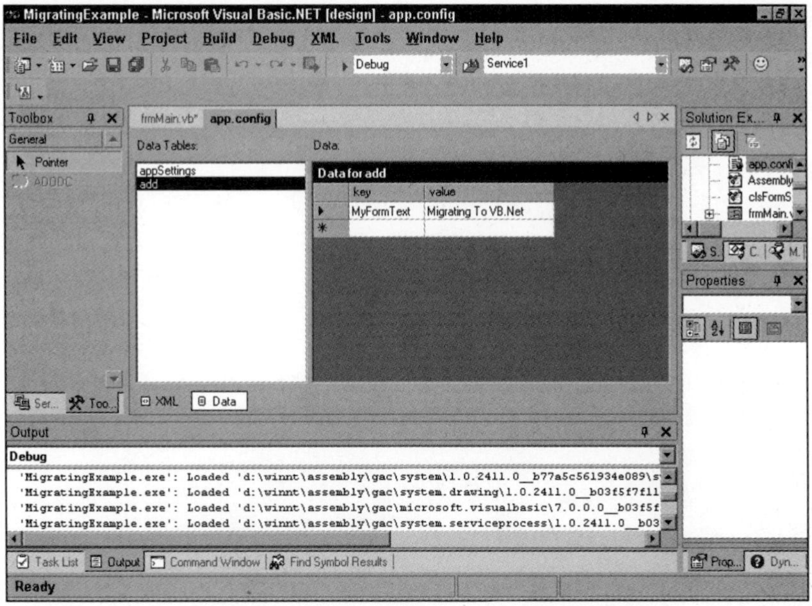

Figure 11-17: The XML application configuration designer in data view.

When you have the configuration file and the data keys in it, you can read the configuration information as shown in the following lines of code:

```
Me.Text =__
  Configuration.ConfigurationSettings.AppSettings.Get("MyFormText")
```

Insert the preceding lines of code in the constructor for the form after the service controller code. At this point, if you were to run the project, you would end up wasting a fair amount of time, because the setup project would be built along with all the other projects in the solution. Bring up the Build Configuration Manager and select the debug configuration, as shown in Figure 11-18. Find the Migrating_Setup project and clear the build check box so that it won't be built in debug mode.

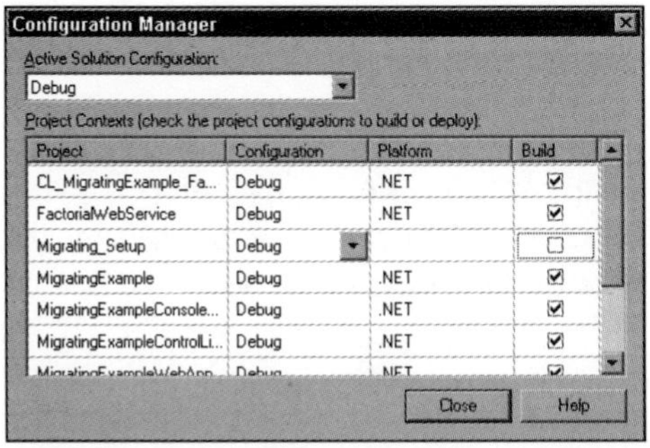

Figure 11-18: The Build Configuration Manager in debug mode.

If you were to immediately run the project, you'd notice that an exception is generated when trying to read the configuration setting. This occurred because the configuration settings haven't been initialized. In the properties window for the form, bring up the Dynamic Properties dialog box as before. Next, select the Text property on the left and pick the MyFormText key mapping from the combo box and click on OK. You'll see that the form's Text property has been updated to the information stored for the key in the configuration file. What this did was to create the proper configuration objects required when the form is created. You can now use the settings in the configuration file on your own. You can delete the mapping under the dynamic properties item in the Properties Window and run the project and notice that the text is properly updated, as shown in Figure 11-19.

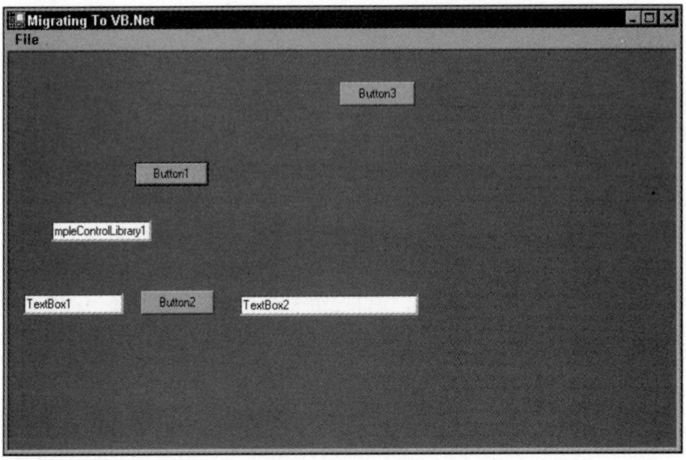

Figure 11-19: Results of reading the application configuration file at runtime.

The preceding example walked you through using the application configuration file to read in and set a property at runtime. The information in the configuration file could be used to specify any configuration information that needs to be able to change at runtime without requiring the application to be rebuilt and distributed with the updated settings. If you give an administrator the information required to change these settings, he could customize certain features of the application without requiring you to rebuild the applications. If you're going to use configuration files, you need to make sure you include the configuration file in the installation program. Now that you know how to manually set and read information from the configuration file, you can experiment with setting dynamic properties to be updated automatically. You can look at the code that's generated to see how the properties are linked and set automatically to the controls and forms.

Because the configuration file is simply an XML text file, proper precautions need to be taken if the configuration file contains sensitive information. The information in the file could be encrypted or could be restricted to certain users by using NTFS file permissions. Although this can require some extra thought, the benefits will easily outweigh the effort required to use these files to store the dynamic configuration information for your applications.

Summary

Visual Basic .NET changes the way applications are deployed from prior versions. The installation programs and requirements are now integrated into the development of the project itself. Certain controls that are in the Components tab of the toolbox need to have installers added for them by right-clicking on them and selecting the Add Installer item from the context menu that appears.

Using the installers and the installation projects will reduce the time and effort required of you when you're ready to deploy the application. As installers are added to a project, you can view and modify the code that is created to handle custom installation requirements if this is required.

Dynamic properties allow an easy way to store configuration information for an application in an XML file that is read in at runtime to configure the application. Configuration information like this would typically have been included in the Registry or in INI files in previous versions of Visual Basic. However, XML files allow you to create hierarchical data structures that map to real-world configurations and don't force the settings to be flattened out to fit a particular format. Registry files were hard to maintain and ship properly with applications, and INI files had their own drawbacks, but they also had the advantage of being able to directly modify over a network with a simple text editor. XML files are the best of both worlds and are easy to use to configure dynamic information for your applications that can change the behavior of an application without having to recompile and redistribute the application each time a setting needs to change.

Part V

Advanced .NET Topics

Chapter 12

Understanding Free Threading in Visual Basic .NET

IN THIS CHAPTER

◆ Thread basics

◆ Disadvantages of threads

◆ Advantages of threads

◆ Using threads in Visual Basic .NET

◆ Getting data to and from separate threads

◆ Synchronization and locking issues with threads

The ability to use threads in Visual Basic .NET is a double-edged sword. If used properly, they can improve the responsiveness of your application and allow your application to appear to be executing more than one piece of code at the same time. Using multiple threads in an application is a critical component of scaleable server-side applications. Throughout this chapter, you'll see how easy it is to use, create, and manage threads in Visual Basic .NET. I also show you some of the problems and workarounds concerning threads. You'll see code in this chapter that will allow you to create a generic class that can be inherited by other classes that need support for threading. You can use this class as a threading framework that will make it easier for your applications to support executing code on multiple threads.

What Is a Thread?

Threads are the basic unit of work for a preemptive, multitasking operating system. When used properly, threads can help your applications be more responsive to user input and scale to more and more clients as the demand increases. When threads aren't used properly, they can quickly bring a computer to a screeching halt by using up the available system memory (which has consequences of its own) or by having too many threads running at the same time, so that no single thread gets enough time to perform any meaningful amount of work. Don't let the preceding statement scare you away from using threads in Visual Basic .NET. When you understand how to properly use multiple threads in your application, you'll be able to design pieces of your applications to take advantage of this ability to execute sections of code concurrently with each other, instead of requiring one section to complete before the next section can start. Visual Basic .NET allows you to create a thread easily and have it execute a certain piece of code. Creating threads is the easy part, as you'll soon understand. The hard part is knowing when, where, and how to use them properly to obtain the many benefits they can provide to your application.

The history of thread usage in Visual Basic

Visual Basic has allowed you to create multithreaded applications since version 5, but in order to do so you had to use some tricks. Version 5 allowed you to use the new AddressOf operator and, with a few Windows API calls, you could run routines in a standard module on a separate thread. However, version 6 changed the underlying architecture a little, and this trick was no longer "safe" to use. A couple of articles were posted on various newsgroups, and some were posted in the various programming journals, showing how you could do it in VB6 — but it was complicated to understand and there was no guarantee that it would work in the next version of Visual Basic. If you wanted to have multiple threads running in the same process, you were probably out of luck, unless you resorted to third-party tools. But again, there was no guarantee that these tools would work in the next version of Visual Basic.

If you were developing in-process or out-of-process components with Visual Basic, you had some limited options available to you by setting the thread model in the project properties. Prior versions of Visual Basic used an apartment-threaded model for using multiple threads within the same component. With the apartment-threaded model, you could choose to use either a thread per object or a pool of threads. The thread-per-object setting allowed each object that was created from the component to have its own thread, but each thread received its own copy of global data within the component. With each object that was created, a new thread would be created consuming more and more resources. The thread pool setting allowed you to specify the maximum number of threads that would be used when creating objects. Each thread in the pool of available threads was assigned to a created object based on a round-robin scheme. This thread-assignment scheme sounded great at first, until developers tried using these features and didn't understand the complications that arise from creating and running an application on different threads, such as deadlocking, race conditions, or no access to shared data.

Drawbacks of threads

Every time a new thread is created on the operating system, it adds additional overhead that must be dealt with. Multitasking operating systems can run multiple threads, but in order to do so, each thread is preempted after so many milliseconds and another thread is given a slice of processing power of the CPU. "Well-behaved" applications should relinquish control frequently so that other threads, whether in the same process space or a separate process space, can be given a chance to use the CPU. When all other threads have had a chance, the cycle repeats and the first thread is given a chance again. If an executing thread doesn't voluntarily release control, it will be preempted and shoved to the bottom of the thread queue. Each time a thread switch occurs, the state of the thread has to be saved, and the saved state of the new thread has to be loaded back into the stacks and registers of the CPU. As you can see, this switching process has a certain amount of overhead associated with it and will force any task to take longer than if it were to have exclusive access to the CPU for the life of the task.

Figure 12-1 illustrates this concept in a graphical format that will help you understand the cost of thread switching. The left column in Figure 12-1 indicates the time it would take two identical threads or applications to run if they weren't running on a preemptive, multitasking operating system. In this scenario, each thread or process would have exclusive use of the CPU while it's running, and the time that it takes for both to complete is twice as long as an individual task. The right column shows what actually happens in a preemptive, multitasking operating system with a single processor.

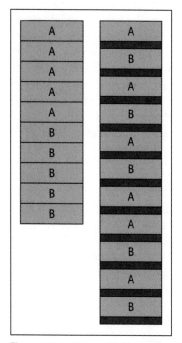

Figure 12-1: The cost of switching threads.

A common misconception about threads is that if the second process were on its own thread, then both processes would run at the same time, and the time that it takes to complete both processes would be the amount of time it takes either one to complete. In a preemptive multitasking environment, the thread switching introduces a small amount of overhead that will actually increase the total amount of time that it takes multiple threads to complete. The only way that both operations could come close to completing at the time required for one task would be if each thread were running on a separate processor.

Using multiple processors is the key to improving performance by reducing the overall execution time of multiple tasks by allowing each thread of execution to be delegated to a separate processor. However, threads don't have to be used to improve the actual timed performance of an application. They can also be used to improve the perceived performance of your application by the user by allowing your application to be more responsive to user input by allowing certain operations to be executed in the background. By executing certain tasks in the background, your application can still be responsive to user input or it can continue to service requests from clients while the specified task is running in the background.

In a Symmetrical Multiprocessing System (SMP) such as Windows NT, Windows 2000, or Windows XP, you can't guarantee which processor will be chosen by the operating system to run the thread at any time. On a multiple-processor machine, two threads may execute on the same processor or different processors. The operating system controls which processor the thread is chosen to run on based on various low-level system resources. Again, the right column in Figure 12-1 shows the additional time required to switch between each thread on a single processor. It doesn't account for any threads that will be running at different priority levels, such as the higher-priority operating system code. The higher priority threads that aren't shown in the figure would be given a chance to execute first, which would only increase the overall execution time for the two threads shown. As more and more threads are used, more and more system resources are used up, and the operating system will spend more time switching between different threads than it does doing actual work.

The benefits of threads

Now that you understand a little more about how threads actually work, you may be wondering why they should even be used at all. The answer is simple: Threads allow multiple units of work to appear to be executing at the same time. A single CPU can only physically execute a single thread at any moment in time. Preemptive multitasking allows each thread to have a small slice of time in which it can use the resources of the CPU before it's stopped and another thread is given the chance to run. The time slice each thread is given is small enough (roughly 20 milliseconds) that it gives the appearance that more than one piece of code is running at the same time. Without preemptive multitasking, a thread would have complete control over the CPU until it was finished, effectively tying up the CPU.

CLIENT SIDE

On the client side, efficient use of threads can keep your application responsive to user input while processing long background tasks and allowing the user to easily cancel those long-running tasks should they desire to do so. One example of a good use of threads on the client side would be a call center application. When the user calls in, the person answering the phone could get the basic information from the client and start a separate thread that checks to see if there is a record or any history for the caller and then populates the forms in the background, while still allowing notes to be entered about why the user is calling.

Another example of a good use of threads on the client side is any time the user or application is going to start a long running process such as a search, an import, or an export of data. By running the process on a separate thread, the user could be allowed to hit a Cancel button, and the thread running the process could be stopped. Threads could also be used to run a monitor process, which would check the state of something in the application and either inform the user when something happened or run another piece of code.

Most developers have used the Visual Basic Timer control to generate events at a predetermined interval without requiring a constant loop. Although this may have worked in most situations, you couldn't guarantee when the event would actually occur. If the queue for the Windows messages were to be backlogged, it would take a little while before the code in the timer event would run. Timers and their events are good candidates to look at to see if the process can be moved into a thread. Threads can be put to sleep for a specified amount of time. When they wake up, they can do any processing they need to do, reset into a loop, and then go to sleep again.

SERVER SIDE

Many clients typically use a single server-side application, but one of the limiting factors is how many clients can concurrently use the application. If a server application doesn't use multiple threads, then only one client can be serviced at a time, and all requests from the other clients will be blocked and serialized to access the application one at a time in the order in which the requests were received. Servers use threads because there are typically many different applications running on a single server, and each application must be given equal access to the processing power. Servers and server-side applications can use threads more efficiently for three primary reasons:

- More RAM on the server
- Multiple processors
- Faster CPU speeds

Servers typically have much more RAM than a typical client workstation does. This alone allows more threads to be created than on a client, because of the memory that each thread requires for saving and restoring its context when switching.

Most servers have more than one processor, which allows multiple threads to be executing concurrently at any point in time. As you now know, only one thread can physically be active on a single processor at a time. Multiple processors allow multiple threads to be running physically at the same time, so the maximum number of threads that can be running on the server concurrently is equal to the number of processors installed and running in the server. This is the primary reason why a server would seem faster or more powerful than a regular client.

The faster CPU speeds typically found on a server allow more work to be done in each slice of time that a thread is given to run. If a thread can complete its work before being preempted, then the thread can terminate, free up the resources, and voluntarily relinquish control before forcing a context switch. If a single threaded application were placed on a single processor client and on a multiple processor computer, where the only physical difference was the number of processors in the computers, the application's performance wouldn't change. The key to taking advantage of multiple processors on a server is efficiently allocating multiple threads in the application that can run on each of the available processors.

Threading in Visual Basic .NET

Now that you understand the basic concepts of threads and how they work, let's look at how you can create a thread and make it do something in Visual Basic .NET. Start a new Windows Application project, and place a button on the form. Thread support is provided by the System.Threading namespace, so you can either use the Imports keyword to import the namespace into the local module, use the Project Properties dialog box to import the namespace into the local project, or completely qualify the objects. Open up the code window for the form and insert the following line of code at the top of the form module:

```
Imports System.Threading
```

This line of code will allow you to declare and create the thread without requiring the System.Threading prefix on all the objects and parameters. Now you'll need a routine that the thread will execute, so within your class declaration for the form, insert the following procedure:

```
Private Sub DoSomethingOnAThread()
    Me.Text = "The thread worked"
End Sub
```

This procedure will simply change the text property of the form in the title bar to indicate that it actually worked. Now in the click event of the button, you'll create and run the thread:

```
Private Sub Button1_Click(ByVal sender As Object, _
  ByVal e As System.EventArgs) Handles Button1.Click

  Dim T As New Thread(AddressOf DoSomethingOnAThread)

  T.Start()
End Sub
```

Run the project, click on the button, and notice how the text changes on the title bar of the form, indicating that the thread actually ran the DoSomethingOnAThread procedure. You should also notice how the routine was within a class module and it was private, yet the AddressOf operator found it and had no problems running it on the thread. From this example, you can see how Visual Basic .NET makes it extremely easy to create a thread and have it execute a piece of code.

If that were all there were to it, then there would be no need for the rest of this chapter and I could've shown you all you needed to know in a chapter at the beginning of this book. What you've done so far was the easy part. The rest of this chapter deals with the other issues you need to understand when using threads.

Getting Down to Business

The code shown in the preceding section will actually only work in the most simple of cases. The major limitation in that example is that, after the thread is running and the click event exits, you have no idea about the status of the thread (such as when it was finished) and you can't supply any parameters to the routine the thread will execute. When the routine that the thread is executing completes, the thread terminates, and trying to start it again will throw an exception – even though the thread object is still alive. You must clean up the thread and create a new one if you want the routine to be executed again. An alternative would be to have a loop within the routine the thread executes and check for some status to jump out of the loop. One of the things you need to keep in mind when working with threads is that they continue to run in the background until they're terminated or the routine they're executing finishes.

What happens if the user tries closing the application or form while the thread is running in a loop? The thread will continue to run, even though the form or application appears to have gone away. The thread will be running in the background and the application will continue to run, but it won't be visible to the user. When it gets in this state, there's no way to end the application without going to the task manager and killing it from there.

How would you know if the thread completes? You can't get an event from the thread object because it doesn't raise any events. You'd need to have some way of tracking the status of the thread to see when it's complete. In this case, you'd have to have a routine that polls for the status of the thread. But how would you keep that routine running in the background?

Creating the ThreadManager

As you can see, there are some issues that need to be addressed when working with threads. The best way to do this is to have a Thread Manager object that's responsible for managing a thread and exposes events that are raised when something happens that the routine or object responsible for initiating the thread needs to know about. The rest of this chapter walks you through creating this object and lets you know how to use it to incorporate thread management in your application.

Start with a new Windows Application project, and add a class named clsThreadManager to the project. At the top of the module, insert the following line of code to use the System.Threading namespace in your class module:

```
Imports System.Threading
```

Next, create the Before and After events for the various control options. As mentioned earlier, threads themselves don't expose events, so we'll provide some events of our own. The thread manager class is going to raise events for ThreadStart, ThreadSuspend, ThreadResume, ThreadAbort, ThreadInterrupt, ThreadSleep, and ThreadJoin. Insert the following code at the beginning of the definition for the class:

```
Public Event BeforeThreadStart(ByRef Cancel As Boolean)
Public Event AfterThreadStart()
Public Event BeforeThreadSuspend(ByRef Cancel As Boolean)
Public Event AfterThreadSuspend()
Public Event BeforeThreadResume(ByRef Cancel As Boolean)
Public Event AfterThreadResume()
Public Event BeforeThreadAbort(ByRef Cancel As Boolean)
Public Event AfterThreadAbort()
Public Event BeforeThreadInterrupt(ByRef Cancel As Boolean)
Public Event AfterThreadInterrupt()
Public Event BeforeThreadSleep(ByRef Cancel As Boolean, _
    ByRef Interval As Integer)
Public Event AfterThreadSleep()
Public Event BeforeThreadJoin(ByRef Cancel As Boolean)
Public Event AfterThreadJoin()
```

The Before events expose a Cancel property that can be set to True to prevent the event from occurring. Creating the working object using the WithEvents syntax will allow it to trap these events as the code is running. We need to add one more event to indicate when the thread has finished executing:

```
Public Event ThreadFinished(ByVal FinishedNormally As Boolean)
```

Next, we need to have a private module level variable that will contain the thread object that we'll use to execute code and manage its state. Insert the following line of code after the event declarations to hold a reference to the Thread object:

```
Protected mThr As Thread
```

You should also note the use of the Protected keyword instead of the Private keyword. You'll see shortly why this was used, but the main reason is that this class will be inherited from when you need to use a thread, and if the thread were declared as `Private`, then it wouldn't be accessible from the derived class. As you already know, the thread must have a routine to execute, so we need to create this. However, if you created this here, then you'd have to include all your code within this routine. Because we're trying to create a generic thread manager, we're just going to stub out the function. Through inheritance, if a class has a same function as its base class, the derived function will be the one that executes. This is what we want, so when we declare our function, we must use the `MustOverride` attribute:

```
Public MustOverride Sub CodeToExecute()
```

Using the `MustOverride` attribute will force the inherited class to override the function and will provide the real work in the overridden function in the derived class. However, by having a `MustOverride` function declared, it forces us to make a similar statement on the class itself:

```
Public MustInherit Class clsThreadManager
```

You must add the `MustInherit` attribute to the class to ensure that the `Thread Manager` is used correctly. This will require that a derived class is created and it must inherit from the `ThreadManager` base class.

The next thing we must do is initialize the `Thread` object when we initialize the `ThreadManager` object. We'll do this in the default constructor for the `ThreadManager` class:

```
Public Sub New()
    mThr = New Thread(AddressOf CodeToExecute)
End Sub
```

This will properly initialize the `Thread` object by pointing to the `CodeToExecute` procedure that we declared. Remember that, through inheritance, the actual procedure that will be run is the one that overrides the abstract procedure in the base class. Therefore, the thread will actually run the procedure in the derived class, which is where you'll write the code that actually performs the work. One of the events we declared was to indicate when the thread was finished. Because the actual work will be performed in the base class, we need a way to raise this event, and derived classes cannot raise events from the base class. In order to raise the `ThreadFinished` event, we need to expose a method on the base class that will fire the event:

```
Protected Sub RaiseThreadFinished(ByVal FinishedNormally As Boolean)
    RaiseEvent ThreadFinished(FinishedNormally)
End Sub
```

We used the Protected keyword because we only wanted this routine to be called from within the inherited class and not from outside it. Next, we'll expose a ReadOnly property that can be used to query the thread's state:

```
Public ReadOnly Property ThreadState() As ThreadState
    Get
        Return mThr.ThreadState
    End Get
End Property
```

The ThreadState property is a *bit mask,* which allows the thread state to represent combinations of the individual thread states. The individual thread states are Aborted, AbortRequested, Background, Running, Stopped, StopRequested, Suspended, SuspendRequested, Unstarted, and WaitSleepJoin. Figure 12-2 shows a thread state diagram so you can see how the states are related.

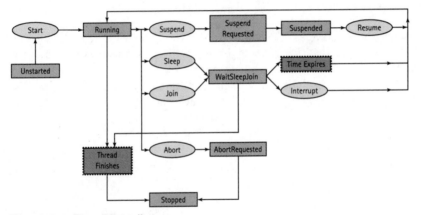

Figure 12-2: Thread state diagram.

Next, threads can have different priorities and can be changed, so we'll expose a property that maps to the thread object and allows the priority to be queries or set:

```
Public Property Priority() As ThreadPriority
    Get
        Return mThr.Priority
    End Get
    Set(ByVal Value As ThreadPriority)
        mThr.Priority = Value
    End Set
End Property
```

Now we just need to be able to start, stop, and manage the thread's actions. You don't want to expose the Thread object directly outside the class, because you'll allow operations on the thread that doesn't come through your object and, as a result, you'll lose the event capabilities this class exposes. We could expose several methods, each of which map to the individual control functions on the `Thread` object, but I chose to expose a `ControlThread` method that accepts a control-type parameter, which determines what function should be called. The control types are an enum listing, so insert the following enum where the other public properties and events are located in the class module:

```
Public Enum ControlThreadOptions
    StartThread = 1
    SuspendThread = 2
    ResumeThread = 3
    AbortThread = 4
    Interrupt = 5
    Sleep = 6
    Join = 7
End Enum
```

Now the heart of the `ThreadManager` class comes from the `ControlThread` method, which is shown here:

```
Public Sub ControlThread(ByVal ControlThreadOption _
    As ControlThreadOptions, Optional ByVal SleepInterval _
    As Integer = 0, Optional ByVal JoinInterval _
    As Integer = 0)

    Dim blnCancel As Boolean
    Dim intSleepInterval As Integer = SleepInterval

    Try
        Select Case ControlThreadOption
        Case ControlThreadOptions.StartThread
            RaiseEvent BeforeThreadStart(blnCancel)
            If Not blnCancel Then
                Try
                    If mThr.ThreadState = ThreadState.Suspended _
    Then ControlThread(ControlThreadOptions.ResumeThread)
                    ControlThread(ControlThreadOptions.AbortThread)
                Finally
                    mThr = New Thread(AddressOf CodeToExecute)
                    mThr.Start()
                    RaiseEvent AfterThreadStart()
                End Try
            End If
```

```
Case ControlThreadOptions.SuspendThread
    RaiseEvent BeforeThreadSuspend(blnCancel)
    If Not blnCancel Then
        If mThr.ThreadState = ThreadState.Running Then
            mThr.Suspend()
            RaiseEvent AfterThreadSuspend()
        End If
    End If

Case ControlThreadOptions.ResumeThread
    If mThr.ThreadState = ThreadState.Suspended Then
        RaiseEvent BeforeThreadResume(blnCancel)
        If Not blnCancel Then
            mThr.Resume()
            RaiseEvent AfterThreadResume()
        End If
    End If

Case ControlThreadOptions.AbortThread
    RaiseEvent BeforeThreadAbort(blnCancel)

    If Not blnCancel Then
        If Not mThr.ThreadState = ThreadState.Unstarted Then
            Try
                mThr.Abort()
            Finally
                Try
                    mThr.Join()
                Finally
                    RaiseEvent AfterThreadAbort()
                End Try
            End Try
        End If
    End If

Case ControlThreadOptions.Interrupt
    RaiseEvent BeforeThreadInterrupt(blnCancel)
    If Not blnCancel Then
        mThr.Interrupt()
        RaiseEvent AfterThreadInterrupt()
    End If

Case ControlThreadOptions.Sleep
    RaiseEvent BeforeThreadSleep(blnCancel, _
        intSleepInterval)
```

```
            If Not blnCancel Then
                mThr.Sleep(intSleepInterval)
                RaiseEvent AfterThreadSleep()
            End If


        Case ControlThreadOptions.Join
            If Not mThr.ThreadState = ThreadState.Unstarted Then
                RaiseEvent BeforeThreadJoin(blnCancel)
                If Not blnCancel Then
                    If Not JoinInterval = 0 Then
                        mThr.Join(JoinInterval)
                    Else
                        mThr.Join()
                    End If
                    RaiseEvent AfterThreadJoin()
                End If
            End If
        End Select


    Catch e As Exception
        'Do something with an exception that may occur
    End Try
End Sub
```

The logic is pretty simple for the preceding function. When a request is called to control the thread, the function checks to see if the request makes sense for the current thread state. This routine makes use of the new Try...Catch...Finally structured error handling and should give you an appreciation for handling the errors that may occur. Think about how you'd have to code for the errors using the On Error...Goto syntax if you couldn't use structured exception handling. From the diagram in Figure 12-2, you can see why the tests are included. If you attempt to call a method on the thread that doesn't make sense for the state that it's in, an exception will be thrown, which will be caught in the outer catch block.

Now let's discuss the various thread-control options available. When a thread is created, its initial state is Unstarted. In order to move from this state, the Start method must be called, which will transition the thread into the Running state. After a thread has transitioned from the Unstarted state, there is no way for it to ever have that state again until the thread is destroyed and re-created. From here, there are several different paths that the thread can take. If no other method is called and if the routine that the thread runs doesn't contain an infinite loop, then when the routine is finished, the thread will finish the code it was executing and the thread state will end up in the Stopped state.

From the Running state, there are four different methods that you can call to transition to another state. The first method is the Suspend method, which will cause the thread to be paused. The thread isn't paused immediately, because the runtime must get the thread in a safe state before it can be paused. During this time, the thread state will be SuspendRequested. When the thread reaches a safe state, it will be paused and the thread state will become suspended. At this time, the thread will remain suspended until the Resume method is called, at which point the thread can pick up from where it left off. It's important to realize that the runtime will suspend all threads except the active thread while it performs a garbage collection, so it can walk the reference tree. The Start method can't be used on a thread that's already running, because an exception will be thrown. If you call the Start method on the Thread Manager, the thread will be aborted and then destroyed and re-created, essentially giving you a restart capability.

The next method is the Sleep method, which will put the thread in the WaitSleepJoin state. This state is similar to the Suspended state, except that there are a couple of different ways for the thread to exit this state. The first way the thread can exit out of this state is for the timeout specified in the Sleep method to expire. When this happens, the thread will resume back to the Running state. The second way the thread can exit this state is if another thread, typically the calling routine, calls the Interrupt method. The Interrupt method will force the thread to "wake up" and will throw a ThreadInterrupted exception. This exception needs to be explicitly caught if you want to be able to resume at a particular point in the code. Otherwise, an Unhandled exception will be generated. You'll see that, in the thread manager, the code that's executing will catch all unhandled exceptions, execute a finally block, and terminate the thread.

A word of caution is needed here because of the way the Sleep method on the Thread object is implemented. Calling the Sleep method will put the currently executing thread to sleep not necessarily the thread itself. If the sleep method were to be called from within the Thread Manager by code that is executing on the active thread, the thread would go to sleep. If the ControlThread method was called from outside the active thread, the calling function would be put to sleep for the specified interval. If you wanted the managed thread to go to sleep for a specified period of time, then you would need to call the Sleep method on the Thread object directly. When the thread was declared, it was declared with the Protected keyword. This will allow the code that is placed in the CodeToExecute routine to call the Sleep method on the defined mThr variable.

The Join method is similar to the sleep method, because it will put the thread into the same WaitSleepJoin state. The Join method can either be called with or without specifying a timeout interval. If no interval is specified, then the Join method will wait for the thread to die by completing its work normally, and then execution will continue on the line following the Join method call. If an interval is specified, then the Join method call will wait for the thread to finish in the specified amount of time. If the thread doesn't finish in the specified amount of time, then the method will return after the timeout interval. The Interrupt method could be called from a different thread, and the thread will behave in the same way as was described in the previous paragraph with the Sleep method.

The last method that can be called on a Running thread is the Abort method, which will throw a Threading.ThreadAbortException in the executing code. If the exception is caught, then the executing code will be given a chance to perform any cleanup filtered exception block or in the finally block. After any code in these blocks is executed, then the thread will transition to the Stopped state.

That is basically all there is to the ThreadManager object, but you need to understand how to use it and how to get data to and from your thread. The next section explains how to do this and outlines some issues that you may encounter along the way.

Using the ThreadManager

In order to use the ThreadManager, you need to define a class that inherits from the ThreadManager class. In this class, you'll need to override the CodeToExecute function as explained in the previous section where you built the ThreadManager class. This is the function that will perform the work for your Thread object. Within this function, you need to wrap the code around a Try...Catch block to catch the interrupted or aborted exceptions that may be generated. You can insert the following class definition within the main form for the application (as a subclass):

```
Public Class ThreadWorker
    Inherits clsThreadManager

    Private mblnFinishedNormally As Boolean = False

    Public Overrides Sub CodeToExecute()
        Try
            'Main work is done here
            'May include additional try catch blocks
            mblnFinishedNormally = True
        Catch e As Threading.ThreadAbortException
            'Do something with the exception like cleanup code
        Catch e As Threading.ThreadInterruptedException
            'Do something with the interrupted exception
            'Could clean up or
            'Could restart by jumping to line label
        Finally
            MyBase.RaiseThreadFinished(mblnFinishedNormally)
        End Try
    End Sub
End Class
```

That's all that's required in order to create a Worker Thread object that uses the ThreadManager support you created. Now, in order to use your Worker Thread object, you just need to create it using the With Events keyword within your code. Insert the following line of code after the Inherits statement at the top of the code module for the form.

```
Private WithEvents MyWorker As ThreadWorker
```

Now in the `Load` event of the form you can initialize the thread worker:

```
MyWorker = New ThreadWorker()
```

Place a button on the form and in the `Click` event you can start the worker thread:

```
MyWorker.ControlThread( __
    clsThreadManager.ControlThreadOptions.StartThread)
```

By declaring the `Worker` `With` events, you can trap for the events that are exposed from the `clsThreadManager` base class. If you sink the `ThreadFinished` event, you will know when the thread is complete and whether it completed normally or whether there was an error by checking the `FinishedNormally` parameter in the event. The other events give you indications of the thread status and allow you to cancel certain events from occurring, if you need to. Sometimes your `Worker` object may be exposed to different threads of execution, and you may not want another thread to abort your operation. Right now, there is no meat to the worker `CodeToExecute` procedure, so if you ran the project and clicked on the button you wouldn't see any evidence that it worked. In the `CodeToExecute` method of the worker class, add a hard loop in the `Try` block where it states "Main Work Is Done Here":

```
Dim I As Integer
For I = 1 To 50000
    frm.Text = I.ToString
Next
```

The preceding code will update the text in the title bar of a form with the value of the counter as the thread is running. We need some way of passing in the form reference, so add the following as a class-level variable to the `ThreadWorker` class:

```
Public frm As Form
```

Now change the `Click` event of the button you placed on the form so that it reads:

```
MyWorker.frm = Me
MyWorker.ControlThread(_
        clsThreadManager.ControlThreadOptions.StartThread)
MessageBox.Show("Hi")
```

Now if you were to run the project and click on the button, you'd see that the text in the title bar of the form is constantly updated even while the message box is displayed. Furthermore, after you clear the message, you can move the form around on the screen and the thread will continue to update the text in the title bar of the form. When the counter reaches 50,000, you'll see that the text stops changing, and if you look in the Output window, you'll see the following message that indicates the thread completed successfully:

```
The thread '<No Name>' (0x5d0) has exited with code 0 (0x0).
```

If you were to click on the button a few times, you'd see that the thread is restarted each time but continues to function. This is the benefit of the Thread Manager managing the state of the thread for you. If you looked back at the `ControlThread` routine, you'd see that in order to accomplish the automatic restarting of the thread, the Thread Manager has to abort the thread and clean it up before it can be restarted. To verify this, place the following code in the `ThreadAbortException` catch in the `CodeToExecute` routine of the worker thread:

```
MessageBox.Show("Aborted")
```

Restart the application and click on the button a couple of times and you'll see the message appear stating that it was aborted. Recalling the discussion on the sleep method, you could force the counting thread to sleep at any time by calling the `Sleep` method on the actual `Thread` object. In order to demonstrate this, place the following code after the line of code in the loop that sets the Text property of the form:

```
If I = 25000 Then mthr.Sleep(5000)
```

If you were to run the project, you'd see the counting pause for five seconds when it reaches 25,000, but the form can still be moved around – which indicates that the worker thread is asleep and not the main thread. Change the preceding line of code to use the `ControlThread` routine as follows:

```
If I = 25000 Then _
 Me.ControlThread(clsThreadManager.ControlThreadOptions.Sleep, 5000)
```

If you were to run the project again, you wouldn't see any difference from the previous code. Here, both ways will work because the `Sleep` method is being called from the thread itself. Place another button on the form and in the click event of the second button attempt to put the thread to sleep using the `ControlThread` method as shown:

```
MyWorker.ControlThread(_
    clsThreadManager.ControlThreadOptions.Sleep, 5000)
```

Run the application again and start the thread running by clicking the first button. When the thread is running, click the second button and observe what happens. First, the form can no longer be moved around the screen and the counter stops as well. After five seconds have passed, you can move the form again and the counter resumes. However, if you observe carefully, you'll see that the counter didn't continue executing this time. When you called the `ControlThread` to put the thread to sleep, the main thread of the form (the calling thread) went to sleep. When the main thread of the form went to sleep, it blocked all calls made to it until it woke up. The counter didn't continue counting because it was on a separate thread, which was blocked from calling onto the thread that executes the code for the form.

Putting threads to sleep can be very valuable to the design of your application. Putting a thread to sleep and then waking up and executing a certain piece of code can be used like a timer. However, remember that timers are based on the Windows messages, which may not be that accurate if there are a lot of messages or events being fired. A thread is controlled by the operating system so it should be more reliable than a timer. Worker threads can be used to check for messages, items to process, statuses, and so on by performing these tasks in the background, sleeping for a specified period of time, and then waking back up and starting the cycle over.

Getting data to and from the worker thread

Now that you know how to use a worker thread, you'll typically need to pass data into and out of the worker thread object. The best way to do this is to provide local variables in your worker thread object, and set these variables using either properties or methods on your worker thread object, as you did in the preceding example – by setting the reference to the form so the text in the title bar could be updated with the counter value. You simply need to set these values before you start the thread, and then when the thread-finished event occurs, you can read these values back. As a general precaution, you shouldn't try setting properties while the thread is running and attempting to set the same values. If you need to change the data that's being used by the thread while the thread is running, you should suspend, interrupt, or abort the thread before you set the values. If the thread is suspended and the local variables are changed, then you may put the logic within the thread in an invalid state. If you must keep the thread alive, then you should have a way of indicating that the variables have changed and restore the thread to a known state.

Using local variables and exposing those values as properties is the best way to share data with your `Thread` object. This way the thread gets a copy of the values it needs to work and won't be trying to update data at the same time as another piece of the application. If you can't get away from using data that can be changed by something other than the worker thread, you need to use the thread synchronization methods available to you in the .NET Framework. The `Threading.` `Interlocked` class exposes a couple of methods that will increment or decrement an Integer or a Long shared variable in an atomic operation and will prevent anything else from changing the data until the operation completes. There are also a couple of methods that allow you to set a variable to a specific Single, Integer, or

Object value and return what was stored in the variable before the exchange, and one that will compare the same types of variables with a value and replace it with a different value if the comparison is equal:

```
Threading.Interlocked.Increment(Variable)
Threading.Interlocked.Decrement(Variable)
Threading.Interlocked.CompareExchange(Location1, Value, Comparand)
Threading.Interlocked.Exchange(Location1, Value)
```

If there is a section of code that needs to access an object and needs to block anything else from accessing the object, then you can use the `Threading.Monitor` class to place a lock on an object by calling the `Enter` method on the object. Anything else that needs to access the same object would need to call the same `Enter` method on the object. The second call to the `Enter` method will be blocked until the first lock is released by calling the `Exit` method of the `Monitor` object supplying the same object that was locked in the `Enter` method. If you need more control over the threading synchronizations, you can look at the documentation to understand the other synchronization classes within the `Threading` namespace and how they can be used to produce the results you need in your application. You can also look at the documentation for the `Threading.ThreadPool` class that provides a way to use a pool of threads to queue items to be completed on `Thread` objects in a round-robin fashion. The `Thread Pool` object handles the creation and management of a pool of threads based on the computer properties, such as available memory, number of processors, number of active threads, and so on. If you don't use this, then you'll have to create your own pool manager for your worker threads based on your application requirements.

Summary

Because Visual Basic .NET includes support for creating your own threads and makes it extremely easy to do so, many developers will start diving in headfirst, without knowing how deep the water is. The hard part of using threads is how to manage the threads and the interactions with the other threads in your application after you create them.

There is a reason why Microsoft has held off on giving Visual Basic developers inherent support for threads until now. Threading is an advanced subject and can introduce hard-to-find bugs in an application, such as deadlocks and race conditions, which may not appear until the application is compiled. With all the synchronization issues and management issues that Visual Basic developers will have to face when working with their own threads, many will become overwhelmed or confused with the new terminology and requirements.

The support for threads in Visual Basic .NET is not intended for beginning- to intermediate-level programmers. Understanding and using threads is a vast, complicated subject, and complete books could and will probably be written on the subject. The purpose of this chapter is to give you enough background so that you can choose whether you really want to use threading in your applications. If you choose to do so, this chapter should serve as your introduction to threading in Visual Basic .NET. I would strongly encourage you to seek out further information on threading in Visual Basic through other books, magazine articles, and MSDN articles.

Chapter 13

Working With and Understanding the Windows Forms Designer

Visual Basic .NET has overhauled the original forms engine that was created for Visual Basic. Although prior versions made gradual modifications to the engine, the changes required for the engine to support the .NET Framework are pretty drastic. The purpose of this chapter is to bring you up to speed on the new forms engine and show you how it creates Visual Basic code to display the various controls on the form both at design-time and at runtime. This chapter shows you how and why you can modify the code that's created by the Windows Forms Designer and also explains some of the direct modifications that you should avoid trying to make.

An Overview of the Windows Forms Designer

Since Visual Basic was first released, its primary feature has been its rich forms engine, which allowed developers to create applications for Windows without having to understand the intricacies of the Windows API. Before Visual Basic, a lot of plumbing was required just to display and allow a user to interact with a graphical user interface–based application. Visual Basic allowed developers to concentrate on solving the business problems instead of the plumbing that's required in every Windows application. It did this by providing a forms engine that allowed the interfaces of applications to be created by simply dragging various controls onto a form and setting some properties on the controls. The forms engine actually generated text files that described the forms and the controls on the form. Any code that was created to respond to events of the controls and forms would then be placed in the same file after the description header. The forms engine and the integrated development environment would then parse out the information and the development environment would display the code while the forms engine would display the interface of the form. As a result, there was one description language for the forms themselves and another language for responding to events of the controls defined in the description language.

Although hiding the inner details allowed developers to concentrate on solving the business problems, it did have some disadvantages. Sometimes developers needed to change the behavior of the form for any number of reasons, such as creating a workaround for a bug in the forms engine, providing enhanced capabilities not present, or modifying an existing piece of functionality so that it provided a different behavior. In cases like these, developers were often stuck because they couldn't figure out how to change the way the forms designer was parsing and displaying the interface description code.

Since its initial release, Visual Basic had relied on the same basic forms engine and description language to describe a form. This situation has changed in Visual Basic .NET, because it provides a new forms engine called Windows Forms, which provides the functionality to standard client applications. Through the .NET Framework, these Windows Forms can be created and run on other platforms provided there is a common language runtime and .NET Framework created for other platforms. To simplify things and give developers more control and power over the behavior of the forms, the new forms engine generates actual code that will create the window in the language in which it's being developed. So in our terms, the forms engine creates and writes Visual Basic code that describes and creates the interface of the form within the form itself. This code is inserted into the normal event handling code and is constantly updated by the forms designer.

By now, you know that everything in Visual Basic .NET is an object, and that all objects use constructors to initialize the object. When a form is initialized, its constructor is called when it's created, and it's the constructor's responsibility to create the object and initialize it properly. When you're working with Windows Forms, the constructor actually calls a routine in each form called InitializeComponent.

Figure 13-1 shows the code behind a new form that's added to the project. The code that's there looks pretty simple right now. The code simply defines a class definition for the form. The class is named, and you'll see that the Inherits statement is included to inherit the behavior of a form from the System.Windows.Forms. Form base class. The only other code in the code window is a collapsed region that contains the code generated by the forms designer. If you expand the region, you'll see the code that manages the creation and destruction of forms, as shown in Figure 13-2.

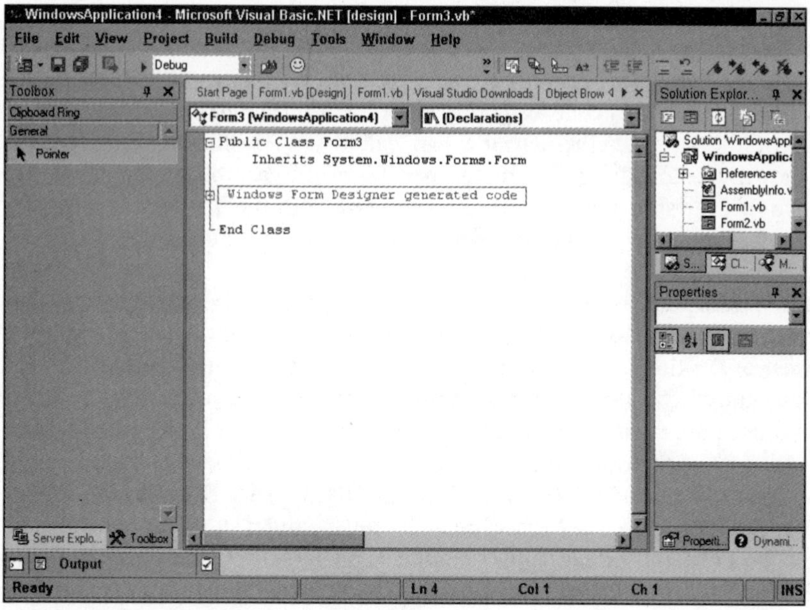

Figure 13-1: Code behind a new windows form.

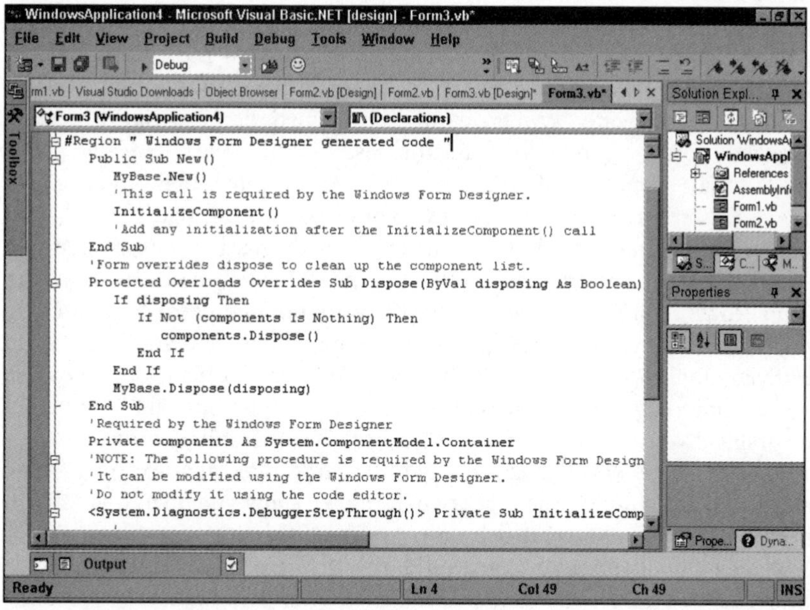

Figure 13-2: Windows Forms Designer–generated code.

As you can see, the Windows Forms Designer creates quite a bit of code that manages the creation and management of the form. The Windows Forms Designer places code in the `InitializeComponent` routine to create all the graphical elements on the form. This code is then executed at runtime to create and display the image of the form on the screen when called for. The forms designer also uses the code in this location to set any properties for the controls whose values are not the default values for the property. As you work with the designer surface, the code in this procedure is constantly updated to reflect your changes to the visual interface of the form.

In keeping with the ease-of-use theme that has made Visual Basic so popular, the code that the forms designer generates is hidden by default in a collapsed region. Most of the time, you won't need to dig any deeper in this area except for creating specialized constructors for the form object. However, there may be times when you'll need to at least look at the code in the initialization procedure in order to figure out how a particular feature is implemented. Remember that everything you see on your forms is created through Visual Basic code. There are no longer any hidden details of how the form is created and the order in which the controls are created. You can use the example code that's generated from the forms designer and implement the same features in your code elsewhere in the form's lifetime.

One of the first things you may notice about the code in this region is the warning telling you not to modify the code using the code editor. For the strong-headed developers out there (myself included), a warning like this telling you not to do something is just an open invitation to see what'll happen if you do. How many times have you heard that you can't do something in Visual Basic? For each of those times, how many times did you try to figure it out or prove that it could be done? Sometimes the only way to learn about something is to tinker around, experiment, and try new approaches or techniques.

Most people may simply restate the warning that's provided, telling you not to modify the code that's generated by the forms designer, fearing that the new feature will give you a small electric shock from your keyboard if you change this code. Most of the time, this rule will hold true, but there will be cases as you're learning and programming in Visual Basic .NET when the rule needs to be broken. However, if you get caught breaking a rule, there are consequences and this is no exception. Even though you can change the forms designer information in the code window, it should only be changed here for specific reasons that you could encounter — typically as a reaction to something that isn't working correctly.

A warning like this is just like the standard warning that Microsoft or anyone else states about not modifying the registry before they show you how to modify it. Although errors that may be created by directly modifying the code won't be as serious as deleting or incorrectly changing a key in the registry, they can cause some nasty, hard-to-find problems. If you make an error or omission in the code, you may not be able to get the form to display again, and the error message you receive may not lead you to the changed code in the forms designer. Instead of letting you figure this out on your own, I'm going to tell you how to modify the code created by the forms designer and some of the things that you shouldn't do (because I've already done them and the results weren't pretty) as well as some things that you *can* do.

Although modifying the code using the forms designer is easier, you can modify the code in the code editor and the changes will be reflected when you view the form again. There are a few cases in which the form may need to be closed and then reopened for the changes to take effect, so you need to try this if the changes you make are not reflected back in the forms designer window.

The most likely reason that you will modify the code here directly is if you change the name of the form after it's created in your project. Visual Basic .NET doesn't have a name property for forms that you can set in the Properties window as you could in the past. Ideally, as you create your forms for your application, you should try to make sure you name the form correctly when it's added to the project. Renaming the file in the Solution Explorer will only rename the file and not the internal object name. However, things change and don't always happen ideally in the real world, and there will be a time when you'll need to change the name of a form after it's already been created.

If you look closely at the forms designer code in Figure 13-3, you will see that the form does have a Name property that's set at runtime when the form is initialized. The Name property needs to match up with the name that was declared for the form in the class declaration statement. By replacing these two values with the new name for the form, you'll be able to change the name of the form after it's been created. After you change the object name of the form, you should also make sure you change the filename to match up with the new form name. You can rename the file by simply right-clicking on it and then renaming it from within the Solution Explorer window.

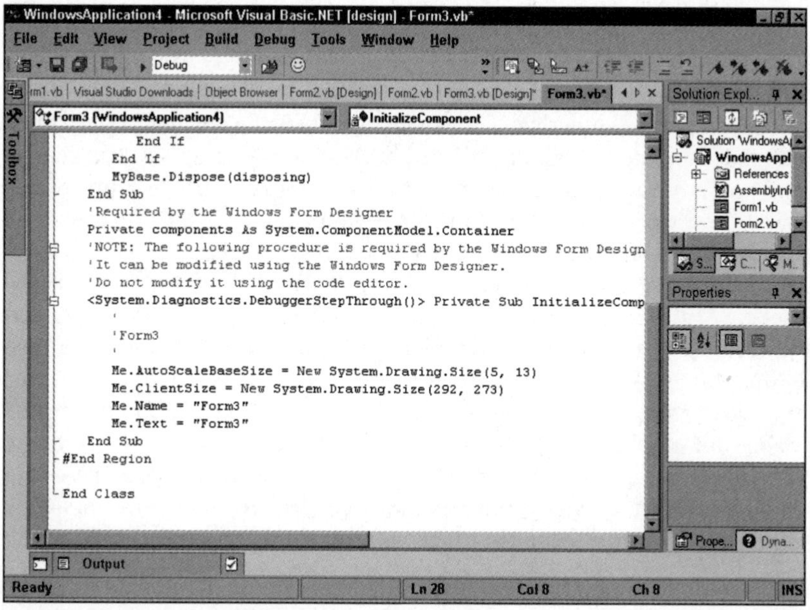

Figure 13-3: Properties set during form initialization.

Another reason why you may need to change the code directly is if you need to customize or change the order in which the controls are added to the forms collection. This could be required if you want to initialize a control based on some value of another control or for an advanced optimization. Each time you add a new control to the form, the forms designer simply appends it to the end of the control list and adds it to the controls collection at runtime in the order in which they were placed on the form. If you were to change the order of the controls as they were created, you could make the code easier to read and understand if all the controls of the same type were located next to each other.

In addition to readability, you could also modify the code that's generated for performance reasons. However, a word of caution is in order here: You must be very careful about what you modify – otherwise you may lose some required code. You'll notice that the forms designer doesn't use any With statements in the code it generates. With statements improve performance because each object layer doesn't have to be determined every function call. However, you shouldn't try to add With statements to improve performance of the form creation.

Keep in mind that there are two forces at work here. The first is the standard runtime instance that will generate the form when the program is running; a With statement falls into this category. On the other side is the forms designer that must be able to read the file and parse the information to create the form that's displayed in the designer window. If you make any changes to the code in the InitializeComponent procedure, you must realize that the code is not actually executed to display the form in design mode. The forms designer will get confused, won't be able to display the form in design mode, and may eliminate the code within the block when the file is saved. This is the main reason why the warning about not modifying the code directly is included. You must understand how the parser works to display the design-time form and the templates that it expects when you modify the code that is presented. Otherwise, you may lose your work or the form may not be able to be displayed in design mode.

As a short example to prove that you can change the code created by the forms designer and that the changes will be reflected back on the designer surface, change the Me.Text property to something else in the InitializeComponent procedure, and then view the form again. You'll notice that your changes were reflected back to the designer window and the appropriate properties were updated.

Right now there isn't much to the runtime initialization of the form in the InitializeComponent method. Switch back to the design view of the form and add some controls to the form. First, add a button, a label, a picture box, and then another button to the form. Switch back to the code window and review the changes that were made to the form-creation code. The forms designer created object variables for each of the controls and declared them using the WithEvents keyword, which is what allows the events for the controls to be trapped and coded for. Next you'll see that the object variables that were declared have to be assigned to something, which is a new instance of the control, as shown in Figure 13-4.

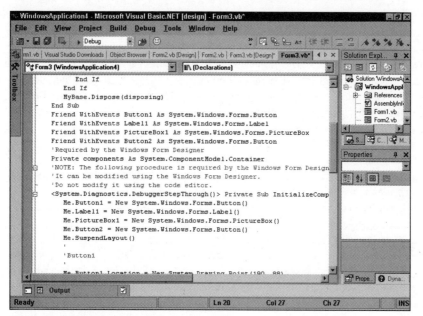

Figure 13-4: Creating controls through code.

Next, the properties are set for each control that was added to the form, and then the controls have to be added to the controls collection of the form. As you can see, all this code was generated for you using the forms designer, which is typically the most efficient way to create the controls on the form. A lot of plumbing is required in order to create and place a control on a form, and Visual Basic .NET now allows you to view and modify it if required.

I mentioned earlier that the code generated by the Windows Forms Designer could be used to figure out how to do something. For example, say you wanted to add another label to the form at runtime when the first button is clicked. By following the example in the code created by the forms designer, you could accomplish this by inserting the following code into the click event of the first button:

```
Dim lblNew As New Label()

With lblNew
    .Location = New System.Drawing.Point(0, 0)
    .Name = "lblNew"
    .Text = "This is a new label"
    Me.Controls.Add(lblNew)
End With
```

On the line of code that sets the location of the label, note what is happening. In order to set the position of a control, you must now set the `Location` property, which is a compound property that exposes an `X` and a `Y` property. The `Location` property must be set to a `Point` object, which can either be created on the fly or could be an existing point object such as the `Location` property of another control. A `Point` object is simply a two-dimensional coordinate that must be created using a constructor. Here you can see that one of the benefits of using constructors is that the object will always be initialized properly, because you must supply both the `X` and `Y` coordinate values in order to create the object. This will prevent a `Point` object that has not been initialized from being supplied to the location property. You'll learn to use this new convention when calling certain functions in the .NET Framework that need an object of a specific type in their own constructors.

Running the project and clicking on the first button will create a new label at the top-left corner of the form with the specified caption. As you can see, it's now much easier to load controls to a form at runtime by creating the control, setting its properties, and adding it to the form's control collection. This was just a simple example where we weren't concerned about the events of the label. If you wanted to trap events from the control that was added, you would need to sink the events from the control using the `WithEvents` keyword from the control before it was added to the controls collection.

New Events on Forms

Visual Basic .NET introduces many new event procedures for the Windows forms as well as changes the name of some of the events that existed in prior versions. This section discusses each of these events and what they're used for, but first you'll need to know how to access these events. In prior versions of Visual Basic, you'd simply click the form object in the Object combo box at the top-left of the Code window and the event of interest in the Events combo box at the top-right of the Code window. If you click on the form name in the Object combo box, you'll only see events for which you have explicitly declared.

Forms are simply classes with a visual interface that's created at runtime. Forms are also inherited from a base class, so, as a result, you need to select the `Base Class Events` object in the top-left combo box before you'll see all the available events. When you select an event for the base class in the top-right combo box, the event procedure will be created for you. When working with the base class events in the code editor, you must realize that upon selecting the `Base Class Events` item in the left combo box, you'll be given a list of all the events in the inheritance hierarchy, not just the immediate base class. If you look at the Form object in the Object Browser, you'll see that it inherits from the `ContainerControl` object. If you continue drilling down to the root base class, you'll see the events that become available to you through each base class. By understanding where the events originate and how they're inherited, you'll begin to understand why there are exposed events that don't make sense for a form object (for example, the TabStopChanged and TabIndexChanged events make sense for a control but not for a form).

Earlier in this book, you learned that any procedure could handle an event procedure by using the Handles keyword, as long as the parameters of the procedure matched those of the event. The procedure naming follows the standard object underscore event syntax that you were used to in prior versions. However, you'll notice that at the end of the procedure declaration, the Handles keyword is used, and the base class event is selected by using the Mybase.Event syntax. As mentioned earlier in the book, event procedures have a new common syntax in which the event procedure has two arguments. The first argument is the Sender object and the second parameter supplies all the additional information in a structure that depends on the event procedure. The majority of the argument procedures will be of the type System.EventArgs.

Activated and Deactivate

The Activated event fires every time the form becomes the active window. It's important to realize that the act of displaying a message box causes the window to deactivate while the message box dialog is displayed. The Activated event will be fired again when the message box is cleared. This may or may not cause a problem, but it's something you need to be aware of if you're writing code for the Activated event. This event maps to the Activate event in prior versions of Visual Basic except that displaying a message box doesn't cause the form to be reactivated. Similarly, the Deactivate event will fire every time another form becomes the active window.

Closing, Closed, and Disposed

The Closing event is fired when a request for the form to be closed has been received but before the form is actually closed. Again, by the use of the Sender parameter, the object that requested the form to be closed can be determined, and on the arguments parameter the Cancel property can be set to True to prevent the form from closing. If the Cancel property is not set to True, then the Closed event will fire. The Closed event behaves like the Form_Unload event of prior versions except that through the Sender parameter, you can determine which object initiated the closing of the form. You should note that the Closed event will fire immediately after the Closing event, but the form is still visible at the time the event occurs. After the code in the Closed event executes, the interface of the form is destroyed and the Disposed event is fired. The Disposed event is actually exposed from the base control class and allows you to clean up any resources such as open files, databases, or communication ports that aren't managed by the Common

Language Runtime. When the form is disposed, only the visual interface is destroyed and any private or public variables and properties still remain in memory until the object variable referencing the form can be freed up by the garbage collector of the Common Language Runtime.

MdiChildActivate

This event will fire whenever an MDI child form in an MDI parent container is either activated or closed. You may be wondering why the event fires when the child form is closed. If there is more than one child form open, then closing one form will activate another form. Typically, you would need to know when a form was activated because you may need to enable or disable certain features on a menu based on the active form. Because there is no deactivate event, the activate event needs to fire if the child window is closed and there are no other child windows to activate.

MenuStart & MenuComplete

The `MenuStart` and `MenuComplete` events are fired when the menu of a form receives focus and loses focus, respectively. This only applies to main menu controls on a form, not context menus. Otherwise these two events are pretty straightforward.

BackColorChanged

This event is an example of the property-changed events that will fire when the corresponding form property is changed. This event is actually exposed several base classes down in the `Control` object, but it does make sense for the form because a form has a `BackColor` property.

There are several types of these events, and they all behave in a similar manner. With these events, the thing to remember is that when they're fired, the property has already changed. So if you access the property from within the event procedure, you'll be reading the new value. Also, these events appear to fire only if the property is actually changed. If the property is set to the same value as it currently is, then the property event won't fire. Most of these property-changed events are obvious, but you should keep in mind that not all the events will make sense for a form object, because they could be inherited from the base classes.

SystemColorsChanged

Although this event again comes from the base control object, it's worth noting that it can be used on the form object itself. As its name implies, this event will be fired when the system colors have changed. Most of the time, you won't need to be concerned with this as long as you use the system color properties for the colors of the controls and forms. Using the system color properties will allow your forms to automatically adjust to the changes. However, there may be times when you may need to do something in your application in response to the color changes.

New Properties on Forms

From the previous section, you now understand how the base class events of a form object appear on the form itself through inheritance. The same thing applies for the properties on the form, except that the form object itself provides more properties than events. Some of these properties are new and can save you a great deal of effort, while others you should already be familiar with. This section will highlight some of the new properties and explain how they can be used in your applications.

AcceptButton and CancelButton

The `AcceptButton` and `CancelButton` properties allow you to set what used to be the `Default` and `Cancel` properties on buttons in prior versions of Visual Basic. These properties now make more sense, because they're properties on the form itself. The properties allow you to choose which buttons on your form, if any, will exhibit this behavior.

ContextMenu

The `ContextMenu` property allows you to specify which context menu control should be displayed automatically when the user right-clicks on the form itself. By setting this property, you no longer have to write code in the mouse-down event of the form to display a context menu.

DockPadding

`DockPadding` is a compound property that allows you to set an offset from each edge of the form for which docked controls will be positioned. This allows you to have the ability to set the dock position of a control but also to have other non-docked controls placed before the docked control. In order to demonstrate this, on a form, set the `DockPadding` property to 100 pixels for the left edge of the form. Next, place a couple of buttons in a vertical row along the left edge of a form. Then place a picture box to the right of the buttons and set its `Background` color to red and its `Dock` property to left, as shown in Figure 13-5.

Without this property, the picture box would be docked to the left edge of the form. By setting the `DockPadding` property, you can still have the features of docking controls, but you now have more control over where the controls will be docked. In prior versions, you had to use multiple container controls that were aligned to the same side, and the first container would provide any offset or controls similar to this example.

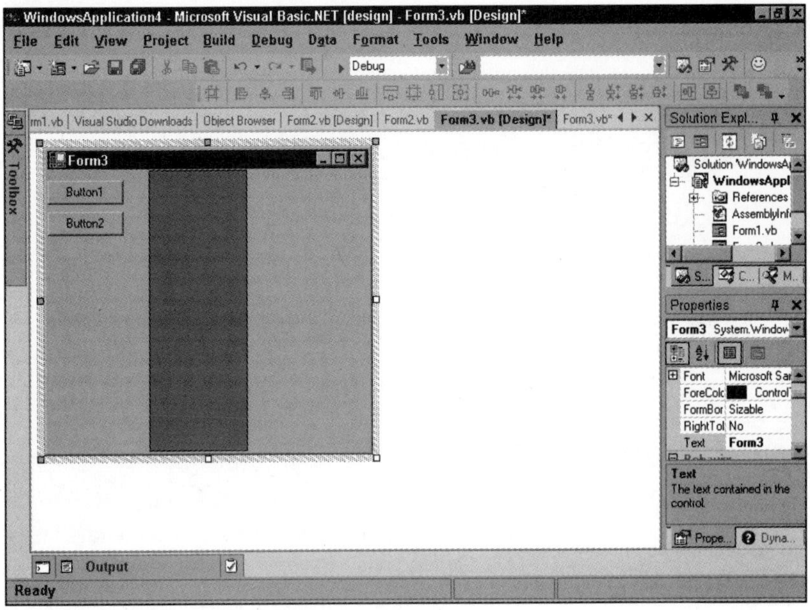

Figure 13-5: Using the DockPadding property.

DrawGrid, GridSize, SnapToGrid, and Locked

These properties allow you to override the environment settings on a form-by-form basis. By default, these properties have an initial value of whatever the environment settings are, but you can change them on each form. It allows you more control over the layout and positioning of controls on a form.

IsMdiContainer

This property allows you to set whether a form is an MDI container form. Prior versions of Visual Basic required you to add an MDI form to the project, and you could only have one in each project. Visual Basic .NET allows you to have multiple MDI forms in an application. Any form can be an MDI container form by setting this property either at design time or runtime. Along with this, you may notice that there is no longer an MdiChild property on the forms. In order to make any form that's not an MDI container form into a container form, you only need to set the MdiParent property of the form at runtime when the child form is created. You can even move a form from one MDI container to the other by setting this property to different MDI container forms in your project.

Location and Size

The `Location` and `Size` properties are compound properties, and each one replaces two properties that existed in prior versions. Previously, you could set the `Left` and `Top` properties for the position and the `Width` and `Height` properties for size. The `Location` property now has two sub-properties called `X` and `Y`. The `X` sub-property replaces the `Left` property, while the `Y` sub-property replaces the `Top` property of forms in prior versions. Similarly, the `Size` property contains two sub-properties `Width` and `Height`, which behave the same as in prior versions. When setting the properties through code, keep in mind that the sub-properties are read-only and you can only set the compound parent property. The `Location` property will return a `Point` object, and the `Size` property will return a `Size` object, both from the `System.Drawing` namespace. For example, in order to set the location of a form or control, you now need to write the following code:

```
Me.Location = New Point(500, 500)
```

The same principle is also used to set the size of a form or control, but you would specify the `Size` object and then supply the appropriate values for the constructor.

Opacity and TransparencyKey

Forms in Visual Basic .NET can now be semitransparent instead of just opaque as they have been in the past. The `Opacity` property allows you to specify a value between 0 and 100 percent, where 100 is completely opaque and 0 is completely transparent. The `TransparencyKey` property is used to define a color that will show through anything that's underneath the form.

SizeGripStyle

This property allows you to specify whether the size grip hashes that appear in the lower-right corner of a sizable form should be visible. This property can be set to `Show` to indicate to the users of your application that the window can be resized. Using this in conjunction with setting the `Anchor` property of the controls on your form, you can easily create sizable forms in which the controls adjust their sizes automatically to display more information to the users when more screen real estate is available.

Topmost

This property is used to force the form to be on top of all other windows. In order to do this in prior versions, you had to use the set window position API call. Topmost forms are typically used for splash screens, about windows, or other dialog boxes that can be or need to be displayed on top of all other windows on the desktop.

Summary

You'll probably use the Visual Basic forms designer most as you create applications, so you need to be thoroughly familiar with it. Forms created in Visual Basic .NET are now created through Visual Basic code in the forms' constructors. Although the default constructor is provided, you could provide your own constructors for initializing your form to a known state when it's created.

Through the .NET Framework and inheritance, a form in Visual Basic .NET is just another class, except that it inherits from the `System.Windows.Forms.Form` base class. The form base class also inherits from many other classes along the way. In order to understand what a form can and can't do and how it works, you need to understand the base classes that a form is inherited from. This also emphasizes the importance of inheritance and how it's used extensively in Visual Basic .NET. When used correctly, inheritance can save you time and effort in your applications. When working with forms, you'll need to remember that a form or any other object can only inherit from a single base class. As a result, after you create a form object, you'll need to perform the procedure required to inherit from a form that you've already defined in your project.

Developers now can see exactly how the forms are created and managed, because the forms are created by Visual Basic code in the constructor of the form itself. The forms designer will create code that can be adjusted as needed to react to special situations that may arise. One of these situations involves changing the name of an existing form after it's been created. Whenever you change the code generated by the Windows Forms Designer, you must remember that the code is used by two different components in the application. The forms designer parses the code to display the form in design mode, and it expects the code to be in a certain format. The runtime library actually executes the code to display the form at runtime. Changing the code that the forms designer generates may work in runtime, but it may actually cause your code to be lost at design time, when the form is saved.

Chapter 14

Graphics Programming in Visual Basic .NET

IN THIS CHAPTER

- ◆ An overview of graphics programming in .NET
- ◆ Graphics namespaces
- ◆ Graphics objects, methods, and effects

As you progress in your journey toward understanding Visual Basic .NET, you'll eventually need to perform some type of graphics manipulations. You may simply need to display an image on a form. Or you may need to perform more complex operations, such as drawing objects for a game.

If you've only used the graphics commands that were directly available to you in prior versions of Visual Basic, you'll probably be lost at first. However, if you've ever had to use the Windows API calls to perform some low-level graphics manipulation, you'll have a head start in understanding how graphics programming is handled in Visual Basic .NET.

The purpose of this chapter is to introduce you to the new requirements for direct graphics manipulation in Visual Basic .NET. The examples provided here will give you a basic knowledge that you can apply to your own unique requirements.

An Overview of Graphics Programming

Prior versions of Visual Basic included several limited graphics routines and some shape controls that allowed you to create lines, ellipses, and rectangles, as well as individual pixel manipulations. However, these functions were limited, slow, and not very intuitive to use. The perfect example of this lack of intuitiveness is shown in the following line of code that draws a red square on the form:

```
Me.Line (0, 0)-(1000, 1000), vbRed, BF
```

Each object was required to provide the same functions in order to support direct graphics manipulation of its user interface. Although it wasn't very intuitive, it did get the job done for objects that supported these methods, such as forms and picture boxes. However, if you wanted to draw a box on something that didn't support these methods, you were out of luck – unless you wanted to resort to a handful of API calls.

As discussed in the beginning of this book, one of the reasons the .NET Framework was created was to bring more organization to the language and to allow Visual Basic to have the same capabilities as other languages, such as C++. In order to do this, the graphics capabilities along with other functionalities were grouped together in a hierarchy of related classes. If you were to open the Object Browser and expand the System.Drawing assembly, you would see the following namespaces, as shown in Figure 14-1:

- ◆ System.Drawing
- ◆ System.Drawing.Design
- ◆ System.Drawing.Drawing2D
- ◆ System.Drawing.Imaging
- ◆ System.Drawing.Printing
- ◆ System.Drawing.Text

These namespaces group the related objects and methods together, making it easier to understand the relationships and the use of the various graphics objects. The System.Drawing namespace is where the majority of the graphics routines are located.

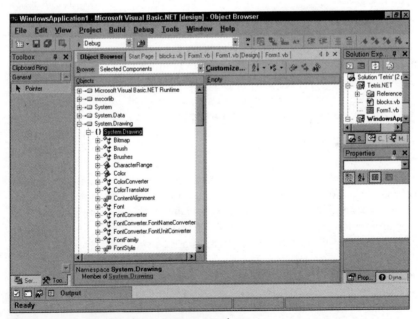

Figure 14-1: System.Drawing namespace members.

The `Color` object in the `System.Drawing` namespace provides the various color constants and functions and would be used when setting the color properties on the forms and controls. In prior versions, the color constants weren't organized and were prefixed with `vb` and then the color name. In Visual Basic .NET the color constants are grouped together and would be used as in the following code that sets the background color of the form to red:

```
Me.BackColor = Color.Red
```

Some of the objects and methods in the listed namespaces are declared using the `Shared` attribute. When a namespace contains shared members and is imported into the local namespace, it isn't necessary to create an object before the shared members can be used. As long as the `System.Drawing` namespace is imported into the local namespace, the shared `Color` object can be used without declaring an object variable, as in the preceding line of code. The import can be explicit by declaring it at the top of the code module by using the `Imports` keyword, or it can be set at the project level in the Project Properties dialog box.

In order to draw anything directly, you need to have an initialized graphics object. The graphics object can be initialized in two ways. First, all `Paint` events have an argument of the following type:

```
ByVal e As System.Windows.Forms.PaintEventArgs
```

This object exposes a graphics object that has already been initialized properly. The graphics object is linked to a specific window by the window handle. Forms are windows, but so are text boxes, buttons, picture boxes, and other controls that have a user interface at runtime. A single graphics object is linked to a single window and, as such, any methods that are called on the graphics object will only apply to the window it is linked to. As a result, the coordinate system on the graphics object is the local coordinate system of the local window object. The X coordinate of a command button's graphics object is relative to the X coordinate of the command button's location property. If you were to draw something outside the visible region of the local window, it wouldn't be visible on the parent window.

The second way to obtain an initialized graphics object is to explicitly create it linking it to a window. Calling the `CreateGraphics` method on the object that will be drawn upon will return an initialized graphics object:

```
Dim G As Graphics

G = Me.CreateGraphics

G.DrawRectangle(New Drawing.Pen(Color.Red, 3), New _
    Drawing.Rectangle(2, 2, 20, 20))
G.FillRectangle(New Drawing.Pen(Color.Green).Brush, New _
    Drawing.RectangleF(7, 7, 10, 10))
```

The preceding code will create an outline of a square with a border width of three pixels and a color of red. It will then create a smaller solid green square within the red square. These squares will be placed in the top-left corner of the form, because the graphics object was created from the Me keyword, which is the form. If you were to create the graphics container using a button, you would achieve the same results except that the squares would be in the top-left corner of the button, as shown in Figure 14-2.

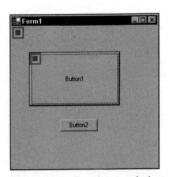

Figure 14-2: Drawing to windows directly using the graphics object.

 When working with the graphics objects to explicitly draw upon a window, the graphics that were drawn won't reappear when the obstruction is removed, unless the code is placed within the Paint event.

Creating Graphics

In this section, you'll see a sampling of the various graphics commands available to you as they're combined together to effectively "paint" a picture on a form. When you understand the basics, you should be able to expand upon them and will be able to understand how to use the other graphics methods that aren't covered here.

Start with a new Windows Application project. Set the background color of the form to white for a blank canvas; set the width of the form to 800 and the height of the form to 600. Then open up the code window for the form. In order to save some typing, insert the following line of code at the top of the code module:

```
Imports System.Drawing.Color
```

This line of code will allow you to specify colors directly by name without the Color prefix and enable you to use the other features of the Color object like transparency effects. Using the `Paint` event is the easiest way to draw graphics directly and to have them automatically redrawn when needed. Open up the `Paint` event of the form and insert the following code:

```
'Space
e.Graphics.FillRectangle(New Pen(Black).Brush, 0, 0, 800, 600)
```

The preceding line of code creates a solid rectangle that is the same size as the form. The `FillRectangle` function has four different overloaded definitions, but they all require a `Brush` object as the first parameter. If you were to try creating a `Brush` object using the `New` operator, you would see that the `Brush` object can't be created in this manner. The first thing to realize about using the graphics routines is that a `Pen` object is used to draw lines and a `Brush` object is used to paint or fill in an area. Furthermore, a `Brush` object is obtained from a `Pen` object, which can be created using the `New` operator.

In the preceding line of code, you're using a new feature in Visual Basic .NET that allows you to create temporary objects inline instead of requiring them to be declared, initialized, and then passed into the function. You'll soon see that this is a shortcut and isn't a requirement. There may be situations in which it's easier to declare the object and pass it into the function instead of the inline temporary object creation. In fact, you'll see an example of this later on in the chapter when the various pens and brushes are reused instead of creating new ones each time.

The second item needed for the function is a definition of a rectangle that it's supposed to fill. This is where the overloaded functions take effect, because you can use one of four different styles to define the rectangle. You can define the rectangle using integer coordinates, or you can use floating-point coordinates for the rectangle. If you use integer coordinates, then a `Rectangle` object would be used. Similarly, if you supply floating-point coordinates, then a `RectangleF` object is created or supplied to the function. In order to define either type of rectangle object, which is characterized by a location and a size, you could specify the four parameters separately, or you could supply an actual `Rectangle` object that has its own set of constructors available. In the preceding sample, the rectangle parameters were supplied individually.

In order to illustrate some of the various graphics capabilities, the examples in this section will create a simple space scene, so the black background is going to represent the void of space. When using the graphics methods, the order in which items are drawn is important. As a result, you should always start with the items that are at the bottom or the farthest away, as you would do if you were painting a real picture. At this point, if you were to run the project, you would see that the form is now black, proving that the function worked. But a black screen isn't very interesting, so we'll move on and start adding other objects to the picture.

The next thing we'll add is a bunch of stars in random locations on the form. In order to create a star, we'll use an `Ellipse` object. The `Ellipse` object needs the same information as a `Rectangle` object before it can be drawn on the form. We're going to use a constant size of two pixels wide by two pixels high for the ellipse, which effectively creates the smallest circle that can be drawn on the form. Now that we have the size of the ellipse, we need to define the point at which it will be displayed and the color that will be used by placing the following code in the `Paint` event for the form:

```
'Stars
Dim Stars() As Point
Dim StarCounter As Integer
Dim RNG As New Random(CInt(Timer))
Const StarCount As Integer = 400
Randomize()
ReDim Stars(StarCount)
For StarCounter = 0 To StarCount
    Stars(StarCounter) = New Point(CInt(RNG.NextDouble * 800), _
        CInt(RNG.NextDouble * 400))
    e.Graphics.FillEllipse(New Pen(FromArgb(CInt(RNG.NextDouble _
        * 255), White)).Brush, New Rectangle(Stars(StarCounter), _
        New Size(2, 2)))
Next
```

The first thing the preceding code does is to define an array of points that will represent the stars, and a counter variable that will be used to loop through the array to define and draw each star. After the array has been initialized to the proper number of points representing the stars, the counter variable is used to loop through the elements in the array. The random number generator is used to generate a Double value, which will be between 0 and 1. The result is then multiplied by the full-scale width of the form to get the X coordinate of the point, and the next random number is multiplied by two-thirds the full scale height in order to obtain the Y coordinate. The full-scale height is not used here because it would place stars in an unwanted region that we'll be filling in with other graphics.

When you have the point for the star, you can proceed to draw it on the form using the `FillEllipse` method. Again, if you look at the code, you can see that you're creating a Brush object for the fill and you're specifying a color, but you're also specifying another property for the color. Because you used the Imports statement, you can call shared functions on the Color object, of which one is the `FromArgb` function. This function has several different signatures that allow you to specify an `Alpha` value along with a Color value. The Color value can be supplied using a named color, as you're doing here. Or you could supply the individual red, green, and blue components of the color separately. The `Alpha` value is used to indicate a transparency effect for the color, which will allow the colors behind the object to show through. By setting this parameter to 255, the color is opaque; setting this parameter to 0 allows the color to be transparent. The code uses the same technique with the random number generator to adjust the transparency of the color, which gives the illusion that some stars are farther away than others in the picture.

Next, you create the moon in the picture. The first tool is used to easily create gradients between multiple colors. Gradients are used quite often when drawing graphics, because they have many uses. They can make two-dimensional objects look three-dimensional by creating highlights, shadows, and blends of colors that mimic the way light bounces off real-world objects. Prior to Visual Basic .NET, you had to create gradients from scratch. You may have created a routine that determined the appropriate color based on a percentage value, but you still had to write all the code that determined the percentage location and managed the gradient steps and then filled the appropriate lines or boxes with the color value. Visual Basic .NET introduces a new type of brush that can be supplied when the various Fill functions are called, and it will automatically perform a gradient as the region is filled.

The following code declares and creates a linear gradient brush, which is located in the Drawing2D namespace:

```
'Earth Atmosphere
Dim GB As Drawing2D.LinearGradientBrush

GB = New Drawing2D.LinearGradientBrush(New Point(0, 300), _
          New Point(0, 600), FromArgb(50, Black), SkyBlue)

e.Graphics.FillEllipse(GB, -400, 301, 1600, 600)
```

A linear gradient brush will create a gradient between two colors along the line defined between two supplied points or the upper-left and upper-right corners of a supplied rectangle. Supplying the two points allows you the freedom of having a gradient along a diagonal line or a vertical line. Supplying a rectangle to the constructor will only allow you to create a horizontal gradient.

The other required parameters for the gradient brush constructor are a starting color and an ending color. The colors can be supplied by names or the individual color components, and they can have transparency effects as well. In the preceding example, the gradient is defined along a vertical line that is the lower half of the form. An important thing to realize is that the gradient line definition doesn't have to be in the actual area where the gradient brush will be used. The gradient line is the definition for the gradient fill pattern. In the preceding example, we set the line along the Y axis, but the same vertical line could be used with any X coordinate value, and the results would be the same. With the vertical gradient line defined as the lower half of the form, any area that is filled in this region will have a color gradient defined by the gradient definition. The gradient brush definition is actually a repeating pattern, and if anything is drawn outside the original gradient with the gradient brush, you'll see that the pattern is repeated. To illustrate this point, you could change the Y coordinate of the ellipse to 201 instead of 301, and you would see the repeating gradient pattern occur. In the preceding example, we used a two-color gradient that starts with a semitransparent black and ends with a shade of blue resembling the color of the sky. This will allow the stars that were previously drawn to appear through the black and a small portion of the blue section of the gradient, giving the appearance that the atmosphere is very thin in this region. Another thing to notice about the definition of the ellipse is that we used coordinates to make the left, right, and bottom edges of the ellipse appear off the edges of the form, so we only see a small portion of the ellipse actually visible on the form.

We'll also use the same technique to draw the moon as a circle with a color gradient, except that the moon will have a diagonal color gradient:

```
'Moon
GB = New Drawing2D.LinearGradientBrush(New Point(375, 100), _
     New Point(425, 150), White, Black)
e.Graphics.FillEllipse(GB, 375, 101, 50, 49)
```

The preceding code will draw the moon with a gradient from white to black along a diagonal line from upper-left to lower-right. The diagonal gradient was chosen because, in this picture, the light source is going to be toward the top of the form and to the left. The light source is also farther back in the depth of the picture, so part of the moon won't be visible and we need to black it out.

The following code illustrates one way that you can create arbitrary shapes and fill these shapes in:

```
Dim Path As Drawing2D.GraphicsPath = New Drawing2D.GraphicsPath()
Path.AddLine(New Point(375, 150), New Point(425, 100))
Path.AddLine(New Point(425, 100), New Point(425, 150))
Path.CloseFigure()

e.Graphics.FillPath(New Pen(FromArgb(160, Black)).Brush, Path)
```

As you can see, the code creates a GraphicsPath object and then adds two lines to the path. These lines start in the lower-left corner of the ellipse boundary rectangle and then travel up to the upper-right corner and then from the upper-right to the lower-right corners. The next line closes the path, which causes a line to be drawn from the ending point to the starting point. In this example, a final line is drawn for the path that travels from the lower-right to the lower-left corner of the ellipse boundary rectangle. Finally, we filled in the triangle that was created from the path with a black that is more opaque, but it still allows some light to show through, which allows you to barely see the dark side of the moon. At this point, if you were to run the project, the form would look similar to the one shown in Figure 14-3.

The GraphicsPath object is a very useful graphics tool, because it allows you to create Path objects in a variety of ways. In the example shown here, adding lines to the object created a Path object. But lines are just one of the objects that can be added to a Path object. Arcs, beziers, curves, closed curves, rectangles, ellipses, polygons, strings, and pie wedges are some of the other ways you can create a Path object. In fact, we could have created the dark side of the moon by adding a single pie object with a –45-degree start angle and a 180-degree sweep angle. You can even add separate path objects to the path object, and the resulting path will be the combination of the paths. The resulting path could then be filled with a single command instead of having to fill each individual path.

Figure 14-3: A drawing of space, stars, moon, and the edge of the atmosphere.

Next, we'll add the sun to our painting using a series of concentric circles with layered transparent colors. The following code will create the sun in our picture:

```
'Sun
Dim CircleCounter As Integer
Dim CircleRect As Rectangle
Dim NewPoint As Point = New Point(274, -1)
For CircleCounter = 1 To 30
   NewPoint.Offset(1, 1)
   CircleRect = New Rectangle(NewPoint, New _
      Size(30 - 2 * CircleCounter, 30 - 2 * CircleCounter))
   e.Graphics.FillEllipse(New Pen(FromArgb(CInt(CircleCounter / _
      30 * 24), Yellow)).Brush, CircleRect)
   e.Graphics.FillEllipse(New Pen(FromArgb(CInt(CircleCounter / _
      30 * 16), Orange)).Brush, CircleRect)
   e.Graphics.FillEllipse(New Pen(FromArgb(CInt(CircleCounter / _
      30 * 50), White)).Brush, CircleRect)
Next
```

The main things to notice about the preceding example are the use of layered colors that have varying degrees of transparency, and the use of the Offset method on the Point object. Interesting effects can be obtained by layering mostly transparent colors on top of each other. The end result is dependent on the order in which the colors are layered. You can experiment with these techniques by changing the transparency level and the order in which they're drawn to understand the effects.

In the preceding example, the ellipses get more and more opaque as they get smaller and smaller toward the center of the circle. This effect produces a circle with fuzzy edges but a more defined center. The Offset method on the point will move the point to a new location based on the supplied values for the individual offsets. The Offset method allows you to work with the points in a more efficient manner without having to calculate the absolute locations for the coordinates of the point. The easiest way to use the Offset method is to have two Point objects. Set the location of the first point and then set the second point equal to the first point. Then call the Offset method on the second point and draw a line. Next, set the first point equal to the second point and then call the Offset method again on the second point. Repeat this process until the desired path is completed:

```
Dim P1 As Point
Dim P2 As Point

P1 = New Point(0, 0)
P2 = P1
P2.Offset(50, 50)
e.Graphics.DrawLine(New Pen(Red), P1, P2)

P1 = P2
P2.Offset(50, 0)
e.Graphics.DrawLine(New Pen(Red), P1, P2)

P1 = P2
P2.Offset(0, -50)
e.Graphics.DrawLine(New Pen(Red), P1, P2)
```

The preceding code was just an example of how to draw lines using the Point objects and the Offset method on the object. If you insert this code to test it, you will need to remove it before proceeding, because the variables names will be used in the next examples. The next example shows how you can create a graphics container that can be rotated around the origin. This allows you to draw rectangles, ellipses, lines, and so on in a normal manner in which they're oriented along the X and Y axes. Then you can rotate the graphics container by a specified number of degrees around the origin to achieve the proper angle. You can even shift the drawing points of the graphics container instead of rotating them. For this example, we'll draw a simple satellite object in the normal coordinate system and then rotate it to provide a tilt to it. This example illustrates one of those times where it makes sense to hold on to the objects that are created so they can be reused later, without having to be re-created each and every time:

```
'Satellite
Dim GC As Drawing2D.GraphicsContainer
Dim SatBodyL As New Rectangle(150, 200, 13, 76)
Dim SatBodyR As New Rectangle(163, 200, 13, 76)
Dim SatPanelL As New Rectangle(SatBodyL.Location.X - 155, _
        SatBodyL.Location.Y + 30, 150, 25)
Dim SatPanelR As New Rectangle(SatBodyR.Location.X + _
        SatBodyR.Size.Width + 5, SatBodyR.Location.Y + 30, _
        150, 25)
Dim CellCounter As Integer

GC = e.Graphics.BeginContainer
e.Graphics.RotateTransform(-15)

'Left half of Sat.
GB = New Drawing2D.LinearGradientBrush(SatBodyL.Location, _
     New Point(SatBodyL.Location.X + SatBodyL.Width, _
     SatBodyL.Location.Y), Peru, White)
e.Graphics.FillRectangle(GB, SatBodyL)

'Right half of Sat.
GB = New Drawing2D.LinearGradientBrush(SatBodyR.Location, _
     New Point(SatBodyR.Location.X + SatBodyR.Width, _
     SatBodyR.Location.Y), White, Peru)
e.Graphics.FillRectangle(GB, SatBodyR)

'Left solar panel
GB = New Drawing2D.LinearGradientBrush(SatPanelL.Location, _
     New Point(SatPanelL.Location.X, SatPanelL.Location.Y + _
     SatPanelL.Size.Height), SkyBlue, MidnightBlue)
e.Graphics.FillRectangle(GB, SatPanelL)

'Right solar panel
GB = New Drawing2D.LinearGradientBrush(SatPanelR.Location, _
     New Point(SatPanelR.Location.X, SatPanelR.Location.Y + _
     SatPanelR.Size.Height), SkyBlue, MidnightBlue)
e.Graphics.FillRectangle(GB, SatPanelR)

'Cells of both panels
For CellCounter = 1 To 15
    e.Graphics.DrawLine(New Pen(Black), SatPanelL.Location.X _
```

```
              + CellCounter * 10, SatPanelL.Location.Y, _
            SatPanelL.Location.X + CellCounter * 10, _
            SatPanelL.Location.Y + SatPanelL.Size.Height)
      e.Graphics.DrawLine(New Pen(Black), SatPanelR.Location.X _
            + CellCounter * 10, SatPanelR.Location.Y, _
            SatPanelR.Location.X + CellCounter * 10, _
            SatPanelR.Location.Y + SatPanelR.Size.Height)
Next

'Text
Dim F As Font = New Font(Me.Font, FontStyle.Bold)
e.Graphics.DrawString("Hello VB .NET", F, _
        New Pen(Green).Brush, 0, 550)


e.Graphics.EndContainer(GC)
```

In this example, we first created a graphics container object and then rotated the container –15 degrees (counterclockwise) to provide the tilt. Then the gradient brushes were used to draw the satellite body and solar panels. Next the lines were drawn to represent the individual cells or sections of each panel. Finally, the DrawString method was used to place some text on the screen, and then the graphics container that was created was closed. If you were to run the project at this point, the form would look similar to the one shown in Figure 14-4.

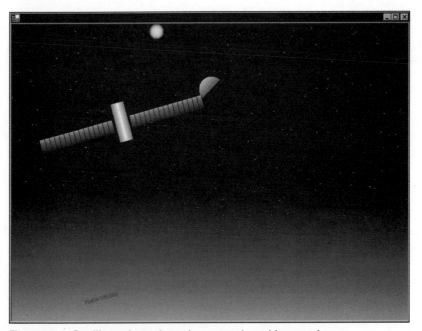

Figure 14-4: Satellite and text drawn in a rotated graphics container.

The code in the next example is included to show you some of the various ways of creating polygons and paths. It also shows you how you can use the `ScaleTransform` function on a graphics container. This allows you to draw an image using a particular set of coordinates and then either scale the image larger or smaller. When you scale the contents of a graphics container, you can use either the same or different values for the X and Y scalars. The following code will produce the graphics image, as shown in Figure 14-5.

```
GC = e.Graphics.BeginContainer
e.Graphics.ScaleTransform(5, 5)

Dim InfPoints5(5) As Point

InfPoints5(0) = New Point(5, 0)
InfPoints5(1) = New Point(10, 0)
InfPoints5(2) = New Point(20, 10)
InfPoints5(3) = New Point(20, 15)
InfPoints5(4) = New Point(15, 15)
InfPoints5(5) = New Point(5, 5)

e.Graphics.FillPolygon(New Pen(FromArgb(225, Yellow)).Brush,
InfPoints5)

Path = New Drawing2D.GraphicsPath()
Path.AddLine(New Point(0, 5), New Point(10, 15))
Path.AddLine(New Point(10, 15), New Point(5, 15))
Path.AddLine(New Point(5, 15), New Point(0, 10))
Path.CloseFigure()
Path.AddLine(New Point(15, 0), New Point(20, 0))
Path.AddLine(New Point(20, 0), New Point(25, 5))
Path.AddLine(New Point(25, 5), New Point(25, 10))
Path.CloseFigure()
e.Graphics.FillPath(New Pen(FromArgb(128, Blue)).Brush, Path)

Path = New Drawing2D.GraphicsPath()
Dim Path2 As Drawing2D.GraphicsPath = New Drawing2D.GraphicsPath()
Path.AddLine(New Point(0, 5), New Point(5, 0))
Path.AddLine(New Point(5, 0), New Point(10, 0))
Path.AddLine(New Point(10, 0), New Point(0, 10))
Path2.AddLine(New Point(15, 15), New Point(25, 5))
Path2.AddLine(New Point(25, 5), New Point(25, 10))
Path2.AddLine(New Point(25, 10), New Point(20, 15))
```

```
Path.AddPath(Path2, False)
e.Graphics.FillPath(New Pen(FromArgb(128, LimeGreen)).Brush, Path)

Dim P1, P2 As Point
Path = New Drawing2D.GraphicsPath()
P1 = New Point(5, 15)
P2 = P1 : P2.Offset(5, 0) : Path.AddLine(P1, P2)
P1 = P2 : P2.Offset(10, -10) : Path.AddLine(P1, P2)
P1 = P2 : P2.Offset(0, -5) : Path.AddLine(P1, P2)
P1 = P2 : P2.Offset(-5, 0) : Path.AddLine(P1, P2)
P1 = P2 : P2.Offset(-10, 10) : Path.AddLine(P1, P2)
e.Graphics.FillPath(New Pen(FromArgb(128, Red)).Brush, Path)

e.Graphics.EndContainer(GC)
```

Figure 14-5: Filling paths and polygons and using scaling.

The resulting image from the preceding code example should be pretty familiar to you. Scaling the graphics containers allows you to zoom in and out of an image as well as to compress either the width or the height of the displayed image.

Summary

This chapter discusses the basic graphics library routines that you can use to create more-advanced graphics easier than you could have ever done in prior versions of Visual Basic. When you understand the basic graphing routines, you can use them to draw items on the form. Although you may not be using Visual Basic .NET to create graphics such as those that have been demonstrated in this chapter, you'll probably end up using some of these methods to draw some simple things on forms.

Because you no longer have the shape controls in your toolbox as you had in prior versions, you may need to know how to draw these simple objects for visual separation on your forms. You may want to draw a three-dimensional line to separate related controls on a form where you don't want an entire panel around the controls. In this case, you'd need to draw two lines and use the `SystemColor` objects to select the appropriate color for each line. Or you could simply pick any standard color for the line. Another reason you may need to use the graphics routines is if you want to have a progress bar or panel that has a color gradient or a smooth fill to it, instead of the choppy progress bar control. Now that you have the capability, you may want to create special graphics within a control, such as a button or other controls, and you don't want to have to load images into the control each time they need to change.

As you can see, there are many reasons why you may have to eventually use the graphics library objects. When you know the basics, you should be able to do most things you may encounter. However, there may be times when you need to do something that isn't covered in this chapter. If this occurs, the best resource will be to use the Object Browser and view the various objects in the drawing namespaces to see if there is something there that you would need. If you think you've found what you may need, look at the documentation if you don't understand how it works.

Chapter 15

Enhancing IDE Productivity

IN THIS CHAPTER

- ◆ Customizing the development environment

- ◆ Window layout, style, and positions

- ◆ Toolbars and menus

- ◆ Macros

- ◆ Add-ins

- ◆ Templates

- ◆ Moving customizations between computers

By now, you should have a good feel for the standard Visual Basic .NET development environment. Visual Basic has supported some minor customization features in the past—such as the commands on the toolbars, some options in the code editor, and placement of windows—but that was about it as far as the things that could be customized from the basic package. Visual Basic .NET on the other hand allows just about every aspect of the common Visual Studio .NET development environment to be customized to fit the needs of the individual developers.

Visual Basic .NET still allows you to change the same basic features as prior versions have, but some of these customization features have many more options and others are totally new. Visual Basic .NET will allow you to change the keyboard shortcuts for any of the menu items and will allow you to execute commands from the Command window, for which you can create aliases. These command shortcuts can save time by not requiring you to use the mouse or the Alt access keys for the menu structures.

Visual Basic .NET now includes a macro editor that you can use to record your own timesaving macros, which can eliminate repetitive work you may have had to perform in the past. Another new feature is a fully user-customizable template manager that will allow you to create your own folders and items to store in those folders. These folder templates will appear along with the standard templates in the dialog boxes that appear as you add or create files in the project.

This chapter introduces you to the various features within the integrated development environment that you can customize to improve your productivity. This chapter also introduces you to some of the other productivity enhancements in the development environment that you may already be aware of.

Customizing the IDE

You can customize the Visual Basic .NET development environment in several ways. Customizing the development environment will allow you to be more productive, because you can create various shortcuts and leverage other features that will allow you to take advantage of the screen real estate limitations you may encounter.

Tabbed windows

Not every developer has the privilege of working on 21-inch monitors with extremely high resolutions. Prior versions of Visual Basic allowed you to display or hide windows as needed, but every time you had to do this it would take a small amount of time away from being productive. Even if it only took two seconds each time, the time eventually added up. Microsoft realized this and incorporated several new window-management features into the integrated development environment to automate some of these tasks. They've also provided a way to have many more windows open at the same time.

In order to allow more open windows at the same time, Visual Basic now uses tabbed windows that can be moved to various locations in the development environment to take advantage of space or personal preferences. If you've used other Microsoft development environments before, you're probably already familiar with these windows. Tabbed windows provide an easy way to navigate between different windows in the environment, including the form and code designer windows.

As you can see in Figure 15-1, tabbed windows are everywhere in the new development environment. Notice how the code and the form designers appear as tabs in the main working window in the center of the environment. The arrows at the top of this window allow you to navigate back and forth among the open windows. These are used like a sliding window scale would be used, in that you only have a few tabs visible at any one time. Clicking on the actual tab of the desired window will bring it into view in the main window. Next to the arrows you'll see an X. This behaves a little differently from the other Xs in the development environment, so it's worth pointing out. Clicking this X will only close the active tab, unlike the other Xs, which close the entire window if they're clicked.

All the other tabbed windows in the development environment have certain common behaviors that can be used to modify the development environment based on your preferences. You're not restricted to the default locations of these windows. You can drag a tab to virtually anyplace in the development environment. You can drag a window into another tab group, or you can create your own tab groups by dropping the window anyplace that isn't part of a tab group.

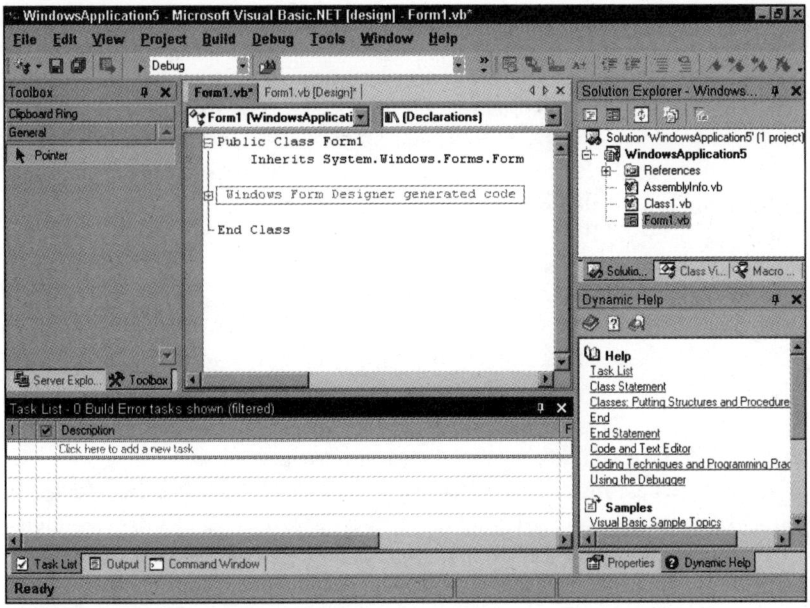

Figure 15-1: Tabbed windows in the development environment.

The tab windows have another feature that allows them to be automatically hidden and displayed when needed to save screen real estate. Each tabbed window has an icon of a pushpin, which controls this setting. When the pushpin is pointed downward, the auto-hide feature is off; when it's pointed sideways, the auto-hide feature is on. The auto-hide feature works on a grouping of tabbed windows and will cause the window associated with a tab to slide into view. When focus moves off the displayed window, it will slide back to its hidden location. In order to move a window to a different location, you first have to turn the auto-hide feature off for the originating tab group to pin the window. When the window is pinned, you can drag it to another location in the development environment and then restore the auto-hide feature of the originating tab group by unpinning the group. You'll gain the most benefit from moving windows around if you have a lot of screen real estate to work with. This will allow you to have more windows visible at the same time and to do things like having the windows you use most frequently open all the time so you don't have to switch between them and have other less-frequently-used windows in the auto-hide mode ready to go at a second's notice.

When you take the time to set up the environment the way you like it, the positions and attributes of your windows will be saved when you exit the development environment and will be restored the next time it's opened. The tabbed windows will take a little getting used to at first, but when you understand how they work and how to customize them, you'll soon welcome this new window-management feature.

Toolbars and menus

Along with the tabbed windows, Visual Basic .NET also incorporates customizable toolbars. Prior versions of Visual Basic allowed you to customize the toolbar by selecting which ones were visible and then adding commands to or removing them from the toolbar. Due to the common development environment, many more toolbars and commands are available to you. However, not all the toolbars make sense at any given time, so Visual Basic .NET will automatically turn on the toolbars when it makes sense to do so. For example, when you're working with the design-time view of the windows forms, the Layout toolbar will become visible and the Text Editor toolbar will disappear. You can customize the toolbars by adding, removing, or rearranging buttons, and you can set the properties for each button by right-clicking a button after it's in customize mode. If you don't know how to customize the toolbar, simply right-click the main toolbar and select Customize. You can even create your own new toolbars, just as you could in prior versions.

Menu items can be customized the same way you customize a toolbar. However, Visual Basic .NET puts a new twist on this: You can now create your own menu items and place them anywhere inside the existing menu structure. In order to create your own menu, you first have to be in the customize mode. When you're in this mode, select the Commands tab. At the bottom of the categories list, there is a New Menu item, and on the commands list there is also a New Menu item. Drag this command to the menu structure, and drop it where you want the menu to be placed. You can even have your new menu exist as a submenu of another menu by simply placing it at the desired insertion point. When the menu is created, you can right-click on it and change the name to whatever you want. You can then add any other commands to your new menu just as you would with any other existing menu structure. Visual Basic .NET, along with prior versions, also supports a little-known feature that allows you to move the toolbars and dock them to any edge of the development environment, not just the top.

Command window

As mentioned in Chapter 2, the new Command window can be used to quickly perform almost any function in the development environment by typing commands in the Command window while it's in command mode. The Command window can be in immediate mode, which functions similarly to the Immediate window in prior versions, or it can be in command mode. The command mode of the window allows you to execute commands by typing them in rather than having to click through the menu structure.

Figure 15-2 shows the Command window with a function typed in. If the Command window is not in command mode, you can type >cmd at the prompt to switch from immediate mode to command mode. Similarly, if you type **immed** at the prompt in command mode, you can switch to immediate mode. If you created the keyboard shortcuts as discussed in Chapter 2, you could switch modes by using the shortcuts as well. If you're in the immediate mode, you don't have to switch to command mode to execute a command. By simply inserting the greater than sign

(>) before typing, you can execute commands in the Command window while in immediate mode.

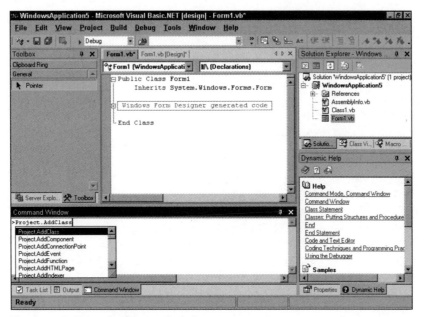

Figure 15-2: Using the Command window.

As you can see, the Command window uses IntelliSense to display a list of available commands just as it would if you were typing in the Code windows. As soon as you type the first letter, IntelliSense shows all the matching commands that start with the specified letter. This allows you to use the Command window without having to type in the entire command by hand. Select the `Project.AddClass` item as shown in the figure, and press the Enter key. You'll see the Add New Item dialog box, as shown in Figure 15-3.

As you can see, the dialog box already has the class selected and is just waiting for you to enter a name for the class. You may be thinking that typing the commands is harder than clicking the mouse a couple of times – and if that were all that the Command window did, you would probably be right. However, the Command window has a feature called *aliases,* which is used to define a shortcut for the command so you don't have to type the entire command in. The Visual Basic .NET development environment already has a predefined set of aliases that you can use. You can view this list by typing **Alias** in the Command window and pressing Enter. The first item on each line is the alias, and the second item is the command that the alias will execute. You can also create your own aliases for the commands as well by typing the keyword **Alias** followed by a space, the alias name followed by a space, and then the actual command name. This will create your alias, and from this point forward you can execute the command by typing your alias and pressing Enter. You should also note that some features may be accessible only by the Command window and are not on any menu or toolbar. In this case, your only way of knowing about or using them is through the Command window.

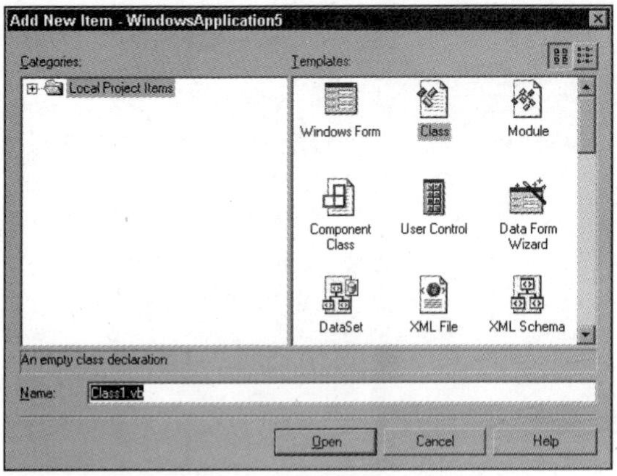

Figure 15-3: The Add New Item dialog box from the Command window.

Code window

When working in the Code window, there are several new features that you should know about. In Chapter 2, you read about the use of collapsible regions and functions. Visual Basic also creates an outline of your code with plus and minus signs to the left of the code, showing you where the classes and functions begin and end. If you right-click in the Code window, you will see an Outlining menu item at the bottom of the menu. There are several choices in this submenu that give you more control over the automatic outlining functionality. Here you can turn the outlining on and off, as well as control the expansion of the outlines. Another feature of this menu will allow you to select a block of code and hide it. The selected code will then appear as three ellipses, indicating that there is code that can be expanded. This feature will work on blocks of code within a function, an entire function, or several functions at the same time. You can even have nested hidden pieces of code. You could use this feature to hide certain plumbing code or code that has already been debugged, allowing you to concentrate only on the code that you need to work with.

Along with the outlining features and the user-definable regions, you can also customize the Code window by changing the fonts, colors, and sizes for the various items in the text editor. Although prior versions allowed you to change the same things, Visual Basic .NET allows you to have more control over each item in the Code window. You're also no longer restricted to using the supplied 16 colors. You can choose any color in the available color palette using the standard Windows Color dialog box.

Keyboard shortcuts

Visual Basic .NET allows you to create and use keyboard schemes, which lets you decide what the shortcuts should be for the various functions. You can access these mappings by selecting Tools → Options and then selecting the Keyboard item in the Environment folder. You'll see the Keyboard Mappings dialog box, where you can view all the commands available in the development environment, as shown in Figure 15-4. If you want to change the scheme or shortcuts, you'll have to save your scheme as a new custom scheme. This will allow you to easily restore the default mappings to their original values if you need to do so.

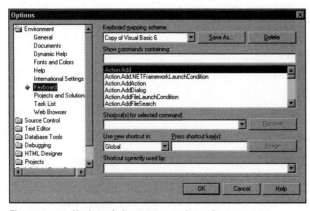

Figure 15–4: Keyboard shortcut mapping schemes.

Creating and Using Macros

The Macro Manager in Visual Basic .NET is a welcome feature that's long overdue. If you've programmed macros in any other application, you should feel right at home with the Macro Manager in Visual Basic .NET. Developers will find themselves performing a series of repetitive keystrokes as they're working with the code windows or forms. By creating a macro, they can either reduce or eliminate the number of keystrokes or mouse clicks and movements required. Macros can be created from scratch, but the easiest way is to record a macro and then manually edit it if the result doesn't meet the original requirements.

The majority of the time, when a macro is created, it's only intended to be temporary or only works at the moment in time the macro was created. Other times, the macro may not work at first, and it takes a couple of tries to get the macro just right. Visual Basic .NET has a convenient way of handling these issues when recording macros. Any macro that gets recorded is saved directly to a single temporary macro and will replace anything that is stored in it. If you want to save the information that's in the temporary macro, you simply need to rename the macro to something else before you record a new macro. This temporary macro that's used by the development environment will be saved if you save the macro project and file in which it was recorded when you're prompted to do so in the Save Project dialog box. If you save the Macro project, the temporary macro can be played again the next time the project is opened.

To illustrate the power and flexibility of recording and using macros within the development environment, I will show you how you can use a macro to turn the following line of commented code:

```
'PropAName Integer
```

into a full-fledged property procedure, shown below:

```
Private mPropAName As Integer
Public Property PropAName() As Integer
    Get
        Return mPropAName
    End Get
    Set (ByVal Value As Integer)
        mPropAName = Value
    End Set
End Property
```

Because it's impossible to show you how to record the macro in this book, I've included the code for the macro, which can be inserted into the temporary macro procedure.

Open a new Windows Application project and bring up the code window for the form. Record a temporary macro by pressing Ctrl+Shift+R. You'll notice that a floating toolbar appears with an icon of a cassette tape. Move the cursor around and type a single character comment to make sure that something is recorded in the macro. Now press Ctrl+Shift+R again to stop the recording.

The Macros menu is located under the Tools menu and contains items that let you record and manage macros. Click on the Macro Explorer item to bring up the Macro Explorer window as a tab in the Solution Explorer window space. Here you'll see a hierarchical view of the macro projects and the macros. Find the module that has the temporary macro within it, and double-click on the module. Don't click on the temporary macro, because when you click on a macro itself, the macro is immediately executed. This feature can be used to easily name and pick a macro from the list instead of having to remember the keyboard shortcuts if you assign them to macros. Double-clicking on the module will bring up the Macro Explorer, where you'll see your temporary macro. Replace the code within the temporary macro procedure with the following code:

```
With DTE.ActiveDocument.Selection
    .EndOfLine()
    .StartOfLine(vsStartOfLineOptions.vsStartOfLineOptionsFirstText)
```

```
            .Delete()
            .Text = "Private m"
            .WordRight()
            .Text = "As "
            .WordLeft(False, 2)
            .CharRight()
            .EndOfLine(True)
            .Copy()
            .EndOfLine()
            .NewLine()
            .Text = "Public Property "
            .Paste()
            .WordLeft(False, 2)
            .CharLeft()
            .Text = "()"
            .EndOfLine()
            .NewLine()
            .LineUp()
            .StartOfLine(vsStartOfLineOptions.vsStartOfLineOptionsFirstText)
            .Indent()
            .LineDown(False, 2)
            .StartOfLine(vsStartOfLineOptions.vsStartOfLineOptionsFirstText)
            .Indent()
            .LineDown()
            .StartOfLine(vsStartOfLineOptions.vsStartOfLineOptionsFirstText)
            .Indent()
            .LineDown(False, 2)
            .StartOfLine(vsStartOfLineOptions.vsStartOfLineOptionsFirstText)
            .Indent()
            .LineUp(False, 4)
            .Indent(3)
            .Text = "Return m"
            .Paste()
            .WordLeft(True, 2)
            .Delete()
            .WordLeft(True)
            .Copy()
            .LineDown(False, 3)
            .Indent(3)
            .Paste()
            .Text = "= Value"
            .LineDown(False, 2)
            .NewLine()
            .LineDown()
        End With
```

When you've recorded a temporary macro, it can be played by pressing Ctrl+Shift+P. To save the macro to something other than the temporary macro, you can right-click the macro in the Macro Explorer and rename it, or you can click on the Save Temporary Macro item in the Macros menu. It may seem like a lot of work just to create one property procedure, and if one is all you're doing then it would be easier to create the property procedure another way. However, think about when you're implementing the design of your class for the first time. Typically, you'd have many property procedures to create, and if you follow a set convention for creating and naming property procedures, you could use this macro to drastically reduce the amount of time required to code the property procedures. All you'd have to do is put each property's name and data type in a commented line:

```
'ID Integer
'FirstName String
'LastName String
'Address String
'City String
'State String
'Zip String
```

Creating a list in this manner and then positioning the cursor anywhere on the first commented line and running the macro as many times as there are commented lines in the preceding format only takes a few seconds. Macros can be as simple or as complex as you want, and they can be saved in external Macro projects as well. Saving your macros in external projects allows you to create various macros that you can take with you on a configuration disk. Creating a configuration disk will allow you to save all your environment settings in one convenient place, in case you work on different computers or have to rebuild or reinstall your development environment.

Any time you find yourself repeating keystrokes or commands or are about to, you should probably record a macro with your next set of keystrokes and then just replay the macro as often as you need. Your fingers and wrists will thank you for doing so. Macros are also an excellent way to learn about the extensibility model of the development environment if you're going to create your own add-ins for Visual Basic .NET.

Using Add-Ins

Prior versions of Visual Basic have had an extensibility model for the development environment that would allow you to install specially designed components called add-ins. An *add-in* is typically a productivity tool that you can use to reduce the amount of work required by the developer. Add-ins can be used to sink certain events from the development environment and provide specialized behavior for those events. Until now, creating an add-in was your only choice for any type of productivity tool that could be used from within the development environment. Microsoft put a huge effort into making the extensibility model more powerful and easier to use, with the goal of significantly increasing the number and complexity of add-ins that are created for the development environment. The powerful macro capabilities available within the development environment are mainly a by-product of the improved extensibility model that was enhanced to foster the commercial add-in market.

This section walks you through creating a basic add-in for your development environment so you can see how it's done in Visual Basic .NET. Create a new Visual Studio .NET add-in project by clicking its template in the Other Projects. . . Extensibility Projects folders, as shown in Figure 15-5.

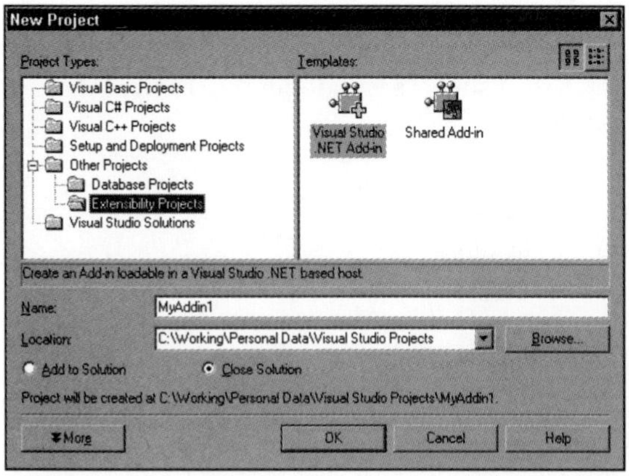

Figure 15-5: Visual Studio .NET add-in Extensibility Project.

Name the Add-In project PropertyGenerator_AddIn and click OK. You'll see the Add-In Wizard Welcome screen appear, as shown in Figure 15-6. The Add-In Wizard will walk you through a few steps as it gathers required information about your add-in. The first step allows you to choose which language the add-in will be developed in. You have your choice of creating an add-in for the common Visual Studio environment in Visual Basic, Visual C#, or Visual C++/ATL. Click the Visual Basic option, and then click Next.

The next screen allows you to choose the host environment that the add-in will run under. You can create an add-in to run in the Visual Studio macros development environment or the regular Visual Studio development environment. For now, just select the Microsoft Visual Studio .NET development environment and click Next.

The next screen allows you to specify a name and a description for your add-in. In the name text box, type **Property Generator**. In the description text box, type **Allows custom property procedures to be created.** Click Next.

Figure 15-6: The Add-in Wizard Welcome screen.

The next screen, shown in Figure 15-7, displays several options that you can set to customize the behavior of the add-in.

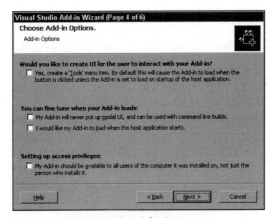

Figure 15-7: Add-in Wizard Options screen.

You're given the choice of whether your add-in will load on startup or when the button is clicked from the Tools menu and whether the add-in displays any modal dialog boxes. If the add-in doesn't produce modal dialog boxes, then it can be used with command line builds as well — as long as the Add-In is set to load when the host application starts. You can also control whether all users or just the user that was logged in when the add-in was installed into the development environment have permission to run the add-in. For this example, select the option to have a Tools menu item created and allow the add-in to be used by all users of the computer. Then click Next.

The next screen allows you to have information supplied for an About box for the add-in and the icon that would be used. Click Next to continue to the next screen, which is a summary of the options that were chosen. Click Finish to create the initial framework for the add-in based on the options you've chosen.

At this point, you'll see two projects in the Solution Explorer. The first project is for the add-in itself, while the second project is used to install the add-in into the development environment. In the code window that will appear for the `Connect` module, you'll notice that it uses the `Implements` keyword, which forces the add-in to support the interfaces required by add-ins for use within the Visual Studio development environment. You'll see that there are already several functions that are inserted into the code module. The first set of routines are used by the `IDTExtensibility2` interface and are used to load and unload the add-in from the development environment. Currently, there is only code in the `OnConnection` event, which will be fired when the add-in is loaded using the Add-In Manager in the development environment. The `OnConnection` event has several parameters that allow you to determine the instance of the add-in that is running (there could be more than one instance running if multiple copies of the development environment are loaded), as well as other pieces of information that are needed to properly install the add-in into the development environment.

In the `OnConnection` event, you'll need to make a couple of modifications. The example that follows won't care about how the add-in was loaded so remove the `If...End If` statement but leave the code that was in the `If` statement code block. After minor reformatting, you should have the following code in the `OnConnection` event:

```
Dim objAddIn As AddIn = CType(addInInst, AddIn)
Dim CommandObj As Command

applicationObject = CType(application, EnvDTE.DTE)
addInInstance = CType(addInInst, EnvDTE.AddIn)

Try
    CommandObj = _
    applicationObject.Commands.AddNamedCommand(objAddIn, _
    "PropertyGenerator_AddIn", "PropertyGenerator_AddIn", _
    "Executes the command for PropertyGenerator_AddIn", _
    True, 59, Nothing, 1 + 2)

CommandObj.AddControl(applicationObject.CommandBars.Item("Tools"))
Catch e As System.Exception
End Try
```

The preceding code stores a module level reference to the `ApplicationObject` and the `AddInInstance`. The `ApplicationObject` is used to communicate with the development environment, and you can see that the code tries to add a command to the Tools menu that will be used to perform some action on your Add-In. When the Add-In is disconnected and unloaded from the development environment either by the Add-In Manager or by the development environment shutting down, it will need to remove the command that was added to the Tools menu. This is accomplished by inserting the following lines of code into the OnDisconnection event:

```
applicationObject.CommandBars("Tools").Controls _
        ("PropertyGenerator_AddIn").Delete()
```

Now that your Add-In can be loaded and unloaded from the development environment, it will need to do something when the menu item that was added is clicked. If you look farther down in the code, you'll see a routine called Exec, which is fired when a menu item in the development environment is clicked. In this routine you'll see that it checks to see what the command name is and if it matches with the name of the item that was added to the Tools menu when the add-in was connected. This is where you would insert code to start your add-in in motion. For now, just insert the following code in the Exec routine for the menu item click:

```
MsgBox("Menu item clicked")
```

The example here is just going to pop up a message box when the menu item is clicked, but you could insert code that would interact with the development environment and the active windows and documents, as well as with the project and solutions. You could even add Windows Forms to the add-in project, and you could display forms that display information to and receive information from the user.

At this point, you're ready to test your add-in to see if it works properly. When testing an add-in, it has to be compiled and a setup application has to be created for it, because it has to be compiled and run under a new instance of the development environment so that you can debug it as needed. Run the add-in and you'll see the build process start, which may take a minute to complete. When the build process completes, another copy of the Visual Studio development environment will launch. On the new instance of the development environment, click on the Add-In Manager from the Tools menu, and you'll see your newly created add-in in the list of available add-ins. Click the check box next to your add-in and click OK. At this point, your add-in will be loaded into the development environment, and it will add a menu item to the Tools menu. If you were to click on the menu item that was added, you would see the message box appear stating that you clicked on the menu item. When you're finished debugging your add-in, you need to close the second instance of the development environment, and the running project in the first instance will stop allowing you to make changes to the code for the add-in.

This is just a simple example showing you how easy it is get an add-in running in the Visual Studio .NET development environment. If you're going to be creating add-ins, you'll need to look at the documentation and review the object models for the extensibility interface so you can see how to work with the various windows, toolbars, documents, and so on. An add-in is a very powerful tool that integrates with the development environment to enhance the user's productivity, but don't forget about macros. Add-ins are more powerful than macros, but they also take more effort to develop and debug. Unless you're creating a productivity tool for commercial release, you'll probably be able to get more accomplished with less time involved by using macros in the development environment.

Managing Templates

Templates are discussed in detail in Chapter 2, so I won't cover them again here. However, you should make sure you understand how they're used in Visual Basic .NET. By spending the time to create and manage your templates for code, documents, images, or any other documentation required for your projects, you'll be able to access these documents or files from directly within the development environment. This allows you to use the other features of the development environment on the files like storing them in the project directory or using version control systems on the files. Take the time to understand templates and customize the folders and items and where they're stored on the hard drive, and you can help reduce the overhead of working with many different applications and files for a single project.

Saving Customizations

When you get your development environment set up and customized the way you want it, you'll probably want to save your configuration information so you can easily restore it if you have to rebuild your computer or if you lose your settings for any reason. You may even want to save your configuration information, so that if you have to go to another computer, you can debug an application or help another developer. When you get to the other computer, you simply need to save any settings that are currently in use and then import your settings and launch the development environment. You'll then have complete access to all your shortcuts, window positions and layouts, and so on. When you're done, you can simply restore the settings that were on the computer when you arrived.

At this point, you may be thinking about where the settings are stored in previous versions and think that saving the settings isn't going to be easy. However, Visual Basic .NET changes the way settings are saved and does make it extremely easy to save off your settings and restore them on any other computer running Visual Basic .NET. The settings and customizations for the development environment are stored as several files in your documents and settings folder. You can find these settings in the `Root:\Documents And Settings\UserID\Application Data\Microsoft\VisualStudio\7.0` folder on your hard drive. By simply copying the files in this and all subdirectories to a safe place, you can save off your settings and then be able to restore them on another computer. If you're working on a network that maps this information to a network drive, and all data is stored there and not on the local hard drives, then all you would have to do is log on to another computer and your development environment would appear the same as it was on the original computer. Most of the files that save configuration information store the data in a simple text format, which you can read using Notepad. You can even change the data in some of the files, like the aliases file, instead of having to do it through the development environment. However, if you do this or need to restore information onto another computer, make sure that the development environment isn't running at the time. When the development environment exits, it will overwrite any data that is stored in these directories and files, and you would lose any of the changes that you made.

In addition to the configuration settings, you may also want to store your macro projects in the same location so you can easily load them into another development environment. A macro project is almost like any other development project and will have a project file along with the various code modules that are in the project. The only difference with macros is that no executable files are created.

Summary

Prior versions of Visual Basic have had a few features that can be customized, but they primarily dealt with either the appearance of the Code window or the positions of the windows and items on the toolbars. Visual Basic .NET gives you much more control over how the environment is configured so that you can be more productive in your day-to-day activities. When you configure your development environment, you can use various shortcuts and customizable features that will make your programming effort a little simpler.

Furthermore, your customizations can be saved off and restored on any development machine with Visual Basic .NET installed when you understand where the configuration settings are stored. Many developers spend the time required to get their development environment just right and will typically have better productivity levels as a result. However, if these developers have to switch machines for any reason, before now they would have had to re-create their development environment by repeating the customizations all over again. If a developer were working with another developer's computer to help solve a problem or debug a piece of code, the developer would often times have to fumble around a little bit to get used to the other developer's settings. In this case, it would not be wise to mess with the other developer's computer just to make it fit your own preferences. However, with Visual Basic .NET, you can easily save off the current developer's settings and then import your own settings and probably be as productive on a different machine as you are on your own computer. When the work is done, the original developer's settings can be restored.

Part VI

Architecture and Design

Chapter 16

Recognizing the Importance of Good Design and Documentation

IN THIS CHAPTER

- ◆ Project failure rates and reasons

- ◆ Application development scenarios

- ◆ Tiered application design

- ◆ Designing and documenting applications

In a recent study of more than 23,000 application development projects, only 26 percent were completed within the original time and budget constraints. Twenty-eight percent failed outright, and the remaining 46 percent were completed over budget or past the original deadline. A few root causes of failure were common to the 74 percent of projects that weren't completed within the original time and budget constraints. The top root causes of errors were:

- ◆ Separation of goal and function

- ◆ Separation of business and technology

- ◆ Lack of a common language and process

- ◆ Failure to communicate and act as a team

- ◆ Processes that were inflexible to change

Functionality in an application should exist only to help achieve a particular goal or to solve a problem. Often, functionality that may be "cool" is created in an application, but it doesn't solve any of the problems that the application was being developed to solve. The technology goals must be aligned with the business goals of the company in order to successfully deploy an application. For example, if a company wants an application developed that will replace several manual processes and serve the needs of the entire organization, but the company forces the application to run on a server that is over five years old, the project will more then likely fail.

Technology needs are not strictly hardware needs, but can be software needs as well. Forcing developers to write applications using and operating system or tools that aren't the latest versions is another path that can lead to project failure. When developing any business software application, you must realize that there will probably be bugs in it. The time and cost involved in searching for and eliminating all the bugs in an application follows the principle of diminishing returns. There comes a point in most application development lifecycles when the cost to eliminate each additional bug outweighs the benefits of eliminating the bug. At this point, known issues and any workarounds are documented, and the application is ready to start the deployment process.

Effective communication between the development team members as well as with the customers or users of the application is critical in order for the application development project to succeed. Common languages and processes are used to help team members communicate effectively throughout the project. Having proper communication between team members and getting individuals to move beyond individual effort and work effectively as a team are critical factors in the success of the project.

The computer and application development industries are so chaotic that application development teams and processes must be able to adapt to the ever-changing needs of their customers and users. If applications and processes don't adapt to changes, then applications are built that don't meet the needs of the users when the application is deployed. If an application is completed but never used because it's out of date, too hard to use, or doesn't meet the needs of the users, it's a failure. The only thing the application was successful at was wasting money and resources. Application developers and managers must be open to new ideas as they come along. The we've-never-done-it-that-way-so-it-can't-be-right mentality is one sure way to get stuck in a rut and get so far behind the technology curve that your project may fail. However, new thought processes and ideas must be tested and tried before they're implemented. Otherwise, you may commit to a new idea or technology early on in the project and then realize toward the end that it doesn't work properly, forcing part or all of the application to be rewritten to accommodate the change.

Having good design and documentation procedures can help improve your chances of success when developing an application. This chapter explains the typical application development scenarios in use and the various application architectures and how they can be used to help make your application development process successful. Good documentation is critical when developing an application, because it helps ensure effective communication between current and future team members. If you develop a great component or function that saves a lot of effort, but no one knows how to use it because there is no documentation, your component or function probably won't be used. And an application or functionality that isn't used indicates failure. This chapter covers the various ways that Visual Basic .NET can help you in documenting your application to help ensure effective communication between all parties involved in the application development process.

Identifying Application Development Scenarios

There are three main types of scenarios or processes that are used when an application is being developed. The first scenario is what I call the *waterfall,* in which each step has to be completed before the next step can begin. The second scenario is what I call the *prototype and hack.* In this scenario, a prototype is completed, and then the prototype is forced into being the actual product. The final method is the *incremental waterfall,* or versioned releases, scenario.

Waterfall

The waterfall scenario originated in the mainframe era and isn't very successful anymore. The waterfall splits projects out into multiple phases, and the work in each phase has to be complete before the next phase can begin. The typical order of the phases is analyze, design, develop, test, and deploy. If you imagine a cascading waterfall where the water has to fill each cup before it can start flowing into the next cup, you can visualize why this scenario is called the waterfall method. No work can be done on any other phase until the previous phase has been completed.

The only real benefit to this approach is that it forces the application to be thoroughly documented. Typically, different organizational units complete each phase, and the only way for these different units to work on the project is to have the application thoroughly documented. The waterfall approach has many downsides, including long project lead times, which can render the application obsolete before it can even be completed. This forces many of the applications that are actually developed to be huge monolithic beasts that can outlast the long lead times and typically try to do everything under the sun. Another downside to this approach is that these types of applications aren't flexible to changing requirements as the applications are being developed. In the days of the mainframe, people really didn't have any choice and were forced to use the system even if it didn't meet their needs. This approach was carried over to the first applications that were created for Windows and, due to the complexities involved, it required skilled developers to create an application for Windows.

Prototype and hack

When visual programming languages such as Visual Basic arrived, a new generation of developers was created that could create an application to run under Windows simply by putting controls on a form and then writing code to respond to the events of the controls. These developers may or may not have had any formal application development training.

As Visual Basic evolved, fewer and fewer applications had any design work completed on them and prototyping became the norm for application development. Prototyping typically involved the cyclic process of creating a form and then checking with the users to see if the form met their needs. If the form didn't meet the users' needs, refinements would be made until it did. Often, users wanted to see some live data in the forms so they could actually see how it worked. So code was quickly created that would get some data and navigate between forms with the intention that the developers would just get something working and then go back and do it right later. After the prototype was approved, the users wanted to know when they could have their application. After all, they thought, it has the forms and the data is being displayed in the forms, so there isn't much else to do. Users didn't understand the shortcuts that were used to get the prototype done, and they wanted to have the finished application right away. As a result, the shortcuts remained and the application was constantly hacked and patched to get it to work.

The prototype-and-hack scenario is actually worse then the waterfall method for many reasons. First, too much emphasis is placed on prototypes. A prototype should be used when a quick proof of concept is needed to explain something visually to the user. In fact, most prototypes could effectively be presented as a series of screenshots on paper, with markups describing the action or navigation. If users only see screen shots and are informed that this isn't the actual application, they're less likely to think that the final version is just around the corner. The common theme of the prototype and hack was just to get it working and fix it later. How many times have you actually had the opportunity to fix something and do it right later? Later never comes, and there's always something more pressing that needs attention. When prototypes are forced into the application, it forces the application development to be in hacking mode, which causes other problems. Hacking typically causes another piece of the application to break when something is changed to fix yet another problem. This constant hacking cycle creates a big plate of spaghetti code, which no one can understand – even the original developers, who won't even touch the application because it's so unstable. The ship date can never be predicted accurately in a prototype-and-hack scenario. The application is finished when the last hack doesn't appear to break something else. As a result of this, the documentation (if any exists) is incomplete and inaccurate, forcing the next poor sap who has to work on the program to understand the entire application before he can make a change to it.

Incremental waterfall

The incremental-waterfall scenario is often referred to as *incremental versioned releases*. The Microsoft Solutions Framework and the Rational Unified Process both use this concept in their application development process. You can visualize these processes by thinking of a spiral staircase that's used to move from the bottom to the top level. If it were to take four steps to complete a circle, you would be back at the first step again but you wouldn't be at the same level. By completing one revolution around the staircase, you've moved a little closer to the top of the stairs.

The incremental versioned releases process involves identifying as many requirements as you can and then negotiating with the user which features are the core features and must be completed first. As soon as the core features have been included, code is developed that meets the next set of requirements. This process repeats until all the requirements for the application have been met. An incremental versioned release isn't the same as the release that will be given to the user. In the staircase example, the release that would be given to the user would be the one at the top stair of the staircase. The releases at each revolution around the center pole would typically be internal releases that build up to the final release to the customer.

This application development scenario has proven to be the most successful and has many benefits. First, the entire application doesn't need to be designed up front. Only the current versioned release needs to be designed. However, care must be taken to identify dependencies before development begins on a project. If feature A must interact with feature B, the interaction must be thought out, and feature B should be developed first.

The next major benefit is that the process is very open to changing requirements and allows changes to be incorporated into the process easily. One of the changing requirements could be the delivery date of the application. Without this model, an earlier delivery date could force the application into hack mode in order to get everything that was put off until later completed. With the incremental versioned releases process, there's always a version ready to ship when the core features have been completed. By prioritizing the versioned releases so that the higher priority items are done first, an earlier delivery date will simply force lower priority features to be cut from the final release to the customer. These features can be the first things to be included on the next major version of the product.

If the deployment team takes and uses the latest completed release, development can continue with the other features and may even be complete before the user even uses the application. The users will find things wrong with the application or things that they want changed, and then these are prioritized and a new development process begins to fulfill the new requirements.

Another benefit to this approach is that a minimal amount of documentation is inevitable as the requirements are analyzed and prioritized to be included in each incremental versioned release. More thorough documentation can be incorporated easily, because there is a lot less documentation required for each versioned release than there is when you're trying to document the entire application. The documentation for the entire application is basically the sum of the parts of each incremental versioned release that is incorporated.

Using a Tiered Approach

Now that you understand the various application development scenarios, you can move on to the various types of applications. These types of applications are often referred to as a *tiered approach,* where a tier contains certain pieces of the application. Any piece of code in an application will typically fit into user services, business services, or data services categories. The user services category contains code and pieces that interact with the user of the application. The business services typically contain all the business logic, which makes the application unique. The data services category contains the pieces of the application that interact with data sources for the application.

Most business applications interact with a data store of some type, whether it's a relational database, a text file, a messaging system, or even hard-coded lookup tables within an application. Tiered applications separate the various user, data, and business services from each other. This makes the code more maintainable, and reusable. If the user services are properly split from the business and data services, then it makes reusing the business and data services in another application easier. Similarly, if the data services are separated from the user and business services, changing data stores without affecting the rest of the application is easier.

A common misconception is that a tier represents a physical computer and that each component runs on different computers. The different application service tiers are logical, not physical. A logical tier is just a separation between the other tiers; all three tiers of a typical three-tier application could be running on the same computer. If applications are developed using logical tiers, the physical implementation can change without changing the application.

Types of tiers

When discussing tiered applications there are three main categories that applications fall into: single tier, two tier, and n-tier. These categories describe how the application is developed and where the functionality resides in each client. The single-tier applications were created first and were huge monolithic applications where each piece of functionality was intertwined with the other functionality pieces and typically required client machines to be pretty powerful. As time passed, developers realized that if the data for the application could be moved to a central server, then all the clients could access the same data and the processing power of the server could be used to reduce the demands on the client machines by sharing the workload of managing the data. Eventually, developers realized that if the application was divided into separate tiers and a clean interface between each tier was provided, then the code that was developed for the application could be reused and could also make it easier to maintain an application.

SINGLE TIER

A typical single-tier application is one that is contained in one or more monolithic executables. These applications will have user interface code mixed in with the data access code and the business logic code; there is no clear separation of the three different sets of services. These types of applications would typically either have internal lookup tables or access a file system database such as Access or any data file on the local computer or even on a network. Single-tier applications are often synonymous with *fat clients*, because without a clear separation between the different layers, there is typically a lot of duplicate code. Making a single change may require making that change in many different places throughout the application, and the application is tied to a particular operating system due to its structure.

TWO TIER

A two-tier application is often referred to as a *traditional client server application*. The server is typically a relational database server, such as SQL Server or Oracle, and it actually uses the processing power of the computer where the database is located. Although it's typically the case, the database server doesn't have to be on a separate physical computer from the application. However, the application and the database server are separate processes or applications.

In a typical two-tier client-server application, the server contains some data access code and some business logic, as in the case of stored procedures, views, or triggers. The client would typically have the entire user interface portion and would have some business logic and some data access code. In the ideal case, the server would only have data access services and logic, such as having all the SQL statements for the entire application stored on the server in a combination of views and stored procedures. The client then would have only the user interface and the business logic. But this separation doesn't occur for many reasons. For performance reasons, sometimes putting business logic on the server in stored procedures makes sense, because the data is local to the server and can be accessed faster for complex data operations. Furthermore, servers are typically more powerful than traditional client desktops and can process more information in a shorter amount of time than the client could. As a result, most real-world two-tier systems end up being very tightly coupled systems that would have to have a major rewrite if the database server were to switch from one vendor to another.

N-TIER

An *n-tier* application has the user services, business services, and data services completely segregated within the application. It is called *n-tier* because there may be more than one item in each service category. For example, there may be many different layers within the business services tier and/or the data services tier. Sometimes, applications need to retrieve data from several different data sources or access business logic from external or legacy systems. Microsoft has elaborated on this and has an architecture guideline called Windows Distributed interNet Applications Architecture (Windows DNA) that can be followed to develop robust, scalable, and maintainable distributed applications on the Windows platform.

The presentation layer includes devices from a rich client, such as a standard PC, to a thin client, such as a handheld computer. Obviously, there could be a couple of groupings in the presentation layer — one for the traditional rich client and another for a Web-based thin client. Both of these present the information to the user in different ways, but they both belong in the presentation layer.

The business logic is in the middle layer, and it may or may not be guarded by a firewall. If the application is just a local intranet-based application and does not have any outside support, a firewall may not be needed. However, depending on the security needs of the organization, a firewall may be included and configured to allow communication from the presentation layer to the business logic layer. The business logic layer is the real heart of the system, because it controls who can see what information, where it's retrieved from, and any validation rules or constraints on the data.

The business logic layer of an application may need to retrieve information from several different services in order to process a request or provide information to the user. The business logic layer should be the only direct link into the data services layer in the application. This allows all logic and rules to be confined in one place, which allows the business logic to be changed without affecting the rest of the application. Typically, the business logic of an application is what changes the most to adapt to the ever-changing needs of an organization. By separating the business logic out from the presentation layer, a change in business logic can be made and updated and the installed application bases don't need to be updated at the same time. The business logic layer allows business rules to be easily identified and shared between different applications in the organization.

The data services layer contains the components of the application that store and retrieve information for the application to work. The data layer typically contains relational databases such as Oracle or SQL Server, but it could also contain legacy databases, mail systems, external applications or data feeds, directory services, or even files in a file system.

In a Windows DNA application, the operating system services provide the plumbing and communication channels between the various layers at a low level. The tools that are used include the various application-development tools that are used to create the components and the interactions at a higher level. These interactions ride on the low-level system services communication channels and make it easy for a developer to write a component that talks to another component without worrying about where the second component actually resides. The second component could reside on the local computer, or it could reside on a server or a server farm with fail-over support.

.NET PLATFORM

Microsoft has recently introduced a new approach that is similar to Windows DNA called the .NET initiatives. The Windows DNA approach to architecting an application solves many problems when creating distributed applications, but it has one drawback: It's tied together with COM, which makes it limited to running on Microsoft platforms. The Microsoft .NET initiative was created to allow applications to communicate and share data over the Internet as well as a local intranet using XML-based Web services. The .NET platform is a family of products that are based on XML and other Internet standards and provide for each aspect of developing, managing, using, and experiencing XML Web services. The tools are what tie all the pieces of the .NET platform together. The tools include the Microsoft .NET Framework and Visual Studio .NET and are used to allow developers to quickly build XML Web services and applications using the language of their choice.

The servers in the Microsoft .NET platform are used to provide the infrastructure for deploying, managing, and orchestrating XML web services. The server products include the following:

◆ Windows 2000 Server family

◆ Application Center 2000

- Biz Talk Server 2000

- Commerce Server 2000

- Content Management Server 2001

- Exchange Server 2000

- Host Integration Server 2000

- Internet Security & Acceleration Server 2000

- Mobile Information Server 2001

- SharePoint Portal Server 2001

- SQL Server 2000

These server products provide extensive support for storing, retrieving, and translating data in the industry-standard XML format.

The XML Web Services are intended for application-to-application communication, as opposed to Web sites that are intended to actually interact with a user. Applications communicate with other applications internally or across the Internet using XML to represent the data and Simple Object Access Protocol (SOAP) as the protocol based on HTTP that allows the data to be transferred from one application to another. SOAP allows applications to communicate with other applications, even through firewalls, because the transport method is HTTP, which is a text-based protocol. Because most firewalls are configured to allow HTTP traffic, SOAP can pass through these firewalls and applications can communicate with other applications on the local network as well as across the Internet. The data is packaged up into an XML package, which again is text based, and then data can be transferred to the other application. By relying on the standards already in place for secure communication between Web sites, such as the HTTPS protocol, the information traveling between applications can be encrypted for security reasons if so desired.

The benefit of XML Web Services is that as long as an XML Web Service follows the established standards for communication, it doesn't matter what operating system or platform is providing the service. This allows for Web Service applications to be developed on a Windows platform and communicate with an XML Web Service on a UNIX platform transparently to the developer or user. Microsoft is currently developing the first set of Web Services code-named "Hailstorm." Hailstorm is based on the Microsoft Passport authentication scheme and delivers relevant information, as needed, to the devices that a user is running based on the user's preferences.

Clients can be PCs, cell phones, handheld computers, laptops, tablet PCs, and other smart devices. A *smart device* is distinguished by its ability to access and consume XML Web Services. A *smart client* runs software that will allow you to access information regardless of the type of information or the device you're using.

The benefits of an n-tiered approach

Regardless of whether you use the Windows DNA or the .NET platforms, both follow the n-tier architecture guidelines. The n-tier architecture provides many benefits when developing applications. By separating the application into logical tiers, it allows the application to scale as the demands upon it increase. For example, let's say you start with a traditional rich client that runs on computers on the local network. As the application grows, business needs change and now the sales force needs access to the application over the Internet. If the application were properly segregated, only the Web site and Web pages would need to be created. Both the rich client and the ASP pages on the Web server could call into the same business logic components, allowing code to be reused in a binary form and making the application more maintainable. If a business logic rule needs to change, it simply needs to be changed in one place, and both types of clients immediately start using the new rules. Without the proper segregation, the business logic would end up being repeated, which increases the chances that errors could be introduced or that there could be two different versions of the same rule running at the same time, which is just asking for problems and headaches.

Coming Up with a Good Design

The importance of having a good design for the application cannot be stressed enough. Without a good working design, your chances of falling into the inescapable prototype-and-hack trap are greatly increased. A design doesn't have to be a long, drawn-out process as in the waterfall method, where everything is designed and documented before application development can begin. However, the design needs to be sufficient based on the size of the project, and you'll only be able to understand the amount required as your skill level progresses in your programming tasks.

The best approach to take when designing an application is to first identify and document the high-level requirements that the application will need to do. Tasks such as exporting the order history, entering a new order, editing an existing an order, entering contact information, editing contact information, and searching contacts on certain types of criteria are all types of tasks that should be documented at this level. When you have the high-level tasks, review them with the intended customer or user and come up with the related subtasks for each high-level task. This approach helps the users concentrate on what they need in order to do their jobs effectively, instead of asking them what they want the application to do in general terms. After the requirements have been gathered and documented, switch to prioritizing the requirements so you can start with the incremental-waterfall or versioned-release design.

The requirements will probably not be complete at this point and will likely change a little as the application is developed, based on the users' feedback.

Continually receiving user feedback as the application is developed is important. If there is a problem with your understanding of the process or if the user forgot to mention something to you, finding out early on in the process, before the complexities or dependencies have been added, is better than finding out later on. If you have a prioritized list of how the features will be included, you can determine with the user's help where the requirement should be included in the development process. It may seem very important to have this particular feature included right away, but when the user reviews the list of his other requirements and priorities, it may not seem as important compared to the other requirements.

When you have your list of requirements, look to see if there are any reusable pieces or requirements that have a similar functionality. If you come across any similar pieces, document them and identify where they're first needed in the development process. At the time when they're first needed, take a little extra time to make sure that you design the piece correctly, accounting for the other dependencies or similar functions. Taking a little extra time now will save you from having to rewrite code later to make it work with the other component.

After you've documented any foreseeable reusable components, you should design and document the overall architecture of your application. In this step, you should make sure to include any communications with external programs or other components that have already been developed. Also think about how many users your application will have and how quickly it may grow. This information should be documented so that when you're designing each smaller piece, if you have a question or concern about the best way to do it, you can first look at the scalability requirements and see if that answers your question. Often, it may be easier to create an object that maintains state through properties than to provide functions that accept all the requirements as parameters. However, if your component could ever be reused in something like Microsoft Transaction Server or Component Services, you should take the extra time to code the function so that it accepts all the required parameters as arguments to the function to avoid the performance hit that you would incur if you developed the component using stateful properties.

One of the benefits of the incremental versioned releases method is that you only have to document small pieces at a time. As you design each small piece of the application, you need to think about whether there is anything that can be reused by other pieces later. If you think that something may be reused, it's better to take a few extra minutes and see if the code could be broken out somehow so that it can be reused with ease later on in the process.

Another benefit to the incremental versioned releases process it that the requirements are already broken down into manageable pieces that can be estimated better. As far as project management is concerned, taking the individual estimates and adding them up to get the overall project schedule is easier than trying to estimate the project from a top-down approach. Furthermore, if individual pieces are assigned to different developers, it's easier to know how much buffer time should be added based on past experiences with each developer.

Documenting the Design and Application

The sole reason for providing any documentation for an application is to help the communication process. At the beginning of this chapter, you read that the absence of effective communication processes is one of the root causes for project failure. Documenting an application actually involves documenting several key steps in the application development process and this section highlights the more important pieces of documentation and how Visual Basic .NET can help in your documentation efforts.

Documentation requirements

It doesn't matter if an application is designed well if no one else can understand the design. The same is true with the requirements. If all the requirements aren't documented, precious time can be wasted reworking code to fit a forgotten requirement when it could have been avoided if the requirement had been documented in the first place.

Documenting an application has typically been put off until the end for many reasons, but the reason given most often is that there is no time to document the application as it's being developed and that it will be documented after the application is completed. Developers often fall into the trap of thinking that because they wrote the piece, they can come back to it later and either document it or modify it and they'll remember exactly what the code was doing. This reason is similar to, and often a result of, the prototype-and-hack method.

With the incremental versioned releases process, there is no excuse for not documenting the application. The purpose of documentation is so that whoever is working on the application at any point in the future can quickly get up to speed with the intended purpose of the application or component and why it was done a certain way. It doesn't matter if the user is yourself or another developer — the documentation should always be done.

Forms of documentation

Documentation doesn't have to be a long, drawn-out process. In fact, there are several types of documentation that you can use to communicate your intentions effectively with other members of the team or with yourself at some point in the future.

EXTERNAL DOCUMENTATION

Although comments in source code are probably the most useful form of documentation for developers, almost every project needs to have some documentation that is external to the source code. This documentation is typically used to communicate effectively with customers, users, managers, or any other interested parties. (**Remember:** One of the root causes of project failure is lack of or ineffective communication among team members and other interested parties outside the team.) External documentation is also required for other developers if they're consuming a binary component in their applications. In this case, they would not have access to the source code or the comments in the source code, so they would have no idea what the binary component is or how it's supposed to be used.

Visual Basic .NET has some interesting features that can help in creating and managing external documentation. Earlier in this book, you saw how you could use templates to create bitmaps from within the development environment. These bitmap templates could be toolbar button images, background images, or anything else that your application may need. You could save time by creating basic templates that have certain colors or sizes already defined, and all that has to be done is add the specific information that makes the image unique. The same principles can be applied to external documentation templates as well. External documentation templates can be created and used to generate a document based on any installed application on your computer. You could create templates for scripting files, databases, Word documents, Visio documents, Rational Rose modeling files, or anything else. The beauty of creating these documents from templates is that they're automatically added to the project file and will be saved and managed through the project directory in the Solution Explorer. Anytime you need to view or update a certain document – whether it's a Word document or any other file – simply double-click on the item within the Solution Explorer and the file will be launched in the default editor. You aren't limited to the default editors for the file based on the file extensions. You can right-click on the item and open it with any registered application on your computer. Another advantage to working with documents based on templates is that if you're using source code control within your project, then the files can be uploaded and checked out through the source code control integration from within Visual Basic.

External documentation is often the type of documentation that's dreaded the most. This type of documentation has typically been comprised of documents that are written, compiled, printed, and stored in binders on a shelf somewhere after the application has been completed. The accuracy of this type of documentation is short-lived because of bug fixes and other enhancements that are completed in the application without the external documentation being updated. However, not all external documentation fits into this category and some types are very useful.

Documentation is provided to effectively communicate information between parties. In the application-development process, there are several parties that will need to have some high-level documentation for the application so they can perform their duties as it relates to the application. Managers need to know why the application is being developed so they can approve resources for the development process. Deployment personnel need to know what files should be distributed and where they should be installed. Help Desk people need to know about any bugs and how the application should work so they can assist end users. External documentation is important and should be completed, but only if it can be maintained with minimal effort and can evolve as the application evolves during its lifetime.

COMMENTING SOURCE CODE

After the external high-level documentation is complete, the best source of documenting an application is through comments in the source code. Putting a comment at the end of a line of code as you're writing the code takes a minimal amount of effort. This end-of-line comment quickly indicates precisely what the line of code is doing. I'm a strong advocate for having a comment on every line of code except for the obvious Next, End If, Loop, and Exit statements. If the line is obvious to understand because of the naming conventions used, and if the line is not complex, then a comment can be spared. Otherwise, commenting the code through function headers, module headers, and inline comments is essential for communicating the purpose of the code. Having the code thoroughly documented is the easiest way for anyone, including you, to look at the code and quickly understand what it's doing. Furthermore, there are many inexpensive utilities on the market that will analyze the source code and extract the important information in the source code, including the comments, and place them in external files with automatic screenshots that you can save or print out for your external documentation binders.

COMMENT WEB PAGES

Visual Basic .NET provides several features that can help minimize the effort required when documenting your application. Visual Studio .NET supports a new tool that will generate a set of Web pages for selected projects or an entire solution. You can generate these comment Web pages by going to Tools → Build Comment Web Pages. The resulting Web pages are stored by default in a subdirectory of your solution files. The solution comment home page displays all the projects in your solution. Clicking on a project will drill down into the projects and display the various modules, classes, forms, and so on, as well as the members of each one.

Figure 16-1 shows the basic comment Web page for a form with two buttons. In Figure 16-1, you can see the members that are in form1. To the right of the members, there is a description field. This field would display description information for each member using XML tags in comments. The documentation lists several types of tags that can be used to describe the functions members and arguments and provide more meaningful information in the comment Web report pages. However, there is a catch: Currently, the only language that will process the tags is C#. The documentation indicates that this will probably be provided in Visual Basic in the future. When support is provided for the comment tags in Visual Basic, it will make it relatively easy to document the structure of the project with detailed descriptions of what the functions and parameters actually do. These comment Web pages could be placed on a common server for reference by the other team members, or they could be printed out to include in external documentation sets for your applications.

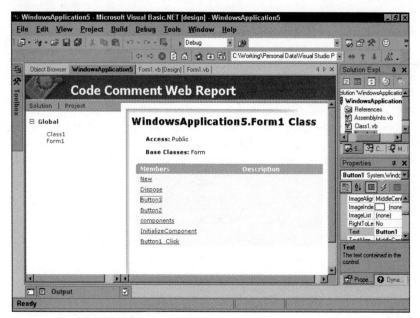

Figure16-1: Comment Web pages.

Summary

With the many new features in Visual Basic .NET, such as inheritance and multi-threading, having a good design and solid documentation for your application becomes even more important. Many projects have failed in other object-oriented programming languages because these features were misused. Up until now, Visual Basic developers didn't have to worry too much about these types of issues. Because Visual Basic .NET is a full-fledged object-oriented development language, you must take care to understand when and where to use these new features. Typically, this will only be done correctly through good upfront design. Without these design efforts and principles in place, you may get too far down one road before you realize that your application won't work or is too fragile, and you could very easily end up in the dreaded hacking mode if you haven't already arrived there.

In the beginning of this chapter, you learned the top root causes of project failure. One of the underlying issues that is common to the root causes is failure to communicate effectively. In order for a project to be successful, everyone involved must communicate effectively and as a team. Like it or not, the most effective way to communicate with the different parties involved in an application development project is through documentation. In a successful project, documentation will consist of both internal documentation and external documentation. Internal documentation is intended for use by the developers and other team members and can include (but is not limited to) source code documentation through the use of good commenting procedures and practices. External documentation is typically used to communicate with other interested parties outside of the project development team and typically includes documents and various diagrams in order to make the documentation clear. Many of the readers of external documentation may not be developers and won't understand the technical terms and documentation that is for the internal team.

Even the most well-designed project will probably fail if the design isn't documented clearly. As a result, design and documentation go hand in hand and should not be put off or skipped. Doing so only increases the odds that the project will fail.

Chapter 17

Microsoft Solutions Framework: Project Lifecycle Development

IN THIS CHAPTER

◆ An overview of the Microsoft Solutions Framework

◆ The team, process, risk management, and application models

The Microsoft Enterprise Services Framework (shown in Figure 17-1) consists of three framework families: Readiness, Solutions, and Operations. Each framework is a family of models, principles, and guides that have been collected from Microsoft's product developers, information technology groups, customers, and partners. This information was collected and analyzed to determine the best practices that can be used to deliver repeatable success rates.

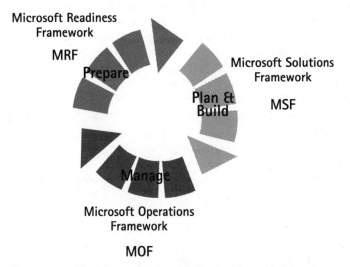

Figure 17-1: The Microsoft Enterprise Services Framework.

The Microsoft Solutions Framework (MSF) consists of the plan and build phases of the application development lifecycle. Microsoft offers several courses that cover the information in the various frameworks, but for Visual Basic developers, the one that's most useful is the Principles of Application Development course in the Microsoft Solutions Framework. In Chapter 16, you learned the root causes of project failure and the basics of how to design and build an application to help improve your chances of success. N-tier application design, incremental versioned releases, and concise documentation are key concepts of the Microsoft Solutions Framework, and I don't cover them in detail again in this chapter. However, some of this information will be expanded upon as it relates to the principles in the framework.

You should note that a framework is not set in stone. The purpose of a framework is to provide you with a starting point that can be modified to fit your particular situation. Certain information or topics can be expanded upon, modified slightly, or omitted if they don't apply in your situation. Care should be taken when omitting certain practices or recommendations that are covered in the framework, because they were included for a reason. By not following certain recommendations, you're introducing unknowns in your project that can increase your chances of failure. The best approach would be to follow the framework or modify the information so that it will apply to your situation.

One of the topics of the framework is the team model. In this model, each team member performs different roles. However, you may not have the luxury of working in a team environment and you may be responsible for performing all the described roles. In this case, your primary role will be developer, but you will need to perform the duties of the other roles as well. In this situation, it would be beneficial to think back to your childhood and put on imaginary hats with different titles on them. While you're wearing a particular hat, you'll have to play the role that hat describes. When doing this, write down any information or questions and break the questions up, depending on the role that needs to answer the question, placing each group of questions in a separate folder. When you're playing the other roles, look to see if any questions were directed to this role and answer them. This method may seem a little weird or childish at first, but if you follow it, you'll gain the practice and experience that's required for looking at the same question from many different angles instead of just your usual role. When you get in a practiced routine of switching roles, you'll become more efficient at it and it'll become a habit. This role-playing game is not just for lone developers; it's also required any time there isn't a specific person or team playing each role.

The purpose of this chapter is to give you an overview of the Microsoft Solutions Framework and to let you know how you can apply it to improve your chances of success when developing applications. But keep in mind that there is really no substitute for attending the actual training class that Microsoft offers or reading all the materials and white papers Microsoft has on its Web site. The Microsoft Solutions Framework information can be found at www.microsoft.com/business/services/mcsmsf.asp. Rational Rose has a similar process called the Rational Unified Process. You can find more information on this process at www.rational.com/products/rup/index.jsp.

Microsoft Solutions Framework Overview

Each model in the Principles of Application Development course contains various principles and guidelines that can be followed to increase the success rate of your applications. The team, process, and risk management models form the core MSF models that describe the best practices for managing the people, technology, and processes and the tradeoffs that companies must be aware of when ensuring that the company's information technology solutions effectively meet the business needs of the company. Although each model focuses on a different area of project management, when used together they provide a basic framework for successful project management of application development projects.

Team model

Microsoft developed the team model after recognizing the inefficiencies and problems with a hierarchical team. A hierarchical team has many problems associated with it due to the high overhead involved in the processes and communications within the team. Unclear goals and roles lead to misunderstandings and possible duplication of effort. They also typically result in team members becoming disengaged from the team and focusing more on individual effort and accomplishments than the goals and effort of the team. When indirect communication occurs between many parties, the resulting information is often incomplete, vague, or different from the original intent of the message. To illustrate this point, think back to when you probably played the childhood game where everyone was in a circle and the first person whispered something into the next person's ear. This repeated until the information worked all the way back to the first person, who revealed the original message to the group. How many times was the message correct by the time it got back to the first person? When this occurs in application development, the developer is often instructed to code something that doesn't meet all the requirements, because certain people opted to eliminate information that they thought wasn't necessary or for which they thought they had an understanding in place.

The MSF team model for application development has an organizational structure where each role is on an equal level in a circle and direct communication can occur between any of the roles within the circle at any time. Figure 17-2 shows the different roles that need to be represented in a successful application development project. The roles shown are those that are required through an entire project lifecycle. Sometimes resources are brought in for a specific task such as design work, or because the individual has expertise with a particular piece of technology being used in the application. Again, the MSF team model is a starting point and not the final answer. The team model is flexible and can be adjusted based on the number of members in the team and each team member's skills, as well as the scope of the project. For small projects, one person may play several roles, whereas on large projects there may be a whole team of people assigned to each role.

Figure 17-2: The MSF team model for application development.

PRODUCT MANAGEMENT ROLE

The product management role is the role that kicks off the project. This role is responsible for the features that are included in the application. Product managers meet with
the customers and users of the product and are the primary point of communication
between the team and the customers or users of the product. A *customer* is one who
is actually paying for the application to be developed, whereas the *user* is the one
who is going to actually use the product. Sometimes customers and users are the
same people; other times they're different. If the customer and user are different and
have differing opinions as to what features should be included in the application, it's
up to the product manager to balance the wants and needs of both groups.

The product manager starts by determining the requirements and establishing
a shared project vision between the team and the customer. This person or team
also obtains the management's buy-in for the project by establishing the business
case and showing how the product will fill the business needs and solve business
problems. The product manager serves as the customer advocate to the team as well
as serving as the team's advocate to the customer. This team member is responsible
for managing customers' expectations, which can determine whether the project is
a success or a failure.

PROGRAM MANAGEMENT ROLE

The program manager is responsible for delivering the right product at the right time.
The program manager is what most people would think of as the project manager,
however a typical project manager will try to fill both the product and program
manager roles (you'll see why this isn't a good idea later on). The program manager
is strictly responsible for driving the overall project process by managing the resource
allocation, project schedule, product scope, and other critical tradeoff decisions. In
a team of peers, program managers are supposed to lead and not be the boss.
Effective program managers will also be able to delegate authority based on the team
members' abilities, so they aren't responsible for making all the decisions.

DEVELOPMENT ROLE

The development role is the role that you're probably most familiar with. A developer is responsible for building and unit testing features that relate to functional requirements and customer expectations. Developers should participate in the design process of the application and should be responsible for estimating the amount of time required to complete each feature.

TESTING ROLE

The testing role is responsible for developing and managing the testing strategy, scripts, and plans for the application. In order for the testing role to function properly and in conjunction with the rest of the team, the testers need to understand the users' needs and how the application is supposed to meet those needs. On small projects the testers will typically manage the build process for the application and possibly build the install program for the application, whereas on large applications, there may be a dedicated team for the build process. Testers should be able to accurately determine and document the state of the application at any time. This involves keeping track of bugs as they're reported and either resolved or closed, as well as documenting the features that are missing, in progress, or complete that are supposed to be in the current version.

USER EDUCATION ROLE

The user education role is responsible for delivering a product that the users can and will use and one that requires as little product support as possible. If an application is developed and delivered to the users, but they don't use the application because it isn't user friendly or they can't understand it, then the project is a failure. In order to prevent this from happening, the user educator is the main point of contact between the users and the team members. User educators need to participate in the design process with the goal of minimizing the need for user support. Minimizing the need for support materials and personnel minimizes the overhead required to support and manage the application, leaving more revenue that can go toward profits.

The user educator is also responsible for testing and tracking usability issues and working with the developers and other team members to address and resolve these issues as much as possible. By involving the user educator in the design process, usability issues can be identified and resolved before the product or feature is actually developed, minimizing the amount of effort required to rework the application or feature.

LOGISTICS MANAGEMENT ROLE

The logistics manager is responsible for communicating with operations in order to support the various stages of product deployment. The logistics manager provides the team with important feedback from the operations group about past and current product deployments. In certain environments, the logistics manager would have to inform the operations department of the computers, platforms, installed applications, and all supporting files and dependencies an application needs in order to run. Often the developers won't have access to the production environment and will require the support of the operations staff in order to move the application from development to testing to production environments. Some production environments are so controlled that the operations team members must test and research the dependencies to make sure that deploying the application won't break other applications that are currently in place.

Another responsibility for the logistics management role is to train the support personnel for the product release. It's important for the logistics manager to inform the operations department of all the requirements and needs of the application early in the process so the operations department can plan for any changes or purchases that are required in order to support the needs of the application. The operations department may inform the logistics manager of the server that the application will be running on and the physical characteristics of the server. If the development server and production server are too different, then you won't be able to judge the true performance of the application. If performance is not acceptable on the proposed server, then arrangements would need to be made for another existing server to be used or for a new server to be purchased and supported.

SCALING THE TEAM MODEL FOR SMALL PROJECTS

Not all development projects will have enough people for each to serve a particular role. Often, individuals will need to perform multiple roles on a project. But care needs to taken to avoid conflicts of interest between the different roles. If a team member is responsible for multiple roles, they need to make it clear to the other team members which role they're speaking for when they're answering questions or offering guidance.

Figure 17-3 depicts the roles that could be combined together when there aren't enough team members to represent each role.

	Product Management	Program Management	Development	Testing	User Education	Logistics Management
Product Management		N	N	P	P	U
Program Management	N		N	U	U	P
Development	N	N		N	N	N
Testing	P	U	N		P	P
User Education	P	U	N	P		U
Logistics Management	U	P	N	P	U	

P Possible		U Unlikely		N No

Figure 17-3: Scaling the MSF team model for small projects.

The most important thing to realize about the matrix is those roles that should not be shared with other roles the same person already has. The most noticeable is that resources that are actually developing the application shouldn't have any other roles in addition to the developer role. The reasoning behind this is that the developers are the only resources that are creating the application that the other roles manage. Distracting the developers will probably cause the development schedule to slip, which will affect all the other roles and the project schedule. Due to the many unknowns in application design and development, the development schedule could be affected in an adverse way. By keeping the developers focused on their primary task, you have the ability to eliminate one schedule buster that is more than likely to occur if the developers serve multiple roles.

The only other roles that shouldn't be crossed are the product management and program management roles. These roles represent a conflict of interest, because the product manager tries to get all the requested features into the product while the program manager has to manage the features against the other constraints such as budget or time.

Sometimes these recommendations cannot be followed, especially when you're the sole person or one of only two members on a project team. In situations like this, you'll have to perform multiple roles. Each of the roles listed must be filled in order to increase your chances of delivering a successful product to the end users. So you can't just drop one or more roles. If you must play different roles throughout the project, be aware of the amount of time involved in performing the duties and responsibilities of the other roles. Even if you accurately estimate the development effort for the product, you won't finish the product on time if you don't estimate and account for the time involved in performing the other roles.

SCALING THE TEAM MODEL FOR LARGE PROJECTS

Just as the team model can be scaled for small projects, it can also be scaled for large projects. The best way to scale the model for large projects is to divide large teams into smaller teams, which have less overhead and faster implementations. These smaller teams are often referred to as *multidisciplinary feature teams* and are organized around a particular product feature such as printing, user interface, database, or application core. The feature teams are composed of the same roles except that the product management and logistics management deal more with the whole than the individual pieces. These feature teams then receive direction and provide deliverables to the lead team, which is responsible for the overall product.

Process model

The process model for application development uses the concept of versioned releases and divides each versioned release into four different phases, where each phase has an overall milestone associated with it and may contain one or more interim milestones. The MSF process model for application development is shown in Figure 17-4.

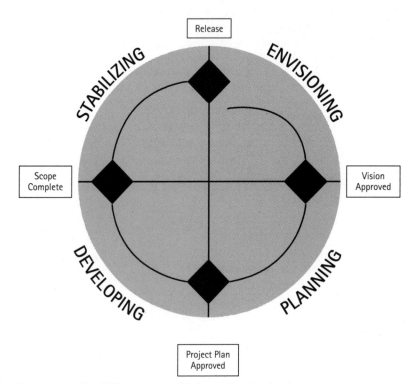

Figure 17–4: The MSF process model for application development.

As you can see in the figure, the process model contains four repeating phases, each with a milestone at the end of each phase. Milestones are used to establish transition and assessment points. These phases are not necessarily equal amounts of time or effort, but there is one main cycle for the external project release and multiple smaller cycles within the developing phase that represent the incremental versioned releases. During the smaller incremental versioned release phases, the envisioning phase will be negligible if the overall requirements for the product have been developed and prioritized as discussed in Chapter 16.

ENVISIONING

The main purpose of the envisioning phase is to get an early, high-level view of the project goals and constraints. The envisioning phase allows the team to coalesce and get behind the vision of the product. The planning done during the envisioning phase provides a springboard for more detailed planning to occur in the next phase. The vision-approved milestone signals agreement on:

◆ The reason for the project

◆ The expected outcome

- ◆ Project feasibility

- ◆ Project goals and constraints

- ◆ Opportunities and risks

- ◆ Project structure

The product manager typically runs the envisioning phase and discusses with the customer the initial requirements of the application. As the product manager and customer agree upon the business requirements and overall goals of the project, the team can begin to be formed by choosing who will be working on the project based on skills and availability.

PLANNING

During the planning phase, the vision scope is used to define the actual requirements of the project. These requirements are then analyzed to determine how they can be broken down and estimated. During this phase, the initial design work is completed on the application, which gives enough direction for the project that it can start when the planning phase is complete. Putting effort into the design work is important, because it's a lot easier and less expensive to fix design problems in the design phase than in the developing or stabilizing phases. During the planning phase, the initial project risks are documented as well as the project trade-off strategy that will be used to determine what limiting resource will be sacrificed when one of the others changes. The project trade-off strategy is a triangle (see Figure 17-5) where a project constraint is one of the sides.

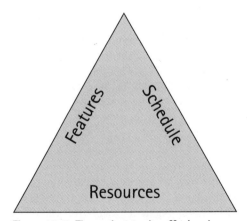

Figure 17-5: The project trade-off triangle.

After the project plan has been agreed upon, the initial trade-off triangle becomes fixed. At this point, when one side of the triangle changes, one or both of the other sides have to be adjusted. For example, say that the resources side is reduced because a developer was pulled off the project. In order to keep the triangle balanced, either the features have to be decreased or the schedule has to increase. Similarly, if the schedule is shortened, then either the features would need to decrease or the resources would have to increase. The trade-off strategy determines what is fixed in making project decisions and which one or ones are able to adjust. The project plan–approved milestone completes this phase and signals agreement on:

◆ Project trade off strategy

◆ Project risks

◆ What will be built

◆ When it will be built

◆ How it will be built

◆ Who will build it

DEVELOPING

The developing phase is when the team accomplishes all the new development and documentation for the products. The developing phase completes with the scope complete milestone, signaling that no new features will be included in the application after this point. This milestone is often referred to as *code complete,* but sometimes *code complete* can be confusing because it doesn't mean that there is no more coding going on. In reality, there is still coding that will be done, but it's not including new features. Instead, the coding that will still be done is to eliminate as many bugs as possible.

STABILIZING

During the stabilizing phase, the features of the application have been developed, but there will be bugs that need to be fixed that come in from the testers. In this phase, all the teams' efforts are directed toward addressing all known issues including bugs and mismanaged expectations. No new development is done during this phase, which completes in the release milestone. At this point, the product shifts from development to operations and support.

Risk management model

According to the dictionary, a *risk* is defined as anything that may happen that would cause a loss. Defined in these words, it's easy to see how any development project that is undertaken will have inherent risks associated with it. A loss could be anything from missed deadlines or diminished quality, to incomplete features or even project failure. Because there is no way to eliminate all risks from a project, you must have a plan in place to identify and minimize the chances that the risk will occur, or minimize the loss that would occur if the identified risk were to happen.

The main purpose of the MSF risk management model is to proactively identify and address the risk and its impact on the project. In order to proactively manage risks, you must anticipate problems (instead of reacting to them), address root causes (instead of addressing symptoms), prevent and minimize the risk through mitigation (instead of reacting to consequences), and prepare for consequences to minimize their impact (instead of reacting to a crisis).

The risk management process, as shown in Figure 17-6, produces a living risk assessment document that's continually managed and updated throughout the entire project. The first step in the process is to identify a risk. This forces the risk to become visible to the entire team so it can be dealt with before it impacts the project. The second step in the process involves analyzing the risk statements to convert the risk into information the team can use to make decisions. Information that is needed is the probability that the risk will occur and the impact the risk will have if the risk does occur. The third step involves devising plans to know when the risk has happened and what to do about the risk if it occurs. The fourth step involves tracking the risk, which monitors the defining factors and trigger points for the risk and any actions that have been taken to mitigate the risk. The fifth step is controlling the risk by moving it into the project management activities. This step ensures that risk management remains a high-priority, high-visibility activity in the overall project. Risks can either be retired or be analyzed again along with any new risks that have been identified. Reanalyzing the risk allows the probability and impact to be adjusted based on past and current activities in the project. The risk may either become a higher or lower priority risk to be managed when compared with the other identified risks and statuses.

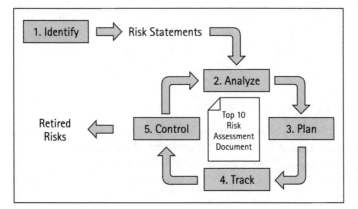

Figure 17-6: The MSF risk management process.

IDENTIFYING RISKS

Risks are identified best through using a collaborative approach. This allows any assumptions and viewpoints to be understood by a team as a whole. Risks can be identified by examination from two different directions. You should look at potential issues and their likely consequences as well as the potential consequences and their likely causes. Risk management as a whole, and risk identification in particular, should be viewed by the team members as a positive activity and not a negative one. Identifying potential problems for the project and implementing a process to manage those risks only increases the chances of a successful project. A risk statement needs to be clearly stated and must include both a condition and a consequence.

ANALYZING RISKS

Analyzing risks involves converting the risk statements into a probability and an impact. Assessing the probability of a risk is and can only be an estimate, because no one can predict the future of the project and whether the risk will occur. By defining and using a simple numeric scale across all the risks for a project, calculations can be made that will determine your overall risk exposure. Probability assessment is very subjective, so it's best to use a simple scale like 1 to 3, where 3 is the highest probability. On this scale, it's easy to determine whether a particular risk is a 2 or a 3 (whereas if you were using a scale from 1 to 20, determining whether a risk would be a 17 or an 18 is difficult). Using a simple three-step scale, you can also use subjective wording such as high, medium, and low, with 3 being assigned to the high item.

When the probability of the risk has been determined, you need to assign a risk-impact value. *The risk-impact value* represents the amount of loss that would occur if the risk happens. Use the same scale that you have for the probability, and assign the impact for each risk. When you've identified all the probabilities and the impacts of each risk, you can calculate your exposure to the risk by multiplying the two items together — the higher the resulting number, the higher your exposure to the risk.

By using the 1-to-3 scales, you could have a result between 1 and 9, with nine being the highest exposure. By identifying the exposures for all the identified risks, you can see which risks should be given priority to manage. You can't identify or manage all the risks in the project. But you should continually evaluate and plan for the risks with the highest exposure levels as you progress through the project lifecycle.

PLANNING FOR RISKS

Risk planning involves prioritizing and devising preventative as well as corrective actions for a risk. This can help minimize the chances that the risk will occur. Or, if the risk does occur, it will minimize the impact that the risk will have. There are five key areas that you should understand about the highest priority risks you have identified:

- ◆ **Research:** Do you know enough about the risk?

- ◆ **Acceptance:** Can you live with the consequences?

- ◆ **Avoidance:** Can you avoid the risk?

- ◆ **Mitigation:** Can you reduce the probability?

- ◆ **Contingency:** Can you reduce the impact?

When planning for a risk, you must balance the consequences of the risk against the effort needed to avoid it. Sometimes avoiding the risk may require much more effort than either accepting or reducing the consequences that may occur.

An important part of risk planning is identifying and setting contingency triggers. *Contingency triggers* are used to identify when a particular contingency plan should be activated. These triggers could be a point-in-time trigger or a threshold trigger. A *point-in-time trigger* identifies a date on which the contingency plan is either effective or ineffective. An example of this would be if a team member quits or is removed from the project. What is the latest date a replacement can be hired and trained? Otherwise, something else in the trade-off triangle will need to be adjusted. A *threshold trigger* relies on things that can be measured or counted, such as a bug count or performance measurement.

TRACKING RISKS

Tracking a risk is an ongoing process in project management. The risk needs to be monitored for any change in conditions or consequences as well as the contingency triggers. If the contingency trigger is not monitored, you'll have no idea when you need to take corrective action to either reduce the probability that the risk will occur or to reduce the effect the consequences of the risk would have on the project. One of the best ways to track a risk is through the creation of a top-ten list, which identifies the highest priority risks in a list format, with the highest priority risk at the top. This list should be reviewed regularly and updated to show changes in priority through the risk exposure calculations.

CONTROLLING RISKS

Controlling the risk is achieved through incorporating the risk management process into the project management activities. This allows the project plan to be adjusted as various risks occur or are retired. A risk is retired either because the risk occurred and you are now in contingency phase, or because the risk has been resolved. Retiring a risk can either remove it from the risk management process completely or the risk and its management plan are archived. If the risk and management plan were archived, then you would have it available for future projects. If it applied to another project, you wouldn't need to spend as much time identifying and planning for the risk. You would only have to make a few changes that may be required for the new project. Another benefit to archiving the risk would be in case something were to happen later on in the project that would force the risk to become active again. All the information would already be there, and it would just have to be prioritized and tracked based on the new information.

Application model

The MSF application model consists of developing an application based on the Windows DNA or .NET architecture guidelines. Discussed in more detail in Chapter 16, the application model consists of a logical network of cooperating services, meaning both consumers and suppliers. The emphasis is on logical separation rather than physical separation of the user, business, and data services. As long as the separation is defined logically, it shouldn't matter to the application where the physical implementation of the reusable service is. It could be on the local machine, or it could be across the network invisible to the application itself. This allows the application the flexibility that's needed in order for it to scale as the demands on the application change over time.

Figure 17-7 shows the differences between the traditional view and the services view for application architecture. The traditional view has each application contain information required to support a particular feature. In this model, business logic, user interfaces, and data services are often repeated in each application that needs them. Compare this to the services view, where applications share common functionality and the information isn't duplicated. The services approach provides many benefits including encapsulation, reuse, and improved maintainability.

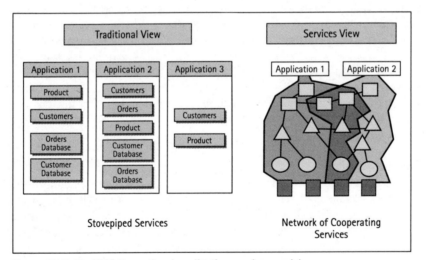

Figure 17-7: The MSF three-tiered application services model.

An important point to understand is that the three-tiered services model is a concept based on logical design. If this concept is taken too literally, the application could still end up being the very huge monolithic application the model is intended to prevent. The sought-after benefits of the three-tiered approach would be lost.

Summary

This chapter provides you with a brief overview to the principles in the Microsoft Solutions Framework and was compiled from the various white papers on Microsoft's

Web site as well as from the courseware documentation. I strongly suggest that you read the materials on Microsoft's Web site, as well as the articles that are presented in the Microsoft Developer Network libraries.

The Microsoft Solutions Framework is compiled from a best-practices approach to software development. The information in this chapter provides you with the basics to their framework and can help you as you're developing applications. One of the best features about the framework is that it's flexible enough to incorporate additional features or requirements, as well as changes that enable it to fit your needs better. One of the core principles in the Microsoft Solutions Framework is documentation through living documents. In order to avoid analysis paralysis, the framework suggests baselining documents as early as possible and freezing the documents as late as possible. Another benefit to this strategy is that it establishes a structured change control process as part of the documentation, which will allow all the parties involved to see how the scope and requirements of the project changed throughout the lifecycle as well as the reasons behind the changes.

Migrating Existing Applications to Visual Basic .NET

When you begin to understand Visual Basic .NET, you'll probably come across a situation in which you'll need to port an existing application over to the .NET platform. When this time comes, you have a few options available to you to assist in the transition, but they boil down to either attempting an upgrade or taking the opportunity to start over and do it right from the start with the .NET Framework. This appendix is a primer on the information you need to understand before deciding which path to take.

Upgrading Projects versus Creating New Projects

When comparing Visual Basic .NET to previous versions, you'll notice many changes. Most people realize the benefits of these changes in due time and eventually understand why the changes were made. Some features in the Visual Basic language have been removed. Visual Basic has been rebuilt from the ground up, and Microsoft has taken the opportunity to clean up the language by removing some functions or features that were redundant or obsolete.

One of the biggest hurdles you'll have to face is how you or your company will handle the transition to Visual Basic .NET. You can take one of three paths, but only you will be able to decide the correct path for your circumstances. Your choices are as follows:

◆ Keep your existing applications in Visual Basic 6.

◆ Create new applications from scratch in Visual Basic .NET.

◆ Upgrade existing applications and port them to the .NET platform.

According to Microsoft, both Visual Basic 6 and Visual Basic .NET can be installed on the same system. At the time of this writing, this appears to be the case; I haven't seen any problems with the two coexisting. This approach will allow you to work with both versions in your day-to-day programming activities without requiring a dual boot system or a separate computer, provided that your computer meets the minimum system requirements for Visual Basic .NET.

The first option you have available to you is to keep your existing applications in Visual Basic 6. The COM interoperability layer allows COM components and .NET components to communicate with each other at the expense of a few extra CPU cycles on each call. Provided that you've followed the principles of good design using the scalable Windows DNA approach, you can have Visual Basic .NET applications call into your existing applications using COM and consume the functionality those applications already provide. In fact, developers will probably use this option most often until they become familiar with the .NET Framework and Visual Basic .NET.

When developers become familiar enough with the .NET platform, they'll probably start creating new applications in Visual Basic .NET. These applications can coexist with and use the services provided by existing applications, so this will probably start the transition process of migrating to Visual Basic .NET. Because of the many changes in Visual Basic .NET, developers will be able to start designing applications that will take advantage of the full-fledged object-oriented language, multithreading, Common Language Runtime, and new project types available to them with Visual Basic .NET. Developers will now be able to create services and console applications directly from within Visual Basic. Designing and creating applications from the ground up is the best way to take advantage of the new and changed features in Visual Basic .NET.

Ideal candidates for Visual Basic .NET applications are completely new applications, or components followed by major revisions or releases of an existing application. Because of the learning curve and the possible incompatibilities your application may have, minor revisions of a product aren't very good candidates for upgrading to Visual Basic .NET.

If you decide to upgrade an existing application to Visual Basic .NET, you can either rewrite it or you can attempt to upgrade your application through running the Visual Basic .NET Import Wizard on projects created in earlier versions of Visual Basic. Both choices have advantages and disadvantages.

If you rewrite applications, you know that you'll be compatible with any language changes, and you can take advantage of the enhanced power and features present in Visual Basic .NET. The disadvantage to this approach is that it will require additional programming effort and may introduce bugs into the application through errors or omissions when porting code from a previous version. However, it's important to realize that any time an application is fixed or modified, the chances of introducing a bug or destabilizing the application increase. The best time to fix a bug is when it is first introduced into the application. After that, as time moves on and the complexity of the application increases, fixing a bug becomes much harder, because the piece of code where the bug resides may be called more and more times by different routines or modules. All the dependencies must be properly tested to make sure that the fix didn't break anything else.

Upgrading a project has its own set of advantages and disadvantages. The advantage to upgrading is that you may be able to get the application running in the new environment with less effort then a rewrite. I used the word *may* in that sentence because upgrading won't *always* be the best answer. Each application could have many problems or incompatibilities that must be fixed when upgraded to Visual Basic .NET. The answer depends on how well you understand .NET and your current application. Many white papers will tell you how to upgrade an existing application to Visual Basic .NET, but you must take the information presented in them (and what this book tells you) with a grain of salt. No one can understand all the intricacies of your application but you. Beyond the most trivial of applications, more pitfalls and incompatibilities will probably arise that may or may not be caught at compile time. Even if an upgrade appears to be successful, you will still need to visit every line of code in your application to be sure. Otherwise, you'll be taking a chance in hoping that there are no problems.

When you've made the effort to upgrade the application and get it running under Visual Basic .NET, you still haven't taken advantage of any of the new features in the language, such as inheritance, overloading, and so on. Furthermore, many of the compatibility functions are wrappers around the .NET functions, so your application will be incurring additional overhead that isn't needed if the application is created from scratch in .NET. Although it may seem like less effort to just get it running under the new version, the disadvantages will probably outweigh the advantages of upgrading. By understanding your application and the .NET Framework (and what the incompatibilities are), you'll be in the best place to determine if attempting to upgrade your application is more practical than rewriting it. As an application evolves, many fixes are put in place to handle limitations or bugs that weren't detected early enough in the process to fix them correctly. By rewriting the application, you have the ability to clean up your code base and fix things correctly in the new version, especially for things that were not inherently present in Visual Basic 6.

Suggestions for Upgrading Projects

At this point, I hope I have persuaded you to take an upgrade attempt very cautiously. If you still think you're going to upgrade your application, then read on, because this section gives you the highlights of the issues you'll face. One thing that will help you tremendously is understanding the .NET Framework and Visual Basic .NET as thoroughly as possible before you attempt to upgrade. As you understand more and more about Visual Basic .NET, you should start to look at your existing code base for incompatibilities and, if possible, make the appropriate changes and test them in your existing code base before attempting to migrate it to .NET. Chapter 3 discusses the primary changes to the language and should be your starting point. When you understand the basic changes to the language, you can review your current code base to see where incompatibilities may exist.

In prior versions of Visual Basic, if you declared an object variable with the As New syntax, the object was not created until the first method or property was called on the object. Furthermore, overhead was involved in every call to the object to make this happen, because the runtime had to check to see if the object was instantiated yet – and if it wasn't, then it had to create it. In Visual Basic .NET, an object variable is instantiated immediately if it's declared with the As New syntax. This allows the use of constructors, which can be supplied after the As New X in order to create and initialize the object at the same time.

Visual Basic .NET no longer supports the variant data type or any of the functions that explicitly operated on the variant data type. Functions like the IsMissing function for testing optional parameters are no longer supported. Therefore, you need to be aware of any functions that have optional parameters in them and test to see if the parameter was supplied, because they will need to be changed in order to handle this properly. Another issue with optional parameters in Visual Basic .NET is that all optional parameters must supply a default value for the parameter. This default value is used to initialize the parameter if none is supplied. This has the side effect of not being able to determine if the parameter was missing or if the calling function supplied the default value. In order to get around this, you'll need to modify the logic of the procedure to either accept the default value, set the default value to something that's outside the normal range of values if possible, or use the concept of overloading functions in order to determine which way the function was intended to be called. The object data type in Visual Basic .NET will be used instead of the variant data type. There are a couple of minor differences in the underlying representation of the variable in memory, because an object is strictly a pointer to the data somewhere else in memory, while a variant contains both a type and the pointer in the same block of memory. For all practical purposes the object data type is the replacement to the variant data type.

Visual Basic .NET no longer supports using default properties for non-indexed properties. An indexed property is one like that of the Fields property of an ADO Recordset. The Fields property requires an index to identify which field object in the collection is being used. The value property on the field object is not an indexed value so you still would need to specify the value property if that's what you want. Other non-indexed properties are those that are on controls. In prior versions of Visual Basic, certain controls, such as text boxes, labels, and buttons, use the property that maps to the displayed text on the form as the default property. Without using the set statement, you would be accessing the default property on the controls. Visual Basic .NET requires you to specify the common Text property when setting or reading the displayed text for the control. By doing this, several other things have changed. For example, property procedures no longer have a Property Let to go along with the set and get, and the use of the Set keyword is no longer required in the language when assigning object variable references. You should look for code in your existing applications that uses the default properties and explicitly provides the property value instead of relying on the defaults. This will help as you migrate code using the upgrade wizard to the Visual Basic .NET platform.

Visual Basic .NET only allows one variable type to be declared on a single line of code. Prior versions would allow you to declare more than one variable on the line but there was a catch that depended on how it was declared. If only the variable names were supplied, separated by commas followed by a data type, only the last variable on the line would actually be created as the specified variable type. All other variables would be declared as variant. As a result, you could include the data type along with each variable name and then have the variable data type combination separated by commas. This would create the variables and data types as expected. In Visual Basic .NET, you can have a single variable and type combination, which is done in most cases, or you can have multiple variable names separated by commas and then a single data type. The result of the multiple variables on the single line declaration is that now all variables will be declared as the defined data type.

Visual Basic .NET changes the default passing convention for parameters to functions and procedures. Visual Basic .NET now passes parameters by value as default compared to by reference, which was the default in prior versions. This can lead to some hard-to-find bugs if you're not aware of it. As a result, you should make sure you explicitly specify whether the parameter is to be passed by reference or by value in your existing code base. You could port your applications without doing this, but you'd only make things harder for yourself when trying to track down bugs or missing or incorrect data, because the parameter is not updated in the calling routine when you think it should be (as would be the case in prior versions). This can be a daunting task in and of itself because you need to look through each procedure to see if it's trying to update the parameter to supply a return value parameter to the calling routine as part of the method call. Depending on how much code you have, this may prove to be one of the limiting factors you should consider when deciding whether to perform an import upgrade or when rewriting the code.

Visual Basic .NET no longer supports implicit form instantiation. In prior versions, if you had a form named `frmTest` and someplace called `frmTest.Show`, the form would be loaded and displayed. The reason this worked was because Visual Basic would create a form object for you behind the scenes, and the name of the variable was the same as the form name. In prior versions, a form could be treated as if it were a class with a visual interface. You could add methods, properties, and functions to the form, and it would behave just like a class. In Visual Basic .NET, you'll need to understand that a form *is* a class. The form class inherits from the `System.Windows.Forms.Form` class to provide a visual interface. Earlier in this book, you saw how the Windows Forms Designer actually writes the code out into the form module that creates the visual interface of the form at runtime. Because a form is a class, it needs to be instantiated just like a class would by declaring a variable of the form type and then initializing the form. One of the benefits to this is that you can provide a specialized constructor for your form that will initialize the form based on the parameters supplied in the constructor. This change will catch many developers off guard when they're trying to upgrade or write new applications in Visual Basic .NET.

Visual Basic .NET doesn't inherently support fixed-length strings. There is a compatibility class available that simulates the characteristics of fixed-length strings, but in most cases you should avoid this and use a regular variable-length string object. Even with the compatibility class, fixed-length strings aren't allowed in structures, which are the replacements to user-defined types. Structures are very similar to classes, which are discussed in Chapter 3 and can have property procedures. Property procedures can limit the size of the string if absolutely necessary when the data is supplied using the Left function on the Value parameter of the set statement.

Visual Basic .NET uses pixels as the only graphical unit of measurement. Any code that deals with explicit values for sizing or moving forms or controls will need to be isolated. By isolating the code, you can make the transition to pixels much easier. Visual Basic .NET provides a couple of compatibility calls that will convert pixels to twips and twips to pixels for you, but you need to be aware of why this is happening. If you can effectively isolate your code that deals with twips or other units of measurement, you can ease your transition and eliminate a few extra function calls.

Visual Basic .NET doesn't allow you to call every function possible in the referenced libraries directly. Visual Basic .NET uses namespaces to prevent naming conflicts and to organize functions and modules in an object-oriented hierarchy that will help you understand how all the libraries are used. A namespace also has another use in that any functions that are declared using the Shared syntax will be available to call directly when an imports statement is included for the namespace in which it exists. Without importing the namespaces, the functions can still be called, but they won't show up in IntelliSense until you fully qualify the function.

Visual Basic .NET uses the Common Language Runtime and the .NET Framework to provide you with an extensive set of objects and methods that are grouped together by related functionality. The .NET Framework and Common Language Runtime should have equivalents to all the Windows API calls and should be used instead of an API call. Using an API call in Visual Basic .NET does several things. First, you lose your type-checking and exception-handling capabilities because you're calling into unmanaged code. Furthermore, declaring a Windows API call immediately limits your application, and it will only run on the Windows platform. The Common Language Runtime was created to allow your applications to run on other platforms that support the runtime other than just standard Windows-based systems. If you're using any Windows API calls in your application, you should isolate them so they're called by wrapper functions that ensure proper type checking and isolation if you can't find the .NET equivalent. If you can find the equivalent .NET call, then you only have to make the change in one place to take advantage of it. Often the framework calls may require you to create and pass in certain objects into the constructors in order for them to work properly. The wrapper functions can hide any additional objects or steps that may be required when making the call.

Upgrade Wizard

The Upgrade Wizard is invoked whenever you open a project that was created in an earlier version of Visual Basic. This wizard will run through your code and attempt to identify all the changes that it knows can be changed successfully. The original project is left alone and a new .NET project is created in the path you specify in the

Upgrade Wizard's dialog box. It appears to correct the majority of issues that appear while migrating an application.

You can also use the Upgrade Wizard as you're learning about the changes in Visual Basic .NET. If you aren't sure how something is done in .NET or, more importantly, which namespace the function, method, or constant resides in, you can run the Upgrade Wizard on a sample project. When the upgrade is complete, you can investigate the Visual Basic .NET code to see the equivalent or where the new function is located.

However, you should be aware of some issues with the Upgrade Wizard. The Upgrade Wizard sets `Option Strict Off` for compatibility with code from prior versions. As a result, the code that's generated may not work, especially if you place it in a module that has `Option Strict On` explicitly or implicitly through the project options. `Option Strict` should be on for all the projects you create in Visual Basic .NET. The small time required to ensure that any conversions that may cause a runtime error or lose data are explicitly coded will pay off as the application is developed and maintained throughout its lifecycle. The Upgrade Wizard will also convert data types from prior versions into the .NET equivalents. For example, an Integer data type in prior versions gets converted to a Short in the upgrade process. The result is still a 16-bit value, but the type has changed. On a 32-bit operating system, 32-bit integers are the fastest when performing calculations. As a result you may want to upgrade your data types in your existing application or after the conversion so that the Integer values use the .NET Integer data type (the long data type from prior versions.) The Upgrade Wizard has its benefits and it may take a while to run for complex projects, so be patient.

Index

A

continued

continued

continued